TRUE CRIMES
and
MISDEMEANORS

ALSO BY JEFFREY TOOBIN

Opening Arguments: A Young Lawyer's First Case: United States v. Oliver North

The Run of His Life: The People v. O. J. Simpson

A Vast Conspiracy: The Real Story of the Sex Scandal That Nearly Brought Down a President

Too Close to Call: The Thirty-Six-Day Battle to Decide the 2000 Election

The Nine: Inside the Secret World of the Supreme Court

The Oath: The Obama White House and the Supreme Court

American Heiress: The Wild Saga of the Kidnapping, Crimes and Trial of Patty Hearst

TRUE CRIMES
and
MISDEMEANORS

The Investigation of Donald Trump

Jeffrey Toobin

DOUBLEDAY

New York

Copyright © 2020 by Jeffrey Toobin

All rights reserved. Published in the United States by Doubleday, a
division of Penguin Random House LLC, New York, and distributed in
Canada by Penguin Random House Canada Limited, Toronto.

www.doubleday.com

DOUBLEDAY and the portrayal of an anchor with a dolphin are
registered trademarks of Penguin Random House LLC.

Book design by Michael Collica
Jacket photograph by Andrew Harnik/AP Photo; (spotlight) Firsik/Shutterstock
Jacket design by John Fontana

Library of Congress Catalog Control Number: 2020017608

ISBN: 9780385536738 (hardcover)
ISBN: 9780385536745 (eBook)

MANUFACTURED IN THE UNITED STATES OF AMERICA

1 3 5 7 9 10 8 6 4 2

First Edition

To my fellow journalists

CONTENTS

TRUE CRIMES

and

MISDEMEANORS

The Forgotten Phone

Robert Mueller had never surrendered his cell phone before entering the Oval Office. He had become director of the Federal Bureau of Investigation on the day after Labor Day in 2001, one week before the terrorist attacks that would define his tenure at the bureau. For the next twelve years—the second-longest tenure of any director—he would be a frequent, often daily, visitor to the White House. President George W. Bush looked to Mueller more than to anyone else to protect the United States from another attack like the one on 9/11. From 2009 to 2013, so did Barack Obama. The last thing anyone thought to do in those years was to separate Mueller from a communication device he might need, even during moments when he was conferring with the president.

But on the morning of May 16, 2017, Mueller gave a rueful half smile when he was reminded to place his phone in the box for civilian visitors to the Oval Office. He, of all people, knew the rule and the reason for it; private cell phones could be rigged to record and transmit, even without the owner's knowledge, and it was imperative that the operational security of the president's office be preserved. So Mueller gave up his phone and walked into the familiar territory of the Oval Office to shake the hand of the forty-fifth president of the United States, Donald Trump. They had never met before, and never would again.

Trump steered Mueller to a chair in front of the Resolute desk, the massive English oak partners' desk that was built from the timbers of an Arctic explorers' ship. George W. Bush and Obama had used the same desk, but Mueller never sat there with them. The two previous presidents talked with visitors on the sofas and armchairs on the other side of the room. No one ever came to the Oval Office expecting a meeting of equals, but that end of the room at least offered a pretense of collegiality. Trump, in contrast, placed visitors in chairs opposite the desk, their knees pressed awkwardly against the oak. To sit this way was to know Trump considered you a supplicant, an inferior. To be sure, no one complained, least of all Mueller himself, but the arrangement drew his notice—as Trump intended for all his guests.

The purpose of the meeting was . . . well, like so much else, that became a subject of dispute. And like so many disagreements in the Trump era, the facts were entirely on one side. Mueller told the truth about why he was in the Oval Office, and Trump lied about it. (Rod Rosenstein, the deputy attorney general, who had set up the meeting, was present, too.) A week earlier, Trump had fired James Comey, Mueller's successor as director of the FBI, and Rosenstein had reached out to Mueller to ask him to offer advice to the president about a replacement. Mueller had returned to the White House because he believed that if the president wanted to see you, it was your obligation to show up. This, as Rosenstein confirmed, was the only reason Mueller had come to the Oval Office.

Later, Trump said Mueller came to the Oval Office to ask for his old job back. The president said this over and over again—in public and private, and repeatedly in tweets, like this one: "Robert Mueller came to the Oval Office (along with other potential candidates) seeking to be named the Director of the FBI. He had already been in that position for 12 years, I told him NO." And this one: " 'Bob Mueller was pursuing the FBI Director job when he met with President Trump in 2017, Administration officials say.' @FoxNews Bret Baier and Jake Gibson @seanhannity This is true even though Mueller denied it." These statements by Trump were lies, all of them.

Mueller did not want to return to the FBI. In any event, federal law placed a limit on his tenure and barred his further service in the job. Still, Trump understood the value of repetition even if (especially if) a statement was false in the first place. The president saw most human contact as transactional—the exchange of favors or the pursuit of grievances; policy and principle meant little to him. So it was easiest for Trump to explain Mueller's acceptance of the job as special counsel, which happened the day after their Oval Office encounter, not as an act of public service but as the pursuit of a vendetta.

On the surface, the two men—Robert Swan Mueller III and Donald John Trump—had much in common. Mueller was born in 1944 and Trump in 1946, both to parents of considerable wealth. Mueller's father was an executive at DuPont, and young Bob grew up in Princeton, New Jersey, and on Philadelphia's Main Line. He went to prep school at St. Paul's, in Concord, New Hampshire, where the high Episcopalian values of muscular Christianity still prevailed. He excelled in his academic work, captained the ice hockey, soccer, and lacrosse teams, and won admission to Princeton. Trump's father, Fred, started a real estate business that built apartments for middle-class New Yorkers—he came to own thousands of them—and he raised his family in a mansion in Queens with a chauffeur to take young Donald to school. As a boy, Donald had a rocky trajectory, and his impetuous nature prompted his father to send him off to military school starting in eighth grade. There, the young heir straightened out enough to graduate. He went first to Fordham University but transferred after two years to the University of Pennsylvania. Trump graduated in 1968 and went to work for his father.

It was in the crucible of their generation—the Vietnam War—that their paths first diverged in a dramatic and revealing way. After graduating from Princeton in 1966, Mueller married his high school sweetheart and tried to enlist in the U.S. Marines. He had a knee injury at the time, and the marines made him wait more than a year for it to heal before he was accepted to officer candidate school. It wasn't until 1968, then, that he achieved his goal of going to Vietnam, where he survived several harrowing experiences in combat. In his first major battle, he was shot through his thigh, but he returned to duty, and more combat, soon afterward. His commendations included a Bronze Star (for combat valor), a Purple Heart, and two Navy Commendation Medals. Mueller maintained a lifelong reverence for the values of the U.S. Marine Corps. (Many years later, a friend asked him how he wanted to be introduced before a speech. "Just make sure to say I'm a marine," Mueller said.)

Trump received his first four deferments from the Vietnam-era draft because he was a college student. In 1968, after he graduated from

Penn and thus became ineligible for more educational deferments, he received a fifth—a medical deferment because of bone spurs. (When Trump ran for president, he said he could not remember which foot had the spurs or the name of the doctor who provided the letter about his medical condition to his draft board. It later appeared that the doctor was a podiatrist who was a tenant of Fred Trump's and wrote the letter as a favor to the Trump family.) Trump sometimes bantered about Vietnam with radio host Howard Stern. He referred to trying to avoid sexually transmitted diseases on the dating scene as "my personal Vietnam." "It's pretty dangerous out there," he said in 1993. "It's like Vietnam."

The contrasting experiences with Vietnam serve as a useful metaphor for the course Mueller and Trump took through their adult lives. To compare them is to challenge the conventions of journalistic balance. At every turn, Mueller chose public service over private gain; Trump did the opposite. Mueller earned a reputation for honesty and rectitude; Trump became infamous for his dishonesty and greed. Mueller had one wife and many lifelong friends; Trump had three wives, many business associates, and few friends. Their career paths reflected their values. After Vietnam, the University of Virginia Law School, and a brief stint in private practice, Mueller spent the next dozen years as an Assistant U.S. Attorney, first in San Francisco and then in Boston. After another short time at a law firm, he moved to Washington to serve in George H. W. Bush's Justice Department, where he ultimately became the assistant attorney general in charge of the criminal division.

After Bill Clinton's election, Mueller and his family moved back to Boston, where he returned to a law firm—again, for a brief time. At that point he made a career choice that might have been unprecedented in recent legal history. Even though he had just run the entire criminal division of the Department of Justice—a job that amounted to being the top federal prosecutor in the United States—Mueller moved back to Washington to serve as a line prosecutor in the homicide division of the U.S. Attorney's office. Mueller hungered for public service and the rush of action in a prosecutor's office. (A modest lifestyle, and a measure of inherited wealth, cushioned the pay cut of approximately 75 percent.) Though Mueller was a Republican, Clinton named him in 1998 to be the U.S. Attorney in San Francisco, to straighten out an office that had fallen into disarray. He had just left that job when George W. Bush nominated him to be director of the FBI in 2001. The Senate confirmed him unanimously.

Trump's trajectory is better known. Before winning the presidency, he had only ever worked at his family's firm. There, he parlayed his father's large fortune into a larger fortune of undetermined size. Trump came to prominence in the 1980s, when New York City was emerging from bankruptcy and the real estate market was recovering with it. In this period, he had a pair of notable successes, renovating the Grand Hyatt hotel, next to Grand Central Terminal (with generous support from city government), and building Trump Tower on Fifth Avenue (with help from the labors of undocumented immigrants). At that point, the nature of his business dealings grew more opaque. Many apartment buildings in New York came to bear his name, but the degree of his financial participation in these projects— both in expenditures and in revenue—remained unclear. The turning point in his public life came in 1987, when he published, to great success, *The Art of the Deal,* his first autobiography, which created his image as a glamourous and successful businessman. (His ghostwriter said Trump never read the book, much less wrote it.)

In the early 1990s, Trump made a disastrous foray into the gambling business in Atlantic City, and his empire nearly collapsed in multiple bankruptcies. In his personal life, he marked the decade with a pair of divorces, which the local and national tabloids followed with their trademark mix of celebration and revulsion. After that time, he was not in the real estate business as much as the Donald Trump business. He licensed his name to an enormous number of products—including clothing, wine, water, jewelry, steak, vodka, and a university (of sorts)—though none lasted very long or made much or any money for his partners. Starting in 2004, Trump won greater fame with a television program that defined (or more to the point, reinvented) his reputation. *The Apprentice* (and *Celebrity Apprentice*) revived and expanded the Trump brand as a symbol of business savvy and personal extravagance. Thanks to worldwide syndication of *The Apprentice,* his real estate ventures in recent years tended to be more outside the United States than within, as he licensed his name to any local developer who would put up the money. A handful of projects, like those in Azerbaijan and Panama, actually came to fruition, but in others Trump was paid for use of his name even if the projects were never built. His dream of building in Moscow, which he had pursued longer than any other foreign undertaking, remained just out of reach.

Trump had flirted with runs for political office for decades, but it was his television persona, created on this "reality" program, that made the presidency a possibility. The Trump of *The Apprentice*—steely, decisive, well versed in the ways of business and of the world—was a creation of the producers of the program. But that's who ran for president and won.

The contrasts between Mueller and Trump extended beyond their résumés and even included their appearances. Both were tall, but Trump was taller and created a more imposing presence, with his substantial girth and hypnotizing swirl of orange hair. Mueller had a head like an Easter Island *moai* and a demeanor to match. Trump intimidated with bluster, Mueller with silence. Both men had cutting senses of humor, usually at the expense of others; Mueller laughed little, Trump not at all. Oddly for senior men of their generation, who tended toward sartorial blandness, both had trademark outfits: Trump had his unbuttoned suits, with red ties hanging long in a forlorn effort to camouflage his gut. Mueller always wore white shirts with button-down collars. In his FBI days, he used the shirts as a symbol—to remind agents that even though the bureau was changing its mission from capturing criminals to preventing terrorism, some things remained the same. The white shirt, which was a required uniform in the days of J. Edgar Hoover, was a link to that imperfect past. Trump embraced ostentation and preferred to see his name in gold; Mueller reflected the shabby WASP gentility of a vanishing age. Mueller's wristwatch, a Casio digital model, retailed for about $50.

In the Oval Office on May 16, Mueller received a quick introduction to the nature of conversations with Trump—which meant that Trump talked and Mueller listened. With Mueller as with others, the topic would be whatever happened to be on Trump's mind. On this day, it was the perfidies of James Comey, the magnitude of Trump's landslide victory over Hillary Clinton (a favorite subject), and the excellence of Trump's polling numbers at that moment. Mueller had one message he wanted to impart—that he thought Trump should select an outsider as the new director of the FBI, rather than promote from within. Mueller did manage to interject that advice into the conversation, which ended after about half an hour.

For Mueller, it was a painless if puzzling encounter, but it had an unfortunate aftermath: he forgot his phone on the way out of the White House, and it took a maddening journey through the security labyrinth to get it back.

The next day, Mueller accepted Rosenstein's invitation to serve as special counsel, with instructions to investigate "any links and/or coordination between the Russian government and individuals associated with the campaign of President Donald Trump" as well as any crimes arising from his investigation. It would be the most extensive examination of presidential wrongdoing in a generation. Mueller assembled a team that represented a contemporary spin on the units featured in World War II movies, with their imagined cross sections of the military of that era—a Brooklyn wiseguy, a farm boy, a WASP prince. Mueller put together a team of experienced and elite prosecutors, and they represented a transformed twenty-first-century America. This time a WASP leader, Mueller, oversaw a Muslim daughter of immigrants from Pakistan, a woman born in Seoul, and an unmarried Jewish man, among others. As the investigation proceeded, the cast became sprawling. Mueller operated independently, but congressional Democrats, a cross section of journalists, and certain private investigators pursued many of the same subjects. Mueller had incidental targets around the president—including campaign advisers like Paul Manafort and National Security Adviser Michael Flynn—but there was never any doubt that the special counsel was focused on Trump himself.

Trump, for his part, fixated on Mueller. It had always been Trump's way to personalize disputes, and it was preordained that he would do the same in this one, which amounted to the most consequential threat of his career. Almost from the start, Trump characterized the investigation as a personal contest between him and the prosecutor. In many ways, it was. Both Mueller's team and Trump's operation, during the campaign as well as in the White House, functioned as projections of their leaders' personalities and values. Mueller and his team were disciplined, restrained, and orderly; they avoided publicity, and their presentations to the public—especially the Mueller Report, which closed their work—hewed scrupulously to provable facts. Trump was in every way their opposite, and his public statements were medleys of invective and falsehood. The president's legal team reflected their client and bore considerable similarities to Trump's 2016 campaign staff; his lawyers were disorganized and riven by internal rivalries, and their number was frequently in flux because of the changing moods of Trump himself.

The legal team that President Trump assembled against Mueller bore another similarity to the campaign team that Candidate Trump mobilized against Hillary Clinton. They both won. It's tempting to see the struggle between Mueller and Trump as one between good and evil, and there is much evidence to support that view. But a more useful dichotomy between the two sides might be between old and new. Mueller's team did a brilliant job in the traditional work of prosecutors. They did meticulous forensic examinations, built compelling cases against several important individuals, and extracted guilty pleas from culpable defendants. They also portrayed their public silence and narrow conception of their mandate as obligatory under the rules and traditions governing the work of prosecutors. But these were choices, and costly ones. Mueller's caution and reticence led him to fail at his two most important tasks. Thanks to the clever actions (and strategic inaction) of Trump's legal team, Mueller failed to obtain a meaningful interview with Trump himself. Even worse, Mueller convinced himself—wrongly—that he had to write a final report that was nearly incomprehensible to ordinary citizens in its legal conclusions. By doing so, he diluted, nearly to insignificance, the extraordinary factual record he had assembled. And the opacity of Mueller's report allowed Trump's allies to define it to the president's advantage.

Trump played with modern tools—mass media, social media, and the power of the presidency. He also relied on the traditional tool of demagogues by refining his legal position to a simple slogan—"no collusion and no obstruction." These phrases were, respectively, a half-truth and a falsehood, but they provided an anchor for his supporters' beliefs. Simplicity rarely loses to complexity in battles in the public square. Mueller was burdened with a complex narrative, which involved multiple contacts between Russia and the 2016 Trump campaign, but none of them dispositive enough to prove a criminal, collusive connection between the two. Trump's efforts to obstruct the investigations were clearer, but the president's allies could render them ambiguous or obscure them in the haze of constitutional legal argument. Trump himself played the major role in winning this war of public understanding, but Rudolph Giuliani, his lead attorney at the end of Mueller's investigation, deserved a large measure of credit as well. The facts and opportunities at Mueller's disposal could have led to a different conclusion of his investigation, but Trump and his allies, especially Giuliani, outplayed him in a game in which they made the rules.

But Trump's victory over Mueller was tactical, not strategic. The president and his allies outmaneuvered Mueller, but Trump's character—and his behavior—didn't change. He had muddied the public's understanding of his collusion and obstruction with regard to Russia, but his determination to collude and obstruct for political advantage never waned. Indeed, as it became clear that Trump would survive the Mueller investigation of Russia, the president took that escape as an invitation to undertake the same kind of effort with regard to Ukraine. But now that Trump was the president, not a private citizen running a long-shot campaign, he had vastly greater powers, which he used to collude and obstruct on a grander scale. To put it another way, 2020 was 2016, plus the power of the presidency. In this, Trump was abetted by the man who helped save him against Mueller—Giuliani. With regard to Ukraine, Giuliani steered Trump to disaster, in probably the greatest failure of lawyering in the history of presidential scandals. In other words, no Giuliani, no impeachment.

The two stories—Russia and Ukraine—adjoined on a pair of summer days in 2019. On July 24, Mueller looked feeble in testifying before Congress about his Russia investigation, and his performance served as an exclamation point on Trump's victory over his pursuer. Thus emboldened, President Trump the following morning demanded of Ukraine what as a candidate he could only request of Russia. This was the culmination of a months-long campaign, led by Giuliani and embraced by Trump, to exploit the vulnerable nation. In the elliptical but unmistakable language of a Mafia don, Trump made clear the terms of the trade he wanted to make with Volodymyr Zelensky, the newly installed president of Ukraine, who was locked in a life-or-death struggle with Russian troops on his eastern border. Ukraine would obtain American military aid, and Zelensky would receive an Oval Office meeting, only if Zelensky announced investigations of the family of Vice President Joseph Biden, Trump's leading rival in the 2020 election. It was a grotesque act of extortion on a vulnerable ally.

Through the intervention of an appalled whistle-blower, Trump was caught in this abuse of his powers. The president had by that point learned a cynical lesson from the Mueller investigation, as he demonstrated when Congress began to examine Ukraine. Of course, Trump lied about Ukraine—he always lied—but he also used the powers of his office as no president had before to stymie the efforts of Congress to determine what happened. The Constitution specifically gives the House of Representatives the right to impeach the president, but Trump imposed a blanket refusal to cooperate with the House's investigation. The White House issued a complete ban on the testimony of administration witnesses and the production of executive branch documents. In response, the House passed two articles of impeachment—the first about Trump's exploitation of Ukraine for political gain and the second about his defiance of Congress. After a perfunctory trial, the Senate acquitted Trump. In both the House and the Senate, the votes were cast almost entirely along party lines, which revealed more about the president's hold on the Republican Party than about the quality of the evidence against him.

For three years, Trump led an almost charmed existence as president. He inherited a growing economy, which prospered further under his leadership, and there were no major international emergencies to test him. All of the crises of Trump's first three years, especially those that led to his impeachment, were those he brought on himself.

Then came the onslaught of the coronavirus, which would have been an epic challenge for even the best-prepared and best-intentioned president. But Trump responded to the coronavirus with the same belligerent dishonesty that characterized his treatment of Mueller and impeachment. In the critical early days of the pandemic, when it might have been contained, he behaved with characteristic self-obsession, preferring to hound his enemies on Twitter rather than to learn the facts about the virus and protect the American people.

That Trump had reached this point in his presidency at all—that he had weathered Russia and Ukraine—was itself remarkable. The president triumphed notwithstanding abundant evidence of his personal dishonesty and immorality and the efforts of learned and accomplished adversaries in Mueller's office and in Congress. Moreover, Trump survived these assaults even though everyone—friends as well as enemies—knew what he had done. It was obvious to any sentient observer that he did what he was accused of in the Mueller Report and in the articles of impeachment. Still, for someone who lied as much as Trump did, he was a remarkably transparent figure. He never really pretended to be anything other than what he was—a narcissistic scoundrel. Yet he survived.

How did this happen?

PART ONE

1

October Surprises

I
t may be an overstatement, though not much of one, to say that James Comey was responsible for both the election of Donald Trump and the appointment of Robert Mueller. In light of this, Comey became the most consequential director of the Federal Bureau of Investigation since, and perhaps including, J. Edgar Hoover, even though Comey served less than four years and Hoover reigned for nearly forty-eight. At the FBI, Comey evinced a showy disdain for his authoritarian and bigoted predecessor. In the director's cavernous office on the seventh floor of FBI headquarters (which is still called the J. Edgar Hoover Building), Comey showed visitors a copy of Hoover's directive to conduct wall-to-wall surveillance of Martin Luther King Jr. It was, as Comey often said, a shameful episode in the history of the bureau, and he was determined never to sully the institution in the same way. Comey worked hard to diversify the ranks of the bureau, but he resembled Hoover in that both directors ran the FBI according to their own rules.

Comey wrote a book about his tumultuous tenure, and its title accurately reflected his approach to the job—*A Higher Loyalty*. "There is a higher loyalty in all of our lives—not to a person, not to a party, not to a group," he wrote. "The higher loyalty is to lasting values, most important the truth." Notably, Comey's loyalty was not to the law or to the procedures and hierarchies that supposedly governed his conduct and those of his predecessors. Rather, his loyalty was to his own conception of the truth and of the right thing to do.

Comey always stood out from his peers, not least because he towered over them. He stood six feet eight inches, and as lean and fit as he was, he looked taller. He was used to being the tallest man in the room, but also the smartest. Comey had a glittering legal résumé: Assistant U.S. Attorney, U.S. Attorney, deputy attorney general, general counsel first to a leading defense contractor and then to a huge hedge fund. Comey became famous in 2007 when he testified in Congress about a dramatic confrontation, when he was deputy attorney general, at the hospital bedside of his boss, John Ashcroft, three years earlier. Though Ashcroft was desperately ill, George W. Bush's White House counsel, Alberto Gonzales, and chief of staff, Andrew Card, had come to the hospital to demand that he sign off on a surveillance program. Comey had raced to the hospital to say that Justice Department lawyers regarded some aspects of the program as unconstitutional. Ashcroft sided with Comey and refused to approve the program. At that point, Comey and other Justice Department officials (including Robert Mueller, then director of the FBI) threatened to resign if Bush overrode them. In response, the Bush White House backed down and agreed to changes in the program. This was Comey's starchy sense of his own rectitude at its best.

Comey's bedside confrontation with his superiors in the Bush White House was a major factor in Barack Obama's decision in 2013 to appoint him director of the FBI. He was a Republican appointed by a Democrat, but Comey always aspired to float above politics. In a partisan age, he sought to be a throwback to the days when a generation of men (and they were all men), known as the best and the brightest, served in Democratic and Republican administrations alike. Unlike many figures in law enforcement, and the eminences of prior generations, Comey cultivated an outward-facing style, and he was a careful steward of his own reputation. With Comey, the line between candor and preening—and between earnestness and sanctimony— was often difficult to discern.

Even more than most directors of the FBI—Mueller in particular— Comey paid special attention to investigations that had the potential to affect the reputation of the bureau, and his own. This was especially true in the months leading up to the 2016 election, when the FBI conducted two politically explosive investigations: the first, about

Hillary Clinton's email practices at the State Department, became widely known, while the second, about possible Russian infiltration of the Trump campaign, never became public before Election Day. Comey's dramatically different treatment of the two investigations was just one of several ways his behavior contributed to Clinton's defeat and Trump's victory.

The Clinton email saga began when Congress launched the first of several probes into the deaths of four U.S. government employees in Benghazi, Libya, in September 2012, when Clinton was still secretary of state. After congressional Republicans learned that Clinton had used a private server for emails during her tenure, the FBI began an investigation to determine if Clinton had violated any laws governing classified information. The bureau conducted the probe at the same time as Clinton was running for president, and the email issue, which was relentlessly pushed by Republicans and exhaustively covered by the news media, haunted her campaign. The FBI's investigation, code-named Midyear Exam, dragged on for nearly a year, but the legal issue was always fairly straightforward and the subject of unanimous agreement among both the FBI agents and the Justice Department prosecutors on the case. Other secretaries of state had used private email accounts. There was no evidence that Clinton shared classified information with unauthorized people. There was, in short, no evidence that Clinton had the criminal intent required for a prosecution.

For Comey, the harder question involved public relations—whether and how the FBI should announce the conclusion of its Clinton investigation, which was wrapping up in late spring 2016. The bureau, like the Justice Department as a whole, long operated by a principle of put up or shut up—that is, public disclosure when criminal charges are filed, and silence when no prosecution is merited. The idea behind this practice was simple. If a criminal case is brought, defendants can respond by defending themselves in a public trial, but if the government disparages an individual without going to court, that person has no real recourse except to accept the reprimand. So, in normal circumstances, the way to end an investigation like the one into Clinton's emails would be to say nothing, or almost nothing.

Even in high-profile cases, the Justice Department usually announced, without elaboration, that a case was closed or, on rare occasions, gave a brief, anodyne explanation of the reasons why.

The Clinton matter was also complicated by a bizarre incident that took place just before the end of the investigation. On June 27, 2016, at the airport in Phoenix, former president Bill Clinton paid an unexpected call on Attorney General Loretta Lynch, whose government plane was idling on the tarmac. Both principals later insisted that their conversation amounted to just chitchat, but their encounter, which was deeply unwise on their parts, suggested that Clinton was trying to curry favor with the government agency that was investigating his wife. The tarmac encounter generated a political furor, and as a result Lynch effectively recused herself from the Hillary Clinton investigation. More to the point, Lynch said she would defer to whatever Comey thought should be done about the case. So the whole matter—both the decision about whether to pursue charges and how to make that judgment public—was now in Comey's hands.

Comey saw the issue as a political rather than strictly legal problem, and he came up with a political solution. Comey was always aware that regardless of the outcome of the 2016 presidential election, Republicans were likely to remain in control of Congress and thus responsible for oversight of the FBI and its budget. He knew, too, that Republicans were baying for Clinton's blood, and he recognized that they would not be happy with the customary silence that comes with a closed investigation. In light of this, he decided to improvise his own resolution. His idea was characteristic of his approach in high-profile controversies—one that departed from customary Justice Department policies, tried to keep everyone happy, and placed himself squarely in the spotlight. In a nationally televised speech on July 5, 2016, Comey said he would not recommend bringing charges against Clinton, but then he added that the former secretary of state had been "extremely careless" in her use of a private server for government business. When it came to the laws governing classified information, there was no such legal category as "extremely careless"; that was just Comey's ad hoc evaluation of the facts, which he had no official obligation to make. Comey was giving something to both sides: clearing Clinton of criminal wrongdoing, but also bestowing on Republicans a talking point with which to attack the Democrat. Accepting the Republican nomination for president a few days later, Trump embraced Comey's denunciation of Clinton but said Comey should have authorized a criminal prosecution of the Democrat. "When the FBI director says that the secretary of state was 'extremely careless' and 'negligent,' in handling our classified secrets, I also know that these terms are minor compared to what she actually did," Trump said. "They were just used to save her from facing justice for her terrible crimes."

At virtually the same time as the Clinton email investigation was closed, Comey and the FBI were again thrust into the presidential race, and this time the outcome of their deliberations would be very different. On July 22, WikiLeaks—the shadowy, international collaborative devoted to radical, and often illegal, transparency—posted thousands of emails that had been stolen from the servers of the Democratic National Committee (DNC). The emails showed that DNC officials favored Hillary Clinton over Bernie Sanders, and thus their disclosure poisoned relations between their respective camps on the eve of the Democratic National Convention. Media speculation immediately focused on Russia as a likely perpetrator of the hack. For his part, Trump greeted news of the hacking joyfully and, indeed, called for Russia and WikiLeaks to commit further crimes to discredit his rival. At a news conference at his Florida resort on July 27, Trump stared into the television cameras and made what would turn out to be one of the most famous utterances of the 2016 campaign. "Russia, if you're listening, I hope you're able to find the 30,000 emails that are missing," Trump said, referring to emails Clinton had deleted from the private server she used when she was secretary of state. "I think you will probably be rewarded mightily by our press." (Both as a candidate and as president, Trump frequently accused Clinton of deleting the emails after they were subpoenaed. In fact, shortly after she left her position as secretary of state, her aides went through her emails, which totaled about sixty thousand, and found approximately half were work related and half were personal. The half that were related to her job as secretary of state were turned over to the State Department and ultimately to investigators. The other half were deleted. This all happened before she was subpoenaed.)

Trump might have welcomed the Russians' hack of the DNC

emails—and called for more—but the American intelligence community had a very different reaction. These officials had known for years that the Russian government had been trying to interfere with the American political system, but Russia's efforts had never before been so brazen or so successful. The concerns of American officials were heightened when, shortly after the WikiLeaks release, an Australian diplomat named Alexander Downer reported to American officials about a strange encounter he had had a few months earlier in a London bar with a young adviser to the Trump campaign named George Papadopoulos. Papadopoulos had told the diplomat that the Russians had thousands of emails that, if disclosed, would embarrass Clinton's campaign. When WikiLeaks made Papadopoulos look eerily prescient, Downer told his American contacts about Papadopoulos's statement. The FBI then opened a formal investigation, which was code-named Crossfire Hurricane.

The FBI's worries about the Russians were compounded that summer, when agents learned about a mission to Moscow undertaken by Carter Page, another foreign policy adviser to the Trump campaign. Like Papadopoulos, Page was an obscure figure in foreign policy circles, but as a member of the Trump team he had been invited to Russia to give a prestigious address to the New Economic School. (Obama had spoken there as president in 2009.) In 2016, Page had praised Trump and Putin, called for a rapprochement between the two countries, and generally recited Russian government talking points. He also met with Russian officials. Years earlier, he had already been the subject of FBI surveillance as a possible asset of Russian intelligence. The DNC hacking, the approach to Papadopoulos, the cultivation of Page—what was going on here? That's what the FBI, along with the rest of the intelligence community, set out to learn in the summer of 2016.

Later, critics of the FBI—notably Trump himself in 2020—claimed that the investigation was a sinister act. They asserted that the intelligence agencies, which they sometimes referred to as the deep state, were interfering with a political campaign, and this represented a grave threat to the independence and integrity of the Trump campaign. But these complaints were always misplaced. The FBI is responsible for counterintelligence, as well as criminal prosecutions, in the United States. Crossfire Hurricane was a counterintelligence operation—to find out what Russia was doing, not to find out what the Trump campaign was doing. In other words, in the summer of 2016, the FBI was investigating Russian efforts to manipulate individuals within the Trump campaign, but not the Trump campaign itself. And the clearest proof that the agencies were not attempting to harm the Trump campaign was the fact that the investigation remained secret. The FBI could have gravely damaged Trump by leaking that the bureau was examining the ties between two of his campaign's advisers and a hostile foreign power. But there was no leak, because there was no attempt, by the FBI or any other agency, to undermine Trump's campaign. If the agencies were motivated to elect Clinton, they could have released this news. But they did not.

The absence of leaks was especially notable because it didn't take the intelligence agencies long to figure out what was happening. In August, the agencies reported to President Obama that the Russian government had orchestrated the theft of the emails, in an operation personally authorized by Russian president Vladimir Putin. And the CIA knew that Putin's goal in this effort was clear from the beginning: to defeat Hillary Clinton and elect Donald Trump as president.

At first, Obama ordered the information to be closely held, limiting the revelations about Russia to just a handful of White House aides. (They also did not leak.) Obama faced a difficult dilemma. The president wanted to denounce and stop the Russian interference, but he wanted to do it in a way that would not look as if he himself were trying to take political advantage of the situation. The president and his advisers knew that Putin was determined to help Trump win, but Obama wanted to disclose that fact without looking as if he were trying to help Trump lose. As he often did, Obama thought the answer was in bipartisanship. A united front with Republicans would demonstrate to the world that Putin's interference with the most important ritual of American democracy was unacceptable. But when Obama's aides went to brief the congressional leadership, Mitch McConnell, the Republican leader in the Senate, refused to accept their findings or join in any denunciation of Putin. Weeks passed as Obama and his aides dithered about what to do with the explosive information about Russia.

In the end, Obama hedged. He agreed to some public disclosure about the Russian hacking initiative, but only in vague, veiled terms.

Still wary of appearing partisan, Obama directed that his intelligence officials refrain from revealing the most explosive part of the hacking story—that Putin was trying to help Trump win the presidency. The joint statement would come from the leaders of Obama's intelligence team—the Department of Homeland Security, the FBI, and the Office of the Director of National Intelligence, which represents sixteen intelligence agencies in the government. But there was a holdup at the last minute, because Comey, displaying his trademark independence, decided he didn't want to be part of any joint statement. He gave his reasons in an October 5 email to John Brennan, the director of the CIA, and James Clapper, the director of national intelligence. "I think the window has closed on the opportunity for an official statement, with 4 weeks until a presidential election," Comey wrote. "I think the marginal incremental disruption/inoculation impact of the statement would be hugely outweighed by the damage to the [intelligence community's] reputation for independence." As with his announcement of the closing of the Clinton email investigation in July, Comey was worried about offending Republicans.

Continuing on a note of faux humility, Comey said, "I could be wrong (and frequently am) but Americans already 'know' the Russians are monkeying around on behalf of one candidate. Our 'confirming' it (1) adds little to the public mix, (2) begs difficult questions about both how we know that and what we are going to do about it, and (3) exposes us to serious accusations of launching our own 'October surprise.' That last bit is utterly untrue, but a reality in our poisonous atmosphere." Two days later, Brennan and Clapper issued the statement without Comey's name. And events would soon show that the FBI director's concerns about an "October surprise" would be selective at best.

The statement from the intelligence officials came, at last, on October 7, 2016, which would turn out to be one of the most consequential days in American political history. "The U.S. Intelligence Community is confident that the Russian government directed the recent compromises of e-mails from U.S. persons and institutions, including from U.S. political organizations," the statement said, in opaque, bureaucratic prose. "We believe, based on the scope and sensitivity of these efforts, that only Russia's senior-most officials could have authorized these activities." Also on that day, WikiLeaks surprised those intelligence officials, and everyone else, when the organization began releasing another set of hacked emails, this time from the account of John Podesta, Clinton's campaign chairman. But by the end of the day, the news from the intelligence community and the latest stolen emails were all but drowned out by the biggest bombshell of the campaign—the disclosure, in *The Washington Post*, of a video outtake from the *Access Hollywood* television program showing Trump bragging about committing acts of sexual violence against women. The *Access Hollywood* video strongly reinforced the prevailing conventional political wisdom: that regardless of what happened in the final days of the campaign, Clinton was going to win anyway.

The WikiLeaks provocateurs had learned from their experience in July, when they had dumped all the DNC emails on the same day. In October, WikiLeaks parceled out the Podesta emails in piecemeal fashion—a new set posted each day in the final stages of the campaign—so that the damage to the Clinton campaign would accumulate. As in the summer, Trump embraced the WikiLeaks disclosures, and the drip-drip pace of the Podesta disclosures gave Trump the chance to pump up the revelations each day. He often appeared on the campaign trail waving copies of the newly revealed emails. Trump praised WikiLeaks throughout the final days of the campaign. "WikiLeaks! I love WikiLeaks!" . . . "This WikiLeaks is like a treasure trove!" . . . "Getting off the plane, they were just announcing new WikiLeaks, and I wanted to stay there, but I didn't want to keep you waiting. Boy, I love reading those WikiLeaks!"

Though none of the Podesta emails were especially damaging to Clinton on their own, the steady stream of disclosures guaranteed that they would draw more attention than the intelligence agencies' careful statement about how the emails had been stolen in the first place. Perhaps worst of all for the Democratic nominee, even though the hack of the Podesta emails had nothing to do with the drama surrounding Clinton's own email account, the swirl of attention to email issues, especially for inattentive voters, was a disastrous development during the last days of the campaign.

The Podesta emails produced grist for a question at the final presidential debate, on October 19. One email quoted a private speech that Clinton had delivered sometime earlier, and Chris Wallace of Fox News asked Clinton about it. Instead of answering directly, the Democratic nominee wheeled on her questioner, and on her opponent, and changed the subject.

"You are very clearly quoting from WikiLeaks," Clinton said. "What is really important about WikiLeaks is that the Russian government has engaged in espionage against Americans. They have hacked American websites, American accounts of private people, of institutions. Then they have given that information to WikiLeaks for the purpose of putting it on the internet. This has come from the highest levels of the Russian government—clearly from Putin himself in an effort, as seventeen of our intelligence agencies have confirmed, to influence our election." The Russian president was supporting Trump, Clinton went on, because "he would rather have a puppet as president of the United States."

"No puppet," Trump shot back. "You're the puppet."

Clinton resumed, "It is pretty clear you won't admit that the Russians have engaged in cyberattacks against the United States of America—that you encouraged espionage against our people." Trump then responded by proving Clinton's point, by refusing again to accept the conclusion that Russia had conducted the hacks. "She has no idea whether it is Russia, China, or anybody else," Trump said.

Clinton's claims about Russian efforts to help her opponent—which were more correct than even she knew at the time—found little traction, either with the news media or with the public at large. Her effort failed because the FBI kept up Comey's effort to downplay the Russia story. Shortly after the debate, the bureau leaked a story to *The New York Times* that bore the headline "Investigating Donald Trump, F.B.I. Sees No Clear Link to Russia." The story went on, "Law enforcement officials say that none of the investigations so far have found any conclusive or direct link between Mr. Trump and the Russian government. And even the hacking into Democratic emails, F.B.I. and intelligence officials now believe, was aimed at disrupting the presidential election rather than electing Mr. Trump." As would become clear, this was precisely wrong. The hacking *was* aimed at electing Trump. But the people who knew the truth weren't talking to *The New York Times*.

—

The campaign had one final turn, and it was entirely Comey's doing.

In September, FBI agents in New York opened an investigation of Anthony Weiner, the former congressman, for an illicit online relationship with a minor. (Public disclosures of Weiner's predilection for such behavior had already ended his political career.) On September 26, agents obtained a search warrant for Weiner's iPhone, iPad, and laptop computer. When bureau personnel started examining the computer, they found that Weiner shared the device with his wife, Huma Abedin, who was a close aide to Hillary Clinton. Further, they saw that the computer contained thousands of emails between Clinton and Abedin. (The agents didn't read these emails, because the warrant covered only Weiner's communications.) Were the Clinton-Abedin emails relevant to the Midyear Exam investigation of Clinton? Could they include classified information that would call into question the FBI's exoneration of Clinton months earlier? Or were the emails simply duplicates of emails that had already been turned over to the FBI? At that point, no one knew the answers. The question of what to do with Weiner's laptop worked its way through the FBI bureaucracy.

And then, remarkably, nothing happened for weeks. The FBI administrators in Washington thought the New York agents were processing the laptop, and the New York agents were waiting for guidance from Washington. The matter, a priority for no one, fell between the cracks. The issue of Weiner's laptop might have disappeared altogether, but in late October prosecutors from the Southern District of New York, who were conducting the investigation of the former congressman, asked the FBI what was going on. This bestirred the FBI to refocus on the issue, and it inched up the chain of command until Comey was finally briefed on it on October 27.

Comey's reaction to the news about the laptop differed from everyone else's at the FBI. He fixated on the fact that when he closed the Clinton email investigation in July, he told the congressional leaders that he would advise them if there were any developments that would cause him to reopen the case. This was a kind of boilerplate statement that investigators routinely make when they close a case. But Comey told his subordinates that the discovery of the Clinton-Abedin emails on the Weiner laptop represented the kind of new information he had promised to provide to Congress. Virtually all of his subordinates disagreed. They pointed out that no one had read the newly discovered Clinton-Abedin emails at that point. There was every possibility that they were duplicates of emails that had already been reviewed in the Midyear Exam investigation. Until the newly discovered emails were reviewed, and any new information actually identified, there were no new developments in the case.

But there was an even more important reason to refrain from disclosing the story of the Weiner laptop: the calendar. On Thursday, October 27, when Comey was briefed, Election Day was less than two weeks away. The Justice Department, including the FBI, had a long-standing if unwritten rule that prohibits public disclosure of investigative steps regarding a candidate within sixty days of an election. Comey acknowledged the existence of this custom, but he told his subordinates that he had to make the disclosure to Congress anyway—because the risk of nondisclosure was too great. Comey told his colleagues, and he said later, that if Clinton had won the election and he failed to disclose the new development, the effect on the bureau's reputation would be catastrophic. It was worth violating the FBI's unwritten rules to preserve Comey's credibility with Congress.

In theory, of course, Comey had a boss—the attorney general. And Lynch, as well as her deputy, Sally Yates, had the technical legal authority to overrule Comey's decision to inform Congress of the new development. And Comey did tell his superiors of his decision to inform Congress before he did so. Predictably, Lynch and Yates were as horrified as the others by Comey's decision, for all the same reasons—that it was premature, unnecessary, and politically inflammatory. But thanks to the Phoenix tarmac misadventure, the Justice Department had effectively ceded its authority on the issue to Comey. Through a subordinate, Yates passed a meek protest against Comey's decision, but neither she nor Lynch pursued the matter. Comey ignored them.

So, in the end, on the eve of the election, Comey again violated the traditions and norms of the Justice Department. In July, he had trashed Clinton while closing her case because he was afraid of offending Republicans; in early October, he had refused to join with the other intelligence agencies in calling out Russian interference because he was afraid of offending Republicans; and now, finally, he was announcing the reopening of the Clinton email investigation because he was afraid of offending Republicans. It wasn't that Comey took these actions because he wanted to see Trump win the presidency; it wasn't that simple. Comey wanted to maintain his position as an independent actor between the Democrats and the Republicans. He placed such a high value on preserving his own reputation for even-handedness that he was willing to violate Justice Department norms and fling himself into the middle of the election. And besides, Comey thought, his last-minute lunge for the spotlight wouldn't matter, because Clinton was going to win anyway.

At 11:50 a.m., on Friday, October 28, Comey delivered a letter to the congressional leadership that said he was "writing to supplement" his previous statements about the Clinton email investigation.

He went on:

> In connection with an unrelated case, the FBI has learned of the existence of emails that appear to be pertinent to the investigation. I am writing to inform you that the investigative team briefed me on this yesterday, and I agreed that the FBI should take appropriate investigative steps designed to allow investigators to review these emails to determine whether they contain classified information, as well as to assess their importance to our investigation.
>
> Although the FBI cannot yet assess whether or not this material may be significant, and I cannot predict how long it will take us to complete this additional work, I believe it is important to update your Committees about our efforts in light of my previous testimony.

Comey's letter, of course, caused a sensation and dominated news coverage, all to Clinton's disadvantage, particularly since the message was so tantalizingly vague. The letter prompted Trump, who had been critical of Comey's decision to recommend against charging Clinton, to change his mind about the FBI director. "You know what? It took a lot of guts. I really disagreed with him. I was not his fan," Trump said of Comey at a rally in Michigan. "I tell you what, what he did, he brought back his reputation. He brought it back. He's got to hang tough."

The underlying facts leaked quickly. The world soon knew that Comey had authorized his agents to seek a new search warrant so they could examine the contents of the Clinton-Abedin emails on the laptop; they obtained the warrant on October 30. (Of course, this could have been done a month earlier if the FBI had not simply forgotten about the laptop for most of that time. That so many bureau employees ignored the laptop for so long suggests that Comey's urgency about the matter was misguided.) The laptop was taken to the FBI facility in Quantico, Virginia, where there was a crash effort by a squadron of agents to review the thousands of emails.

On Sunday, November 6, Comey wrote a second letter to Congress, stating, "Based on our review, we have not changed our conclusions that we expressed in July with respect to Secretary Clinton." The entire frantic enterprise surrounding Weiner's laptop had produced no relevant information about Hillary Clinton. The laptop yielded no new evidence.

On November 8, Donald Trump was elected president of the United States. Of course, in a close election, it is never possible to identify with precision the individual factors that tip the balance. But it appears likely, if not certain, that Comey cost Clinton the presidency.

2

Loyalty and Honest Loyalty

Comey had a taste for gallows humor, often at his own expense. Given Clinton's fury about the email investigation, and Trump's criticism of the way the FBI conducted that probe, Comey liked to joke with colleagues that he was going to get fired regardless of who won the election. But he didn't really believe that. When Trump was elected, Comey was only three years into a ten-year term as FBI director. One main reason for the long term was to insulate the director from political interference by the president. (Another was to prevent overlong tenures like Hoover's.) Realistically, then, what could Trump do to him?

Comey and Trump had never met in person before the election, so the FBI director was compelled to ask the same questions that many people in the government, and in the country, were asking. What was Trump really like? How would the burdens of the presidency change him? For Comey, there were high stakes in the answers. Establishing a relationship with the president was a big part of the FBI director's job. Mueller met almost daily with George W. Bush—for years. At Bush's direction, he had reoriented the bureau toward preventing terrorist attacks, rather than just investigating crimes that had already taken place. Bush required constant updates from Mueller on the nation's state of readiness. As the threat of terrorism receded, Obama saw his FBI director less often, but Comey was still a regular visitor to the Oval Office during his first years on the job. The FBI director went to the president with pressing issues—the chances of terrorist attacks, the state of national security investigations, the threat of spying by foreign adversaries in the United States. Trust between the two men was not just desirable but vital to the safety of the nation.

But Trump wasn't like any of his predecessors, and that difference, at a minimum, called for special handling. Trump had never served in government, or the military. He had no experience with national security or terrorism issues. He had only ever worked for his own family business, where he consorted with the seediest of characters in New York real estate and earned a reputation for sharp practices, and worse. In other words, Comey realized, Trump was boss, stranger, novice, witness, possible security risk, potential subject of criminal investigation, and president-elect of the United States. How was the FBI director supposed to navigate all *that*?

Worse yet, Comey had an immediate issue for Trump's attention. At that moment, in the first weeks after the 2016 election, few had heard of the document that became known as the Steele dossier. But Comey had to decide whether to tell Trump about it.

The story of the dossier began with Fusion GPS, a private investigative firm founded by a pair of former *Wall Street Journal* journalists, Glenn Simpson and Peter Fritsch. In 2015, Fusion was hired by the Washington Free Beacon, a conservative political website, to do research on Donald Trump, among others. The leaders of the Free Beacon were Republicans, but they were "Never Trumpers," and they hired Fusion to find dirt on Trump to use to deny him the party's support. By the spring of 2016, though, Trump had locked up the nomination, and Fusion sought out a new buyer for its trove of Trump opposition research. In April, the company signed on with Perkins Coie, the law firm that was representing the Clinton campaign. Now working for Trump's likely Democratic opponent, Fusion decided to look into the ties that were just beginning to be revealed between Trump and Russia. To that end, it hired as a subcontractor Christopher Steele, a former British intelligence official with long expertise in Russian affairs. Over the next few months, during the heart of the 2016 general election campaign, Steele compiled a series of reports based on interviews with knowledgeable sources about Russia. The work was rough and preliminary, totaling about thirty-five pages, and it became known—both famous and infamous—as the Steele dossier.

Steele had a long and fruitful relationship with the FBI. His private investigative work had produced some of the most important evidence in the bureau's successful criminal investigation of FIFA, the international soccer organization. Steele was shocked by what he found in his inquiries about Trump. As he put it in the clipped language of the dossier, "Russian regime has been cultivating, supporting and assisting TRUMP for at least 5 years. . . . Former top Russian intelligence officer claims [Russia] has compromised TRUMP through his activities in Moscow sufficiently to be able to blackmail him." In the summer of 2016, Steele grew so concerned about Trump's potential vulnerability to the Russians that he reached out to his contacts in the FBI to advise them of his findings. The agents never verified all of Steele's claims, but they added his reports to their Crossfire Hurricane investigation—the examination of Russian influence in the election. In addition, Steele, along with his patrons at Fusion, decided to supplement his efforts to prevent Trump from winning the election by sharing his work with a handful of journalists in Washington.

And this created Comey's problem. In the weeks leading up to Trump's inauguration, the FBI learned that CNN and other news outlets had copies of the dossier and were considering reporting on it. One of Steele's purported discoveries was especially problematic. Two sources reported that when Trump stayed at Moscow's Ritz-Carlton hotel in 2013, a pair of Russian prostitutes had urinated on each other for Trump's entertainment. This was supposedly especially appealing to Trump because the pair defiled the bed that had earlier been used by Barack and Michelle Obama—"whom he hated," as Steele put it. According to Steele's sources, the sordid scene had been secretly videotaped by Russian intelligence and thus served as a likely source of *kompromat,* or compromising material, on the future president.

Comey knew that Steele's claim about the "pee tape," even if it was entirely untrue, would create a media storm. The question, then, was whether he should advise Trump of Steele's findings before they became public. At one level, Comey believed that Trump would want a heads-up so the president-elect wouldn't be blindsided when the report came out. No one, especially public figures, likes unpleasant surprises. Moreover, a warning to Trump would be especially prudent because the FBI had known about the dossier for some time. On the other hand, it would be excruciating for Comey to introduce himself to his new boss with this kind of information.

In what became a recurring pattern over the next several months, Comey consulted his top two advisers about his Trump problems. The pair were as different from each other as they were from the director himself. Comey was bluff, outgoing, confident that he could charm or think his way out of any predicament. James Baker—owlish, professorial, absentminded—was the FBI general counsel and a confirmed worrier. Andrew McCabe—the deputy director—was, unlike Comey or Baker, an actual FBI special agent who had had a long and successful career chasing criminals, including mobsters. With his crew cut and unfashionable eyeglasses, McCabe looked the part of the prototypical agent and leavened Baker's bookishness with his streetwise savvy.

The trio thought they had no illusions about Trump. The president was into his eighth decade when he arrived at the White House, and people rarely changed their personalities at that age. They knew about his reputed temper, impatience, lack of intellectual curiosity. But they felt at that point that they had no choice but to give him the benefit of the doubt, to treat him like the other presidents they had served. But Comey and company came to realize—as others would soon learn in the crucible of Donald Trump's presidency—that they had no idea of the magnitude of his flaws, of his narcissism, sociopathy, and ignorance. Trump's only concern was his feral self-interest, his only belief was that those around him existed to serve him. This recognition came gradually to the FBI leaders—it was hard to accept that Trump was really this way—but everyone who was paying attention saw the same thing.

In that early moment, though, Comey and his colleagues had a specific issue before them: what, if anything, to tell Trump about the Steele dossier. As the three men pondered the issue, they thought of J. Edgar Hoover. Even decades after his death, Hoover's ghost still haunted the FBI. Hoover was notorious for hoarding embarrassing information about politicians and using it as leverage; this implicit blackmail helped coerce presidents into allowing him to remain in office for so long. The question, then, was whether Trump would see

Comey's invocations of the Steele dossier as a Hoover-esque act of intimidation.

When Comey and his colleagues were pondering the legacy of J. Edgar Hoover, they had drawn a surprisingly meaningful analogy, except they had it backward. Trump, not Comey, was the heir to Hoover's legacy. In the early 1950s, when Hoover was at the peak of his powers, he led the investigation of Julius and Ethel Rosenberg, who were accused of passing atomic secrets to the Soviet Union. When the case came to trial in New York, one of the prosecutors was a twenty-four-year-old legal prodigy named Roy Cohn. Hoover was impressed by Cohn's work and became a mentor to the young lawyer. He persuaded Senator Joseph McCarthy to hire Cohn as his chief counsel, and Cohn became one of the leading red-baiters in the country. Later, Cohn turned his vindictive and unethical style of lawyering into a private practice in New York. There, in the 1970s and early 1980s, he became a mentor to young Donald Trump, instructing the novice developer in the win-at-all-costs style that he would bring first into business and then into politics. There was, in other words, a straight line of political and ethical descent from Hoover to Cohn to Trump. Its touchstones were paranoia and malice, which were, in practice, little different from the prevailing values of organized crime. Later, when President Trump's legal woes multiplied, he would beseech the heavens with the words "Where's my Roy Cohn?" (Cohn himself was disbarred for unethical behavior in 1986 and died later that year.)

This background was basically unknown to Comey, Baker, and McCabe as they prepared for the director's first meeting with the president-elect and pondered whether Comey should talk about the Steele dossier. Baker, the lawyer, counseled caution. *Say nothing,* he told Comey. *You never know what Trump will say. He may deny it. He may admit it and ask for your help in dealing with it. Someday he may even lie about what he told you. In all those possibilities, you become a witness—which you don't want to be. Silence is safer.* Baker even suggested that if Comey was going to discuss the dossier with Trump, he should bring McCabe along to take notes and produce a 302—the official FBI form for summaries of interviews. McCabe agreed to go but understood that if Comey brought along a G-man, that might look more like an ambush than a heads-up.

Comey rejected Baker's advice and even went a step further. The decision was, in a way, classic Comey—counting on his ample interpersonal skills to talk his way out of a difficult situation. Comey alone was going to tell Trump about the dossier, but he was going to ease the blow with a bit of good news. He would tell Trump that even though the Steele dossier had come to the bureau's attention, the FBI was not investigating Trump's behavior. Trump would want to hear that he, personally, was in the clear. Baker, the general counsel, again warned against Comey's volunteering this information. The Russia investigation—Crossfire Hurricane—had already raised questions about the propriety, if not the legality, of the Trump campaign's dealings with Russia. Even if Trump himself was not at that moment under scrutiny, there was every possibility that he might be in the future. If that happened, Baker warned, the bureau would have to tell Trump that he had become a subject of the investigation—with disastrous consequences for the president's relationship with the FBI. But Comey decided to override Baker's concerns and tell Trump that he was not under investigation. And this was true—at least for the moment.

On December 29, 2016, with the election over and the need for bipartisanship no longer relevant, the Obama administration finally announced some consequences for Russia for interfering in the election. Obama expelled thirty-five Russians from the United States and closed two American estates that the Russian government owned. Trump responded as he had throughout the campaign, by downplaying any Russian role in the election. "I think we ought to get on with our lives," he said. But the president-elect did agree to receive a briefing from intelligence officials about the Russian activities, and it was scheduled for Friday, January 6, 2017, at his offices in Trump Tower in New York.

Comey was among those who attended, and he took advantage of the opportunity to raise the issue of the Steele dossier. When the larger briefing ended, Comey approached Trump and said he wanted to discuss a private matter with him, in a smaller group. Reince Priebus, the incoming chief of staff, offered to participate, but Trump said he would handle it one-on-one with Comey. Trump began by saying

Comey had had "one heck of a year" and that he looked forward to working together. He hoped Comey would stay on, and Comey said he would. Comey said he wanted Trump to know that there was a document circulating that asserted that the Russians had tapes of him with prostitutes at a hotel in Moscow in 2013. (Comey skipped the urination detail.) Trump said he had not consorted with prostitutes in Moscow and then added, in characteristic fashion, that he wasn't the kind of guy who needed to hire prostitutes anyway. Comey said he wasn't asserting that the incident actually took place, only that the report existed and CNN and others had copies and might reveal the story. Comey said he didn't want Trump to be blindsided by the news. And, true to his plan, he made sure to say that the FBI was not investigating Trump himself. (Following the five-minute conversation, Comey raced to an FBI SUV, where he typed up a report of the encounter, as close to verbatim as he could recall. This plan for Comey to record nearly contemporaneous notes was a rough substitute for bringing McCabe along as a witness.) The meeting ended cordially enough, but when the Steele dossier itself leaked four days later, in BuzzFeed, Trump was furious, and he blamed Comey—as the FBI director was about to hear directly.

The relationship between presidents and FBI directors has long been fraught and ripe with potential for abuse. Richard Nixon, who also had long relationships with Hoover and Cohn, used the power of the federal government against his political enemies. He compelled the Internal Revenue Service and other regulatory agencies to audit and harass his adversaries; the Watergate cover-up, which ultimately forced Nixon's resignation, was at its core about the abuse of his authority over the FBI and CIA. As a result of these transgressions, all subsequent administrations honored the procedures put in place that created buffers between the president and the federal investigating agencies. The president and the FBI director were expected to communicate often about potential threats to the country, as well as counterintelligence and criminal justice policy. That was why Mueller went to the White House nearly every day. But if, for example, the president wanted to inquire about or participate in any investigatory decisions by the Justice Department or the FBI in specific criminal cases, those contacts were supposed to go through the White House counsel, who would make his or her own initial judgments about their propriety. The counsel would then pass the request to the Justice Department, which would also review it, and only then would it be passed to the FBI. These customs were norms, not formal legal rules, but they had been accepted and followed by presidents of both parties for decades.

One way this policy manifested itself, Comey knew, was that phone calls between the president and the FBI director had been both rare and choreographed in advance; Comey never had a single telephone conversation with Obama. So Comey was surprised, on January 11, the day after the BuzzFeed story, when Trump called him out of the blue to complain that the FBI had leaked the dossier. As Comey gently reminded his future boss, this was not the case. The dossier was not a government document, and several people outside the FBI had copies of it. Bizarrely, Trump also volunteered a refutation of a part of the dossier that Comey had not mentioned to him. Trump said the urination story couldn't be true because he was a "germaphobe." (Comey thought to himself that the Ritz-Carlton suite was probably big enough so that Trump would not necessarily have been in the line of fire, as it were, but he also thought better than to pursue this line of argument.) In any event, Trump appeared somewhat mollified by the end of the call, but Comey could tell their relationship was off to a shaky start. In those first days, Trump was taking Comey's measure, seeing if the FBI director was trying, like Hoover, to gain leverage. If that was the case, Trump was going to respond in kind, with his own sort of Hoover-esque manipulation. At first, Trump would try to see if he could recruit Comey to his side. If he could, so much the better; if he couldn't, as Comey would soon learn, he would be gone.

In what became a pattern, Comey convened Baker and McCabe for a debrief after the phone call with Trump. They agreed it was weird and awkward, but they thought Comey should shrug it off. Perhaps Trump wasn't trying to intimidate the FBI director. He was just new, they thought—and hoped.

At the time of Trump's inauguration, the FBI's investigation of Russian interference in the election was continuing on a low boil. Agents were looking into the ties of Papadopoulos and Page to Russian interests, and the bureau was also trying to determine who, precisely, was behind the hacking of the DNC and Podesta emails. But then, in a pattern that would recur throughout the investigation, the news media advanced the story further than the investigators had done. This, in turn, prompted the FBI (and later the Mueller team) to accelerate their efforts. At the time, Trump and his allies found this pattern maddening. The zeal and skill of the news media (especially *The New York Times* and *The Washington Post*) kept the Russia story in the headlines nearly every day. In the long run, though, the drip-drip of news coverage wound up working to Trump's benefit. By the time the Mueller investigation concluded, the public already knew much of the story and had become acclimated, if not inured, to its outrages. (In contrast, the story of Trump's corrupt overture to the president of Ukraine was revealed in a single splash and thus retained its shock value.) In the early days of the new presidency, though, the press haunted Trump's world—starting with Michael Flynn.

Flynn had a distinguished three-decade career in the army, where he rose to the rank of lieutenant general. In 2012, Obama appointed him to run the Defense Intelligence Agency, where he earned a reputation for an erratic leadership style, an unhealthy obsession with Islam, and a peculiar fondness for Russia. Obama fired him in 2014, and Flynn became an outspoken critic of the administration and an apologist for Vladimir Putin. Flynn signed on early with the Trump campaign, just after a Russian propaganda outlet paid him a $45,000 fee to travel to Moscow to give a speech and dine with Putin. On the campaign trail, Flynn's behavior bordered on the unhinged, as when, at the Republican National Convention, he stood at the lectern and joined a chant of "lock her up." When Obama met with Trump immediately after the election, one piece of advice the president gave to his successor was to step away from Flynn. But Trump announced soon thereafter that Flynn would serve as his national security adviser.

Flynn's journey to oblivion began on January 12, 2017, when David Ignatius, a *Washington Post* columnist with long ties to the intelligence community, reported that Flynn had spoken repeatedly with Sergey Kislyak, the Russian ambassador to the United States, on December 29—the day that Obama imposed sanctions on Russia because of its interference in the 2016 election. Ignatius's story raised the possibility that Flynn and Kislyak were discussing the sanctions and scheming to have them removed once Trump took office. Such negotiations would have been improper, possibly even illegal, because Flynn was still a private citizen at the time. After the column, various figures in Trump's world—including Vice President elect Mike Pence—pressed Flynn about his conversations with Kislyak, and Flynn denied that any discussions of sanctions had taken place. The denials were repeated to the public by Pence and others, and the statements drew the attention of the Justice Department, where Obama's appointees were serving out their last days.

The Obama officials, like all administrations for decades, had been monitoring the phone calls of the Russian ambassador, so they knew that Flynn had in fact discussed sanctions. So they knew, and the Russians knew, that Flynn had been lying to everyone, and those lies had been repeated to the public. This raised the possibility that Flynn could be vulnerable to blackmail. The FBI quickly mobilized, and Flynn agreed to be interviewed by the agents on January 24, at his new office in the White House. There, Flynn repeated his lies, asserting that he had never talked to Kislyak about sanctions. This compounded the concern at the Justice Department, which now knew that the national security adviser had committed a crime—lying in an FBI interview—as well as opened himself up to being compromised by the Russians. Sally Yates, who was acting attorney general at the time, asked for an emergency meeting with Don McGahn, the new White House counsel, on January 26 and spelled out the problems. McGahn, in turn, briefed the president. He told Trump that Flynn was in trouble with the FBI. The bureau believed people who lied to agents should be prosecuted. Flynn was now in serious legal jeopardy.

Trump reacted in classic Roy Cohn fashion—by inviting Comey, the man investigating Flynn, to dinner.

Comey already had a hint that Trump would not be operating like his predecessors when it came to contacts with the bureau. The phone call after BuzzFeed's publication of the Steele dossier gave Comey an idea of what was coming. Then, on Sunday afternoon, January 22, there had been another peculiar incident. Comey had been invited to what he understood was a private reception at the White House, to thank the law enforcement leaders who helped protect the inauguration ceremony. Comey had been reluctant to go; he didn't want to be publicly perceived as too close to the new president, especially since many people already believed that he had handed Trump the election. But he thought passing on the event would offend both the president and his fellow law enforcement officials, so he showed up at the White House and tried to be inconspicuous, especially since it turned out cameras were present. To that end, the towering FBI director, in a blue suit, made a futile attempt to blend in with the drapes of the White House Blue Room. But Trump spotted him and summoned him, as if he were a courtier, to make the long walk across the room. Trump extended his hand to shake Comey's and then pulled him close for a whisper that almost looked like a kiss. "I'm really looking forward to working with you," Trump said. With a sheepish grin on his face, Comey walked back across the room, his plan to keep his distance from Trump, physically and otherwise, in tatters.

But more, and worse, was still to come. Five days later, on Friday, January 27, Comey's assistant received a phone call from the White House asking that the director join the president for dinner that night. Seeing no other choice, and hoping forlornly that others would be present, Comey showed up, as instructed, at six thirty. He didn't know that Don McGahn had just told Trump that his national security adviser was in serious trouble with the FBI. Nor did he know that Trump's mentor Roy Cohn was famous for saying, "I don't want to know what the law is—I want to know who the judge is." Comey was, in effect, the judge in Flynn's case, and Trump was going to put Cohn's advice to work on him. So as soon as Comey sat down to dinner, he could tell what was on the menu—his own job security. Trump didn't want to talk to Comey about any policy issues—nothing about terrorism, crime, or immigration—just loyalty.

Trump began the dinner by asking Comey if he wanted to stay on as director. Comey said yes, without reminding him that he had already said this twice to Trump. The president said he needed "loyalty" from his FBI director. "I need loyalty," Trump said, "I expect loyalty." Uncomfortable with the formulation, Comey said he would always give "honesty." Awkwardly, given the little standoff, he promised he would give "honest loyalty," whatever that meant. In his conversations with Baker and McCabe, Comey had said he planned to tell Trump about the customs governing White House contacts with the FBI—about the need to go through his White House counsel.

But he never had the chance during dinner, because Trump scarcely ever stopped talking.

By dessert, there was no doubt in Comey's mind about Trump's agenda for the dinner: that in order to keep his job as FBI director, he would have to prove his loyalty to the president—the person, not the institution. Or, as Comey later wrote of the dinner, "To my mind, the demand [for loyalty] was like Sammy the Bull's Cosa Nostra induction ceremony—with Trump, in the role of the family boss, asking me if I have what it takes to be a 'made man.'" At the dinner, Comey failed to prove that he had what it took to serve Trump, but the president would not stop trying, in his distinctive way, to see if his FBI director was right for the job.

3

Lifting the Cloud

Trump received a cascade of bad news following his inauguration. There was widespread mockery for his administration's false claims about the size of the crowd on the Washington Mall. All over the country, massive women's marches took place on the day after he took office. A poorly drafted, and obviously discriminatory, executive order limiting immigration from Muslim-majority countries led to more protests and court reversals. Trump's approval ratings in the polls, which were never high to begin with, dropped to about 40 percent, where they remained. There was, in short, no honeymoon.

Trump's relationship with Comey evolved in this poisonous political atmosphere. The president's natural inclinations toward paranoia and self-pity were heightened in the unfamiliar setting of the White House. In this environment, the FBI director made the classic mistakes when dealing with a bully—offering incremental concessions in the hope of keeping him at bay. When Trump demanded "loyalty," Comey tried to mollify him with "honesty" instead of telling the president that his only loyalty belonged to the law and to the American people. Instead of refusing to tell Trump whether he was under investigation—as he should have done—Comey tried to curry favor with his new boss by volunteering that the president was in the clear. Like any bully, Trump took these gifts from Comey as his due and then demanded more. Comey recognized this process as it was happening; he saw Trump ratcheting up his demands in ever more inappropriate ways. But once Comey let the cycle begin, his efforts to appease Trump's greed and hunger became more futile.

In further bad news for the new administration in these first days, the heat on Flynn became too intense for him to survive. His lies about his interactions with Kislyak led to the national security adviser's resignation on February 13, after a tenure of less than a month. As it happened, Comey was scheduled to be in the Oval Office the next day, for a joint briefing involving several agencies, about the terrorist threat in the United States. Trump's improprieties with Comey had been escalating with each interaction. The phone call blaming him for the leak of the Steele dossier. The forced show of deference in the Blue Room. The demand for loyalty at dinner. But Trump's behavior with Comey on February 14 reached a new level—outright illegality. In their prior dealings, Trump's interactions with Comey might have been sufficiently ambiguous that they fell short of criminal obstruction of justice. But on February 14, all pretense vanished; Trump broke the law.

After the briefing ended that afternoon, Trump asked Comey to stay behind. Jeff Sessions, the new attorney general, and Jared Kushner, the president's son-in-law and adviser, lingered, perhaps sensing that a one-on-one between the president and the FBI director held the possibility for impropriety. But Trump shooed the two men out of the room and faced Comey alone across the Resolute desk.

Trump's first words were, "I want to talk about Mike Flynn."

As Trump and Comey both knew by then, Flynn was under criminal investigation by the FBI. Any presidential request to discuss a pending case was supposed to go first through the White House counsel. Until this point, Comey could say that Trump had walked up to the line but hadn't yet crossed it. He might have been acting out of ignorance of the customs governing relations between the president and the FBI director. But Trump's actions on February 14 eliminated that possibility.

The conversation, as was Trump's habit, soon began meandering over a broad landscape. Trump complained about leaks. He volunteered that "they say I have one of the world's greatest memories." He circled back to the subject of Flynn, saying that Flynn had done nothing wrong in speaking to the Russian ambassador. But the president asserted that Flynn had to be fired because he lied to the vice president. In time, he specifically addressed the subject of the FBI's investigation of Flynn. As Comey wrote in his notes about the conversation, Trump told him, "[Flynn] is a good guy, and has been through a lot." He went on, "I hope you can see your way clear to letting this go, to letting Flynn go. He's a good guy. I hope you can let this go." In the moment, Comey told the president that he agreed that Flynn was a good guy, but he said nothing further about him. (Comey typed up his recollections of the encounter as soon as he left the White House. This had become his practice after interacting with the president because Comey and his advisers felt, with reason, that Trump might someday mischaracterize their dealings.)

In plain terms, the president was instructing his subordinate to drop a criminal investigation of one of his close associates. This behavior was not just inappropriate; it was a crime. It is true, of course, that Comey and the FBI did not follow the president's instruction, and the investigation of Flynn continued. But it has long been established that an act of obstruction of justice need not be successful to be criminal; the crime is the attempt, which Trump had clearly made.

As soon as Comey finished typing up his notes of the meeting in the White House, while still in his FBI van, he called his deputy, Andrew McCabe, who was in his car heading home to a Valentine's Day dinner with his wife.

"You are not going to believe this," Comey told him.

After the February 14 encounter in the Oval Office, something flipped within both Trump and Comey. By this point, Comey saw Trump not as a Washington naïf but as a New York gangster. Trump, in turn, saw Comey as an enemy. Trump's fear and anger were compounded on March 2, when Jeff Sessions, the former Alabama senator who had just been confirmed as attorney general, recused himself from any involvement with the Russia investigation. Under the law, Sessions's decision was clearly correct. Not only had he actively participated in the campaign as a surrogate and adviser, but he had met with the Russian ambassador and misled the Senate about it in his confirmation hearings. It would have been inconceivable for him to have supervised an investigation of the campaign. The very notion of recusal was anathema to Trump, who, in the Roy Cohn spirit, always counted on personal ties to decision makers. The personal connection was why Trump nominated Sessions to be attorney general in the first place. In a conversation with McGahn on the day after Sessions recused, Trump said, "I don't have a lawyer," and he said he wished that Roy Cohn was still around to represent him. The president's lament was revealing at two levels: first, that Trump thought the attorney general was (or should be) his own lawyer, as opposed to one who represented the United States, and, second, that Roy Cohn—a corrupt, unethical, mobbed-up, and ultimately disbarred outlaw of the New York bar— remained the president's role model for legal excellence.

With the arrival of spring came the beginning of congressional oversight—sort of. When Trump won the presidency, Republicans maintained control of both the Senate and the House of Representatives. The Senate, in its traditional fashion, employed a mostly bipartisan process to examine the issues raised by Russian interference in the 2016 election. The Senate Intelligence Committee held hearings on the role of social media in the election. Also in traditional Senate fashion, nothing much came of these hearings.

The House, though, lived up to its reputation as the citadel of partisanship in Washington. The House also pledged to investigate the 2016 election, but the reigning Republicans had a distinctive idea about what that meant. Under Chairman Devin Nunes, the House Intelligence Committee devoted obsessive attention to investigating (and criticizing) the origins of the FBI investigation of Russian influence in the campaign. The facts never changed; the investigation began after Alexander Downer, the Australian diplomat, passed word to the U.S. government that Papadopoulos appeared to have advance notice of the DNC hacks. Still, prodded by Trump himself, the committee nursed conspiracy theories that the Steele dossier—and thus its sponsors in the Clinton campaign—actually prompted the investigation. It wasn't true, but the theory fed years of conjecture on the committee, in the right-wing media universe, and in Trump's White House.

The Intelligence Committee's first major hearing after the election, on March 20, marked the national debut of a heretofore-obscure congressman named Adam Schiff, the ranking Democrat on the committee. A former prosecutor first elected from a district in Los Angeles in 2000, Schiff had taken on unglamorous tasks in the House: serving as the House manager in the Senate impeachment trial of a federal judge, serving on the important but then fairly low-profile Intelligence Committee. At this March 20 hearing, the nation had its first chance to hear, not just see, Schiff talk about the Russia investigation. At that time, with Republicans in full control of the federal government, there was no Democrat with the platform, or the knowledge, to explain what happened in the complicated scandal and what it meant. (This would be true even after Mueller was appointed, because he imposed an extreme version of a media blackout on himself and his staff.) Schiff, on the other hand, relished the spotlight (and the cameras) and had a plainspoken way of explaining complicated subjects. On March 20, he delivered a seventeen-minute opening statement, much longer than customary, to make his case. "Last summer, at the height of a bitterly contested and hugely consequential presidential campaign, a foreign, adversarial power intervened in an effort to weaken our democracy, and to influence the outcome for one candidate and against the other," Schiff said. "That foreign adversary was, of course, Russia, and it acted through its intelligence agencies and upon the direct instructions of its autocratic ruler, Vladimir Putin, in order to help Donald J. Trump become the 45th President of the United States."

It was still very early in the investigation and Schiff was relying mostly on news reports, but he laid out the pattern of contacts between the Trump campaign and Russia. He ran quickly through the stories of Carter Page in Moscow, Paul Manafort in Ukraine, Jeff Sessions in Washington with the Russian ambassador, Michael Flynn's lies about the Russian ambassador, plus, of course, the hacking of the DNC and Podesta emails. "Is it possible that all of these events and reports are completely unrelated, and nothing more than an entirely unhappy coincidence? Yes, it is possible," Schiff went on. "But it is also possible, maybe more than possible, that they are not coincidental, not disconnected and not unrelated, and that the Russians used the same techniques to corrupt U.S. persons that they have employed in Europe and elsewhere. We simply don't know, not yet, and we owe it to the country to find out."

The witness before the Intelligence Committee on March 20 was

Comey, who was coming to the realization that Trump was a great deal worse than a mere neophyte. The FBI's Crossfire Hurricane investigation had not yet developed direct evidence against Trump, but in light of Trump's behavior in their interactions Comey was not going to vouch for him in any way. Comey knew that Trump wanted a publicly announced clean bill of health from the FBI director, but Comey wasn't going to give it to him. On March 20, he stated his position in carefully planned, turgidly bureaucratic prose: The FBI "is investigating the Russian government's efforts to interfere in the 2016 presidential election and that includes investigating the nature of any links between individuals associated with the Trump campaign and the Russian government and whether there was any coordination between the campaign and Russia's efforts. As with any counterintelligence investigation, this will also include an assessment of whether any crimes were committed." Comey refused to say anything more. Most important (especially to the president), Comey did not exonerate Trump himself or confirm or deny that the president was under investigation. His studied ambiguity about the president's status, plus Schiff's damning summary of the evidence to date, dominated news coverage from the hearing. Predictably, the news reports included a great deal of speculation that Trump was under investigation, and these reports made Trump even more furious—"beside himself . . . hotter and hotter," McGahn told his own chief of staff, who served as a scrupulous note taker for the lawyer's day-to-day reflections.

To some extent, Comey brought the problem on himself. Against Baker's advice, and confident as ever that he could talk his way out of any problem, he had volunteered to Trump in their first conversation that he was not under investigation. He repeated the reassurance in subsequent talks. But Comey consistently refused to say the same thing in public, thus enraging the president. Most other presidents—indeed, any other president in the post-Nixon era—would have understood that he needed to back off and let the investigation run its course. But Trump could never process any interest except his own, and he regarded all executive branch employees as working for him personally.

Disgusted with Comey, Trump looked to other members of his administration for exoneration on Russia. In March, he approached Dan Coats, the director of national intelligence; Mike Pompeo, the director of the CIA; and Mike Rogers, director of the National

Security Agency, and asked them all to make public statements clearing him of any involvement with Russia during the campaign. Baffled and put off by this irregular request—and in any event lacking the requisite knowledge of the facts to offer any such assurance—the three told Trump that Comey was the only one who could help him.

Trump kept working Comey. The president called him again on March 30 and asked him to "lift the cloud" of the Russia investigation. Comey put him off, saying that his investigators were working as fast as they could. On April 11, Trump called Comey once more, again asking for a public exoneration. The president tried to leverage his understanding of their agreement at dinner. (Of course, Comey believed he had made no agreement of any kind at dinner.) "Because I have been very loyal to you, very loyal, we had that thing, you know," Trump said, according to Comey's notes. (Comey thought this was an example of Trump's penchant for Mafia talk. When making improper demands, the president, like the gangsters, would switch to a studied vagueness—like "that thing, you know.") After Comey tried to put the issue off on the Justice Department, saying that top officials there would have to approve any public statement about the president, Trump said he would persuade them to do so. (Adding to the confusion at this time was a leadership vacuum regarding the Russia investigation at the Justice Department, because Sessions had recused and Rod Rosenstein, the nominee to be deputy attorney general, had not yet been confirmed.)

During this period, Trump was venting nonstop to McGahn, his White House counsel—about Comey, about Sessions's decision to recuse, about the myriad injustices that were inflicted on him. McGahn was an anomalous figure in the Trump orbit, because he was one of the few people in the White House who might well have had his current position if another Republican had been elected president. McGahn was extremely loyal, but not to Trump; he was a protégé of Mitch McConnell's, the Republican leader in the Senate, who had earlier placed the lawyer on the Federal Election Commission, where he did the senator's bidding by effectively undermining any efforts at campaign finance reform. McGahn arrived at the White House focused on McConnell's other major agenda item—filling the federal judiciary, and especially the Supreme Court, with hard-edged conservatives. He owed McConnell, not Trump, and the president knew it.

McGahn kept his hair unfashionably long, which helped him fit in with his rock band, to which he was devoted. He had a rocker's sneer off stage as well as on, whether he was disparaging softheaded liberals or enduring Trump's self-pitying monologues. McGahn previously served as Trump's lawyer during the 2016 campaign, but the two men never hit it off. (Trump nearly fired McGahn during the race for the White House but relented when he realized that Don's uncle was Patrick "Paddy" McGahn, an old-time Atlantic City lawyer and power broker who represented Trump on real estate matters during his casino days. Trump had a rare sentimental attachment to Paddy McGahn.)

Longtime aides to Trump divided the people around the president into those who "got" Trump and those who didn't—the people who knew when to take the president seriously (and literally), and those who could tell when Trump was just blowing off steam. (This division was also a convenient way of explaining away Trump's bad behavior.) By this rubric, McGahn never "got" Trump. He did his job, which sometimes involved telling Trump no. In other words, McGahn was a real lawyer who understood both the laws and the norms that governed official behavior in the White House. He knew Trump shouldn't be browbeating Comey about his investigation; he recognized that this behavior was at least unwise if not actually illegal. More to the point, Trump's theatrics had the potential to drag down the administration and frustrate McGahn's (and McConnell's) ambitions for this presidency. As the president whined about Comey's failure to exonerate him, McGahn did a poor job of hiding his contempt. For someone like Trump, who expected fawning deference from his staff, McGahn's behavior rankled. And Trump didn't like McGahn's message either—which was that there really wasn't much Trump could do about Comey except fire him.

And that, increasingly, is what Trump wanted to do. The final straw came on May 3, when Comey testified before the Senate Judiciary Committee. His testimony, as ever, was vivid and dramatic, as when he said that the thought that his October letter affected the outcome of the election made him "mildly nauseous." This colorful way of expressing himself was part of what made Comey a compelling figure, and another reason Trump couldn't stand him. There was always an element of projection in Trump's criticism of others, so when he called

Comey a showboat—an accusation with some justification—the president was also speaking about himself. The "nauseous" comment also bothered Trump because it sounded as if Comey wanted Clinton to win the election, which was not what Comey meant. Again, though, what enraged Trump most was that Comey declined to say that Trump was not under investigation by the FBI.

As Trump prepared to leave the White House for a weekend at his New Jersey resort, he began polling his advisers on the wisdom of firing Comey. (He had already directed McGahn to research the legality of ending Comey's tenure before his ten-year term as director expired.) Sessions advised firing Comey, if only to take the heat off himself, since Trump continued to berate the attorney general for his recusal on Russia. Steve Bannon, who was still Trump's chief strategist, gave the opposite advice—that the political storm that was likely to follow a dismissal of Comey was too big a price to pay. And Bannon pointed out further that the FBI investigation would continue even if Comey was gone. So it wasn't worth it.

But by this point, Trump was fixated on getting rid of Comey. Notably, for the weekend in New Jersey, he didn't bring any senior advisers with him—no one who would raise questions about any decision to fire Comey. Trump left his chief of staff, his counsel, and his strategist back in Washington. Instead, the president surrounded himself with his principal enablers—Stephen Miller, his speechwriter, and Jared Kushner, his son-in-law, both of them in their thirties, both inexperienced in the executive branch, both distinguished principally by their devotion to Trump himself. Neither, in any event, was a voice of caution. Miller spent Friday night literally taking dictation from the president for a letter that would go to Comey the following week. Trump's first version began, "While I greatly appreciate you informing me that I am not under investigation concerning what I have often stated is a fabricated story on a Trump-Russia relationship—pertaining to the 2016 presidential election, please be informed that I, and I believe the American public—including Ds and Rs—have lost faith in you as Director of the FBI."

Miller and Trump traded drafts all weekend. What was striking about them was Trump's pervasive dishonesty—even when he didn't have to lie. As president, he could have just fired Comey, but Trump's character led him to lie even in the behind-the-scenes process of creating more lies. From the beginning of the weekend, he told Miller that he wanted the letter to mention prominently that Comey had told him that he was not under investigation, because that would establish that the firing had nothing to do with the Russia investigation. But of course, the firing had everything to do with it. In addition, in the final weekend draft of the letter, which stretched to four pages, he stated that Comey had "asked me at dinner shortly after inauguration to let you stay on in the Director's role, and I said that I would consider it," but Trump had "concluded that I have no alternative but to find new leadership for the Bureau—a leader that restores confidence and trust." As reflected in Comey's nearly contemporaneous notes, Trump had actually asked him several times to stay on as director, but instead Trump had to rewrite history in such a way that he was the all-powerful leader who had placed his subordinate on a kind of prolonged probation. Trump was following his usual custom of portraying himself in the dominant position in all relationships.

Hope Hicks, Trump's personal aide and a kind of surrogate daughter, had spent the weekend with her parents in Connecticut, but she drove to New Jersey to fly back with the president on Air Force One. No one "got" Trump better than Hicks. She was just twenty-eight years old at the time and by her own admission a neophyte in most of the policy issues before the president. But she had come to the Trump Organization, and then the campaign and White House, with a savvy sense of how issues would play before the public, and more important, she knew how to read the man she always called Mr. Trump. Her collegiate appearance and almost spooky reserve lent her a mystique, even among those closest to Trump. They saw Hicks as a kind of Trump whisperer who could divine his moods and intentions better than anyone. Unlike, for example, Priebus and McGahn, Hicks could tell what really mattered to Trump and what was just a passing irritation. Like everyone, she knew of Trump's growing frustrations with Comey, and she also understood the political risks of firing him. She was skeptical that Trump was really going to go through with it.

Hicks knew, too, that Trump was a decisive man, except in one particular circumstance. Trump's public fame soared when he starred in the television reality show *The Apprentice,* where his primary job was to eliminate one contestant each week. He did so with what became his famous catchphrase—"You're fired." But Hicks knew that while in real life Trump often talked about firing people, both in his company and later in the White House, he often had trouble doing the deed. When she arrived at Air Force One, Hicks wondered whether the pattern would recur with Comey—big talk followed by no action.

It didn't take long for the president to satisfy Hicks's curiosity on the issue. As soon as Hicks walked up the steps to the plane, Trump handed her Miller's letter and told her he was going to fire Comey the next day. Hicks could tell he was serious. The decision had been made.

For the participants, and even for the country, what followed were several days of extraordinary chaos and peril. John Le Carré once wrote, "There are moments that are made up of too much stuff to be lived at the time they occur." This, for Donald Trump, was the second week of May in 2017.

4

"I Faced Great Pressure"

On the morning of Monday, May 8, 2017, following his return from his New Jersey resort, Trump summoned McGahn, Priebus, and Miller to the Oval Office. They took their places in front of the Resolute desk, and Trump gave them a dramatic reading of the opening of the letter he and Miller had composed over the weekend. (Hicks listened from the sofas at the other end of the room.) At some point, though, Trump tired of the letter and just started free-associating about Comey's faults. Still, the president's tone was matter of fact as he recounted the multiple grounds for Comey's dismissal.

In the Oval Office meeting, Trump made clear to his subordinates that the issue of Comey's firing was no longer up for discussion. The only remaining questions concerned the mechanics of his departure. Like Steve Bannon, McGahn recognized the political calamity Trump was courting with the firing of Comey, but he was resigned that the president was going to proceed. In hopes of tempering the disaster, or at least delaying it, McGahn told the president that Sessions and Rod Rosenstein, the newly confirmed deputy attorney general, were coming to lunch at the White House later that day. McGahn said the leadership of the Justice Department was also considering Comey's fate, so it might be wise to get a read on their thoughts before taking any action. McGahn figured that if Trump was determined to fire Comey, the top people at the Justice Department might do the job and at least give the president some political cover.

McGahn told Sessions and Rosenstein that Trump planned to fire Comey, and neither man rose to the FBI director's defense. McGahn took their acquiescence as a kind of legal blessing for the dismissal, and he arranged for the two men to meet with Trump later in the afternoon. Rosenstein had never been in the Oval Office or met Trump before this day, and he received a fast introduction to the president's conversational style—the meandering subject matter, the mumbled sentence fragments, the persistent aggression. On this day, Trump was on an extended tear about Comey—that he was "not right" in the head, that his May 3 congressional testimony was a disgrace, and above all that the Russia investigation was a witch hunt and a hoax. It was clear that Trump was going to fire Comey, and the president offered a string of reasons. Rosenstein agreed with some of them. Like many veterans of the Justice Department, he had a starchy aversion to government officials' calling attention to themselves. So Comey's publicity-seeking performances with the Clinton emails—both in July and in October—offended him. But Rosenstein thought some of Trump's other reasons were crazy. The president nursed a strange obsession with Andrew McCabe, the deputy FBI director, and his wife. In 2015, Jill McCabe, who worked as an emergency room physician, had run unsuccessfully for the Virginia state senate, and her campaign had received substantial funding from money controlled by then governor Terry McAuliffe, a close ally of the Clintons'. McCabe had cleared Jill's run with the FBI's ethics office, and he played no part in her campaign; in any event, she had already lost by the time McCabe helped supervise any investigations related to the 2016 campaign. Nevertheless, Trump raged about McCabe and his wife and, even more nonsensically, regarded Comey's decision to keep McCabe as another ground for firing him.

As usual with Trump, there was some confusion about what was actually agreed to at the meeting. Rosenstein was assigned to write a memorandum in connection with the firing, but its substance and purpose were left somewhat vague. According to one set of notes, Trump said he wanted the memorandum to say that Comey was being fired because of his handling of the Russia investigation. Another set of notes said Rosenstein told the group that he preferred to focus on Comey's violations of Justice Department policies in announcing the results of the Clinton email investigation. One thing, however, was clear to everyone. The assignment for writing the memo justifying the firing went to Rosenstein, and his deadline to turn it in to the president was 8:00 the following morning. In less than twenty-four hours, as it turned out, Rod Rosenstein was on the road to becoming the most famous deputy attorney general in the history of the United States.

If Rod Rosenstein had gotten his way at that moment in 2017, he would have been completing his first decade as a federal appeals court judge in Baltimore. He would have been an important jurist, but an obscure one, largely unknown to the public. A life of reading cases, hearing arguments, and writing opinions on the U.S. Court of Appeals for the Fourth Circuit was all Rosenstein wanted. That he didn't reach that goal reflected a theme in his life—that until that moment, he hovered on the periphery of great events, and of celebrated people, without becoming well known himself.

At fifty-two, Rosenstein wore a kind of personal invisibility cloak as well. He was neither tall nor short, neither handsome nor plain, and as colorless as his rimless glasses. He dressed in the blue suit and striped tie uniform of the Washington government bureaucracy. He was a Justice Department lifer, with twenty-five years on the books, and the experience had left him with an improbably jolly demeanor. Rosenstein laughed easily and often. He was the rare person who had found his life's work at an early age and stuck with it.

No one doubted his intelligence. Rosenstein graduated summa cum laude from the Wharton School at the University of Pennsylvania and then went on to Harvard Law School, where he worked as an intern in the Boston U.S. Attorney's office, when Robert S. Mueller III was a senior prosecutor there. After a clerkship with Douglas Ginsburg of the D.C. Circuit (whom Ronald Reagan had unsuccessfully nominated to the Supreme Court), Rosenstein joined the Justice Department as a junior prosecutor in Washington.

At Justice, Rosenstein alternated between positions where he served as a special assistant to senior figures—thus learning to navigate the baroque internal politics of the place—and others where he conducted his own investigations and tried his own cases. He developed an expertise in white-collar crime prosecutions, but unlike most of his colleagues in that field he never made the leap to the private sector and a tripled (or more) salary. In the late 1990s, he joined the staff of Independent Counsel Kenneth Starr in the Whitewater investigation, where his colleagues included a young Brett Kavanaugh, but Rosenstein steered clear of the controversies associated with that office. He helped try a successful fraud prosecution in Arkansas and cleared the Clintons in a long-forgotten miniscandal involving FBI files. After working for Starr, Rosenstein returned to the Justice Department as an Assistant U.S. Attorney in Baltimore. He wanted to try more cases, which he did.

In 2005, George W. Bush named Rosenstein the top federal prosecutor in Maryland, and two years later Bush nominated him to the Fourth Circuit. (Kavanaugh was nominated to the D.C. Circuit around the same time.) Rosenstein should have won easy confirmation to the appeals court—he was a registered Republican but otherwise had no particular ideological profile—but Maryland's Democratic senators took exception to his lack of strong Maryland roots. (Many Marylanders regard the Washington suburbs, where Rosenstein had lived for a decade, as an insufficiently authentic part of the state.) In any event, his nomination lapsed without a vote, and Rosenstein stayed on as U.S. Attorney. In 2009, in an extremely rare occurrence, the new president of the opposition party kept Rosenstein on in the job. Rosenstein had displayed nonpartisan competence as a prosecutor, and the state's two Democratic senators found no reason to recommend that Barack Obama name a replacement. A long tenure of fighting violent crime, prosecuting local corruption, and uncovering a bizarre scandal in Baltimore's ancient jail (the male prisoners were sleeping with the female guards) gave Rosenstein a mantle of competence and integrity. Still, as Donald Trump assumed the presidency in 2017, Rosenstein posted a LinkedIn profile for the first time and prepared to go on the private job market. College tuitions beckoned.

Historically, senators who were nominated by presidents for jobs that required Senate confirmation received almost automatic approval. But this notion of senatorial courtesy had largely vanished in the polarized age of Trump, and his nomination of Jeff Sessions to be attorney general was a bitter insult to the Democrats in the chamber. Jefferson Beauregard Sessions III was a sort of human onomatopoeia—a personification of the Old South, with its history of racial bigotry, which in his case was topped by a modern obsession with limiting immigration. Sessions was also the first senator to endorse Donald Trump, so his selection as attorney general also had the odor of a political payoff. However, the news that Trump (and Sessions) had chosen Rosenstein as deputy met with nearly universal acclaim, led by Maryland's own Democratic senators. Rosenstein was seen as Sessions's near opposite: nonideological, experienced, and fully capable of running the day-to-day operations of the Justice Department in his customary anonymity. He was confirmed by a vote of 94 to 6 on April 25, and he expected the job would represent a quiet culmination of his career in the Justice Department. Then, two weeks later, he had a homework assignment from the president of the United States.

As the sun was setting on May 8, Rosenstein returned to the Justice Department building, recruited two junior lawyers for research help, and set out to write the memorandum for the president. No one had ever been given a task like the one Donald Trump gave him. What was this document supposed to be? It wasn't a legal brief, or a press release, but it also wasn't a formal legal opinion of the kind produced by the Justice Department's Office of Legal Counsel (OLC). It wasn't meant to be a persuasive document, because its audience, the president, was already persuaded of its conclusion—that Comey had to go. And what was it supposed to be used for? Rosenstein wasn't sure. He didn't even know if his document was going to be made public. So Rosenstein decided to take the assignment at face value. He'd heard Trump's reasons for firing Comey, and he thought some of them, like the business about McCabe and his wife, were ridiculous. But Rosenstein did disdain Comey's handling of the Clinton emails. So he decided to write a memo that summarized his own reasons (not the president's reasons) why Comey should be fired. And he knew the president was waiting. At 10:00 p.m., Don McGahn called Rosenstein and demanded to see the memo. Rosenstein assured him that it would be ready by the morning deadline.

In the end, Rosenstein styled the document as a memorandum from him to the attorney general. "The current FBI Director is an articulate and persuasive speaker about leadership and the immutable principles of the Department of Justice," Rosenstein wrote. "He deserves our appreciation for his public service. As you and I have discussed, however, I cannot defend the Director's handling of the conclusion of the investigation of Secretary Clinton's emails." Unlike virtually all other written products from the Justice Department, Rosenstein's memo cited no law, regulations, or government policy; it relied instead on op-ed pieces critical of Comey's decisions in the Clinton email investigation. The memo didn't even conclude with a firm recommendation. "Although the President has the power to remove an FBI director, the decision should not be taken lightly," Rosenstein wrote. "The FBI is unlikely to regain public and congressional trust until it has a Director who understands the gravity of the mistakes and pledges never to repeat them. Having refused to admit his errors, the Director cannot be expected to implement the necessary corrective actions."

Rosenstein's memo was, in short, a shoddy and naive piece of work. In the absence of any actual legal authority, the memo was hardly persuasive as a justification for the firing. And Rosenstein knew it wasn't the real reason Trump was going to fire Comey anyway. Rosenstein remembered (as everyone who followed the 2016 campaign recalled) that Trump praised Comey for announcing the reopening of the Clinton email investigation in late October. In light of that, Trump could hardly agree with Rosenstein's position that Comey's late intervention was a firing offense. Most important, Rosenstein's memo ignored the central fact about Trump and Comey in May 2017. Comey was leading an investigation of Trump's campaign, and perhaps the president himself, at the time that Rosenstein was recommending firing him. To ignore this essential matter of law and politics was malpractice. Still, Rosenstein fulfilled his assignment and submitted the memo the first thing on the morning of May 9 without knowing what Trump would do with it. Soon enough, he would find out.

Don McGahn recognized Rosenstein's memo for what it was—a gift. McGahn knew that the letter that Trump and Miller had produced over the weekend was a mess, full of weak and nonsensical justifications for firing Comey. To have the deputy attorney general vouch for Trump's action would be a big improvement. Trump agreed and cut back his dismissal letter to just a few sentences—but still making the point that Comey had told the president three times that he was not under investigation. Trump then dictated a statement about the firing to be released by Sean Spicer, his press secretary: "President Trump acted based on the clear recommendations of both Deputy Attorney General Rod Rosenstein and Attorney General Jeff Sessions." Around midday, Spicer released both the president's statement and Rosenstein's memorandum.

This was news to Comey and Rosenstein. Comey was leading a training session at the FBI field office in Los Angeles, when he caught a glimpse of a television that was reporting on his firing. (Trump had dispatched Keith Schiller, his personal aide and former bodyguard, to hand deliver the official letter to FBI headquarters, a few blocks away from the White House on Pennsylvania Avenue. Comey's assistant scanned it and emailed it to Comey. McCabe, now the acting director of the FBI, made a quick decision to allow Comey and his security team to take the FBI plane back to Washington.) The announcement threw the national news media into a frenzy, and much of the attention was focused on Rosenstein.

Everyone had the same question: Why—really—was Comey fired? Most of the coverage focused on Comey's leadership of the Russia investigation. The obvious implication was that Trump had fired Comey as punishment for leading the probe. This narrative—in effect, that the president was trying to obstruct justice—was obviously unsatisfactory to the White House, so Trump told Spicer to put out a different explanation. In an impromptu news conference outside the White House press room, as darkness fell, Sean Spicer said, "It was all Rosenstein. No one from the White House. It was a DOJ decision." The press attention grew so frantic that Spicer for a brief time hid from reporters in the shrubs by the West Wing.

Back at the Justice Department building, Rosenstein was nearly catatonic with shock. He knew the White House was putting out a false story. Spicer's statement was absurd on its face. Trump was on the record endorsing Comey's late disclosure of the email investigation. It could hardly be his reason for firing the FBI director. Rosenstein had been used, and he knew it. He should have known it was coming, but in his naïveté about Trump's deviousness—and with just a few days on the job—he had blundered into a fiasco. He was disoriented and out of his depth. He knew his memo was not the real rationale for

Comey's firing. But suddenly Rosenstein had to face the question, What was Trump's real reason?

The president himself soon answered that question. On May 10, just a day after the firing, Trump welcomed Russian foreign minister Sergey Lavrov and Russian ambassador Sergey Kislyak to the Oval Office. (The meeting had been planned in a May 2 phone call between Trump and Vladimir Putin and confirmed on May 5, the day that Trump had dictated his reasons for firing Comey to Stephen Miller.) That Trump went ahead with this meeting under the circumstances demonstrated his peculiar deference to Russia, and his remarks to the visitors were even more incriminating. "I just fired the head of the F.B.I. He was crazy, a real nut job," Trump told the Russians. "I faced great pressure because of Russia. That's taken off." In any event, Trump went on, what Russia did during the 2016 election was no big deal. The United States interfered in the elections of other countries, so we shouldn't be so quick to condemn Russia's attempts to do the same. White House staffers immediately saw these remarks as wildly inappropriate, and they placed the detailed record of Trump's comments in a special computer server, with very limited access. (The White House prohibited the customary U.S. pool photographs of the meeting, so the only pictures came from a Russian Foreign Ministry photographer.)

The next day, Trump gave an interview to Lester Holt of NBC News where he undermined the explanation of Comey's firing that the White House had been peddling for the previous two days. "I was going to fire regardless of the recommendation. . . . [Rosenstein] made a recommendation. But regardless of the recommendation, I was going to fire Comey. . . . When I decided to do it, I said to myself—I said, you know, this Russia thing with Trump and Russia is a made-up story. It's an excuse by the Democrats for having lost an election that they should have won." So in this latest iteration of the rationale, Comey was fired because of the Russia investigation, not for the reason Rosenstein presented.

As part of his effort to justify Comey's firing, Trump pretended that the FBI rank and file had lost confidence in the director. In a press briefing on May 10, Sarah Sanders, who was then the deputy press secretary, said that Rosenstein had decided "on his own" to review Comey's performance and then chose "on his own" to tell the president his views. (Both statements were lies.) In addition, Sanders said, "We've heard from countless members of the FBI" supporting the president's decision. (Sanders later admitted this, too, was a lie.) Also that day, Trump called McCabe, who was now acting director of the FBI, to tell him he had received "hundreds" of messages from FBI employees indicating their support for terminating Comey. This, too, never happened. Trump also excoriated McCabe for allowing Comey to take the FBI jet back to Washington. The president wanted the suddenly former director to suffer the indignity of flying commercial.

The real FBI response to Trump's firing of Comey was taking place in the director's suite, on the seventh floor of the Hoover Building. A day earlier, immediately after Comey was fired, McCabe had summoned the agents who had been working on the Russia investigation and related matters to give him a briefing. He wanted to make a prompt decision about which cases to pursue and which ones to drop. There was a counterintelligence investigation of Russian involvement in the 2016 election—that was Crossfire Hurricane—and then there were separate investigations of Michael Flynn and George Papadopoulos, a former Trump campaign aide, for making false statements to FBI agents. In addition, Paul Manafort, Trump's ousted campaign chairman, was the subject of a wide-ranging probe relating to his representation of Russia-aligned political figures in Ukraine. All those would proceed, McCabe decided.

But there was, on May 10, a more momentous question before the FBI team: whether to open a formal criminal investigation of the president of the United States. Comey had told McCabe about all of his interactions with Trump, and he had shared his memos recounting those conversations, too. McCabe thought Trump's behavior was sufficiently problematic to be investigated, and he told his team to open a case. Given the wild pace of events, McCabe couldn't be sure how long he'd last as director, so he wanted to lock down as much evidence as possible. Most important, he told the investigating agents to place Comey's memos in Sentinel, the FBI's case management software. He knew that once documents were inside the Sentinel system, they were virtually impossible to remove. With Comey's memos in Sentinel, the investigators were certain to have access to them—even if McCabe himself would eventually be gone. Following this meeting in the Hoover Building, McCabe passed the word to Rosenstein: the president was under criminal investigation for obstruction of justice. (Once McCabe became director, FBI officials were so concerned that Trump would try to shut down the investigation that they secreted at least three copies of key documents in remote locations around the bureau. This was to make sure that in the event Trump directed an end to these inquiries, the documents could always be preserved and located, and shared.)

Comey, characteristically, had a more theatrical approach to keeping the investigation alive. At the time he was fired, he had told no one outside the FBI about Trump's inappropriate (or worse) overtures to him over the previous five months. He now wanted Trump to pay a price for this conduct, and he didn't trust the Justice Department to follow through, at least in its current configuration. Comey thought Rosenstein needed to appoint an outside prosecutor, so he took a wild, and arguably improper, step to force the deputy attorney general's hand. Comey told an old friend, Daniel Richman, a professor at Columbia Law School, about Trump's attempts to control the Russia investigation. He also showed Richman one of his contemporaneous memos documenting his interactions with Trump and later shared the rest of them with his lawyers. With Comey's encouragement, Richman told the story of Comey's interactions with Trump to Michael S. Schmidt, a reporter at *The New York Times*. Schmidt's story, which ran on May 11 and chronicled some of Trump's attempts to control the FBI's investigation, was a bombshell, and it did indeed prompt more calls for an independent prosecutor. (Notably, though, Comey did not have a clear legal right to share these records with an outsider like Richman or with his attorneys. Indeed, a later investigation by the FBI inspector general revealed that the memos contained some information that was later deemed to be classified. In other words, Comey unintentionally revealed classified information to unauthorized persons, just as Hillary Clinton unintentionally discussed classified information in her unsecured emails—for which Comey excoriated her. The U.S. Attorney's office in Washington later investigated Comey for these improper disclosures but declined to prosecute—albeit with much less fanfare than Comey's decision on Clinton.)

By the end of this tumultuous week in May, Rosenstein was feeling a combination of rage, embarrassment, and confusion about the whole situation. A week earlier, he had been a respected, if little known, career federal prosecutor. Now he was widely (and justifiably) mocked as Trump's patsy—who had acted as a kind of beard for the president's decision to fire Comey. As he sat in his office in the Justice Department, Rosenstein realized how little he knew about what was really going on. Why *did* Trump fire Comey? The president's comments to the Russians, and to Lester Holt, suggested an improper, and perhaps illegal, motivation. Comey's leak to the *Times* raised the possibility that Trump had been interfering with the investigation for some time, even before he fired the FBI director. And the news from McCabe on May 13—that the FBI had opened a formal criminal investigation of Trump—deepened Rosenstein's unease and foreboding. Then, at the end of the week, Trump posted a provocative tweet in response to the *Times* story: "James Comey better hope that there are no 'tapes' of our conversations before he starts leaking to the press!" Good Lord, Rosenstein thought, were there tapes? He had no idea. *What was going on?*

All in all, Rosenstein decided, it was time to stop being taken for a fool, so he stopped acting like one.

Rosenstein decided to place a call to Robert Swan Mueller III.

PART TWO

5

"This Is the Worst Thing That Ever Happened to Me"

At that moment, Rosenstein was simultaneously in the center of the action in Washington and almost completely alone. He barely knew Sessions, his new boss, and in any case he couldn't talk to Sessions about what mattered most—the Russia investigation—because the attorney general was recused on the issue. Rosenstein didn't know if he could trust anyone at the White House, because the president and his men were the ones who put out the false story that Rosenstein came up with the decision and rationale to fire Comey. For a confidant, Rosenstein could look only to Andrew McCabe, now the acting director of the FBI, who was similarly thrown from obscurity into the vortex of a major national crisis. From May 12 to May 16, they spoke several times a day, usually on the phone, but sometimes in each other's office, on either side of Pennsylvania Avenue.

The pressure started to affect Rosenstein in particular, turning his customary camp counselor demeanor to one that alternated between grim foreboding and manic despair. Rosenstein used the conversations with McCabe almost as therapy sessions. On the surface, the two men had much in common—both fiftyish, both law enforcement lifers, both clean-cut family men whose careers reached their respective pinnacles in unexpected ways and who, just as important, had never faced any sustained public criticism. When they were portrayed in the news media at all, they were invariably the good guys. But while McCabe tried to juggle a new and bewildering set of responsibilities—which included managing thirty-five thousand employees, preparing for his first congressional testimony as director, and launching an investigation of the president of the United States—Rosenstein sank into a state of near paralysis. For McCabe, the experiences with Rosenstein became so peculiar that he started taking contemporaneous notes, in the same way that Comey did for his conversations with Trump.

On the morning of May 12, Rosenstein came to the FBI command center with a small group for a routine meeting. In the three days since Trump fired Comey, Democrats and their supporters had come down brutally on Rosenstein. They said he was a Trump shill who gave the president political and legal cover for his contemptible, and possibly illegal, decision to dismiss the FBI director. But that, Rosenstein explained to McCabe, wasn't what happened at all. After the others left the command center, and it was just the two men, Rosenstein began volunteering to McCabe the story of how his Comey memorandum came to be written. "I didn't know they were going to say the firing was my idea. They had their own reasons for firing him. They were going to do it anyway." Rosenstein's eyes misted over. He had trouble speaking. McCabe asked him if his family was okay and if he was getting enough sleep. After returning to his office, McCabe thought he needed to see Rosenstein again that day—to check on him and to make sure he knew how strongly McCabe and his team felt that Rosenstein should appoint a special counsel.

A meeting the next day was even stranger. This one included a handful of aides, as well as Rosenstein and McCabe, in the private office of the deputy attorney general, just off a large conference room. As McCabe described the FBI's obstruction of justice investigation of the president, Rosenstein said he had an idea. His demeanor on this day was manic instead of mournful. This was at a time when the news media (and the public) still took Trump's tweets both seriously and literally, and the president had just convulsed the capital with this shocking tweet: "James Comey better hope that there are no 'tapes' of our conversations before he starts leaking to the press!" This gave Rosenstein an idea.

"What would we do in an obstruction investigation in a normal case?" Rosenstein asked the group, more or less rhetorically. "Well, the whole point is to capture their intent, state of mind. We'd find an informant to wire up to get admissions. We could do the same thing here. This time we were the targets of the obstruction. So we are the ones who could get evidence on it."

Then Rosenstein explained how the team might go about collecting evidence on the president. "No one searches me when I go to the White House," he went on. "I could wear a wire and get admissions from Trump, no problem."

The constitutional and practical problems with wearing a wire to gather evidence on the president of the United States, in the Oval Office no less, were beyond daunting. That it would be the deputy attorney general acting as the informant ratcheted up the complications even more. But McCabe dealt gently with the idea, which he thought was insane. "Let me run it by my team and get back to you," he said. Rosenstein excused himself to his private bathroom, apparently to compose himself.

Still not exactly deterred, Rosenstein had another idea to address the possible criminality of the president. He said that he might be able to rustle up enough votes under the Twenty-Fifth Amendment to have the president removed from office. (Under section 4 of the amendment, which was ratified in 1967, a majority of the cabinet can remove a president if they find that he is "unable to discharge the powers and duties of his office." This provision has never been invoked.) McCabe let this idea pass altogether. He thought—he hoped—Rosenstein was just spitballing whatever idea popped into his head.

For all the bizarre detours, the conversations did reach one point of resolution. Rosenstein told the group that he had decided he would appoint a special counsel. It was difficult enough to imagine Trump's own Justice Department investigating Trump's campaign for president. But now that Rosenstein had learned that Trump himself was the subject of an FBI probe for obstruction of justice, it became impossible to contemplate any alternative. It was in this fraught context that Rosenstein reached out to Robert Mueller.

Rosenstein had two agenda items for the call to Mueller—gauging his interest in becoming interim FBI director and in being special counsel for the Russia investigation. There was a subtext, too. Rosenstein was desperate.

In 2017, Mueller occupied a rarefied place in the politically polarized capital—as an object of bipartisan support, even veneration. He became FBI director in 2001, after being nominated by George W. Bush, a Republican, and he was confirmed in the Senate with overwhelming support. After taking office a few days before 9/11, Mueller successfully steered the vast bureau from an organization devoted principally to catching criminals who had already committed their offenses to one that prevented crime in the first place. Mueller had accomplished his mission with such proficiency that Barack Obama, a Democrat, took the unprecedented step of asking Congress to extend Mueller's ten-year term by two years, so that a new director would be chosen after the 2012 election. Again, the Senate gave Mueller a bipartisan endorsement. (Obama chose Comey for the FBI job in 2013.) In a city full of public figures who hungered for attention, Mueller had created a mystique with his reticence. The less he said— and he said little—the better everyone liked him. In light of this, Rosenstein thought who better to calm the roiling chaos at the FBI than Mueller himself. Perhaps, Rosenstein wondered, Mueller would accept an interim appointment as director. (Rosenstein thought, perhaps wrongly, that a brief interim appointment would not run afoul of the term-limit issue.)

Rosenstein thought Mueller was also a perfect fit for the special counsel job. That post would require knowledge of both counterintelligence and criminal justice. It would be neither a pure foreign policy assignment nor just a domestic prosecution matter. The special counsel would have to know both areas, and Mueller was one of the few people with those qualifications. As FBI director in the post-9/11 world, he had fought hard in Congress to keep the FBI's preeminence in running counterintelligence within the United States. (Both President Bush and Congress were considering shifting responsibility for counterterrorism to the CIA or an entirely new agency.) Mueller won that bureaucratic battle, so his FBI continued to investigate foreign penetration of American businesses and government, which was apt preparation for examining Russian interference in the 2016 election. Before his tenure at the FBI, Mueller had spent most of his career as a prosecutor, so his credentials in that realm couldn't be surpassed either.

Rosenstein called Mueller at WilmerHale, the law firm where he had been based for the past four years, and asked whether he was interested in either the FBI or the special counsel position. The deputy attorney general received a clipped and definitive response to the first question. Even if the term-limit issue could be surmounted, Mueller would not return to the FBI, even on an interim basis. He said he'd be pleased to offer his opinions about what Rosenstein should be looking for in a director. But as for Mueller himself, the answer was no. Been there, done that.

The question about being special counsel didn't come as a total surprise, and Mueller's response was more equivocal. He said he would have to know more in order to answer, and for starters he had one question in particular. Would Mueller have to resign from his law firm to take the special counsel job? Rosenstein was ready for this one. In the Whitewater investigation, in which Rosenstein had served, Kenneth Starr had tried at first to do both—remain a partner at his law firm and lead the investigation. It was a disaster, Rosenstein told Mueller. Starr's dual roles had led to legal conflicts with clients of the firm, and his divided attention slowed down the work of the office. (Starr eventually quit his firm to work full time on Whitewater.) So it would have to be one or the other, Rosenstein said. If Mueller wanted to accept the special counsel job, he would have to resign at WilmerHale. Mueller said he would think about it.

Rosenstein became so obsessed with the idea that Mueller was the only man for the job that he never really considered anyone else. He made a brief overture to James Cole, who served as deputy attorney general under Obama and earlier did an independent ethics investigation that largely cleared former House Speaker Newt Gingrich of wrongdoing in connection with his outside work. But Cole was never a serious candidate. Rosenstein wanted Mueller—the only person with the gravitas and experience to win acceptance from Democrats and Republicans.

In their conversation, Mueller had a deceptively simple question for the deputy attorney general and thus his own putative boss. What, exactly, was a special counsel?

—

The answer was rooted in the ebb and flow of Washington scandal politics over two generations. The modern history of the subject began in May 1973, when Elliot Richardson, who at the time was President Richard Nixon's nominee to be attorney general, asked Archibald Cox, a professor at Harvard Law School, to be a "special prosecutor" in the Watergate affair. No position by that name existed at the time, so Richardson, Cox, and the Senate essentially made up the rules for the assignment. According to the terms the two men negotiated, Cox would have a free hand to pursue cases related to the 1972 election, and he could be dismissed only for "extraordinary improprieties." Cox had hired a staff and begun building cases when in July 1973, he (and the rest of the world) learned of the existence of the White House taping system. Cox's team issued a grand jury subpoena to Nixon to obtain the tapes, the president objected, and a legal fight ensued. Cox, after winning in federal district court, declined to relent over the tapes issue, and on the evening of Saturday, October 20, 1973, Nixon directed Richardson to fire Cox. Richardson refused, and so did his deputy, William Ruckelshaus. Robert Bork, the solicitor general and third in line at the Justice Department, finally agreed to the president's demand and fired Cox—in an event that gained immortality as the Saturday Night Massacre.

As part of the massacre, Nixon initially attempted to disband Cox's office altogether and fire his staff, but the president relented under political pressure and hired Leon Jaworski, a Houston lawyer, to continue the work of the Watergate Special Prosecution Force. The cascade of events set in motion by the firing of Cox ended ten months later, when Nixon resigned rather than face impeachment in the House of Representatives and conviction in the Senate. In this way, the cause of good government achieved a happy ending in Watergate, but the Saturday Night Massacre itself left a wound that Congress sought to heal. In future scandals, Congress wanted to establish a system that would insulate a special prosecutor from the kind of harassment and even dismissal that Cox endured.

The process took several years, but in 1978, Congress passed the Ethics in Government Act, which created an entirely new system for authorizing and protecting criminal investigations of officials in the executive branch. If the attorney general found a basis for possible prosecution, a panel of three federal judges (all appointed by the chief justice of the United States) would select the independent prosecutor, who would be known as an independent counsel. The counsel could be removed only by a finding by the attorney general of "good cause."

In its early years, under Jimmy Carter and Ronald Reagan, the law proved to be more or less successful. There were only a handful of independent counsels, and they mostly resolved their investigations without filing charges. The first major investigation under the auspices of the Ethics in Government Act was that by Lawrence E. Walsh, a former federal judge, who investigated the Iran-contra matter from 1986 to 1993. The length and expense of Walsh's probe—and especially his decision to indict a prominent member of the Reagan administration on the eve of the 1992 election—soured many Republicans on the entire independent counsel structure. Critics of Walsh and the law thought it gave the prosecutor too much independence and not enough oversight. During the Clinton years, Democrats raised many of the same complaints, as independent counsels spent many years and millions of dollars pursuing relatively minor cabinet members like Henry Cisneros and Mike Espy. But the most ferocious controversy arose over Kenneth Starr's independent counsel investigation, which stretched from 1994 to 2002 and evolved from an examination of the Whitewater land deal in Arkansas to one focused on President Clinton's relationship with Monica Lewinsky, a White House intern. In light of the bipartisan anger about the course of these investigations, the independent counsel provisions of the Ethics in Government Act were allowed to expire, unmourned, in 1999.

But that still left an open issue: what to do about investigations of high-level wrongdoing in the executive branch. Without the procedures established by the Ethics in Government Act, there was no way to address the problem. The Clinton Justice Department attempted a solution with a regulation issued in 1999. It created a new title—special counsel—for a job with less autonomy than independent counsels enjoyed. The attorney general (not a three-judge panel) decided whether to name a special counsel and defined the scope of the investigation. The AG had to approve all major investigative steps, like indictments, and the special counsel was required to follow all Justice Department policies. Perhaps most important, the attorney general possessed broad discretion to fire the special counsel—for "misconduct, dereliction of duty, incapacity, conflict of interest, or for other good cause, including violation of Departmental policies."

Since Sessions was recused, it would be Rosenstein who exercised those powers over the special counsel. In their conversations, Rosenstein gave Mueller his word that he would not interfere with his work. Mueller trusted Rosenstein, but he wasn't naive either. Cox also trusted Richardson, who kept his word not to thwart the Watergate investigation, but it was Nixon who possessed, and used, the ultimate authority over the prosecutor. Rosenstein's promises were meaningful only as long as Trump kept him in the job, and there was no way to know how long that would be. Based on Rosenstein's honest representations, as well as his own research, Mueller recognized that a special counsel enjoyed considerably less independence and job security than a special prosecutor or an independent counsel. His question was whether to accept this job, or any job, with those kinds of vulnerabilities spelled out in advance.

The morning of May 16 provided another bizarre collision of events. As Rosenstein was trying to sell Mueller on taking the special counsel assignment, Sessions's people reached out to Mueller to meet with the president about the FBI job. Mueller again made clear that he wasn't interested in taking the job himself, but he agreed to meet with Trump to talk about the qualities he should seek in a director. Mueller showed up as directed and deposited his phone in the box outside the Oval Office.

Sessions and Rosenstein were running several candidates to head the FBI through the Oval Office on that day, though the task seemed of little interest to the president. He seemed only vaguely aware of Mueller's history and devoted most of the brief meeting to riffing on subjects unrelated to the FBI. Mueller managed to pass along one piece of advice—that the director should come from outside the bureau, not a promotion from within—before he was ushered out. While inside the Oval Office, Rosenstein and Mueller said nothing about their separate, ongoing negotiations over the special counsel job. (As noted earlier, Mueller forgot his phone as he was leaving, which set off its own comedy of errors. When he realized his mistake,

Mueller located a different phone, tracked down Rosenstein's number, and asked him to retrieve the phone. But when Rosenstein went to look in the box, he learned that someone in the West Wing had noticed the phone in the box and grabbed it to try to return it. This person, though, had no way of reaching Mueller, and Rosenstein wandered the West Wing asking random staffers if they had seen Robert Mueller's phone. In time, Rosenstein located the phone and made sure it was returned to Mueller.)

Later that day, Rosenstein tracked down Mueller again and pressed him to take the special counsel job. This time Mueller accepted the offer and said he would resign from WilmerHale the following day, when his appointment would be announced. Rosenstein spent the morning of May 17 finalizing the appointment papers for Mueller. The subject of Mueller's jurisdiction—the scope of his investigation—was a matter of some delicacy. Rosenstein believed that Comey, as a rule, talked and revealed too much, and in particular he thought that Comey should not have revealed the existence of the Russia investigation at his March 20 testimony before the House Intelligence Committee. But Comey had made the disclosure, which could not be undone, so Rosenstein decided to use Comey's words as the model for Mueller's jurisdiction. This way, Rosenstein thought, at least there would be no further disclosures of the scope of the FBI's work. So it was Comey's words that led Rosenstein to define Mueller's scope to include "any links and/or coordination between the Russian government and individuals associated with the campaign of President Donald Trump." Crucially, though, Rosenstein went further and wrote that Mueller could examine "any matters that arose or may arise directly from the investigation." Especially given his broad authority under the special counsel regulation, Rosenstein didn't have to provide this open-ended invitation for Mueller to investigate other matters. But he did, with potentially important implications for the course of Mueller's work.

It was late afternoon on May 17 when Rosenstein called Sessions to tell him that he had just appointed Mueller special counsel. Sessions, of course, had received no hint that Rosenstein was even going to name a special counsel or that Mueller was a candidate for the job.

To Sessions's misfortune, he received this news when he happened to be in the Oval Office, interviewing a candidate for FBI director with Trump. Sessions had excused himself to take the call and returned to inform the president that Rosenstein had just named Mueller as special counsel. At first Trump was just confused.

"Wasn't he the guy who was just here?" he asked, correctly remembering that Mueller had been in the Oval Office the previous day.

But when the implications of the appointment began to sink in, Trump was enraged and, rather uncharacteristically, despondent. He slumped in his chair behind the Resolute desk. "Oh my God," he said. "This is terrible. This is the end of my Presidency. I'm fucked." Trump didn't know a lot of American political history, but he recognized the implications of a full-time prosecutor and staff burrowing through his campaign and presidency. "Everyone tells me if you get one of these independent counsels, it ruins your presidency," he said. "It takes years and years and I won't be able to do anything. This is the worst thing that ever happened to me."

Trump soon turned his fury on Sessions, blaming him for recusing himself and thus exposing him to Rosenstein's decision on the special counsel. "How could you let this happen, Jeff?" he said. As always, Trump had no concern for the merits of Sessions's decision to recuse—whether it was appropriate or required under the law— but only its implications for him personally. Trump neither knew nor cared about the distinction between his personal lawyer and the attorney general of the United States. His models for loyalty, he said, were Eric Holder and Robert F. Kennedy. But of course, his real model as an attorney was Roy Cohn, who was never burdened by ethics or even the law in his zeal. Now with great suddenness, and some justification, Trump felt exposed as never before as an army of prosecutors was arraying against him. Within hours of Mueller's appointment, the FBI, acting on its own initiative, sent Don McGahn a demand that all documents relating to Comey's firing be preserved.

At the offices of WilmerHale, just a few blocks from the White House, it hardly felt like the massing of an army. Mueller had no staff, no offices, no FBI agents assigned to him, and no idea of how much work had been done in the investigation. As FBI director, he could send dozens of agents to descend on a major crime scene. As a partner at Wilmer, he could scramble a team of some of the finest lawyers in the country to conduct an investigation. Mueller was held in such high regard that some judges saw him less as an advocate than as a quasi-judicial figure himself. As it happened, at that moment in 2017, Mueller and a team from Wilmer were completing work, at the direction of Judge Charles Breyer in San Francisco, as the special master charged with settling more than five hundred cases against Volkswagen, as a result of its diesel emissions scandal. Now, suddenly, in the most important moment of his career, Mueller was alone.

So he started to build a team, one lawyer at a time. He began with Aaron Zebley, who had worked as both an FBI agent and an Assistant U.S. Attorney, before he became Mueller's chief of staff at the bureau. He followed Mueller to Wilmer, and Mueller asked him to replicate his FBI role in the special counsel's office—as the administrative head of the office and as Mueller's eyes and ears. James L. Quarles III was an anomaly in a high-powered corporate law firm like WilmerHale, because he was still practicing full time in his mid-seventies. But his status as a peer and a friend of Mueller's was part of his appeal to the special counsel, of course. And even though he had spent the last several decades mostly handling intellectual property cases, Quarles had another credential that made him stand out. Shortly after he graduated from Harvard Law School—where he wrote his third-year paper for Archibald Cox—the professor hired him as a junior member of the Watergate Special Prosecution Force. Quarles had a rarefied, if dated, bit of experience: he had investigated a president.

As the news of Mueller's appointment, and Zebley's and Quarles's hiring, swept the firm, their colleagues wandered by to offer congratulations.

"Investigating the White House again!" one lawyer said to Quarles.

A smile spread below Jim Quarles's snow-white mustache.

"And maybe getting fired again," he said.

6

Patriots Plaza

When Andy McCabe was working his way up the FBI bureaucracy, he attended countless meetings in Director Robert Mueller's conference room on the seventh floor of the Hoover Building. McCabe knew that Mueller always presided from a seat on the short end of the rectangular table in the room. Now, suddenly and unexpectedly, McCabe himself was the director, and he was going to host Mueller and his embryonic special counsel team at that very table. For that first meeting, McCabe decided, as a gesture of respect, that he wouldn't occupy what he still regarded as Mueller's seat. Instead, after he welcomed Mueller, Zebley, and Quarles to the seventh floor, McCabe officiated from the middle of the wider side of the table. Mueller, sitting opposite him, noticed the gesture.

There was a long agenda for this meeting, which took place a few days after Mueller took over as special counsel. For starters, Mueller needed to address a host of logistical matters. His team had no place to work, and the special counsel's offices could not be located just anywhere. Their investigation would include a great deal of classified information, so any space for them would have to be kitted out as a SCIF—pronounced "skiff"—a Sensitive Compartmented Information Facility. Mueller was beginning the process of hiring a staff of prosecutors, but he also needed FBI agents and analysts assigned to his team. Rosenstein had not given the Office of Special Counsel (OSC, in a newly christened acronym) a specific budget, but Mueller needed at least rough guidelines, as well as support staff, to organize his inquiries.

McCabe had anticipated many of these issues. The FBI controlled some underutilized rented space in a newish commercial building in a booming but still unfashionable part of Washington, near the Nationals' baseball stadium. The building was called by the resonant name, especially under the circumstances, of Patriots Plaza, and McCabe was ready to install the OSC there. McCabe brought with him to the meeting a special agent named Peter Strzok (pronounced "struck") who was already leading Crossfire Hurricane, the investigation of Russian influence in the 2016 election. At forty-seven, Strzok was probably the most highly regarded agent of his generation and had been rewarded with assignments to supervise two politically explosive investigations. In addition to Crossfire Hurricane, he had been the lead agent on Midyear Exam—the FBI's investigation of Hillary Clinton's email use at the State Department. Strzok and his team of agents on Crossfire Hurricane would now report to Mueller.

All of these matters were important, of course, but they were preliminary to the real purpose of the meeting, which was to describe the FBI's Russia investigation to date and to outline the possible path ahead for Mueller's team. Historically, the work of the FBI had been rigidly divided between counterintelligence and criminal cases, with both legal and practical impediments prohibiting information sharing between the two sides of the divide. As Rosenstein recognized when he decided to hire Mueller as special counsel, the Russia investigation had both counterintelligence and criminal elements. At the meeting in his office, McCabe made clear from the outset that as far as Russia was concerned, Mueller's agents would be free to roam in both areas.

Then, at length, McCabe turned to the state of the investigation, starting with its origin. Much later, the story of the beginnings of the Russia investigation would turn out to be controversial, especially among the president's supporters. But at this moment, McCabe and Strzok gave a brief introduction, though the story always had its twists and turns. McCabe recalled what it was like to brief Mueller on a case—the way he inhaled information and spit back a constant series of questions demanding more details. For that reason, McCabe provided a warning at the outset. "We will not get through the whole story in this one meeting," he said. "It's too long and complicated. We will tell you how we got here.

"As you know," McCabe went on, "Russia is an existential threat to the United States." Here McCabe was repeating back what he knew Mueller already believed. Mueller's career in the Justice Department stretched back to the days of the Cold War against the Soviet Union, so he hardly needed lessons on the malign intentions of the government in Moscow. McCabe said Crossfire Hurricane began shortly after the hack of the Democratic National Committee emails in July 2016. It was then that the Australian government reached out with word that George Papadopoulos, from the Trump campaign, had told Alexander Downer, the Australian diplomat, earlier in the spring that the Russians were planning to release hacked emails related to the campaign. "The Australians hadn't done anything when they first heard about it, but once the hacking took place, they told us about the conversation," McCabe explained. "We've known for years that the Russians were probing our political systems. But July is when we say, fuck, this is actually happening."

McCabe went on to say something else that Mueller, of all people, already knew—that the FBI investigates people, not political campaigns. But in light of the hacking and the Australian disclosures, the bureau started looking at Trump campaign officials who had ties to the Russians. "In those early days, we were asking, who are the people who are associated with the campaign who appear to have connections to Russians?" McCabe said. That included Papadopoulos, of course, and Carter Page, whose pro-Russian activities had drawn the interest of the FBI as much as a decade earlier. There was also Paul Manafort, who served for a time as Trump's campaign chairman and who also had long-standing financial and political ties to the pro-Russian political party in Ukraine. The link between Michael Flynn, the ousted national security adviser, and the Russians appeared to be the weakest, but he was the one who lied to the agents about his contacts with the Russian ambassador.

And then there was the question of the candidate—now the president—himself. "We have no idea that Trump knows anything about these connections," McCabe said. "Or were these people just rogue morons?" Still, regardless of Trump's connections, if any, to the Russians during the campaign, there was the issue of possible obstruction of justice once he became president. The issue arose from Trump's bizarre interactions with Comey. McCabe gave the Mueller group a brief introduction to those meetings, which Comey had already mostly succeeded in leaking to the press through his friend Dan Richman at Columbia Law School. "On the loyalty pledge at dinner," McCabe said, "we just thought, this is weird. In that first interaction, you could tell yourself, Trump is new and doesn't know how it all works. But then the Flynn moment completely erases all that—when he kicks everyone out of the Oval Office. He knew he shouldn't do it. That's why he kicks everyone out." The Comey-Trump encounters led to the opening of the criminal investigation of the president himself.

Mueller and his team had lots of questions, of course, and they were only beginning to absorb the background facts. Still, that first meeting at the FBI was enormously consequential for the future of the special counsel's investigation—both for what was said and for what wasn't. McCabe and his team gave Mueller five targets—Papadopoulos, Page, Flynn, Manafort, and Trump. This gave Mueller a focus, but the new special counsel took it as a limit as well.

This message was reinforced when the Mueller trio went to meet with Rosenstein for an introductory meeting at the Justice Department. The deputy attorney general had regained a measure of equanimity since he named Mueller as special counsel. The choice was as roundly applauded as Rosenstein's Comey memo was broadly condemned. Rosenstein didn't know the evidence in anywhere near the detail that McCabe and his team did, but he had a more general piece of advice for Mueller. And given that the deputy attorney general was Mueller's boss, the guidance had a measure of command. It was drawn from Rosenstein's own experience in outside investigations of the executive branch.

"I love Ken Starr," Rosenstein told Mueller. "But his investigation was a fishing expedition. Don't do that. This is a criminal investigation. Do your job, and then shut it down."

Temperamentally as well as professionally, Mueller was a receptive audience for this advice. As stammering aides learned to their misfortune, Mueller had little patience even in the best of circumstances, and he especially disdained investigators who lingered over their work. As special counsel, he wanted to complete his assignment and move on. (That he was seventy-two years old added to his sense of urgency.) Mueller shared Rosenstein's view of Starr. Indeed, for Mueller, the Starr investigation served as a kind of reverse North Star—a model of everything not to do. The very notion of a criminal investigation lasting almost eight years was repellent to Mueller, as was a prosecutor's meandering, seemingly desperate search to find something, or anything, to pin on a target. The persistent news leaks from Starr's office, as well as Starr's frequent news conferences on the driveway of his home in suburban Virginia, were anathema to Mueller as well. From the day he was hired, Mueller imposed a press blackout from his office that was the most successful in modern Washington history. He hired as his press "spokesman" a genial Justice Department veteran named Peter Carr who might have set a record for the number of times he told reporters "no comment." From day one, Mueller determined to do a limited, tailored investigation, and to do it in secret.

Those first meetings with McCabe and Rosenstein left Mueller with a clear agenda of what to do and what not to do. There looked to be prosecutable cases for false statements against Papadopoulos and Flynn and for financial improprieties against Manafort. McCabe had just opened an investigation of Trump for obstruction of justice in the White House. Mueller decided to take on all of these cases, but that's just about all he took on. He did not use the FBI information as a jumping-off point for a deeper examination of Trump's history and finances—to explore, for example, why Trump had a special affinity for Russia and its leader. Indeed, on this first day the FBI investigators said nothing about Trump's personal finances or his taxes, and Mueller never explored those subjects himself either.

Mueller's determination to pursue only a limited agenda never wavered over two years of investigation. The prolonged public silence of his team fed rumors about the supposedly vast scale of Mueller's ambitions. Over that time, Mueller became an object of hope, even obsession, among Trump's political adversaries. There were "Mueller Time" T-shirts and Robert Mueller action figures—G.I. Joes for the MSNBC set. If anything, these fixations steeled Mueller's desire to do less, not more. He was not hired to write Trump's biography or to bring him down. Mueller was hired to complete an ongoing investigation that was already begun by the Justice Department. This former marine was hired to do a job and follow orders, which he did, and nothing more.

Twenty-four hours or so after he was appointed, Mueller showed up at the door to Jeannie Rhee's office at WilmerHale. "I don't know what I'm getting myself into," he told her. But did she want to join the team? Mueller didn't have to ask her a second time. Rhee spent a weekend extricating herself from her clients at the firm and reported for duty on Monday. She was the fourth lawyer on the team, but while the first three were still setting up the office, Rhee became the first to start actual investigating. She began looking for people to prosecute, and to flip.

Jeannie Rhee's résumé looked like those of many people at Wilmer-Hale, which long prided itself on the lofty pedigrees of its lawyers. Rhee went to Yale College and Yale Law School, which she followed with a prestigious clerkship on the D.C. Circuit. She tried criminal cases in the U.S. Attorney's office in Washington and did stints in the Clinton and Obama Justice Departments. In her forties, she was ascending the partnership ranks at WilmerHale and heading toward a leadership role at the firm.

In reality—that is, in background, demeanor, and personality—Rhee little resembled her colleagues. She was born in Seoul to parents who had the first non-arranged marriage in the history of either family. When Jeannie was five, her father took what was supposed to be a two-year assignment with Westinghouse in western Pennsylvania. They never returned to live in Korea. Westinghouse was a dying business in those days, and Jeannie's parents drifted for a time into the restaurant business, to join a cousin who operated a Japanese place near Pittsburgh. Rhee learned a lesson at the restaurant that led, indirectly, to her first memorable interaction with Robert Mueller.

Shortly after Mueller left the FBI and arrived at WilmerHale, he was retained by the National Football League to investigate its handling of a domestic violence incident involving the Baltimore Ravens' Ray Rice. Mueller first asked Zebley and Quarles, his usual team members, to work on the case with him, but he recognized that an all-male team for this kind of investigation would not be appropriate.

So he asked Rhee to join them. She wasn't wild about serving as "the woman" on the team, but she had handled dozens of domestic violence cases at the U.S. Attorney's office, so she knew the field, and she was curious about working with Mueller, so she said yes.

The assignment involved a good deal of time spent in a hotel in Baltimore, and it was at the restaurant there that Rhee explained to Mueller her philosophy of the buffet, which she had learned from her parents. One should always order the buffet, Rhee asserted, but then load up one's plate with proteins—especially meat—and avoid carbohydrates, like rice. Proteins were expensive, and carbs were cheap. As a customer, the best bang for your buck were the proteins, and Rhee could be found at the hotel buffet every morning with her plate full of bacon and sausage. Mueller found Rhee's dollar-based intensity on the subject of food fascinating and bizarre, and he proceeded to needle her about it relentlessly over the course of their time together. Mueller's subordinates often said that they could tell they remained in his good graces if he continued to tease them about something. For Rhee, it was the "boo-fay," as Mueller pronounced it, as if it were some exotic culinary passion rather than a staple of high school cafeterias. Mueller despised all forms of pretension, including in food, where his tastes were relentlessly bland. Rhee's passion on the subject, and her intensity generally, marked a significant contrast to Mueller's aristocratic reserve.

In making hiring decisions, at the Office of Special Counsel and elsewhere, Mueller often said he was looking for people who were "sparky"—that is, dynamic and energetic. This was notable because Mueller himself rarely exuded spark—a kind of looming intensity, to be sure, but not in a way that was any more colorful than his white shirts. Rhee, in contrast, was all spark, all immigrant hustle, always looking for an edge. She was loud, aggressive, and opinionated, which was not to everyone's taste, especially since she rarely dialed down the sparkiness. But that kind of attitude was exactly what Mueller wanted.

In the same way that McCabe and Rosenstein defined the scope of the special counsel investigation, Mueller himself defined the tactics. His team would be aggressive but conventional. In the words of a famous Supreme Court opinion, Mueller thought that while a prosecutor "may strike hard blows, he is not at liberty to strike foul ones." Mueller would use the FBI but not the news media. He believed in stealth but not deception. He would prosecute individuals but not humiliate them. He would play by the rules he had always known.

Mueller would, as the saying went, try his cases in the courtroom and not in the press, but first he needed a case to try or, better yet, a guilty plea. He needed a victory, and he needed it fast. So after Rhee passed her security clearance and a drug test, she demanded binders full of the existing evidence from the FBI agents on the case. With characteristic certainty, she settled quickly on an initial target: George Papadopoulos.

There was always something preposterous about the idea of George Papadopoulos at the center of a major national scandal. When Mueller eventually announced charges against him, Trump supporters dismissed him as "the coffee boy." And they had a point—almost. Given his age, maturity, level of accomplishment, and judgment, Papadopoulos should have been the coffee boy on a national campaign for president. But it was characteristic of the shambling, improvisational nature of the Trump operation that Papadopoulos really did travel around the world as the candidate's representative. And in doing so, Papadopoulos carried the transactional, ethics-free values of the candidate with him. Papadopoulos didn't want to change the world as much as he wanted to change his life. As a first target of the Mueller team, he offered a kind of trailer of what was to come. The evolution of the case against him, as well as those against several others, would show how different from other Washington scandals this investigation turned out to be.

Papadopoulos was born in 1987 to parents who were immigrants from Greece, and he grew up in the suburbs of Chicago. His father was active in the Greek American community, and that ignited in George a budding interest in foreign policy, which he pursued in a passing way, when he went to college locally, at DePaul. After graduating in 2009, he spent a year in London and then began drifting around the think tank world, mostly as an unpaid intern, writing occasional op-ed pieces for foreign publications. On his LinkedIn page, he called himself an "oil, gas, and policy consultant," which was a stretch. There was nothing untoward in his behavior, nor anything particularly distinguished, as he looked to find his place in the world.

For someone with his background, it was not surprising that Papadopoulos tried to connect with a presidential campaign in 2015. He managed to catch on briefly with Ben Carson's short-lived undertaking, but as that campaign was winding down, in early 2016, he reached out to the ascendant effort of Donald Trump. The Trump campaign was disorganized in the best of circumstances, and its policy apparatus was an especially neglected corner. ("Policy" on the campaign was whatever Trump happened to say on any given day.) Still, there was a thought that the campaign should at least pretend to have an infrastructure of experts and advisers. Following a Skype interview with a campaign official when Papadopoulos was in London, he was "hired" as an adviser. His job with Carson came with a modest stipend, but Trump's campaign, in characteristic fashion, wasn't offering any pay at all. But Papadopoulos got to call himself part of the campaign, and the campaign got to put his name on a list, so the situation had advantages for both sides.

What mattered, though—especially, in time, to Rhee and her colleagues at the OSC—was what happened after Papadopoulos became publicly affiliated with the Trump campaign in the spring of 2016. Papadopoulos had a connection to a fledgling legal institute in London, and in mid-March he traveled with a group to Rome to attend a conference at Link Campus University, a for-profit school that had close ties to intelligence operatives from around the world. There Papadopoulos met with a shadowy figure named Joseph Mifsud, a professor and citizen of Malta who took a strong interest in the American visitor when he found out he was working for Trump. Mifsud boasted to Papadopoulos of his close ties to Russian officials, and Papadopoulos welcomed any intelligence from Mifsud that he might be able to pass back to the campaign.

A week later, Papadopoulos had lunch with Mifsud in London, and the professor brought along a guest, Olga Polonskaya, a woman whom Mifsud described as "Putin's niece." (She wasn't.) According to an email Papadopoulos sent to several people on the Trump campaign, Mifsud wanted to arrange a meeting between Trump and Putin, as well as campaign officials and "the Russian leadership," at a neutral site or in Moscow. Ambitious young people gravitate to political campaigns all the time, and many obtain positions of real responsibility. But they don't, as a rule, negotiate for meetings between the candidate and foreign leaders. So it was astounding how seriously Papadopoulos's superiors took his effort on behalf of the campaign. Sam Clovis, Papadopoulos's boss, emailed back, regarding the possible Putin-Trump summit, "Great work."

On March 31, 2016, Papadopoulos had his one and only meeting with Trump, a photo-op convening of the candidate's alleged foreign policy advisers at the Trump International Hotel in Washington. (Jeff Sessions was the nominal leader of the group.) When Papadopoulos piped up about Putin's interest in meeting with Trump, the candidate expressed enthusiasm for the idea. Though Papadopoulos didn't know it, he had touched a long-standing obsession of Trump's. At least as far back as 2013, when Trump hosted the Miss Universe pageant, which he then owned, in Moscow, Trump had been longing to meet Putin in person. By this point in the campaign he had already noted, in both speeches and tweets, his admiration for Putin. Papadopoulos took Trump's words as an invitation to continue his talks about a preelection summit when he returned to London.

There Papadopoulos had more meetings and phone calls with Mifsud and the Russian leader's supposed niece. After Mifsud paid a quick visit to Moscow in April, he gave Papadopoulos some startling news. Not only would Putin like to meet with Trump but the Russians had "dirt" on Hillary Clinton in the form of thousands of emails. At that point, Papadopoulos didn't know if this was true—that is, if the Russians really had such dirt—but he knew he had a hot piece of gossip to pass along to his contacts in London. On May 6, he had a boozy evening in a London bar with Alexander Downer, the Australian diplomat, where he shared Mifsud's claim that the Russians had negative information on the Democratic candidate. Downer also had no way of checking out the story at that point, but it was confirmed two months later, when the "dirt" materialized in the form of the DNC emails, released by WikiLeaks on the eve of the Democratic National Convention.

Even before Mueller was appointed, the FBI team conducting the Crossfire Hurricane investigation had focused on Papadopoulos and his connections to the Russians. On January 27, 2017, agents showed up without prior notice at Papadopoulos's mother's home in Chicago, where he was visiting. Papadopoulos agreed to follow the agents to the FBI field office downtown and answer questions, and he told them a series of lies. He acknowledged that he had spoken to Mifsud, and he agreed that the professor had told him the Russians had dirt on Clinton. But Papadopoulos said the conversation took place *before* he had joined the Trump campaign. He also said he understood Mifsud was "a nothing," "just a guy" with no special connections to Russia. He said it was a "very strange coincidence" that Mifsud had told him about the Clinton emails before he had any connection to Trump's campaign. In fact, Papadopoulos's role in the campaign was the focus of his conversations with Mifsud, who appeared to have significant contacts within the Russian government. Indeed, it seems that the only reason Mifsud spoke to Papadopoulos at all was because of his role in the Trump campaign. Papadopoulos repeated his lies in a second interview with the FBI a few days later. (His lies hampered the FBI's investigation because agents had their one and only chance to interview Mifsud on February 10, 2017. Because Papadopoulos had lied to the agents, they didn't have enough facts to conduct a real interrogation of the mysterious Mifsud. In any case, after that interview, Mifsud disappeared, presumably somewhere in Europe, and has never been seen again by American law enforcement.)

This, then, was the background Jeannie Rhee uncovered in the FBI files as she began Mueller's investigation in May 2017. The evidence raised as many questions as it answered. Why did Mifsud and "Putin's niece"—whoever she really was—try to make connections between the Russian leadership and the Trump campaign? How did Mifsud know that the Russians had the "dirt"? What else did Mifsud, or the Russians, do for the Trump campaign? Papadopoulos told Downer, the Australian, about the Russian dirt on Clinton, but did he pass the same information to his superiors in the campaign? Who else in the Trump campaign had connections to Mifsud or his Russian friends? Did they seek out dirt on Clinton from anyone else—especially any Russians?

Better yet, Rhee and the FBI had the prospect of real leverage over Papadopoulos. He had lied to the FBI agents in their interview, and that was a federal crime. Mueller authorized Rhee to obtain a sealed complaint against Papadopoulos, with the hope that a sudden arrest would prompt him to tell the FBI a true story this time—or better

yet, to flip and testify against others. The FBI's initial inquiries suggested that Papadopoulos would be returning to the United States
soon. So Rhee told the agents to set up an ambush.

First, though, she had to obtain an arrest warrant, and this, too,
established a pattern for Mueller's office. Mueller decreed that there
would be no leaks to, or even informal contact with, the news media.
But like any prosecutor, he would have occasion to file legal documents with the court—complaints, affidavits in support of search and
arrest warrants, and, ultimately, indictments. Prosecutors have a lot
of leeway in how they frame these documents. They can be terse,
revealing little about the progress of an investigation, or they can be
expansive, laying out the scope and progress of a prosecutor's work.
"Speaking indictments," as the longer versions are known, are written
to command respect from the public and to inspire fear in possible
targets. And notwithstanding Mueller's showy silence, his office used
its legal documents as unofficial press releases, and the first one was
the complaint against George Papadopoulos.

The complaint, in the form of an affidavit by FBI agent Robert
Gibbs (but written, as is customary, by the prosecutors), opened
with a primer on Russian recruitment techniques. "I am aware that
the Russian government and its intelligence and security services
frequently make use of non-governmental intermediaries to achieve
their foreign intelligence objectives," Gibbs stated. These intermediaries include professors and think tank academics—people like Joseph
Mifsud. The affidavit went on to quote the email exchanges between
Mifsud, Putin's alleged niece, and Papadopoulos to demonstrate the
degree of interest the Trump campaign, through its representative,
showed in meeting with the Russians, especially Putin himself, and
the Russians' interest in Trump. Papadopoulos wrote to Clovis that
his Russian contact "said the leadership, including Putin, is ready
to meet with us and Mr. Trump should there be interest. Waiting
for everyone's thoughts on moving forward with this very important
issue." In a later email to the campaign, Papadopoulos wrote, "Russia
has been eager to meet Mr. Trump for quite sometime and has been
reaching out to me to discuss." Polonskaya, the supposed Putin niece,
wrote to him, "We are all very excited about the possibility of a good
relationship with Trump. The Russian Federation would love to welcome him once his candidature would be officially announced." (This

email was sent on April 12, 2016, well after Trump announced, but the Russians sometimes evinced a fuzzy understanding of the details of American politics.)

The Gibbs affidavit, which ran to twelve pages, was meant to do a great deal more than just outline the false statement charge against Papadopoulos, which was its official purpose. When it became unsealed, it would show the intensity of interest on both sides of the Trump-Russia relationship. By 2017, of course, the world knew that a campaign summit between the American candidate and the Russian leader had never taken place, but nor did anyone know the effort that had been extended to make one happen. The affidavit was suggestive, but not proof, of "collusion"—a word that came to have totemic significance in public perception of the Mueller investigation.

Rhee's purpose in ordering Papadopoulos's arrest was to shock him into disclosing what went on in his role as an intermediary between the campaign and the Russians. The FBI was able to track Papadopoulos's movements across Europe and learn that he would be returning on a Lufthansa flight to Washington Dulles International Airport on July 27. On that day, FBI agents were waiting for him before he reached customs. They took him to a side room and placed him in handcuffs and told him he was under arrest. He spent the night in detention before he was told the charges the following morning. At that point, the complaint was still under seal. For the moment it was to be read only by Papadopoulos, who would consider the strength of the government's case against him and, the Mueller team hoped, decide to cooperate.

"If the plan was to scare the hell out of me," Papadopoulos later reflected, "it works."

7

"Do You Think Putin Will . . . Become My New Best Friend?"

Mueller's early moves were invisible to Trump. (The complaint against Papadopoulos, as well as the fact of his arrest, was initially kept secret, while Mueller's prosecutors tried to persuade Papadopoulos to cooperate.) The prosecutor's public silence unnerved the president almost as much as his appointment did. Trump's psychological deficits—his narcissism, his lack of empathy, his short attention span—were almost comically conspicuous, and so, too, was his tendency to project his deficits onto others. In this way, it was fitting that the president became obsessed with the notion that Mueller should not serve because he had conflicts of interest.

In the first days after Mueller became special counsel, Trump complained to Reince Priebus, Steve Bannon, and Don McGahn about Mueller's purported conflicts. In characteristic fashion, he rewrote the story of Mueller's conversation with him on May 16. He said Mueller had "begged" to be named FBI director again. Trump's refusal to reappoint him meant Mueller had a grudge against the president. He said WilmerHale represented other people in the case (including his son-in-law, Jared Kushner). According to Trump, this also represented a conflict. And most of all, Trump fixated on the fact that Mueller had once been a member of Trump National Golf Club, outside Washington, and had then resigned and requested a refund. This, too, meant Mueller had a preexisting grievance against Trump. As even his close advisers acknowledged, Trump's claims against Mueller were frivolous. They knew that Mueller had not sought out the FBI job. Mueller himself had nothing to do with his firm's representation of Kushner. And as for Trump National, Mueller and his wife had realized he was not using the golf club in 2011, so he asked for a prorated portion of his membership fee to be returned, as was his right. It was a routine transaction. (On May 23, the Department of Justice made a formal ruling that Mueller had no conflicts and could serve as special counsel.)

Still, in private at first, then later in tweets and public comments, Trump returned obsessively to Mueller's "conflicts." Of course, he himself had the most egregious conflicts of interest of any president in modern history. His family continued to run and profit from the Trump Organization as the president, directly and indirectly, drove business their way. Trump's criticisms were a reliable window into his own flaws. He was the man who said he wasn't Vladimir Putin's puppet; Hillary Clinton was. He was not the corrupt politician, but his adversaries were. Trump's taunts of Mueller for conflicts of interest fit the same pattern.

Trump's paranoia and rage were heightened by Comey's first public appearance as the former director of the FBI, on June 8, when he testified before the Senate Intelligence Committee. There, Comey recounted his dealings with Trump from the first postelection briefing until the day he was fired. Much of the story was already public, thanks to Comey's leaks through Richman, the law professor, but the cumulative effect of the leaks and the testimony was devastating. In Comey's account, Trump came across as a near gangster, his words lightly coded with menace. The testimony was also Comey's chance to respond in public to Trump's tweet about the possibility of tape recordings of their conversations. Comey provided the memorable reply: "Lordy, I hope there are tapes." (There were no tapes.) By this point, both Democrats and Republicans had complaints about the former FBI director, but in light of his demeanor and his contemporaneous notes it was very difficult for anyone (except Trump himself) to believe that he was lying about his interactions with the president.

A report in *The Washington Post,* on June 14, that Mueller was investigating the president for obstruction of justice produced even more fury from Trump. On the morning of June 15, before 8:00, he tweeted, "You are witnessing the single greatest WITCH HUNT in American political history—led by some very bad and conflicted people! #MAGA" and "They made up a phony collusion with the Russians story, found zero proof, so now they go for obstruction of justice on the phony story. Nice." Two days later, on Saturday morning, June 17, the president took his rage a step further. He called Don McGahn and ordered him to have Mueller fired—on the one-month anniversary of his appointment. (This, too, was an act of obstruction of justice by the president.) McGahn, as he later recounted, tried to stall, telling Trump he would see what he could do. But McGahn resolved that he was not going to pass along the instruction to Rod Rosenstein to fire Mueller. As he later told Mueller's investigators, he wanted to be more like Judge Bork—the hero of conservative jurisprudence—than "Saturday Night Massacre Bork," the man who followed the order to fire Archibald Cox.

But Trump wouldn't relent. He called McGahn a second time on that Saturday and again demanded that he see that Mueller was removed. "Call Rod, tell Rod that Mueller has conflicts and can't be Special Counsel," Trump said. "Call me back when you do it." Once again McGahn did his best to get Trump off the phone without responding directly to his demand, but he felt trapped. McGahn wasn't going to fire Mueller, and he didn't know what he was going to tell Trump about it. He called his personal lawyer and said he had to resign as White House counsel. He called his chief of staff (and note taker), Annie Donaldson, and told her he was leaving. She told him she would resign too. He went to the White House and packed up his belongings. But when he saw the president the next week, neither man said anything about their conversations over the weekend, and McGahn remained in his job. There was no doubt that Trump told McGahn to fire Mueller, but did he mean it? As Hope Hicks, the Trump whisperer, recognized, Trump talked about firing people more often than he actually did the deed. But McGahn thought Trump's intention was clear—that he wanted Mueller gone and he wanted McGahn to make it happen.

But Trump wasn't finished trying to get rid of Mueller. On the following Monday, June 19, the president met with Corey Lewandowski, his former campaign manager, who was now an outside adviser. After some small talk, Trump told Lewandowski to take down some dictation—something Trump had never done before with him. The president said he wanted a message passed to Jeff Sessions, who was a friend of Lewandowski's. Trump said that Sessions should give a speech with the following words:

> I know that I recused myself from certain things having to do with specific areas. But our POTUS . . . is being treated very unfairly. He shouldn't have a Special Prosecutor/Counsel b/c he hasn't done anything wrong. I was on the campaign w/ him for nine months, there was no Russians involved with him. I know for a fact b/c I was there. He didn't do anything wrong except he ran the greatest campaign in American history.

People around Trump, and eventually the whole country, would come to expect that the president would describe himself and his efforts with these kinds of superlatives. Trump's proposed speech for Sessions went on to say that Mueller would be banned from any further investigation of the 2016 campaign, but the special counsel would be permitted to monitor future election interference. In other words, Trump wanted Lewandowski to pass along orders to Sessions to unrecuse himself and then truncate Mueller's jurisdiction. (This, too, was obstruction of justice by Trump.) Lewandowski was known as a ferocious partisan—and he wasn't even a lawyer—but he knew enough to put the crackpot speech draft in his pocket and forget about it. (Much later, he made a halfhearted attempt to pass it through an intermediary to Sessions.) Both the campaign operative and the ideologue attorney had the intelligence and integrity to save Trump from himself. The president told them both to participate in his scheme to obstruct justice, and they both, in similar ways, managed to turn him down while avoiding a direct confrontation.

Trump always believed that he was his own best advocate, but he also recognized that Mueller's appointment meant that he needed a lawyer. This was not a new issue for him. By one analysis, Trump and his businesses had been the subject of approximately 3,500 lawsuits in the thirty years before he became president. He was the plaintiff in 1,900, the defendant in 1,450, and involved in about 150 other cases that related to his various bankruptcies. The subjects included disputes with casino patrons, complaints from unpaid contractors, personal injury cases from his resorts, libel lawsuits against journalists, and sexual harassment claims by women. *USA Today,* which conducted the study, could figure out the resolution to only about 1,300 of the cases. Among these, Trump won about 900, settled 175, and lost 38. (There was some other conclusion to the others.) Even by the standards of prominent businesspeople, this was an enormous amount of litigation. Thanks in part to the tutelage of Roy Cohn, his first lawyer and the one he admired most, Trump approached the courtroom with his customary cynicism. All that mattered was winning, regardless of what norms, or people, he had to trample in the process.

This was especially true in a special counsel investigation. Trump was no student of history, but he knew enough to recognize the peril in which he found himself. He knew that the Starr investigation led to Bill Clinton's impeachment; he knew that Watergate led to Richard Nixon's resignation. Given those precedents, Trump had good reason for his initial reaction to Mueller's appointment: "This is the end of my Presidency. I'm fucked."

Trump had a well-deserved reputation for disloyalty, especially to employees and business partners, but he did have a small core of associates, if not friends, who managed to hang on for a long time. Allen Weisselberg, the chief financial officer of the Trump Organization, had been with the company since the 1970s. Alan Garten, the company's chief legal officer, had been with him for more than a decade. And Marc Kasowitz, who had his own law firm, had represented Trump in various pieces of litigation since the 1980s. Kasowitz had handled only civil matters for Trump, but just after Mueller was appointed, the president turned to him to lead the criminal defense.

Kasowitz had much in common with the people who remained in Trump's good graces. For one thing, he looked the part. With his white hair immaculately barbered and his suits tailor made, Kasowitz projected the prosperous look that Trump required. He was also a success. Since splitting off from an old-line law firm in the early 1990s, he had built his own firm into one of 250 lawyers. His firm operated as a sort of on-call service for Trump's legal needs, whether he was a plaintiff or a defendant. Kasowitz Benson Torres & Friedman wasn't in the very top rank of New York law firms, but it was just below—a rough counterpart to Deutsche Bank, Trump's longtime lender, which agreed to do business with Trump when leaders in the industry refused. Trump's ties to the Kasowitz firm were deep. As president, Trump named David Friedman, another partner who frequently represented him, as his ambassador to Israel.

Kasowitz spent the 2016 campaign as Trump's legal firefighter. Representing Trump was as much a matter of mollifying the client as it was filing and winning cases. Kasowitz threatened to sue *The New York Times* when the newspaper published excerpts from Trump's 1995 tax returns. After the *Access Hollywood* video surfaced in the final month of the campaign, several women came forward to the *Times* to claim that they had been sexually harassed by Trump. "You are a disgusting human being," Trump told Megan Twohey, the *Times* reporter on the story. Kasowitz followed up with a letter to the *Times*'s editors asserting Twohey's article was "reckless, defamatory and constitutes libel per se." But in neither case did Kasowitz actually file a lawsuit or do anything except send a threatening letter. After years of representing Trump, Kasowitz understood that his job was to make indignant noises that sounded as if Trump were prepared to sue. The point of these letters was to have them quoted in the media. Kasowitz was savvy enough to recognize that once that mission was accomplished, it was usually the better course to let the matter drop. Trump, of all people, understood the value of bluster. (On one occasion, Kasowitz did file a libel suit on Trump's behalf, against Timothy O'Brien, who wrote a biography of Trump in 2005. The core accusation against O'Brien was that he wrote that Trump was not a billionaire, but rather worth in the neighborhood of $200 million. Nothing enraged Trump as much as assertions that he was not as rich as he claimed to be. After years of litigation, Trump's case was dismissed.)

Kasowitz had for years been a respected member of the New York legal community, known for his hard-edged and often successful litigation tactics. But once he became enmeshed in the Trump presidency, he suffered the fate of nearly everyone who became identified with this president: public humiliation. Cabinet members (like Jeff Sessions and Rex Tillerson, Trump's short-lived first secretary of state), White House aides (like Reince Priebus and his successors as chief of staff), and even outside advisers (like Kasowitz) saw their reputations damaged by their association with Trump. In many cases, like those of Sessions, Tillerson, and the chiefs of staff, they suffered because

Trump himself turned on them. For Kasowitz, the problem was a level of media scrutiny that he had never faced as a law firm partner. He dealt awkwardly with questions from the press, and, even worse, ProPublica ran a detailed story asserting that Kasowitz had for a time abused alcohol. The claim was dubiously relevant to Kasowitz's work as Trump's lawyer, but it prompted him to seek to return to his lucrative anonymity at his law firm. After that first burst of attention, both Kasowitz and Trump thought it best for the president to have a Washington-based criminal defense lawyer leading his effort.

Kasowitz led the search, guided by Trump. As in all areas of his life, the president had a preference for big names, so Kasowitz went after some of the biggest. He reached out to Brendan V. Sullivan Jr., who became famous as Oliver North's defense attorney in the Iran-contra scandal. Sullivan declined, citing a conflict. (At the firm of Williams & Connolly, Sullivan's partners included David Kendall, who had long represented Bill and Hillary Clinton. This was not perhaps a technical conflict of interest but certainly awkward enough for Sullivan to decline.) Kasowitz also called Theodore Olson, who was solicitor general in the George W. Bush administration, as well as the victor in *Bush v. Gore* and a leader in the fight for marriage equality. Olson agreed to meet with Priebus and Steve Bannon, but he also begged off, citing a conflict. There was also an approach to Robert Bennett, who represented Bill Clinton in the Paula Jones case. He declined outright. In most circumstances, the opportunity to represent the president of the United States is highly coveted, the kind of assignment that would lead many lawyers to find a way around conflicts. But Washington's top lawyers formulated reasons to say no to Donald Trump.

In time, John Dowd found his way to Kasowitz. Dowd was not an obvious choice. At seventy-six, he was somewhere between partially and totally retired. He had a blood sugar condition that frequently waylaid him in the afternoon. But Dowd had once been a prominent lawyer in Washington, mostly during the 1980s, when he conducted a high-profile investigation of gambling by Pete Rose for Major League Baseball. Dowd was a former marine and a political conservative, both rarities in the Washington legal community. He had a martial, peremptory style that led him to make unlawyerly denunciations of his (and Trump's) legal and political adversaries. Dowd wanted the job, emailing one of Kasowitz's partners, "Happy to help DJT quietly behind the curtain. . . . I am not sure he needs counsel but it would not hurt to keep an eye on it and independently advise him." (Importantly, for the always-thrifty Trump, Dowd was willing to work for free.) When they met for the first time, the president enjoyed Dowd's full-throated contempt for Democrats and the news media. (That Dowd was a generational peer of Trump's didn't hurt him at first either.)

But Dowd's best quality, as far as the president was concerned, was that he was an old friend of Mueller's. In line with his education from Roy Cohn, Trump thought a personal relationship with a decision maker was more important than any legal argument, and he assumed everyone else felt that way, too. Dowd could appeal to Mueller marine to marine, and that sounded good to the president. Trump thus chose Dowd as his lead defense lawyer in the Mueller investigation.

By this point in late spring, the president had tired of his press secretary, Sean Spicer, who had become a figure of mockery for his exaggerations and outright lies. (Spicer's ill-fitting suits also offended Trump.) White House officials began scouting around for a replacement, and they started making appeals to Mark Corallo, who had been the chief spokesman for Attorney General John Ashcroft in the period after 9/11. Like Don McGahn, Corallo was the kind of professional who might have been hired in any Republican administration but who had no ties to the Trump universe. He was living the prosperous life of a consultant, and he'd promised his wife he would reject any offers to return to government, but he agreed to meet with Priebus, McGahn, and Bannon.

The Trump advisers realized that Corallo had a particular corner of expertise, and they wanted to exploit it. At the Justice Department, Corallo had worked closely with Comey (who was Ashcroft's deputy) and Mueller (then the FBI director), and he had strong feelings about both. He revered Mueller—a straight shooter, he said, with no political agenda: Mueller will listen to legal arguments and take them seriously. The White House should strongly consider reaching out to him and offering to cooperate. Corallo's view of Comey was very different. He saw Comey as a sanctimonious phony—an attention junkie with a Messiah complex. And contrary to popular (and Trump's own) belief,

Mueller and Comey were not particularly close, Corallo said. Mueller would not defer to or necessarily believe his successor as FBI director.

This was news to Trump's advisers, and they decided that the president himself should receive the same briefing, so they marched Corallo into the Oval Office and then into the president's small private dining room for a face-to-face briefing. (Corallo noticed that no one in the White House, including the president, seemed to have a schedule of appointments, but rather they seemed to roll into each other's office when they had something to say.) "The best thing you can do is be quiet, be president, and let Mueller do his thing," Corallo told him. "It'll be fine. Bob Mueller doesn't do agendas." Trump was skeptical but attentive. Priebus and the others asked Corallo to return in the late afternoon. (He agreed, on the condition that someone feed the meter where his car was parked.) By the end of the day, Bannon was haranguing him to become communications director and White House press secretary. Mindful of his promise to his wife, Corallo said no, but he ultimately agreed to be hired as the spokesman, outside the government, for the president's legal team.

Soon enough, Corallo became a regular in the West Wing, and in the Oval Office, and he became attuned to the peculiar rhythms of the Trump White House. He would have meetings with the president about legal strategy with Kasowitz and Dowd, but Jared Kushner and Ivanka Trump would invite themselves to sit in. "How's the Dream Team going?" Ivanka would chirp pleasantly. Attorney-client privilege covered only conversations between lawyers and clients, so Jared and Ivanka's presence meant that the conversations with Trump's lawyers would not be privileged. But no one seemed to care, least of all the president. Indeed, he would often rhapsodize about his daughter. "She brands the Trump name," the president told Corallo. "It used to mean hotels and golf courses, but now it means class and dignity and the presidency and power."

It was clear, too, that Kushner and Ivanka enjoyed privileges that were not extended to other staffers. It was, for example, unspoken that Kushner would continue to be afforded access to classified information, even though he had not received a security clearance and the resubmissions of his applications continued to include errors, particularly about his contacts with hostile powers, like Russia. But the real crisis of the spring—which began with Kushner and nearly consumed the president—involved what became known as the Trump Tower meeting.

The roots of the Trump Tower meeting went back to the Miss Universe pageant of 2013, which was held in Moscow. Trump had been interested in building a branded property in Moscow since the days of the Soviet Union. Starting in the 1980s, he had visited once a decade, though he had nothing to show for it. The closest he came to doing business in Russia was in 2007, when he signed a distribution deal for his Trump-branded vodka to be sold there. (It flopped in Russia, as it did elsewhere.) In later years, Trump and his sons frequently bragged about how many buyers of the apartments in their New York buildings were Russian nationals, but his dream of building in Moscow remained unfulfilled.

In 2013, Trump's prospects in Russia began to look more promising, thanks to a music video featuring a pop star named Emin Agalarov. Emin's father, Aras, had made a fortune as a real estate developer in Moscow, and Emin had put the family money to work for the benefit of his singing career. The Moscow music scene favored hard-edged rap, but Emin found a degree of success as a crooner in the mold of Enrique Iglesias. Emin never caught on in the United States, but he drew thousands to concerts in Russia, eastern Europe, and especially Azerbaijan, where he was born. In 2013, Emin had high expectations for a danceable tune called "Amor," and he wanted an especially beautiful woman to star in the accompanying music video. He and his publicist, Rob Goldstone, a former tabloid journalist from Great Britain who was hired to promote Emin's singing career outside Russia, approached the Miss Universe Organization and asked if they could cast the reigning champion, Olivia Culpo, the former Miss USA.

Emin and Goldstone also suggested that the Agalarovs host Miss Universe in Moscow in 2013 so that Emin could perform for the pageant's global audience. That June, Emin and Aras traveled to Las Vegas to close the deal with Trump, who had owned the pageant since the mid-1990s. On June 18, 2013, just after Trump announced that the Miss Universe pageant would take place in Russia, he tweeted, with a kind of desperate giddiness, "Do you think Putin will be going to The Miss Universe Pageant in November in Moscow—if so, will he become my new best friend?" That fall, before the pageant, David Letterman had Trump as a guest on his program and asked him if he had ever met Putin. "I met him once," Trump replied, falsely.

The pageant was held on November 9, 2013, in the Agalarovs' vast complex, which is known as Crocus City. The faux triumphal arch that greets visitors established the grandiosity of the Agalarovs' operation. It included three separate but connected malls. One, dubbed Vegas, featured moderately priced retailers. A second consisted of dozens of luxury shops, and a third offered home-improvement products. There was also an aquarium, a hotel, a heliport, and Crocus City Hall, the six-thousand-seat theater where the Miss Universe pageant was staged. At the end of the show, Olivia Culpo handed her crown to Gabriela Isler of Venezuela, who became the seventh winner from that country since 1979. Following the ceremony and an after-party, Trump returned for his second night at the Ritz-Carlton hotel, a few steps from the Kremlin walls. It was there that Christopher Steele's sources asserted that the Russian intelligence services obtained *kompromat* on Trump, in the form of a videotape of him with two prostitutes. This, of course, was never proven. (Trump was supposed to stay in Moscow somewhat longer, but he cut his trip short to attend Billy Graham's ninety-fifth birthday celebration.)

As a presidential candidate, Trump continued working on a plan to build in Russia. This project was based on a proposal by Felix Sater, a Moscow-born convicted felon who was Trump's sometime business partner on real estate deals. Through the summer and fall of 2015, while Trump was running for president, Sater negotiated the details of the deal with Michael Cohen, who was Trump's personal lawyer at the Trump Organization. In October 2015, a time when he had already been running for president for several months, Trump signed a non-binding letter of intent to license the Trump name to a potential office tower in Moscow. Around the time that Sater and Cohen agreed to the deal, Sater sent Cohen a remarkable email that spoke in exuberant tones about the possibility of a Trump-Putin alliance. "I will get Putin on this program and we will get Donald elected," Sater wrote. "Buddy our boy can become President of the USA and we can engineer it. I will get all of Putins team to buy in on this." Cohen, who negotiated on Trump's behalf, recalled, "The licensee was intent on developing the tallest building in the world, 120 stories or so, with commercial space, a hotel, and residential. But the most important requirement we had was that Felix find the right piece of real estate for it, because the Trump brand is all about location, location, location." Sater never found the proper site, and the deal never came to fruition.

Even without a Moscow building to show for it, the ties between the Agalarov and the Trump families endured. Trump appeared in a couple of Emin's music videos, and the Agalarovs would stop by Trump Tower when they visited New York. The most important subsequent connection between the two families came at the height of the 2016 presidential campaign. On June 3, 2016, Rob Goldstone, Emin Agalarov's publicist, sent the most infamous email of the Trump era. He offered Donald Trump Jr. damaging information about Hillary Clinton. Goldstone wrote,

Emin just called and asked me to contact you with something very interesting. The Crown prosecutor of Russia met with his father Aras this morning and in their meeting offered to provide the Trump campaign with some official documents and information that would incriminate Hillary and her dealings with Russia and would be very useful to your father.

This is obviously very high level and sensitive information that is part of Russia and its government's support for Mr. Trump—helped along by Aras and Emin. What do you think is the best way to handle this information and would you be able to speak to Emin about it directly? I can also send this info to your father via Rhona [Rhona Graff, Trump's longtime executive assistant], but it is ultra sensitive so wanted to send to you first.

Donald junior replied,

Thanks Rob I appreciate that. I am on the road at the moment but perhaps I just speak to Emin first. Seems we have some time and if it's what you say I love it especially later in the summer. Could we do a call first thing next week when I am back?

Six days later, Trump junior, Jared Kushner, and Paul Manafort, then the chairman of the campaign, followed up on Goldstone's email by welcoming a group of visitors to Trump Tower, led by a Russian attorney named Natalia Veselnitskaya. She wanted to talk to the campaign officials about the Magnitsky Act, which was an American law that punished certain Russians, by prohibiting them from entering the United States or using its banking system, because of Putin's human rights abuses. In response, Putin prohibited Americans from adopting Russian children. Later, the Trump aides in the meeting would assert that it was a waste of time over a trivial issue. But in fact Veselnitskaya was raising an issue of major concern to Vladimir Putin. The meeting was the very definition of collusion, in at least the colloquial sense of the term, between the Russian government and the Trump campaign.

Shortly after Trump was inaugurated, the Senate Intelligence Committee began an investigation of Russian involvement in the 2016 campaign. As part of this effort, the committee sent a document request to the Trump campaign for all emails relating to Russia. In early June 2017, lawyers for the campaign located the emails between Goldstone and Don junior, and they began circulating among the participants in the Trump Tower meeting and their lawyers. In light of this widespread distribution, it wasn't surprising that rumors about the existence of incriminating emails began reaching journalists at around the same time.

A series of panicked meetings, with a rotating cast, sometimes including the president, ensued about what to do. The emails spoke for themselves. They showed that a close adviser to a leading Russian oligarch family offered the help of the Russian government to Trump in the 2016 election. The candidate's son welcomed that assistance. There was no such criminal offense as "collusion," but it was difficult to imagine clearer proof, in email form, of at least an attempted collaboration between Russian interests and the Trump campaign—and at most a crime.

Because the emails were soon going to be turned over to congressional investigators, there was little question that they would become public, sooner rather than later. In light of this, some people in the Trump camp, like Corallo and Hope Hicks, advocated releasing the emails and getting in front of the story. As a part of the president's own legal team, Corallo felt that the damage to Trump personally would be minor, because he himself was not on the email chain and asserted that he never saw the emails at the time. Trump's refusal to use email often worked to his advantage in legal matters.

The president rejected the advice to disclose the emails. He wanted as little released as possible. The issue came to a head on July 8, when he and his team were flying home from Europe after the G20 meetings. The *Times* was about to write a story about the Trump Tower meeting, though its reporters did not yet have the emails. The *Times* wanted a comment from Don junior. On the plane, Trump was shown a draft of a statement to be released by Don junior. The statement said, "We discussed a program about adoption of Russian children that was active and popular with American families." Don junior changed the statement to say, "We primarily discussed . . . ," and the president approved its release in that form. The statement said nothing about the Magnitsky Act or the promise of derogatory information about Clinton. On July 8, 2017, Don junior's statement ran with the first *New York Times* story about the Trump Tower meeting. Back in Washington, Corallo and Kasowitz had been working on their own response to the prospect of the disclosure of the Trump Tower meeting, and they also issued a statement to the *Times* about the meeting. They asserted that Veselnitskaya, the Russian lawyer at the meeting, also had ties to Fusion GPS, the firm that hired Christopher Steele to compile his dossier. In light of this, they speculated, the meeting at Trump Tower might have been contrived as a setup to embarrass the Trump campaign.

Corallo had not coordinated his response to the *Times* with the White House—he thought private lawyers should not be sharing this kind of information with government employees—but he quickly discovered he had made the wrong decision. On the morning of Sunday, July 9, he was folding laundry at home when the president and Hicks called him. They excoriated him for coming up with a "conspiracy theory." As Corallo scrawled on a nearby pad, Trump said, "The meeting was about adoption. That's a good thing." Hicks said the whole thing would probably be just a one-day story. There was no need to prolong it. Corallo tried to explain that adoption was related to the Magnitsky Act, which involved sanctions on Russia. "It's something Putin cares about," Corallo said. And there were documents about the meeting, he said, referring to the emails. Not to worry, the president responded. "They'll never get out."

But in keeping with the general chaos of the Trump defense effort, just two days later Don junior himself posted the emails online, because he knew the *Times* was about to report on their contents. Of course, the emails told a very different story from the anodyne statement about adoption that Don junior had put out, with the president's approval, just a few days earlier. The *Times* story caused a sensation, not just because the emails contradicted Don junior's explanations but because they offered the clearest proof yet of coordination—collusion—between the Trump campaign and Russia.

The Trump Tower story, in July 2017, represented a genuine crisis for Trump, and his reaction was especially revealing. Trump had long believed that the best response to a political attack was not just a denial but a counterattack, preferably to accuse an enemy of a worse version of his own alleged misdeed. (Trump was a master of projection.) So that's what Trump did about Russia. He didn't just deny that Putin helped him in 2016; he said it was his opponent who had been aided by another country. Trump asserted that it was Hillary Clinton who benefited from foreign assistance, and it came from Ukraine.

The idea—that Ukraine schemed to help Clinton win in 2016—originated with Paul Manafort. During Manafort's brief, tumultuous tenure with the Trump campaign in 2016, he was tormented by news out of Ukraine. Of course, Manafort had spent years there, serving the pro-Putin president Viktor Yanukovych and his Party of Regions, and Manafort had made both a great deal of money and a great many enemies. By the time Manafort went to work for Trump, Yanukovych was out of power, and their political adversaries controlled the government. So some of Manafort's detractors in Ukraine likely settled an old score with him by leaking the so-called black ledger to *The New York Times*. The ledger detailed Manafort's massive income from his political patrons in Ukraine and led to his compelled departure from the Trump campaign. Manafort's time with Trump also overlapped with the first big WikiLeaks disclosures of emails from the Democratic National Committee. Manafort believed that his enemies in Ukraine had forged and leaked the black ledger to damage him. Likewise, in conversations with his deputy, Rick Gates, and with Trump himself, Manafort pinned the DNC hack on the Ukrainians, not the

Russians. So even as far back as the campaign, when Manafort was on his way out, he had planted the idea that the government of Ukraine was out to get him—and by extension Trump.

After Trump became president, conspiracy theorizing about Ukraine acquired a new focus. After the Democratic National Committee emails were hacked, the party brought in an internet security firm called CrowdStrike to work with the FBI and do an analysis of what happened. In 2017, a theory emerged in remote corners of the conspiracy-mongering right-wing internet that CrowdStrike was somehow affiliated with the government of Ukraine. Thus, the theory went, the DNC brought in CrowdStrike to cover up Ukraine's role in the election. Trump raised it in an interview with the Associated Press in April 2017. "They brought in another company that I hear is Ukrainian-based," Trump said.

"CrowdStrike?" the reporter said.

"That's what I heard," Trump went on. "I heard it's owned by a very rich Ukrainian, that's what I heard. . . . Why didn't they allow the FBI in to investigate the server? I mean, there is so many things that nobody writes about. It's incredible." This comment went largely unnoticed at the time—for the mainstream news media, many of Trump's comments, whether in interview or in tweets, were too bizarre to debunk—but the story stayed alive in right-wing circles. And in Trump's moment of crisis after the Trump Tower meeting came to light in July 2017, he and his media enablers turned to the blame-Ukraine theory for relief.

As usual, Sean Hannity of Fox News took the lead. Throughout July 2017, he returned to the idea that the real scandal of the 2016 campaign was Ukraine's secret assistance to Hillary Clinton. "Democrats, the mainstream media, are hysterical over the story," Hannity said on July 11, regarding Trump Tower. "But they have completely ignored an example of actual election interference." On a graphic behind Hannity were the words "Ukrainian Election Interference," against a backdrop of a Ukrainian flag. Hannity's evidence of Ukrainian interference was thin to nonexistent. It consisted of a single months-old article in *Politico* that asserted that one member of the Ukrainian embassy in Washington provided some information critical of Trump to a Democratic consultant. Hannity spun that disclosure into a Ukrainian conspiracy that matched, or outdid, Putin's efforts on behalf of Trump. In response, Trump tweeted admiringly, "Ukrainian efforts to sabotage Trump campaign—'quietly working to boost Clinton.' So where is the investigation A.G. @seanhannity."

In the chaos of the Trump White House—and the equally frenetic news coverage of the president—this particular chapter passed without much notice. In response to the disclosure that the Trump campaign had colluded with Russia, the president and his allies claimed that the Clinton campaign colluded with Ukraine. Most reporters, as well as their audience, quickly forgot this exchange, if they ever even heard it in the first place. Considering how little evidence there was to support the blame-Ukraine hypothesis, ignoring the subject was a rational reaction. But Trump himself never forgot a slight or discounted a conspiracy theory. Ukraine had brought down Manafort, Trump's campaign chairman. CrowdStrike had hidden Ukraine's role in the DNC hack. The Ukrainian embassy in Washington had schemed against Trump's campaign. Trump himself, now the president, brooded on this nation's misdeeds and filed away his grievances for use at a later date.

8

"This Dumb Meeting Which Your Father Insisted On"

Of course, Mueller and his team had no idea how close he came to being fired in June. News of Trump's overtures to McGahn and Lewandowski didn't leak until sometime later. So Mueller continued to go about the business of putting together a staff. He had only looked down the hall at WilmerHale for his first three lawyers—Zebley, Quarles, and Rhee—but then he started to cast his net more widely, though not by much. The next hire was Andrew Weissmann, who had been Mueller's general counsel at the FBI, as well as a prosecutor on the Enron task force and in the U.S. Attorney's office in Brooklyn. At that point, Mueller turned over the screening of prosecutors to Beth McGarry, who had been a top aide to Mueller when he was U.S. Attorney in San Francisco. McGarry narrowed down finalists, but in order to be hired, everyone had to pass Mueller's own test for sparkiness.

In organizing the office, Mueller followed Rosenstein and McCabe's advice and modeled the special counsel operation roughly on the existing lines of inquiry at the Justice Department. This was not just bureaucratic convenience. It reflected Mueller's conception of his role—as a surrogate for the current Justice Department prosecutors, not as a roving sleuth in search of wrongdoing in the Trump administration. As special counsel, Mueller would be outside the customary chain of command at the Justice Department, but he regarded his mission as pursuing the same people and subjects, with the same tactics, as the original team would have done if he had not been appointed.

This was perhaps the greatest difference between the perception of the Mueller investigation and the reality of it. Trump's legion of critics looked to Mueller almost as a savior—as an instrument of deliverance from a president they despised. (Ironically, Mueller's critics came to see him with a similar kind of mandate—as a renegade dispenser of vigilante justice.) Mueller's resolute public silence allowed both sides to project their fantasies onto him, and both were wrong. He was always doing a narrower job than Trump's adversaries hoped for and the president's allies feared.

The structure that Mueller devised in those early days remained more or less intact for the full two years of his tenure. He established four investigative teams: Team Obstruction, for Trump in the White House; Team F, for Flynn; Team M, for Manafort; and Team R, for Russia. (Creativity with team names was not a strong suit for the office.) Jim Quarles was assigned to run the team investigating obstruction of justice by Trump in the White House. He was soon joined by Andrew Goldstein, who had made his name as a prosecutor of political corruption in the Southern District of New York in Manhattan. Weissmann took over the Manafort investigation. Jeannie Rhee had Russia.

Mueller was also fastidious about informing Rosenstein, his superior in the Justice Department, about his investigative priorities and, perhaps more important, about obtaining his permission to pursue these cases. Throughout Mueller's tenure, Rosenstein never turned Mueller down, but there was never any doubt about who ultimately had final say over targets and charges—it was Rosenstein. On August 2, for example, Rosenstein sent Mueller a memo approving his current investigative subject areas. Rosenstein had approved the White House investigation, and he also gave Mueller permission to look at Carter Page, for his ties to Russia (that probe went nowhere); Paul Manafort, for his ties to Russia and his financial dealings in Ukraine; and Papadopoulos, for his Russian connections that Rhee was already exploring.

In the memo, Rosenstein also gave Mueller permission to look at Michael Flynn, the ousted national security adviser. Specifically, Rosenstein said Mueller could examine allegations that Flynn "committed a crime or crimes by making false statements to the FBI when interviewed about his contacts with the Russian government." Mueller thought Michael Flynn was a likely candidate to plead guilty—he had clearly lied to the FBI agents about his conversations with the Russian ambassador—so he assigned Zainab Ahmad to try to make it happen. Assistant U.S. Attorneys normally toil in anonymity, but Ahmad had become almost famous as a federal prosecutor in Brooklyn. Born in 1980 to Muslim parents who immigrated to the United States from Pakistan, she had changed her ambitions from medicine to law after the 9/11 attacks. She became perhaps the leading terrorism prosecutor in the country, luring targets back to the United States or orchestrating their arrests abroad. She possessed a particular gift for turning defendants into cooperators—for flipping people. Along with Brandon Van Grack, who came to Mueller's staff after working on Flynn's case in the Justice Department, Ahmad's job was to close a deal with the former national security adviser—and fast.

Mueller convened two daily meetings at the special counsel's suite at Patriots Plaza. The morning meeting, often in Mueller's office, concerned internal operations, and it included Mueller, Zebley, Beth McGarry, and occasionally others. The agendas included hiring decisions, requests for staffing to the FBI contacts with Congress (basically nonexistent), relations with the Justice Department (Rosenstein kept his promise not to interfere in Mueller's investigation), and media contacts ("no comment"). Mueller then spent the rest of the morning and afternoons interviewing prospective hires, reviewing court documents before they were submitted, coordinating with other government agencies, and meeting with his staffers about the details of individual cases.

The afternoon session—known as the Daily Ops Meeting—took place at 5:00 every day in room 3023. This was where the team leaders, and sometimes others, discussed the progress of the investigation. (Given the sensitivity of information about Trump and his close White House advisers, the obstruction team sometimes met with Mueller separately and thus avoided sharing their work with the rest of the office.) At the Daily Ops Meeting, the prosecutors reported what they and their FBI colleagues had learned from witness interviews and document reviews and discussed their plans for next steps. If there was one theme, it was Mueller's impatience. He was not going to be doing this job for years; he would not turn into Ken Starr or Lawrence Walsh. Whenever he heard temporizing or hesitation from his prosecutors, Mueller defaulted to his needling style and a favorite question: "Are you done playing with your food?" The Daily Ops Meeting was scheduled for forty-five minutes and rarely took more than an hour. (A mythology arose about the length of Mueller's workdays—which included a rumor that he slept in his office—but the truth was more mundane. His typical hours were roughly 8:00 a.m. to 6:00 p.m.)

Even though Mueller and his staff didn't give interviews, or leak, they were avid students of media reports about their own investigation. Peter Carr, Mueller's press person, became famous among reporters for his good-natured but insistent refusals to answer questions. But Carr was a valuable member of the Mueller team, because he kept careful track of the reporters' questions, which often led to productive lines of inquiry for the special counsel. In truth, journalists, especially those at *The New York Times* and *The Washington Post,* sometimes knew more than Mueller did about the underlying facts of his investigation. Their stories provided a road map for the prosecutors and FBI agents.

This was especially true of the *Times*'s scoops about the Trump Tower meeting. When those stories came out, in early July 2017, the Mueller team hadn't yet gotten around to subpoenaing the emails from the Trump campaign, so the infamous exchange between Donald Trump Jr. and Rob Goldstone, the British publicist, was news to Mueller, too. Jeannie Rhee jumped in to follow up, as part of her leadership of the Russia team.

The *Times*'s stories about Trump Tower illustrated how Trump and his team neutralized bad news. The emails were indeed shocking in both the explicitness of the Russian offer of help to Trump and in his willingness, through his son, to accept it. Goldstone: The meeting was to feature "very high level and sensitive information that is part of Russia and its government's support for Mr. Trump." Trump junior: "If it's what you say I love it." But the disclosure gave Trump and his allies plenty of time to put their spin on the story. Through sheer repetition of the Trump gloss on the Trump Tower story, it lost much of its ability to appall and outrage.

The Trump party line on the meeting was straightforward. The three witnesses from the Trump campaign—Don junior, Manafort, and Kushner—gave consistent accounts of the conversation. For one thing, they agreed the meeting on June 9, 2016, was brief—maybe twenty minutes. As a statement from Don junior's lawyer put it, "Ms. Veselnitskaya mostly talked about the Magnitsky Act and Russian adoption laws. . . . There was never any follow up and nothing ever came of the meeting." Even better, Jared Kushner had real-time evidence of his feelings about the meeting. To Kushner's great relief, his lawyer discovered, in reviewing his texts and emails from the time, that Kushner sent one to Manafort during the meeting calling it a "waste of time." Also during the meeting, Kushner sent two emails to his assistants, asking them to call him so he would have an excuse to escape the meeting. (Kushner had forgotten about these messages until his lawyer found them and refreshed his recollection.)

Within days, then, of the *Times*'s disclosure of the Trump Tower meeting, the participants from the Trump campaign, and the president's allies in the news media, had succeeded in defusing what at first appeared to be an existential crisis. The emails might have suggested an appetite for collusion on the part of both the Russian government and the Trump campaign, but that was not how the facts played out. It was a brief meeting in the middle of a busy day, and nothing came of it. The verdict: no big deal.

In further proof of their interpretation, the Trump defense offered Rob Goldstone as a kind of exhibit. How could an international criminal conspiracy feature in a central role a ridiculous figure like Rob Goldstone?

Goldstone did provide a measure of comic relief in an otherwise dour story. A cherubic Briton with no discernible political history or views, Goldstone had lived by his wits in London, Bangkok, and Australia, engineering public relations stunts for pop bands and record stores. (Most of his friends were liberals, and he enjoyed twitting them by checking in on Facebook when he visited Trump Tower.) Goldstone also knew little about politics or law, as illustrated by his overwrought email to Don junior. (For example, his email made reference to the "Crown prosecutor" in Russia; that's a position in Great Britain, not Russia.) In his days as a tabloid reporter, his greatest claim to fame was as the only journalist to cover the entirety of Michael Jackson's tour across Australia in 1987.

Goldstone's fortunes turned in 2012, when he went to work as Emin Agalarov's public relations man. Goldstone and Emin traveled the world together and shared a madcap sense of humor—Emin once told a reporter in London that his hobby was eating human flesh—but Goldstone knew that the singer always had a single, serious priority: pleasing his father.

Goldstone saw the Trump Tower meeting as fundamentally an Oedipal drama. Since the preparations for Miss Universe in 2013, he had spent a good deal of time with both the Agalarov and the Trump families, and he noted a similar dynamic at work in both. Emin worked in his father's construction business as well as conducting his singing career; Aras was as taciturn and withholding as Emin was ebullient. Likewise, Don junior worked for his demanding father and struggled to prove his worth. Emin's gift to Don junior of dirt on Trump senior's political rival would have allowed both men to please their fathers in ways they had never before done. By this account, then, the Trump Tower meeting was more about two rich boys with daddy issues than about foreign interference in the democratic process.

So there was the defense case. The Trump Tower meeting, like Goldstone himself, was no big deal, even kind of a joke.

To which Jeannie Rhee replied: *Bullshit.*

Almost as soon as the *Times* broke the story of the Trump Tower meeting, Rhee's team set out to do a deep dive on what actually happened, and this phase of the operation was up and running in July. Based on what they'd found, Rhee took the opportunity at the Daily Ops Meeting to push back on the notion of the Trump Tower meeting as a trivial bust. It was hardly incidental to note that the meeting was, first of all, a *crime*—or at least *possibly* a crime. Campaign finance law prohibited the receipt of any "thing of value" from a foreign source, and the Goldstone email could hardly be clearer that the information came from a foreign source, the Russian government. True, this was a so-called intent crime; that is, the defendants had to know their actions were against the law in order to be prosecuted. It was not clear they could make that case against Don junior, Manafort, or Kushner. But the point remained: the very act of receiving opposition research—which has value—from a foreign government was against the law.

And the Trump team did receive opposition research. In their accounts of the Trump Tower meeting, Don junior and company found it convenient to mention that Veselnitskaya had focused mostly on the Magnitsky Act and adoption—major priorities of the Putin regime. Based on the interviews conducted by Rhee's team, it was clear, too, that Veselnitskaya did provide some of the dirt promised in Goldstone's email. The Russian lawyer said that Ziff Brothers Investments, business partners with William Browder, had broken Russian tax laws and might have made illegal contributions to the Clinton campaign. (Browder, who was once a leading American investor in Russia, had since become a major critic of the Putin regime, and he led the effort to persuade Congress to pass the Magnitsky Act.) Veselnitskaya's information did not produce useful dirt on Trump's opponent; there were no such illegal campaign contributions to Clinton. But that didn't obviate the fact that the Russian lawyer had delivered information purportedly damaging to Trump's rival, as she had promised.

Then there was the role of Goldstone. It was easy to dismiss him as a negligible figure, but that wasn't the point. Goldstone was a conduit, and he did his job. By definition, conduits may not know the ultimate source or value of the information that they pass along. And where did that information come from? The answer to that question became clear in emails between Emin Agalarov and Goldstone from the period after news of the meeting broke. Goldstone complained to Emin that his reputation was "basically destroyed by this dumb meeting which your father insisted on." So the meeting wasn't some lark conjured by a flighty public relations man or his crooner client. The meeting was ordered by Aras Agalarov, a major Russian oligarch with close ties to Vladimir Putin. And the focus of Veselnitskaya's remarks was the Magnitsky Act—that is, the American government's sanctions on Russia—and the Russian response of cutting off adoptions. This issue was a major preoccupation of the Russian government. Indeed, it was exactly what Trump and Putin talked about at the G20 a year later, as Trump himself acknowledged in an interview with the *Times* shortly after the Trump Tower story broke. The reporters asked about the moment at the summit when Trump had risen from his seat at the group dinner and walked over to have a lengthy chat with Vladimir Putin. What, the reporters wondered, had the two men discussed? "We talked about Russian adoption," Trump said. "Yeah. I always found that interesting. Because, you know, he ended that years ago. And I actually talked about Russian adoption with him, which is interesting because it was a part of the conversation that Don [junior] had in that meeting."

So there was every reason to believe that the Trump Tower meeting, far from being a pointless one-off, was an attempt by Vladimir Putin's government to push a major Russian priority in the campaign of (perhaps) the next president of the United States. Then, too, there was the matter of timing. This Russian offer of dirt on Hillary Clinton came in June 2016—a few weeks after Joseph Mifsud, the Maltese academic, told George Papadopoulos that the Russians had email dirt on Clinton and a few weeks before WikiLeaks released the hacked DNC emails. That was a lot of Russian attention to the Trump campaign to be purely coincidental.

Finally, it was true that the meeting had no direct follow-up. Veselnitskaya's dirt on Clinton didn't prove to be useful, and the Trump campaign officials didn't do anything about her complaints about the Magnitsky Act, at least during the campaign. But spycraft is about more than just obtaining and sharing information at a single time and place. Just because nothing came immediately to fruition in Trump Tower didn't mean that nothing happened. The Russians saw the campaign's receptivity to future contact and future support, and there would be future support for Trump's 2016 campaign. The meeting itself created a measure of vulnerability in the campaign, as the ensuing controversy demonstrated. The Trump Tower meeting told the Russians a great deal about the Trump campaign, and it told the Mueller investigation a lot, too.

To be Donald Trump's lawyer was to manage competing crises. News of the Trump Tower meeting materialized seemingly out of nowhere in early July, but that story didn't crowd out the one that caused Rosenstein to hire Mueller as special counsel in the first place—the firing of James Comey as FBI director. Kasowitz was on his way out the door as Trump's criminal lawyer, hastening back to the profitable relative anonymity of his New York law firm. Still, he wanted to lay down a marker before he left, to make a legal point that he knew his successors on the Trump legal team would continue to stress. The argument was simple: it could not be a crime for Trump to fire Comey, because he had the legal right to fire Comey for any reason, or for no reason.

The question raised profound issues under Article II of the Constitution, which defines the powers of the president. Congress established the ten-year term for FBI directors as part of a law enacted in 1976. The law decreed that the president had to nominate the director, and the Senate had to vote to confirm the choice. Under the law, there were two ways to remove the director, before he completed his term. He could be impeached by the House and removed by a two-thirds vote of the Senate (like the president, federal judges, and other high-ranking federal officials), or the president could remove the director himself. Since Trump had the legal right to fire Comey, and that's what he did, the issue would seem to be simple. The president merely did what the law and the Constitution allow. It can't be obstruction of justice, or any kind of crime, for Trump to do what he is allowed to do.

That, in essence, is what Kasowitz argued in a confidential memo to Mueller. "The Constitution leaves no question that the President has exclusive authority over the ultimate conduct and disposition of all criminal investigations and over those executive branch officials responsible for conducting those investigations," he wrote. "The President cannot obstruct himself or subordinates acting on his behalf by simply exercising these inherent Constitutional powers." The hint that the issue might be more complicated than Kasowitz let on came in the form of one of the principal authorities he cited—Alan Dershowitz. To burnish Dershowitz's credibility, Kasowitz described him as an "outspoken critic of the President." Dershowitz had recently retired as a professor at Harvard Law School, where he earned fame and notoriety as a pugnacious civil libertarian and defense lawyer. But after Trump's election, Dershowitz quickly emerged as a prominent voice, on cable news and elsewhere, in defense of Trump. And the Dershowitz quotation hinted at some of the complexity that the Kasowitz letter elided. Dershowitz had written, "Throughout United States history—from Presidents Adams to Jefferson to Lincoln to Roosevelt to Kennedy to Obama—presidents have directed (not merely requested) the Justice Department to investigate, prosecute (or not prosecute) specific individuals or categories of individuals." Thus, the argument went, not only could Trump fire Comey, but he had the absolute right to tell his successor, and others in the Justice Department hierarchy, what they could and could not investigate and prosecute. According to this theory, every single decision by a presidential appointee could be overruled by the president, for any reason at all. As Kasowitz put it, Trump "has Constitutional authority to direct the Justice Department to open or close an investigation, and, of course, the power to pardon any person before, during, or after an investigation and/or conviction. Put simply, the Constitution leaves no question that the President has exclusive authority over the ultimate conduct and disposition of all criminal investigations and over those executive branch officials responsible for conducting those investigations."

Implicit in this argument was that the president could put his own behavior outside the reach of prosecutors to investigate, much less prosecute, even if the behavior would have been criminal for an ordinary civilian. During the campaign, Trump had famously said, "I could stand in the middle of Fifth Avenue and shoot somebody, and I wouldn't lose any votes." Kasowitz, in effect, was saying he couldn't be investigated or prosecuted for it either, if he issued orders to that effect.

Was that the law?

To answer, Mueller called Michael Dreeben.

Dreeben's formal title was deputy solicitor general, but that hardly captured his role or his influence. At that point, in 2017, he had been with the department for forty years, nearly all of them in the SG's office, which represents the federal government before the Supreme Court. The solicitor general himself (or herself) is a presidential appointee, as is one of the deputies, but there is always another deputy, a civil servant, who is in charge of all criminal appeals in the federal courts. Dreeben had that role through presidencies of different parties, and that meant that every time a federal prosecutor lost a ruling in a district court and wanted to appeal, Dreeben had to give permission. So Dreeben's job was to review hundreds of cases a year, covering every imaginable area of criminal law—"a short-order cook," he called himself. If so, Dreeben was a prodigiously learned one.

But that was only part of his job. He was also the government's chief advocate in criminal cases before the Supreme Court. In 2016, Dreeben became only the second person in the century to make one hundred arguments before the justices. ("I distinctly recall your first argument in January of 1989," Chief Justice John G. Roberts Jr. said when the Court paused to offer a tribute to Dreeben on the occasion. Small wonder that Roberts remembered. He was Dreeben's opposing counsel in the case, which Dreeben won unanimously.) Like most experienced Supreme Court advocates in the modern era, Dreeben had a low-key, conversational style. Lean and nearly bald, with a wispy gray beard, he talked to the justices as a near equal, and, more notably, they talked to him that way, too. Dreeben was far from undefeated— the government sometimes has a weak hand before the justices—but few advocates were treated with more respect, even deference, than Dreeben.

So Mueller, as a Department of Justice veteran himself, knew where to go for a nearly definitive answer to the question of whether there were any limits on the ability of the president to fire the FBI director. Mueller sent Kasowitz's letter to Dreeben for a confidential evaluation. (The chance to draw on this kind of expertise was one advantage of being a special counsel, inside the department, rather than an independent counsel, outside it.) But before Dreeben could answer, Kasowitz had another letter for Mueller.

Part of representing Donald Trump involved pleasing Donald Trump. Sometimes Trump wanted letters written, or motions filed, or even lawsuits brought, that had little chance of success. But he wanted his point made. (For instance, Kasowitz knew that Trump's libel suit against Tim O'Brien for writing that Trump was not a billionaire was a likely loser. But at Trump's insistence, he brought the case anyway— which was, indeed, ultimately rejected.) In that spirit, then, Kasowitz followed his letter to Mueller about the president's prerogative to fire the FBI director with one about Comey himself. The eleven-page single-spaced letter was an outright diatribe, written as much for

Trump's reading pleasure as for Mueller's. Kasowitz branded Comey a leaker and a liar whose testimony should not be relied on by Mueller. As he put it, "There is no question that Mr. Comey improperly used the privileged and confidential information he obtained from the President as FBI Director to retaliate against the President after he was terminated. Mr. Comey is not a credible witness, and no potential investigation should be pursued based on claims he has made." (Kasowitz's bill of particulars against Comey included criticism for his letter to congressional leaders, reopening the Clinton investigation, on the eve of the election. Of course, at the time, Trump himself praised Comey's letter.)

In light of both letters from Kasowitz, Dreeben had to make his call: Under Article II of the Constitution, could the president be charged with obstruction of justice for firing Comey or interfering with a criminal investigation? Dreeben knew how to put this argument to rest—by starting with a single word in the laws prohibiting obstruction of justice. In order to be found to violate those laws, a defendant must act "corruptly." As Dreeben later wrote, this requires "a concrete showing that a person acted with an intent to obtain an improper advantage for himself or someone else, inconsistent with official duty and the rights of others." In other words, Article II did not shield the president's decision to fire Comey if Trump acted "corruptly."

Dreeben went on, "A preclusion of 'corrupt' official action does not diminish the President's ability to exercise Article II powers. For example, the proper supervision of criminal law does not demand freedom for the President to act with a corrupt intention of shielding himself from criminal punishment, avoiding financial liability, or preventing personal embarrassment." If Dreeben were inclined toward more vivid examples, he might have added that Article II does not allow a president to fire (or hire) an FBI director in return for a suitcase full of cash. Likewise, a president could not stop a criminal investigation because it might implicate a friend or a relative. History, as well as law, bore this out. In Watergate, the so-called smoking-gun White House tape showed Richard Nixon telling an aide to instruct the CIA to tell the FBI to stop the investigation of the Watergate break-in. This conduct was widely seen as justifying Nixon's impeachment and removal, even though the president had supervisory authority over both the CIA and the FBI. Nixon acted "corruptly" and thus, even as a president, violated the law.

So Mueller's investigation of Trump's firing of Comey would continue. And the White House had to find another line of defense.

9

"I Would Love to Speak, I Would Love To"

Ty Cobb had the serene demeanor of a man who had answered, without complaint, the exact same question every single day of his adult life. Yes, he was distantly related to the baseball player of the same name. But this Ty Cobb had grown up in Kansas, far removed geographically, as well as temperamentally, from the irascible star known as the Georgia Peach.

In addition to his famous name, Cobb had a waxed mustache, like a silent movie villain, but he was in other respects a standard-issue Washington corporate lawyer. After growing up on the Great Plains, where his father owned radio stations, he went east to Harvard. (There, perhaps inevitably, he played on the baseball team.) After knocking around for a few years after graduation, he went to Georgetown for law school and then to the U.S. Attorney's office in Baltimore. After a successful stint as a prosecutor, Cobb migrated to the firm now known as Hogan Lovells. There, he tried cases now and then, but his real duty was to do what most big-firm litigators do in the capital—represent large corporations that are under federal investigation and try to minimize the damage. For such lawyers the agenda is always clear: accept fines, if unavoidable, but under all circumstances avoid prosecution of top executives. Cobb was good at his work.

This was why Cobb received a call from a White House operator in early July, saying Trump was on the line. Cobb, who was vacationing with his wife, was aware that it was customary to accept a phone call from the president of the United States at any time. He also knew that Trump was calling to make a formal job offer—to be the White House official in charge of responding to Mueller's requests for interviews and documents. Cobb wanted the job but still hesitated to take the call. "Mr. President," Cobb said at last, "we probably shouldn't talk too long, because I'm in Russia and we're probably not the only ones listening."

If there was such a thing as a "normal" Washington scandal, that's what the Russia matter still was in July 2017. Trump had denied wrongdoing, as other presidents had at an early stage, but he had also agreed to cooperate with the investigation, or, more precisely, he had not said that he would not cooperate. His representatives said the Trump White House had nothing to hide; reflecting what became the president's mantra, the White House officials asserted that there had been no collusion (with Russia) and no obstruction (of the FBI or other investigations). Thus, Trump would allow Mueller to interview White House officials and review documents from his campaign and administration. As with Iran-contra in the 1980s and Whitewater in the 1990s, the White House needed a facilitator for contacts with the prosecutor. That person would be a member of the White House staff, of course, but he would also serve as a kind of honest broker whose goal would be to foster cooperation rather than thwart it. Cobb was a Republican, if not an especially partisan one, but he was also a skilled advocate, so he made a logical choice for the role in 2017.

Cobb reported for work on July 31, and he quickly learned that there would be nothing normal about his tenure. Three days earlier, Trump had fired Reince Priebus, his first chief of staff, whose tenure lasted just six months. (The president fired Priebus by tweet, even though they were both on Air Force One at the time. Trump then left Priebus on the tarmac at Andrews Air Force Base, forcing him to find his way home alone in the rain.) Priebus had been instrumental in Cobb's hiring. On the day that Cobb arrived at his office in the West Wing, John Kelly, the new chief of staff, fired Anthony Scaramucci, the director of communications, after a tenure of ten days. (Earlier in the week, Scaramucci had engaged in an obscene on-the-record tirade with Ryan Lizza, of *The New Yorker,* which included the statement

"I'm not Steve Bannon, I'm not trying to suck my own cock.") Bannon himself, whose title was chief strategist, would be fired two weeks later. Sean Spicer, the press secretary, had been fired earlier in July, and the departed staff members—Spicer, Priebus, Scaramucci, and Bannon—all had one thing in common. They had run afoul of Ivanka Trump and Jared Kushner, the president's daughter and son-in-law, and they were soon gone. Cobb resolved to keep a respectful distance from the couple.

All of this would be disconcerting enough for a new arrival, but what really mattered to Cobb was his relationship with Don McGahn, the White House counsel. Cobb was not technically part of the counsel's office; he reported, rather, to Kelly, the new chief of staff. But Cobb expected that McGahn and his subordinates of more junior lawyers would be a resource that he could use in his work. Cobb's domain included issues of executive- and attorney-client privilege and security classification, as well as the responsibility to assemble documents for review and distribution. It was the kind of assignment that only lawyers could complete, and Cobb expected he would receive the assistance of those who already worked at the White House.

But as soon as he started work, he learned that McGahn refused to have anything to do with the response to the Mueller investigation or with Cobb himself. McGahn didn't even return Cobb's phone calls. Worse yet, he also prohibited his staff from assisting Cobb. This was an apt symbol of the general dysfunction among the White House staff, but it also reflected a more specific problem. Cobb started his job a little more than a month after Trump had tried to persuade McGahn to have Mueller fired; McGahn had refused because, as he later said, he didn't want to be part of another Saturday Night Massacre. Indeed, McGahn thought the president's approach was so obviously improper that the counsel had planned to quit in response. When Trump appeared to let the matter drop, McGahn had stayed on, but the incident poisoned the relationship between them. In response to this standoff with the president, McGahn essentially absented himself from much of the work of the administration and, to the extent he could, from Trump personally. McGahn instead focused on working with McConnell and other Senate Republicans in confirming as many federal judges as possible. In April, he had shepherded Neil Gorsuch to confirmation as Trump's first Supreme

Court appointment, and McGahn was building a pipeline to fill the lower courts as well. Trump was generally aware of McGahn's efforts in this area—and the president often boasted about his success with judicial appointments, especially to conservative audiences—but that record did little to thaw the frost between the two men.

When Cobb was hired, he didn't know this history; it wasn't until much later that he learned that Trump had tried to order McGahn to oust Mueller. Cobb's first clue that all was not well between the president and his counsel came when Trump gave Cobb one of his first specific assignments. A summons for jury duty in Manhattan had worked its way from Trump's home in Trump Tower to the White House. Though the matter belonged in McGahn's domain, the president asked Cobb to deal with it. "If you can't get me out of jury duty, you're not a very good lawyer," Trump told him, with reason. Cobb succeeded in that mission, but other assignments proved more challenging. And for the first month, Cobb was on his own—literally. He had not a single staff member working for him, so he made the acquaintance of the keepers of the electronic records at the White House and started to learn their system.

To prepare for his job at the White House, Cobb read transcripts of the White House tapes from the Nixon era. He was particularly interested in the role of John Dean, the White House counsel who later gained fame for turning on Nixon and testifying about the Watergate cover-up. The indelible moment in Dean's story came when he told Nixon that the cover-up represented a "cancer" on the presidency. But what drew Cobb's attention were the earlier tapes, when Dean was an enthusiastic participant in the conspiracy. Dean became a whistleblower only after he was guilty of the underlying crimes. Cobb took Dean's story as a warning. He vowed that he wasn't going to make the same mistake—to say yes too often, to lie, or to encourage others to lie. Cobb knew Trump's reputation for ethical laxity, which the president had lived up to in their earlier meetings. He heard Trump's rhapsodies about Roy Cohn, whose loyalty and ferocity remained forever Trump's lodestar for professional excellence. Cobb heard the rants about Mueller and Trump's other enemies and how he wanted to destroy them all. Like others before him (Comey, for example),

Cobb excused Trump's passion for extralegal activity as a product of inexperience rather than sociopathy.

This pattern of making excuses for Trump—for his dishonesty, ignorance, racism, immorality—extended well beyond Trump's subordinates and served as a critical asset in the crises of his presidency. The justifications included "That's just how Trump talks," and "It's just his tweets," and "He really doesn't know the rules," and "He's never worked in government." In addition to staffers like Cobb, other enablers included Trump's political allies, elected officials, and even ordinarily skeptical journalists who wearied of calling out every single one of Trump's outrages.

Cobb had one condition for accepting the job with Trump. The president had already been grousing about the Mueller investigation, calling it a witch hunt, but he had not yet gone after Mueller personally. (Trump had aired his complaints about Mueller's purported conflicts of interest only to his aides, not yet to the public or on Twitter.) Cobb said he would work for Trump only if the president held off on attacking Mueller publicly. In part, he insisted on this condition because of his personal experience. He had known Mueller since they were both line prosecutors in the 1980s, and he had always respected him in his various roles since that time. More important, though, Cobb thought that a cooperative posture with Mueller was in Trump's best interests. He recognized the burden that the special counsel placed on the White House; such investigations dominate the news, and they preoccupy the officials involved, starting with the president himself. Thus, Cobb thought speed was of the essence and cooperation was the best route to a fast resolution.

Cobb thought the president had a strong factual and legal position. Based on what he had seen, he accepted Trump's claim that there had been no collusion with Russia during the campaign. And as for obstruction, Cobb believed in the legal position that Kasowitz had laid out in his letter to Mueller—that the firing of Comey was within Trump's constitutional prerogatives as president. (At this point, of course, Cobb thought the obstruction investigation began and ended with the Comey firing. He had no idea that Trump importuned McGahn and Lewandowski to oust Mueller in June.) In addition, Cobb took comfort from a pair of Justice Department legal opinions, from 1973 and 2000, that said a sitting president could not be indicted. In light of these opinions, Cobb believed there was no chance that Mueller would indict Trump, so the risk of turning over even incriminating documents seemed modest. All in all then, at the time of his arrival in the White House in July, Cobb thought the sooner the documents were out the door and the interviews were completed, the faster Mueller could wrap up his work and give Trump a clean bill of health.

Also early in Cobb's tenure in the White House, he began thinking about an issue that would in many ways define the Mueller investigation and Trump's response to it—the issue of whether the president himself would answer the prosecutors' questions. Trump was probably the most experienced witness ever to become president. Not surprisingly, given his litigious history, he had testified many times in the past, usually in depositions in civil lawsuits. (He once estimated that he had given a hundred depositions.) Witnesses in civil depositions are placed under oath, so they are, at least technically, subject to prosecution for perjury. As a practical matter, however, prosecutors almost never bring cases based on false statements in civil depositions. Since most of Trump's cases had settled before trial, most of his deposition transcripts had never been revealed to the public.

Still, enough of his depositions had surfaced to provide a sense of Trump's style as a witness, which bore a great deal of similarity to his behavior as a public speaker. He was boastful, vague on details, and conveniently forgetful. He filibustered to waste the limited time allotted for the sessions. As with political debates with his rivals, Trump had coasted in preparation for these encounters. A lawyer named Deborah Baum represented the celebrity chef Geoffrey Zakarian, who broke a lease with Trump after he disparaged Mexicans during his announcement of his candidacy for president. Baum took Trump's deposition in a case arising out of the dispute over the lease. It included this exchange about his preparations:

BAUM: What did you do to prepare for the case today, for the deposition?

TRUMP: I would say virtually nothing. I—I spoke with my counsel for a short period of time. I just arrived here, and we proceeded to the deposition.

BAUM: Thank you. So you didn't look at any documents or

TRUMP: No, I didn't.

BAUM: anything.

Of course, it was reckless to wing it the way Trump did, but it had worked out well for him—in both the courtroom and the political arena. Trump's deposition style worked better than it might initially appear. It's difficult to cross-examine vague bluster, especially since Trump didn't use email or keep notes, which are customarily the best impeachment material on a witness. It's unlikely that Trump was ever serious about wanting to testify before Mueller, but it would be understandable if he had a measure of confidence about the process. As with so much else in Trump's life, his dodgy style under oath had not yet caught up with him, and he had reason to believe that his luck would continue.

As soon as Mueller was appointed, reporters began asking the president if he would sit for an interview with the special counsel. Trump's answers followed one of his familiar patterns. At a media availability in June, he was asked, "Would you be willing to speak under oath to give your version of those events?" Trump answered categorically: "One hundred percent." On another occasion, he said of prospective questioning by Mueller, "I'm looking forward to it, actually. I would do it under oath." In other answers to the same question, Trump said, "I would love to speak, I would love to, nobody wants to speak more than me," and "I would love to go, nothing I want to do more." But Trump also hedged on the issue. On some occasions, he said he thought the weakness of the evidence against him on the issues of collusion and obstruction would obviate the need for an interview with Mueller. "When they have no collusion," he said, "it seems unlikely that you'd even have an interview." Still, most of the time, his public comments indicated general agreement that he would answer questions—sometimes with the caveat "subject to my lawyers and all of that." Trump's answers on the subject were reminiscent of those he offered, during the 2016 campaign, about the release of his tax returns—a firm commitment to do so, followed by a hazier agreement to follow through, ending with a complete refusal. In neither case, regarding his tax returns or his possible testimony, did Trump suffer any real negative consequences for his disingenuous public statements.

Over the next year and a half, Trump's possible testimony was the subject of frequent discussion between Trump's rotating cast of lawyers and Mueller's prosecutors. What began as a fairly straightforward issue—will Trump testify?—evolved into a complex mosaic of considerations. There were questions about the scope of the questioning: What subjects could be raised, covering what time period? Would Trump answer questions about his actions during his presidency or just about the campaign? There were questions of logistics: Where would the examination take place, and how much time would be allowed? There were issues of format: oral questions (videotaped or not) or written questions (with follow-ups or not). But through all these discussions, there was one overarching assumption, shared by representatives of both sides, even if it wasn't always uttered out loud. It was this: everyone knew Trump would lie. Trump lied constantly and compulsively. Some of his friends, in generous moments, would assert that Trump actually believed many of the falsehoods he uttered, even if the facts turned out to be otherwise. The real story was probably more mundane. Trump had been lying for his entire adult life, and far from being brought down by this pervasive dishonesty, he had been elected president of the United States. Why change what was working so well? And in any event, what man in his eighth decade changes such a fundamental aspect of his character? Not Trump.

Trump had managed to skate through his various civil depositions, but the possibility of testimony under oath before Mueller's grand jury, or even just an interview with prosecutors, presented a much greater element of risk. Even if Mueller couldn't prosecute Trump, as a sitting president, the special counsel could call out his lies, which would have, at a minimum, disastrous political implications. Bill Clinton had agreed to testify on videotape before Kenneth Starr's grand jury, and the experience turned out to be one of the low points of his presidency and thus a cautionary tale for Trump. One of the articles of impeachment against Clinton rested on his alleged false statements to the grand jury; the article said Clinton committed a high crime and misdemeanor by "willfully committing perjury by providing false and misleading testimony to the grand jury in relation to his relationship with an employee"—that is, Monica Lewinsky. Almost as bad, Clinton's grand jury testimony became notorious, and an indelible part of his legacy, for his unseemly hairsplitting. In an earlier statement,

Clinton had said "there is nothing going on between" Lewinsky and him. In testimony before the grand jury, he insisted that the statement had been truthful because he had no ongoing relationship with Lewinsky when he made it. Clinton said, infamously, "It depends upon what the meaning of the word 'is' is." In light of Trump's propensity for falsehood, he could expect at least as bad an experience as the one Clinton had endured.

No one around Trump knew if he was telling the truth when he said he wanted to testify for Mueller. (He went back and forth on the issue in private, in front of his lawyers, as well as in public.) But in case Trump was telling the truth about wanting to testify, his lawyers felt it was their obligation to protect him from himself. This effort, too, would stretch out over many months, but it began with Ty Cobb, who took a lesson from the investigation of Bill Clinton's secretary of agriculture.

The multiyear probes by Lawrence Walsh and Kenneth Starr earned greater notoriety, but the worst independent counsel investigation—the most excessive and wasteful—may have been the one targeting Mike Espy, the former Mississippi congressman who went on to serve in Clinton's cabinet. In 1994, *The Wall Street Journal* reported that Espy might have received sports tickets and travel from Tyson, the chicken producer, and other companies that were regulated by the Department of Agriculture. (Espy said the gifts were personal, from longtime friends, which was permissible under the law.) A California lawyer named Donald Smaltz was hired as an independent counsel to investigate, and he spent four years and $17 million to examine this minor scandal. When the Espy story first surfaced, Clinton's White House counsel did an internal investigation of the matter, and Smaltz later issued a grand jury subpoena for documents related to this internal inquiry. The White House produced most of the documents but withheld eighty-four of them on the ground that they were protected by executive privilege. The case went to the D.C. Circuit, and the three-judge panel addressed a fundamental and largely unresolved question of constitutional law: When must a president comply with a grand jury subpoena?

There was, of course, one important precedent on the issue of executive privilege. In 1973, the Watergate special prosecutor issued a subpoena for certain White House tapes, for use in the trial of the defendants in the Watergate cover-up case. In a unanimous opinion the next year, the justices agreed that there was "a presumptive privilege for Presidential communications," founded on "a President's generalized interest in confidentiality." But the privilege had limits. "Neither the doctrine of separation of powers, nor the need for confidentiality of high-level communications, without more, can sustain an absolute, unqualified Presidential privilege of immunity from judicial process under all circumstances." Turning to the precise issue at hand, the Court held that an assertion of executive privilege "based only on the generalized interest in confidentiality . . . must yield to the demonstrated, specific need for evidence in a pending criminal trial." Having laid out the general principles, the Supreme Court then left the trial judge in the Watergate case, John Sirica, to decide which of the tapes were necessary for a fair trial.

In truth, then, *United States v. Nixon* didn't resolve all that much. The Supreme Court recognized that executive privilege existed, but subject to limits. Nor did the Paula Jones case provide a definitive answer to the question of whether Mueller could subpoena Trump. Jones had sued Clinton for sexual harassment, in connection with an incident that took place when Clinton was governor of Arkansas. In 1997, the Supreme Court in *Clinton v. Jones* unanimously rejected Clinton's claim that he should be exempt from having to give a deposition in the case while he was president. But because the Jones case concerned conduct that took place before Clinton became president, the justices had no reason to consider the permissible scope of questioning about his behavior as president, which was likely to be the key issue in a Trump subpoena case. (Justice John Paul Stevens's opinion in *Clinton v. Jones* contained a questionable prediction: "The case at hand, if properly managed by the District Court, appears to us highly unlikely to occupy any substantial amount of petitioner's time." As it turned out, Clinton's enemies converged on the deposition process, as did Kenneth Starr's investigators, and the fallout from the Jones case dominated Clinton's final years in office.)

It was, rather, the Espy case in the D.C. Circuit that provided the best guidance to Cobb about how to proceed. Decided just a couple of weeks after *Clinton v. Jones* in 1997, *In re Sealed Case*, as it was known, provided the most detailed analysis of when and whether presidents had to comply with grand jury subpoenas. The court acknowledged that the "withheld documents likely will contain evidence that is directly relevant to the grand jury's investigation of Espy." But that wasn't enough for the court to order the White House to produce them, because the independent counsel "has not yet made a sufficient demonstration of its inability to obtain this information from alternative sources or an explanation of why it particularly needs to know what evidence is in the White House files." (Smaltz ultimately obtained an indictment against Espy for receiving approximately $33,000 in improper benefits. After a two-month trial, a jury acquitted Espy of all thirty counts against him.)

Cobb thought that this passage in the D.C. Circuit's Espy case was the best guide to the state of the law and thus the key to protecting Trump from a grand jury subpoena from Mueller that the courts would uphold. By Cobb's reading, the D.C. Circuit opinion meant that in order to have a subpoena to Trump upheld, Mueller would have to (1) show that he couldn't obtain the same information from alternative sources and (2) explain with specificity why he needed the evidence. Cobb worked backward. How could he show a court that Mueller *could* obtain the same information elsewhere, and how could he show that Mueller had *no particular need* for the evidence? The answer, Cobb decided, was by making virtually all of the White House witnesses and documents available to Mueller. If Mueller had access to all of this evidence, the theory went, he didn't also need Trump's testimony. What was the question that Trump needed to answer personally that wasn't available from the people and documents around him? Cobb thought there wasn't one.

So all through the summer of 2017, Cobb and his meager staff turned over thousands of documents from the White House to Mueller. The president and his team, in characteristic fashion, exaggerated the extent of his cooperation with Mueller. Not surprisingly, Trump himself was the worst offender, tweeting at one point, "Millions of pages of documents were given to the Mueller Angry Dems." In fact, the Trump campaign turned over 1.4 million pages of documents to Mueller. This was certainly a lot of documents, but it was also true that the campaign had no remotely plausible legal claim to refuse to produce them. All the campaign did was comply with the law. As for the White House, Cobb and his staff reviewed approximately 100,000 pages of documents and turned over to Mueller about 20,000 pages as relevant. These submissions included 1,601 documents totaling 5,079 pages regarding Michael Flynn and Russia, and 1,245 documents totaling 7,799 pages regarding James Comey. Still, even if it wasn't the "millions" of pages touted by Trump, it was a substantial record of cooperation. Cobb dealt occasionally with Mueller himself, but usually with the leaders of the prosecutor's White House team— Jim Quarles and Andrew Goldstein. They had occasional disagreements about individual documents, but by and large the process of document production went smoothly through the summer and fall of 2017.

It took somewhat longer for White House officials to begin making the trek to Patriots Plaza for interviews with Mueller's staff and in some cases for appearances before the grand jury. (Mueller impaneled his grand jury in August.) Many of the relevant Trump associates had to hire lawyers, who then had to negotiate with Cobb about access to documents that were relevant to their clients. Only when the defense lawyers could review the documents with their clients would they agree to let them speak to prosecutors. It was laborious, and it took longer than Mueller wanted, but the interviews did start to happen, and Cobb facilitated them.

Cobb did his job. He played it straight. This allowed the Mueller investigation to continue to follow the pattern of earlier White House scandals. Crucially, too, Mueller's targets chose lawyers who knew the customary Washington game. The lawyers were devoted to helping their clients; they were not, for the most part, determined to sabotage Mueller or help the president. Michael Flynn hired Robert Kelner and Stephen Anthony from Covington & Burling, a firm that has long been a pillar of the Washington establishment. (Their law partners included Eric Holder, President Obama's first attorney general.) Like Ty Cobb, Kelner and Anthony spent most of their time steering large corporations (which could afford their fees) to discreet and successful settlements. The former national security adviser's son Michael G. Flynn was a business partner with his father and an outspoken pro-Trump presence on Twitter and elsewhere. The son's ties to the father, especially with foreign clients, exposed the younger Flynn to the possibility of criminal charges as well. The scrutiny of the son added to the pressure on the father to cut a deal—to plead guilty and cooperate with Mueller. By the fall, Zainab Ahmad, the prosecutor in the case, had things heading in that direction.

Papadopoulos was folding, too. His lawyers, Thomas Breen and Robert Stanley, were experienced ex-prosecutors in Chicago, with no particular political bent. Papadopoulos hired them after he was arrested at Dulles Airport on July 27 and released on bail the next day. The secret complaint charged him with lying to the FBI about his dealings with Joseph Mifsud, the Maltese go-between with the Russians, over the course of two interviews in January. His lawyers promptly forced Papadopoulos to face reality. Papadopoulos would have little chance of acquittal if he went to trial. His best chance—really, his only chance—of avoiding a significant prison sentence was to plead guilty and cooperate with Mueller's prosecutors. The lawyers explained these facts of life to Papadopoulos, and the erstwhile campaign operative followed their advice and agreed to cooperate—sort of.

For a callow youth who had barely ever held a full-time job, Papadopoulos had an extraordinary degree of arrogance and entitlement. In August and September, he had four proffer sessions with Mueller's prosecutors and FBI agents. Proffer agreements, also known by the more colorful title of "Queen for a Day," allow defendants to tell their stories to prosecutors, in hopes of securing a favorable plea deal. Papadopoulos played games in the interviews, coming clean about his connections with the Trump campaign and his Russian contacts only when agents confronted him with his own emails, text messages, and internet search records. Prosecutors were still undecided about using him as a witness when he started giving media interviews, frequently alongside his Italian-born fiancée, an aspiring lawyer with a thirst for attention (and an active Twitter feed) that matched Papadopoulos's own. In light of Papadopoulos's recalcitrant behavior, there was some sentiment on Mueller's staff to file a major indictment against him. But in the end, he was too minor a figure to prosecute in that way. And a guilty plea of any kind would send the message that Mueller meant business. So Mueller's team allowed Papadopoulos to plead guilty to a single count of lying to the FBI on October 5. His case was still under seal at that point, and Mueller's team had the opportunity to decide when to reveal it.

It had been a frantic but productive first summer for the special counsel. Mueller had hired a staff and established an office. He had agreed upon a workable system for interviewing White House officials and obtaining their documents. He had his first guilty plea, from Papadopoulos, and seemed likely to have another, from Michael Flynn. Mueller had imposed a press blackout on himself and his staff—no interviews, no leaks—but he still wanted to make his presence felt. To do so, he began a pattern that would recur through his entire investigation. He would use official court documents to tell the story of his investigation. The first would be the complaint against Papadopoulos, which detailed his connections to Mifsud and, indirectly, to the Russians. This would be the first official acknowledgment that the Trump campaign knew about the Russian effort to defeat Clinton.

But Mueller wanted to make an even bigger splash. For this, he turned to the figure on his staff who had attracted controversy in the way that Mueller himself never did. For the moment, few people outside the insular world of white-collar prosecutors and defense lawyers had heard of Andrew Weissmann. But that was about to change.

10

The $15,000 Ostrich Jacket

W hen Andrew Weissmann was named to the Enron task force, a macabre joke circulated among the white-collar defense bar in New York. Enron, the Houston-based energy trading company, filed what was then the largest bankruptcy in American history in December 2001. Shortly thereafter, Robert Mueller, then the FBI director, and the leadership of the Justice Department formed an elite unit of prosecutors and FBI agents to identify and prosecute crimes that took place in connection with the collapse of the company. At around the same time, one of the company's top executives took his own life. When news that Weissmann would be joining the task force began circulating, his longtime adversaries exchanged knowing smiles and muttered, "There will be more suicides."

Many successful prosecutors enjoy respectful if not warm relations with the lawyers who represent their targets. The rules governing criminal investigations and trials are fairly straightforward, up to a point. In even the most heated prosecutions for the most serious crimes, prosecutors and defense lawyers have to interact with each other a great deal; reputations for candor and straight dealing, or for their opposites, are established in haste and endure for ages. By the time Weissmann went to work for Mueller, he was fifty-nine years old and had spent almost his entire career as a prosecutor. And from the day he arrived at the U.S. Attorney's office in Brooklyn in 1991, he was lustily despised by his adversaries.

No one ever doubted his intelligence. Weissmann grew up on Manhattan's Upper West Side, the son of an eminent physician, and he graduated from Princeton and Columbia Law School. After clerking for a federal judge in Brooklyn, he joined the prosecutors there at a moment when the office was enjoying a great run of success against traditional organized crime—the Mafia. Weissmann's ferocious work ethic was well suited to these grueling, long-term investigations, which required the review of thousands of hours of wiretaps and the cultivation of odious witnesses, most with long criminal records of their own. In this period, the Brooklyn U.S. Attorney's office finally ended the reign of John Gotti as the leader of the Gambino family, and Weissmann won the case that brought down Vincent "the Chin" Gigante, the city's second most notorious Mafia chieftain. Gigante had all but taunted prosecutors for decades by pretending to be mentally ill. He wandered the streets of Greenwich Village in a bathrobe, earning the nickname the Oddfather in the tabloids. All the while he had been running the Genovese family with a firm hand. In a complex series of cases, which featured extensive and conflicting testimony from psychiatrists about Gigante's mental state, Weissmann finally put him away. Gigante died in prison in 2005.

Most of Weissmann's colleagues from this era managed to win their cases without antagonizing opposing lawyers, but Weissmann became notorious. Part of it was style. Dark-haired, bespectacled, and generally soft-spoken, Weissmann had a perpetual half smile that radiated contempt. He didn't hide his disdain for talented lawyers who, in his view, chose to devote their careers to defending the obviously guilty. (As with Mueller, Weissmann's brief turns with private law firms were unhappy interludes in his career.) Weissmann also gained a reputation for inviting witnesses to come in for informal office interviews, and then threatening them with prosecution if they didn't tell what he regarded as the full truth. Even if he didn't follow through and prosecute these witnesses, these sessions sometimes poisoned the relationships between the witnesses and their lawyers, who had permitted the office interviews in the first place, as a gesture of good faith. Defense lawyers regard prosecutors who drive wedges between them and their clients with a special form of loathing.

At the Enron task force, Weissmann brought his organized crime tactics to a white-collar investigation, with a predictable backlash from defense lawyers. The Enron effort had many successes, including the prosecutions of more than thirty people, but the task force became best known for a failure. In 2002, Weissmann led the team that charged the Arthur Andersen accounting firm with obstruction of justice, in connection with its work for Enron. Weissmann won the trial after persuading the judge to offer a jury instruction that said the company could be convicted even if no employees knew they were violating the law. The case involved only the Houston branch of Andersen, but the conviction effectively destroyed the entire firm, which had thousands of employees in offices around the world. Three years later, however, the Supreme Court unanimously overturned the conviction. (That decision, of course, was too late to help Arthur Andersen.) Weissmann's superiors had approved the prosecution, but he was the face of the case, and the repudiation by the justices contributed to his reputation for pushing the boundaries of acceptable behavior.

Mueller, though, admired Weissmann's grit, smarts, and spark, and he brought him to the FBI, first as a special counsel and then in 2011 as general counsel, the top lawyer in the organization. As general counsel, Weissmann surprised some people by taking a dovish line on certain administrative issues. For example, he cooperated with the Innocence Project on a measure to uncover unjust convictions. But Weissmann remained a zealot in cases where he thought the defendant was guilty. So it was no surprise that in the special counsel investigation, Mueller gave Weissmann his most important individual case.

Paul Manafort's businesses and tax returns had been under investigation for some time, at the Department of Justice, when Weissmann took over the case. FBI agents had interviewed Manafort way back in 2013 and 2014. Prosecutors had been using the customary tools of white-collar investigations—chiefly grand jury subpoenas to banks and examinations of phone company records. They had even collected a remarkably detailed picture of Manafort's financial dealings in Cyprus, a frequent transaction point for crooked businessmen around the world. But what did the prosecutors have to show for years of effort? There was still no indictment—no case.

So within weeks of his arrival on Mueller's team, Weissmann

decided to turn up the temperature. Subpoenas, while useful, produced information slowly; recipients often took their time in complying. On the other hand, search warrants—featuring FBI agents banging on doors, then coming inside—produced results overnight. So that was how Weissmann moved on Manafort. In an extraordinary burst of work—at a pace he continued for two years—he assimilated the results of a lengthy investigation and then drafted an affidavit to obtain a search warrant for Manafort's condominium in Alexandria, Virginia, outside Washington. Weissmann did not mince words. "There is probable cause to believe that the Subject Offenses"—a panoply of crimes ranging from money laundering to tax evasion to illegal lobbying—"have been committed by Paul J. Manafort, Jr., the former campaign chairman of Donald Trump for President, Inc., and others known and unknown," he wrote. "Between at least 2006 and 2014, Manafort, a United States citizen, worked as a lobbyist and political consultant for the Party of Regions, a Ukrainian political party commonly believed to be aligned with Russia. There is probable cause to believe that Manafort engaged in a scheme to hide income paid on behalf of Ukrainian politicians and others through foreign bank accounts in Cyprus and elsewhere, to and on behalf of Manafort and related people and companies." A judge signed the search warrant on July 25, and the following morning, shortly after dawn, Manafort heard the proverbial, and literal, knock on the door.

When Paul Manafort joined the Trump campaign, in early 2016, only the most venerable political journalists remembered him. Trump initially hired him to plan delegate strategy for the Republican National Convention, which made a certain amount of sense. Trump was marching through the primaries at that point, but there were rumors that party elders might try to steal the nomination from him at the convention. Manafort had experience as a delegate counter at the last contested Republican convention, but that was back in 1976! He had helped James A. Baker III, then in the early stages of his own political career, steer Gerald Ford to the nomination over Ronald Reagan. Manafort later had a modest role in Reagan's 1980 campaign, but he'd been otherwise nearly invisible in presidential politics.

But Manafort had not disappeared—not exactly. He had essentially invented a new career, even a new industry. There had been lobbyists in Washington since the New Deal, but they were few in number and distinguished in appearance. And the notion of representing foreign governments and corporations was seen as anathema, unpatriotic. But Manafort and his colleagues—notably Roger Stone, an old friend and a colleague from the 1980 Reagan campaign—shattered those norms. Not only did Black, Manafort & Stone represent foreigners, but their clients included some of the world's most repressive and distasteful governments and leaders. The firm represented the Philippines, Nigeria, Kenya, Zaire, Equatorial Guinea, Saudi Arabia, and Somalia and earned the nickname the Torturers' Lobby.

With these clients came riches and a lifestyle rarely seen in the staid Washington of the 1980s. Manafort became partial to a foppish, custom-made wardrobe of jackets and suits in exotic colors and fabrics. In time, he accumulated an estate in Virginia, an apartment in Trump Tower in New York, and a mansion with a putting green in the Hamptons. (There were rumors, never proven, that he walked off with $10 million that Ferdinand Marcos, the dictator of the Philippines, had meant as an illegal campaign contribution to Reagan's reelection in 1984.) As the journalist Franklin Foer discovered, when Manafort's daughter showed an interest in horseback riding, Manafort bought a farm near Palm Beach, then stocked it with specially bred horses imported from Ireland, which required a full-time staff to tend. In 1991, Manafort's firm was purchased by Burson-Marsteller, the public relations giant. After a brief period under this corporate supervision, Manafort struck out on his own, and this time he had fertile new soil to till—the remains of the former Soviet Union, which had just ceased to exist.

The fall of the Soviet Union set off one of the great gold rushes in world history. First under the chaotic reign of Boris Yeltsin, from 1991 to 1999, and then during the more orderly kleptocracy of Vladimir Putin, the Kremlin parceled out to favored oligarchs the assets that formerly belonged to the Communist Party. Vast fortunes were made, but only conditionally. The recipients of Putin's largesse understood that continued fealty to him was the price to be paid for the riches, and even the freedom, that the oligarchs enjoyed.

Russia and most of its former satellites had become democracies of sorts, and that meant they conducted campaigns and elections, even if the results were sometimes fixed in advance. These campaigns needed people to run them, and Manafort and his colleagues saw this vast region as an enticing market for their services. In a typical deal, Manafort's firm ran a referendum that led to the independence of Montenegro. The effort was financed by a young Russian oligarch named Oleg Deripaska, to whom Putin had gifted much of the region's aluminum industry. (The independence of Montenegro was advantageous for Deripaska's aluminum interests.) Manafort followed up this success with another proposal. According to the Associated Press, in 2005 he pitched a contract proposing that Deripaska finance an effort to "influence politics, business dealings and news coverage inside the United States, Europe and former Soviet Republics to bene-fit President Vladimir Putin's government." Manafort's proposal went on, "We are now of the belief that this model can greatly benefit the Putin Government if employed at the correct levels with the appropri-ate commitment to success." This precise deal apparently never came to fruition, but Manafort soon signed another contract to provide a wide range of advice to Deripaska for $10 million per year. It was a great deal of money to Manafort but not to Deripaska, whose net worth was estimated at $28 billion at its peak.

Manafort's work for Deripaska involved a single place—Ukraine, the former Soviet republic that had been coveted by Russia for centu-ries. As Foer observed, "The narrative of Manafort's time in Ukraine isn't terribly complicated. He worked on behalf of a clique of former gangsters from the country's east, oligarchs who felt linguistic and cul-tural affinity to Russia, and who wanted political control of the entire nation." Manafort's finances followed a similarly straightforward tra-jectory. When his party, known as the Party of Regions, was in power, Manafort made (and spent) millions; when the party lost, he strug-gled. When Manafort arrived on the scene in Ukraine, after the turn of the century, the pro-Russian clique was still in control, because its leader, Viktor Yanukovych, was prime minister. In the presidential election of 2004, Yanukovych, who led the Party of Regions, was ini-tially declared the victor over Viktor Yushchenko, a reformer. How-ever, pervasive evidence of fraud prompted street marches in Kyiv, and the rebellion became known as the Orange Revolution. Pressure from the protests, and international outrage, led to a revote, which Yushchenko won with ease. Following a brief period in the political wilderness, Yanukovych returned to politics, this time with a new consultant at his side—Paul Manafort.

In simplified form, the story of Ukrainian politics over the next decade pitted the pro-Russian, thoroughly corrupt Party of Regions, led by Yanukovych and advised by Manafort, against the pro-Western, less corrupt reformist forces. Deripaska and a Ukrainian oligarch paid Manafort princely fees to be Yanukovych's political Svengali, and their collaboration paid off in the 2010 presidential race, when Yanukovych won a comeback victory. These were glory days for Manafort. Assisted by his second-in-command, Rick Gates, who was far less lavishly compensated, Manafort branched out in Ukraine from political consulting into private equity investing. Both ventures were for the most part funded by Deripaska, the Russian oligarch. But Manafort's fortunes turned. In 2014, another public uprising forced Yanukovych out of office and into exile in Russia, and Deripaska lost much of his fortune in the recession. Virtually overnight, Manafort lost his financial and political patrons.

Worse yet for him, the new leadership of Ukraine in 2014 asked for the assistance of the FBI in investigating Yanukovych's pilfering of the public treasury, and the probe came to include Manafort. (The FBI interviews of Manafort took place in the course of this investigation.) Still worse, Deripaska turned on Manafort, accusing him of stealing from him. In 2015, the oligarch even took the rare step of filing a lawsuit in an American court, charging Manafort with fraud. Even though Manafort had made millions in Ukraine, he had spent millions more, and he had borrowed to finance a lifestyle that he suddenly could not afford. In just two years, he borrowed $15 million, and he had no way of paying it back.

Also around this time, Manafort's wife and two daughters found out that he had been having an affair and financing his girlfriend's life in lavish fashion. He rented her an apartment in New York City for $9,000 per month as well as a house in the Hamptons. Bereft in the middle of 2015, Manafort checked into a mental health clinic in Arizona. In a weird preview of what was to come for others, a "hacktivist collective," probably drawn from Manafort's Ukrainian enemies, hacked thousands of his daughter's text messages and posted them on the internet. As her father sought solace in the desert, his daughter Andrea texted a friend, "My dad is in the middle of a massive emotional breakdown."

Bankruptcy, and ruin, loomed. But shortly after Manafort emerged from the clinic, he fixated on a new savior—Donald Trump.

It's unclear if Trump knew of Manafort's perilous financial condition when he hired him for his campaign in March 2016. (Manafort had been recommended to Trump by Thomas Barrack, one of the candidate's billionaire friends, and Roger Stone, Manafort's former partner, who was Trump's longest-tenured political adviser.) Trump might have misread one clue about Manafort's finances. Manafort told Trump he would work for free, which the candidate might have taken as a sign of Manafort's great wealth. (Besides, Trump might have welcomed this news because he never liked spending more money than necessary.) In fact, Manafort took no salary because he thought that a connection to Trump was the only route to escape his predicament. Given the magnitude of his debts, a weekly salary on the campaign would have meant little. For Manafort, his role in the campaign was a marketing opportunity designed to persuade his longtime sponsors in Russia that he was worth backing again.

At that point, then, to a degree probably unprecedented in the history of presidential campaign operatives, Manafort had dual loyalties. He was working to elect Trump as president of the United States, but he was also trying to please Vladimir Putin so that his oligarchs would see fit to hire Manafort again. Manafort brought along his aide Rick Gates as his deputy, and his first assignment to Gates revealed Manafort's priorities. He told Gates to prepare briefing memoranda about the state of the race for Deripaska and the other pro-Putin Russian and Ukrainian oligarchs for whom Manafort used to work. He also told Gates to keep the oligarchs updated with fresh reports of Trump's proprietary polling data.

Manafort was quickly caught up in the chaos of the Trump campaign. At the time, the campaign manager was Corey Lewandowski, a volatile operative with no national experience. He had run afoul of Jared Kushner and Ivanka Trump, whose disapproval was usually a professional death sentence in Trump's world. (Notably, even though

Lewandowski was still campaign manager on June 9, Donald Trump Jr. invited Kushner and Manafort, not Lewandowski, to the Trump Tower meeting with Natalia Veselnitskaya, the Russian lawyer with the supposed dirt on Hillary Clinton. Given Manafort's longing to return to Putin's good graces, he would have been the last person to complain about meeting with a representative of the Russian government; accordingly, Manafort attended without protest.) In any event, Donald Trump dismissed Lewandowski later in June. With no one else of comparable stature and experience remaining on the campaign, Trump named Manafort chairman and chief strategist. As with many of his employees, whether in his company, his campaign, or his presidency, Trump griped about Manafort, especially his work ethic. When Manafort deigned to appear on the Sunday shows, he would do so only from his weekend home. Every time Trump saw Manafort on television with a chyron that showed his location as "Bridgehampton," he was enraged.

When Manafort took over the Trump campaign, its outlook did not look promising. Manafort ran Trump's operation at the Republican National Convention, which took place from July 18 to 21 in Cleveland; Trump accepted the nomination without a floor challenge, but he still trailed Hillary Clinton by a significant margin in the polls. Just before the Democratic convention, which ran from July 25 to 28 in Philadelphia, the Russians made their first overt display of support for Trump. The DNC emails, which had been hacked by Russian military intelligence, were released by WikiLeaks, thus sowing discord within the Democratic Party. Still, Clinton left her convention with the shape of the race basically unchanged.

What happened next, in New York, again revealed Manafort's true priorities. In late July, Konstantin Kilimnik, a Ukrainian who was Manafort's representative in Kyiv for many years, reached out to Manafort and asked for a meeting. Kilimnik was also, according to the FBI, closely tied to Russian intelligence services. On August 2, he came to New York for a rendezvous with Manafort and Gates at the Grand Havana Room, a cigar bar on the top floor of 666 Fifth Avenue. (This building was purchased in 2007, at the height of the New York real estate boom, by Jared Kushner's company for $1.8 billion, then the highest price ever paid for a single building in the city. By 2016, the Kushners' debt on the property, which had lost a great deal of value, threatened to bring down the presidential son-in-law's entire family business.)

Manafort and Kilimnik engaged in some spycraft in their dealings with each other. They avoided entering and leaving buildings together and used code names in emails. (Kilimnik referred to Yanukovych as "the guy who gave you your biggest black caviar jar," or simply, "black caviar." In their glory days, after Yanukovych won the 2010 election, he had given Manafort a jar of caviar worth between $30,000 and $40,000.) On that summer night in New York, they settled into a private room at the Grand Havana cigar bar, which was full of tatty velvet furniture and wheezing overhead exhaust fans. With Gates by his side, Manafort gave Kilimnik a briefing on the state of the race, before Kilimnik brought up his agenda for the meeting. He wanted Manafort to persuade Trump to support a "peace plan" that Yanukovych was pushing. The plan would have locked in Russian hegemony in eastern Ukraine, which was a major goal of Putin's. As Kilimnik put it in a later email, "All that is required to start the process is a very minor 'wink' (or slight push) from [Trump]." Manafort made no commitment about the peace plan, but he had his own request for Kilimnik: that he should lobby Deripaska to drop his lawsuit against Manafort and restore him to good graces within the pro-Putin Russian oligarch community.

In simplified terms, at the cigar bar summit, Putin's emissary delivered his demand, and Trump's campaign chair named a price. There was no definitive resolution, but the messages had been delivered, and the future looked promising. (Shortly after the meeting, Manafort emailed his bookkeeper to say that the spigot of Ukrainian money was likely to open again soon.) Manafort had figured out a way to help Putin, Trump, and himself, all at the same time. The degree of Russian penetration of the Trump campaign in the summer of 2016 can scarcely be overstated. In June, Trump's son and campaign high command welcomed Putin's representatives to hear dirt from them about Trump's opponent; in August, a suspected Russian spy put forward a plan to consolidate Russian rule in Ukraine—with the implied offer of millions of dollars to Trump's campaign chairman. And in between those two events, in July, Russian interests had convulsed the Clinton campaign by releasing emails hacked from the accounts of the Democratic Party.

Still, the complexities of Ukrainian politics soon caught up with Manafort. In mid-August, *The New York Times* began publishing a series of stories about the so-called black ledger, which had been found in Kyiv, apparently by political enemies of Yanukovych, Manafort's longtime client. The ledger revealed that Manafort had been paid $12.7 million in cash by Yanukovych's Party of Regions from 2007 to 2012. The *Times* stories raised a host of questions about Manafort and thus his continued service in the Trump campaign. What, exactly, did Manafort do in return for this money? Did he pay taxes on it? Did he violate money-laundering laws in handling the cash? In light of these payments, should he have registered as a lobbyist for Ukraine? Was he still receiving money from Ukraine?

For a week or so, Manafort and his colleagues on the Trump campaign struggled to answer these questions, but the stories were so damaging that the end was preordained. Manafort resigned from the Trump campaign on August 19. His roles would be taken by Steve Bannon and Kellyanne Conway. Trump kept in touch with many people he had fired, like Lewandowski, and that would be true for Manafort, too. Now freed from his campaign obligations, Manafort could devote even more time to renewing his ties in Russia and Ukraine. Kilimnik and others kept feeding Manafort "peace plans" that advanced Russia's interests in Ukraine, and Manafort had the chance to advocate for them with Trump and others around him.

Through Manafort, then, Trump found his way into the thicket of Ukrainian politics. No one had entirely clean hands in that fraught and complicated country, but Manafort, and thus Trump, became firmly aligned with the side that was more afflicted with the corruption virus. More to the point, Trump became allied with the pro-Russia and pro-Putin forces—the ones dominated by Yanukovych and the Party of Regions. Manafort was on their side, and so was Trump. Indeed, in 2016, Trump had special reason to resent the pro-Western forces in Ukraine, because they were the ones who had brought down his campaign chairman. Manafort's cash windfall had been exposed by investigators from the National Anti-corruption Bureau, which had targeted Yanukovych and his allies.

Twice in a decade, in 2004 and 2014, Ukrainians had risen up against the corruption of the leadership in their country, and the ebb and flow between the pro-Russian and the pro-Western forces would continue in subsequent years. Manafort's role in the Trump campaign was a casualty of this struggle between factions in Ukraine. Trump took notice and remembered. The Ukraine conflict, and the damage it inflicted on his campaign, reinforced his preconceptions. Putin and Manafort were on one side, and the pro-Western reformers were on the other, and they had taken down Trump's campaign chairman. Personalizing the conflict, as he always did, Trump came to see the pro-Western side in Ukraine as his enemies. In the frenzied days of the 2016 campaign, few other Americans had occasion to think about this obscure and distant conflict. Later, that would change.

The search of Manafort's condo on July 26, 2017, produced the bonanza that Andrew Weissmann sought. The records found there allowed FBI agents and prosecutors to heed the venerable advice to law enforcement: follow the money. And it was an extraordinary amount of money: Manafort had received roughly $60 million from his Ukrainian clients. As far as Weissmann was concerned, the important disclosure was that Manafort had parked the money in Cyprus and the Cayman Islands, and thus shielded it from the Internal Revenue Service. (The documents showed that Rick Gates, his deputy, had executed many of these transactions, even if he didn't benefit on anywhere near the scale that Manafort did.) Upon preliminary investigation, it seemed as though Weissmann and his boss, Mueller, had Manafort dead bang at least on the issue of tax evasion.

The contents of the search also offered some insight into Manafort's character and personality. He was handsome, after a fashion, with a barrel-chested build and a head full of thick, dyed hair. But Manafort was awkward in public; that much was clear from his occasional television appearances when he was leading the Trump campaign. He was reserved and secretive in private as well. But the contents of the apartment showed that Manafort had a kind of mania for shopping, starting with electronics. According to the inventory of the FBI's search, there were eighty-three electronic devices in the apartment, including five iPhones and eight iPods. But the real bounty was in clothes. Manafort had done most of his shopping at a New York boutique called Alan Couture, where suits started at $7,500 and most cost about $12,000.* In all, Manafort spent $849,000 at the boutique between 2010 and 2014. (He also spent $520,000 at the House of Bijan in Beverly Hills.) One of his purchases later became famous: a $15,000 ostrich jacket with silk lining.

Of course, it's not illegal to spend a lot of money on clothes, but the search produced clear evidence of crimes. Manafort had paid for all of these purchases (as well as real estate and expensive rugs and watches) with wire transfers from his accounts in Cyprus. He never paid taxes on the money in those accounts. So the purchases represented not just indulgences of a passionate shopper but proof of money laundering and tax evasion. So Weissmann set about turning the evidence produced in the search of the apartment, along with the data assembled by the Department of Justice over the past three years, into a grand jury presentation and thus the basis for an indictment.

Suddenly, in late summer 2017, the whole Mueller office was on a roll. Thanks to Ty Cobb, the White House was starting to produce documents, and administration witnesses were beginning to file into the Patriots Plaza offices for interviews. The investigation of the Trump Tower meeting from the previous June was under way. In Washington's federal courthouse, Weissmann was supervising a grand jury that was preparing to indict Manafort and Gates. Papadopoulos had already pleaded guilty in secret. Michael Flynn was close to admitting his guilt. Even outside events were cooperating. Mueller and his staff did not know how close they came to being fired in June and July, but they had heard rumors of Trump's fury about the investigation. But on August 11 and 12, white supremacist marchers had converged on Charlottesville, Virginia, and one of their number had killed a civil rights counterprotester. In public remarks, President Trump equated the two sides in Charlottesville and drew bipartisan condemnation in response. Politically weakened by the controversy, Trump was now in no position to unleash the storm that firing Mueller would set off.

Mueller would not characterize it as a press strategy—he didn't countenance such vulgar terms—but that's what he had for October 30, 2017, when he made a triple-barreled announcement. First,

---

* It is now, sadly, defunct.

the office unsealed the news that Papadopoulos had pleaded guilty, along with the affidavit that spelled out how he had been told that the Russians had "dirt" on Hillary Clinton. But the big blow was the twelve-count thirty-one-page indictment of Paul Manafort and Rick Gates that was handed down that afternoon. It's rare that an indictment alone, which is just a summary of charges, provides such convincing evidence of defendants' guilt. But Weissmann had crafted a so-called speaking indictment, which spelled out with devastating clarity the way Manafort steered money from Ukraine to Cyprus to the United States—with the tax man none the wiser. In addition, the indictment was phrased in such a way that it was clear that Manafort was far more culpable than Gates. The indictment thus resembled a neon sign inviting Gates to plead guilty and cooperate. A veteran like Weissmann knew that any competent criminal defense attorney would invite Gates to do so with alacrity. With Gates on board with prosecutors, the pressure on Manafort to flip would become over-whelming. And Manafort, if he decided to spill, could deliver . . . who knew?

So after less than six months on the job, Mueller had streams of new evidence coming in the door, guilty pleas, a devastating indict-ment, and the prospect of more in every respect.

What could go wrong?

PART THREE

11

"Being Patriotic"

In the days just after the 2016 election, a phrase came into wide use—"fake news." At that moment, "fake news" had a specific meaning. Later, of course, Trump used the term as an epithet to describe journalism that he didn't like. What Trump called fake news was almost invariably true; the original fake news was really fake. It referred to a certain category of internet post that was designed to draw traffic but bore no relation to actual events. This fake news was created in what were known as content or troll farms, where writers—they were not journalists—developed strategies to use inflammatory headlines and provocative claims to prompt readers to click on their stories. The clicks drove advertising dollars to the fake news sites. Some of the content farms were in the United States. Three days before the election, one fake news site, which called itself the Denver Guardian, posted a made-up story headlined "FBI Agent Suspected in Hillary Email Leaks Found Dead in Apparent Murder-Suicide," which alleged that an FBI agent investigating Clinton had been found dead in a Maryland house fire. The story was immediately shared on Facebook more than 500,000 times and earned more than fifteen million impressions. Other content farms were located around the world, even when their stories were targeted (sometimes in imperfect English) to the American market. One notorious center for the creation of fake news was the small city of Veles, in Macedonia, where teenagers often earned more than their parents for producing scores of fake news stories every day.

The fake news industry was largely dependent on Facebook. The content farms' websites generated little traffic on their own, so their owners depended on gullible readers sharing the stories on social media, which usually meant Facebook. Thus, in the aftermath of the election, the question quickly arose about Facebook's responsibility for serving as the transmission belt for fake news. This was no small issue, because studies showed that more than 40 percent of Americans received at least some of their news from their Facebook News Feeds. At a conference in California three days after the election, Mark Zuckerberg, Facebook's founder and chief executive, dismissed the issue. "Personally, I think the idea that fake news, of which it's a very small amount of the content, influenced the election in any way is a pretty crazy idea," he said, speaking off the cuff. "There is a certain profound lack of empathy in asserting that the only reason why someone could have voted the way they did is because they saw some fake news. I think that if you believe that, then I don't think you have internalized the message that Trump supporters are trying to send in this election."

In fact, at that point, Facebook had little understanding about its role in circulating fake news. The issue had never drawn much attention at the company's headquarters in Menlo Park, California. Facebook had employees who scoured the site for pornography, terrorist recruitment, hacking, malware, spam, and financial scams, among other issues. But no one was assigned to look for propaganda or fake news. At that time, there was no clear definition of fake news, nor a prohibition on its circulation on the site. But many at Facebook knew that Zuckerberg's snide dismissal of the issue was, at a minimum, too glib and possibly inaccurate. So Facebook's security team started trying to figure out the dimensions of the issue. In April 2017, Facebook's security department issued a white paper that more or less acknowledged the problem of fake news but didn't say anything specific about the extent or the source of the problems. Dissatisfied with the company's tepid effort, congressional committees demanded more information.

So Facebook went back to work. They started with the entire universe of Facebook advertising that had anything to do with politics and then sought to find any Russian connection to it. Did the advertising come from a computer that was logged on in Russia? Was it paid for with a Russian credit card? Was there any other hint that there might be a Russian tie to the post? Gradually, then suddenly, the picture started to come into focus. There was a cluster of connections to Facebook in St. Petersburg in Russia. And in midsummer Alex Stamos, the chief security officer of Facebook, decided to place a call to the office of the special counsel. He was routed to Jeannie Rhee, the head of Mueller's Team R, the Russia team, and he had a question for her.

"Have you ever heard of something called the Internet Research Agency?"

The Internet Research Agency (IRA) was housed in a small office building in St. Petersburg that was as nondescript as the name of the organization. The company was founded around 2013 by a Russian oligarch named Yevgeny Viktorovich Prigozhin, who was better known by his nickname—Putin's cook. Like the Russian leader, Prigozhin grew up in what was then called Leningrad, but he didn't join the KGB, as Putin did, instead becoming a small-time gangster and thief. He was still a teenager when he began serving a nine-year prison sentence, and after he was released, he began selling hot dogs, lots of them. From hot dogs, Prigozhin expanded into groceries and high-end restaurants, where Putin became a frequent patron. Thanks to Putin's patronage, Prigozhin and his company, Concord Management, won contracts to feed tens of thousands of students at schools in St. Petersburg and Moscow.

Prigozhin, through Concord, also founded the Internet Research Agency. The IRA appears to have started as a straightforward troll farm, focused on making money from advertising. As Facebook discovered, the workers there created fake accounts for nonexistent people and wrote invented posts about events that never happened. The IRA promptly staffed up to several hundred employees and became a high-tech operation, with separate departments devoted to graphics, data analysis, information technology, and search engine optimization. There was no doubt who was running the show. Emails from an

IRA account directed a person to stand in front of the White House in Washington and hold a sign that read, "Happy 55th Birthday Dear Boss." Two days later, Prigozhin turned fifty-five.

What the IRA didn't have, at least at first, was much of an understanding of what Americans would want to click on and read. And so, like an updated version of *The Americans,* the television series about Soviet spies living under deep cover in the United States, the IRA sent operatives to the United States to learn about its politics. For three weeks in June 2016, two IRA staff members went on an energetic tour, which took them to stops in Nevada, California, New Mexico, Colorado, Illinois, Michigan, Louisiana, Texas, and New York, to gather intelligence. Under the code name "the translator project," the IRA employees talked to people about the hot political issues of the day and learned how these issues resonated on Facebook, Twitter, YouTube, and Instagram. When the pair returned to Russia, they used their expertise, according to an internal document, to employ social media to "spread distrust towards the candidates and the political system in general." The priorities of the IRA were turning more straightforwardly political and more in line with the goals of Vladimir Putin, Prigozhin's patron. By later in 2016, the IRA completed its transformation. The company was no longer sowing random chaos but rather focused on achieving a specific goal—winning the presidency for Donald Trump. As an internal IRA email put it, the company was now to focus on posting content that centered on "politics in the USA" and to "use any opportunity to criticize Hillary and the rest (except Sanders and Trump—we support them)."

Alex Stamos of Facebook gave Rhee a basic picture of the IRA's work for Trump and asked if she thought the special counsel would want to pursue the matter. It wasn't clear that this investigation would be within Mueller's jurisdiction. There was no suggestion at this point that the IRA was connected to the Trump campaign or even any American. It appeared to be an entirely Russian operation. But Rhee told Stamos to proceed. In short order, there were about a hundred technicians and lawyers at Facebook scouring the back end of its site, trying to find the fingerprints of the IRA and, thus, indirectly, of Vladimir Putin.

—

Still, the activities of the IRA raised a simple question: So what? A group of Russians were using social media to try to help Donald Trump win the election. But why was that any business of American law enforcement? What was the violation of U.S. law? Why devote the limited resources of the special counsel and the FBI to this matter? In other words, why make a federal case out of it?

Rhee put those questions to Michael Dreeben and his team of legal scholars on the special counsel's staff. What was the possible crime here? In a way, the question went to the heart of the Mueller investigation. How did Russia insert itself into the 2016 election? And what could be done about it? As Dreeben's team looked at the question, it was clear what the IRA initiative was *not*. It was not a hacking or a traditional cybercrime. They weren't stealing identities (at least not many of them), but rather inventing most of the identities from scratch. But the Russians were contributing to an American political campaign— in an in-kind way, not in cash—and it was illegal for foreigners to do so. The law prohibited contributions of any "things of value," so there was an argument that the law covered support on social media. Dreeben's team reached for one of the broadest criminal laws on the books—the one that prohibited "conspiracy to defraud the United States." How did the employees of the IRA defraud the United States? By interfering with the government's efforts to keep foreigners out of our politics. Or, as the Mueller office eventually put it, "by impairing, obstructing, and defeating the lawful functions of the Federal Election Commission, the U.S. Department of Justice, and the U.S. Department of State in administering federal requirements for disclosure of foreign involvement in certain domestic activities."

Dreeben's theory was a stretch, because there was a big problem with it. Conspiracy is what's known as a specific intent crime: in order to be found guilty, a person must know that what he is doing is against the law. He doesn't have to know which law, or precise details about the law, but he does have to know that his behavior is wrong. And how would Mueller prove that a bunch of Russians in St. Petersburg, most of whom didn't speak English and had never visited the United States, knew they were violating American law? Well, that was a problem for another day—or perhaps never. That was because the unspoken assumption underlying the IRA investigation was that the defendants in the case would never show up to be tried and the

United States could never extradite them. So the case was almost a public relations exercise—an opportunity to show the world how Putin's allies exploited social media to help Trump win. In any event, Mueller gave Rhee the okay to pursue the investigation and find out how far the Russians had traveled on this highway into the American consciousness.

So Rhee, assisted by a quiet and determined young Department of Justice prosecutor named Rush Atkinson, began an investigation of the Internet Research Agency—from forty-five hundred miles away. They called it the "active measures" case—a term long associated with the Soviet Union's efforts to manipulate rival governments with propaganda and other forms of interference. It wasn't just Prigozhin's ties to Putin that made it clear that the IRA was effectively a Russian government operation. It was the scale of the IRA, which eventually came to employ hundreds of people with a budget of at least $1.25 million per month. During the period leading up to the 2016 election, the IRA had no meaningful sources of income—minimal advertising revenue—so the budget came from Prigozhin's pocket. No Russian oligarch, especially one so close to Putin, would spend that kind of money without his authorization or, more likely, his command.

Investigating the IRA long distance was a challenge. Facebook was the easy part. The prosecutors sent the company hundreds of subpoenas, which directed Facebook to reveal the contents and origins of thousands of accounts. The more difficult part was to reach inside the IRA itself, but the prosecutors, and especially the FBI, had access to extraordinary technical means. (Mueller's connections to the intelligence agencies, from his days at the FBI, helped his team get access to these tools.) U.S. government computers could reach into Russia and read the IRA's emails, and even watch the employees type documents, keystroke for keystroke. (The prosecutors were fortunate to have Aleksandr Kobzanets, one of the few Russian-born FBI agents, to translate the IRA documents that they extracted. Kobzanets also specialized in mocking Rhee and Atkinson's attempts to pronounce Russian words.) American surveillance technology made the company's phone calls and financial transactions easy to trace. The Mueller team of prosecutors and agents never met any of their Russian suspects, but they began to emerge as individuals and personalities who knew a lot about American politics.

The Russians had clusters of interests—all designed, in the end, to help Trump win the presidency. Some of their Facebook advertising and posts were straightforward statements of support for Trump and the Republican Party. For example, they set up a Facebook page for "Tennessee GOP," which used the handle @TEN_GOP. The @TEN_GOP account falsely claimed to be associated with the official state Republican Party. Over time, the @TEN_GOP account attracted more than 150,000 online followers. The IRA's posts on Twitter used hashtags like "#Trump2016," "#TrumpTrain," "#MAGA," "#IWont ProtectHillary," and "#Hillary4Prison." The IRA also engaged in more subtle politicking, particularly when it came to African Americans; the company sought to alienate that key voting bloc from the Democratic ticket. An IRA Instagram account called "Woke Blacks" posted the following message: "[A] particular hype and hatred for Trump is misleading the people and forcing Blacks to vote Killary. We cannot resort to the lesser of two devils. Then we'd surely be better off without voting AT ALL." Another account said, "Choose peace and vote for Jill Stein. Trust me, it's not a wasted vote." (Stein was the Green Party candidate for president.) Still other Facebook pages sought to associate Clinton with Muslims and Sharia law; one of them, "United Muslims of America," had over 300,000 followers. "Don't Shoot Us," designed to alienate African Americans from Clinton, had over 250,000. As the campaign heated up, IRA officials stepped up the pressure on its employees. In September 2016, according to an internal IRA message, a lower-level employee was criticized for having a "low number of posts dedicated to criticizing Hillary Clinton" and was told "it is imperative to intensify criticizing Hillary Clinton."

Perhaps the strangest initiatives undertaken by the IRA were a series of Trump campaign rallies in the United States that were organized from the company's headquarters in St. Petersburg. In the later stages of the campaign, the IRA had enough of a following on its social media accounts that they could generate at least modest crowds at events in swing states like Florida and North Carolina. Rhee and her team decided to try to track down some of the purported organizers of these events and find out what they knew about the backstory of their efforts. This was why FBI agents knocked on the door of a man named Harry Miller and asked him about his portable jail.

Miller liked to say that he was ninety-nine years old, but he was really only in his late seventies. The bigger number fit with his cranky old codger persona, which he cultivated online as well as in his community in south Florida. His dyspeptic posts about Hillary Clinton helped him garner as many as 100,000 Twitter followers during the 2016 campaign. He even started a primitive website called Crooked Hillary.com. Harry Miller was, to use a term he would not recognize, an internet influencer.

In August 2016, Miller was contacted by someone from "Being Patriotic," which was a pro-Trump Facebook page. (It is, of course, surreal that the Russians chose the name "Being Patriotic" for one of their American operations.) The message was the beginning of an effort of surprising complexity, to organize a series of rallies across Florida. The message came from the Facebook account of a real person whose identity IRA operatives stole. The message stated,

> My name is [T.W.] and I represent a conservative patriot community named as "Being Patriotic." . . . So we're gonna organize a flash mob across Florida to support Mr. Trump. We clearly understand that the elections winner will be predestined by purple states. And we must win Florida. . . . We got a lot of volunteers in ~25 locations and it's just the beginning. We're currently choosing venues for each location and recruiting more activists. This is why we ask you to spread this info and participate in the flash mob.

Miller responded positively, and he started communicating regularly with "T.W.," who was coordinating the rallies. Miller never met "T.W.," but they had a series of conversations on Facebook and on the telephone. Through the fictitious "T.W." persona, the IRA also bought a series of Facebook advertisements to publicize the flash mob event. The ads reached fifty-nine thousand Facebook users, and eighty-three hundred Facebook customers clicked on the ads, which directed them to the "Being Patriotic" page.

"T.W." also reached out to Trump campaign officials in Florida, to advise them of his plans. One such message to the campaign stated,

> We are organizing a state-wide event in Florida on August, 20 to support Mr. Trump. Let us introduce ourselves first. "Being Patriotic" is a grassroots conservative online movement trying to unite people offline. . . . [W]e gained a huge lot of followers and decided to somehow help Mr. Trump get elected. You know, simple yelling on the Internet is not enough. There should be real action. We organized rallies in New York before. Now we're focusing on purple states such as Florida.

"T.W." asked Miller to lead one of these events, and the two men batted ideas back and forth about how to draw attention. They decided that Miller would build a cage on the back of his flatbed truck and he'd place mannequins dressed as Bill and Hillary Clinton on chairs inside. The tableau would bring to life the "lock her up" theme of Trump's campaign speeches. But there was a problem. Miller didn't have the money to buy the fencing and other material he'd need. No problem, said his contact. "T.W." said he'd wire the $900 that Miller needed, and he did.

The IRA operatives set up several rallies around Florida on the morning of August 20, all under the social media banner of "Florida Goes Trump." Miller paraded his truck down a main drag of West Palm Beach, and even though his mannequins didn't much look like Bill and Hillary, his point was still clear—as was the crowd's chant of "Lock her up." Three other flash mobs around Florida popped up at the same time as part of the same initiative. (The IRA paid another unknowing contact to buy a prison jumpsuit for a Hillary imitator to wear at one of the other rallies.) In all, several hundred people attended. Miller never spoke to "T.W." again. When the FBI approached him in the fall of 2017, he had trouble recalling anything about his interactions with "T.W." He certainly denied knowing that "T.W." was a Russian. Still, there was one thing that Miller did remember. The guy had an accent.

—

Mueller's team was able to assemble a detailed account of the scope of the IRA's political activities. The company, through its various accounts and false names, paid Facebook about $100,000 to purchase 3,519 advertisements. But the paid advertisements were only a fraction of the IRA footprint on Facebook. It doesn't cost anything to start a dedicated page on Facebook, and the IRA created 470 of them and produced eighty thousand pieces of content to post on its pages. In all, roughly 126 million Americans saw some of the IRA content that was posted on Facebook. The IRA also created 2,752 Twitter accounts. Those numbers sounded impressive but were possibly misleading. For a company the size of Facebook, an expenditure of $100,000 would barely register. (During the general election campaign in 2016, the Trump and Clinton campaigns spent a total of $81 million on Facebook advertisements.) Given the vast scale of Facebook's customer base, and the speed at which those customers churn through impressions, numbers in the millions might not mean much either. It was impossible to say how many votes the IRA influenced, so its overall impact could not be determined with any precision. It would certainly be irresponsible to say, even in a close election, that Russia's social media initiative provided the margin of victory to Donald Trump. No one could know for sure.

Still, Rhee thought that those caveats, though accurate, misread the issue of Russia's active measures during the 2016 campaign. The point was not the success of the Russian effort but that it was undertaken in the first place and with such sophistication. The IRA was actually employing a strikingly contemporary form of campaigning. They were using social media to build a network of believers for Trump— using social issues to identify and motivate them. Some of the Russian messages didn't even mention Trump, but they used proxy issues, like fear of Sharia law, to build his coalition. (An IRA proxy found an American to pose for a photo holding a sign with a quotation falsely attributed to Hillary Clinton: "I think Sharia Law will be a powerful new direction of freedom.") And at the same time, the IRA was identifying likely Clinton supporters, especially African Americans, and giving them reasons to stay home from the polls or to vote for

Jill Stein. On February 16, 2018, Mueller's indictment in the active measures case charged thirteen individuals, starting with Yevgeny Prigozhin, Putin's cook, and three companies, including Prigozhin's Concord Management, as well as the Internet Research Agency itself, with conspiracy to defraud the United States. As predicted, no individual defendants showed up to be arraigned. The point of the case, ultimately, was not to prove that the Russians succeeded in electing Donald Trump but rather that they tried so hard, and with such savvy, to do so.

This was even clearer in the hacking case. The Russian hack of the Democratic National Committee emails, which were released through DCLeaks in June 2016 and then through WikiLeaks the following month, set off the original FBI investigation, the one code-named Crossfire Hurricane. After WikiLeaks posted the documents, Alexander Downer, the Australian diplomat, told his counterparts in the U.S. government about his earlier communications with George Papadopoulos. In light of Papadopoulos's disturbing prescience about the hacking, the FBI had been hunting for the source of the hack for more than a year. Department of Justice prosecutors had already made some progress, and they were none too pleased when Mueller's prosecutors took the case away from them in 2017. As with the active measures case, about social media, Jeannie Rhee's Russia team took the lead on hacking.

In several respects, the hacking case was simpler than the active measures case. For one thing, there was no need for prosecutors to come up with a creative legal theory, because it was clear that hacking emails was a crime. Likewise, it was straightforward to attribute the hacks to the Russian government. American intelligence agencies traced the hacks to the Main Intelligence Directorate of the General Staff (GRU), better known as Russian military intelligence. Specifically, Units 26165 and 74455 of the GRU established two websites, known as DCLeaks and Guccifer 2.0, to pass the hacked documents to WikiLeaks, which released them to the public. The GRU was responsible for both major hacks that targeted Democrats in 2016— the first, of the DNC emails, which were released on the eve of the

Democratic National Convention, and the second, of Clinton campaign chairman John Podesta's emails, which were released starting in
October.

The key events had taken place in the spring of 2016. GRU operatives had engaged in what is known as spoofing and spear phishing. They had created fake email accounts that looked like Google
notifications—the spoofing—and then sent official-looking emails to
their targets, notifying them that they had to change their passwords:
the spear phishing. On March 19, a GRU officer named Aleksey Viktorovich Lukashev sent a spoofing email to Podesta's campaign email.
In the email, Podesta was instructed to click on an embedded link
to change his password. He did, and the Russians promptly inhaled
about fifty thousand emails from his account. Similar efforts around
the same time allowed the Russians to hack into other Democratic
Party accounts.

The Mueller team never had any evidence that the Trump campaign encouraged, or even knew about, the Internet Research Agency's activities on the candidate's behalf on social media. "T.W." and
the other orchestrators of the pro-Trump rallies had some interactions
with low-level campaign aides, but there was no reason to believe they
knew they were dealing with Russians. The evidence about Trump
and the hacking was more ambiguous, as Rush Atkinson discovered.

The evidence from the hacking came into the special counsel's office
as a great, undifferentiated mass of material. Texts and emails (many
of them in Russian) as well as technical data about hacking challenged
the understanding of even the most assiduous student. Through many
late nights, Atkinson pored over the material in a struggle to figure
out what the evidence said and then what it meant. Late one night,
he was looking over some translated emails and decided to dig a little
deeper than usual.

The data showed that some unusual things happened on July 27,
2016. As a rule, the GRU operatives made their hacking rounds during regular business hours, but they worked late on July 27. What
were they doing? On that date, the GRU opened new fronts in its
data war on Hillary Clinton. First, they started spear phishing at new
targets—accounts at a domain hosted by a third-party provider used
by Clinton's personal office. In addition, they targeted more spear-
phishing attacks at seventy-six email addresses at the domain for the

Clinton campaign. So Atkinson wondered, why this burst of activity? And why these targets in particular? Why then?

The prosecutor started noodling around on the internet. What was so special about July 27? What else happened that day? Where was Donald Trump? As it turned out, he was at his golf club in Doral, Florida. He had a press conference that morning. What did he say? "Russia, if you're listening, I hope you're able to find the 30,000 emails that are missing," Trump said, referring to emails Clinton had deleted from the private account she had used when she was secretary of state. "I think you will probably be rewarded mightily by our press."

Wait. What?

Atkinson started looking at the timing and time zones. Trump's press conference started at 10:30 a.m. eastern time. That was toward the end of the working day in Moscow, where the GRU hacking units were located. He checked. He double-checked. But the times lined up. It was possible Russia *was* listening and took up Trump's invitation right away.

Atkinson went over to Jeannie Rhee's office with his calculations and walked her through the story. She made him do it twice. Then again.

When she finally understood exactly what Atkinson was saying, she registered her astonishment in a single word: "*Fuuuuuuuck.*"

12

Doing a Frank Pentangeli

Lawyers (and others) have a saying. Correlation is not causation. Just because A preceded B does not mean that A caused B. Trump explicitly and publicly asked Russia to hack Hillary Clinton's emails, and then the Russian military worked late that very night to do so. But that, by itself, didn't prove that the Russians were complying with Trump's suggestions. Nor, of course, did it prove that Trump knew the Russians were listening and responding. It could all just be a coincidence. But still.

The apparent call-and-response to Trump's demand for Clinton's emails raised a fundamental question in the Mueller investigation. What exactly was Trump's relationship with Russia, and especially to its president, Vladimir Putin? There was plenty of circumstantial evidence of a symbiotic connection. Russia's initiatives on Trump's behalf could not have been clearer. The efforts of the Internet Research Agency to mobilize social media, and the hacking initiatives of Russian military intelligence operatives, were unprecedented acts of Russian interference in an American presidential election—all aimed at helping one candidate win. So, too, was the offer of dirt on Hillary Clinton at the Trump Tower meeting in June 2016. For his part, Trump made his admiration for Putin long a matter of record. As far back as 2013, as noted earlier, after Trump secured Russia's invitation to bring the Miss Universe pageant to Moscow, he had tweeted, "Do you think Putin will be going to The Miss Universe Pageant in November in Moscow—if so, will he become my new best friend?" In

2008, Donald Trump Jr. told the audience at a real estate conference, "Russians make up a pretty disproportionate cross-section of a lot of our assets. . . . We see a lot of money pouring in from Russia." He also said that he had made six trips to Russia during the previous eighteen months. In 2013, Trump's son Eric told the sportswriter James Dodson, "We don't rely on American banks. We have all the funding we need out of Russia." (On Twitter, Eric Trump denied having made the remark.) Donald Trump himself had been traveling regularly to Moscow since the 1980s, in hopes of building a tower there.

The question of Trump's financial ties to Russia, of course, occurred to Mueller's prosecutors as well. And unlike the journalists who had delved into the subject, these government lawyers had the tools to obtain clear answers. Mueller could subpoena Trump's financial records—from banks and from the Trump Organization itself. He could also obtain Trump's tax returns from the Internal Revenue Service or from Trump's accountants. In one of the most consequential decisions of his tenure as special counsel, Mueller decided to do neither. He did not examine Trump's personal finances or obtain his tax returns.

Mueller's main reason was somewhat abstract. It concerned the legal concept of state of mind—specifically, the difference between corrupt *intent* and *motive*. Most federal crimes, and certainly all the ones that Mueller was investigating, are what are known as "intent" crimes. In order to be found guilty of an intent crime, a defendant must know that what he's doing is wrong. (This was the issue that made the prosecution of IRA employees problematic. If there was ever a trial, could Mueller prove the states of mind of people in St. Petersburg?) For prosecutors, it's usually pretty easy to prove intent—a defendant's attempts at secrecy, or to lie about or cover up his actions, usually suffice to prove intent. If there was ever going to be a prosecution of Trump, the prosecutors believed, there would be no problem proving intent.

Motive is related to intent, but a much broader concept. A defendant's motive to commit a crime could include financial gain, jealous rivalry, or an unhappy childhood. When bringing a criminal case, prosecutors often find it helpful to prove a defendant's motive, but the law does not require it. It's necessary only to prove intent. Mueller's prosecutors thought Trump's financial records and tax returns went to possible motive, not intent, so they thought they didn't need the evidence. Mueller's limited jurisdiction as a special counsel contributed to his restraint on the issue. Rosenstein had directed Mueller to investigate "any links and/or coordination between the Russian government and individuals associated with" the Trump campaign. Trump's financial records were not directly relevant to that issue. In order to pursue the financial records, and especially the tax returns, Mueller would have had to ask Rosenstein to expand his jurisdiction. Rosenstein never denied any of Mueller's requests, but Mueller couldn't be sure that he could justify this expansion to Rosenstein. Even in fraud investigations, it's unusual for Department of Justice prosecutors to seek their subjects' tax returns, especially when, as here, Mueller had no evidence that Trump had cheated on his taxes. (Of course, Trump refused to disclose his tax returns voluntarily, as all presidential candidates had done for more than a generation; this was suspicious behavior by Trump, but not actual evidence that he committed a crime.) Mueller thought that if he tried to expand his mandate to look at Trump's possible financial misdeeds, that would look like a fishing expedition, which he was determined to avoid.

Moreover, in Trump's July 2017 interview with *The New York Times,* he was asked if Mueller would cross a "red line" if he investigated Trump's finances, "unrelated to Russia." The question was not entirely clear, and neither was Trump's answer. But Trump implied yes—that he would fire Mueller if he went into that area. There's no specific evidence that Mueller was intimidated by this statement by Trump, but the comment did underline the difference between a special counsel, like Mueller, and an independent counsel, like Starr or Walsh. As an employee of the Department of Justice, Mueller had less job security than the independent counsels did, and that had to make him at least somewhat wary of crossing the president's red lines. The president's threat was another reason for Mueller to demur on expanding his investigation to Trump's finances.

Mueller's decision to forgo a financial investigation of Trump was defensible, but that doesn't mean that it was correct or that other prosecutors would have made the same judgment. Mueller reasoned that Trump wanted to win the election in 2016, so that alone was enough for him to welcome the assistance of Russia; thus, it was unnecessary for Mueller to establish Trump's possible financial motive as well. But

Trump's solicitude of Russia, and especially of Putin himself, was so extreme that it suggested something more might have been at play. Trump had been attempting unsuccessfully to develop real estate in Moscow for decades, and Putin had absolute power to grant or withhold permission for such projects. In light of Putin's hegemony in Russia (and because Trump, like virtually everyone else, thought he was unlikely to win the presidency in 2016 and thus would be returning to the real estate business), Trump might well have had a financial motive to cultivate Putin. Many prosecutors would have used their authority to explore that possibility. It's true that motive evidence is not mandatory in the way that intent evidence is, but the line between the two can be blurry. A prosecutor who wanted the full story of Trump's relationship with Russia, especially given the developer's history, would not have walled off financial evidence so completely. But Mueller did. He behaved like what he was—a rule-following Justice Department near lifer who didn't want to step too far outside his assigned lane.

Mueller's decision on the financial evidence did not mean that he abandoned all inquiries into the nature of Trump's relationship with Russia. The decision meant only that if there were going to be any proof of connections between Trump and Russia, it was going to have to come from the testimony of witnesses. The Trump Tower meeting was one clear connection between the campaign and Russia, but it appeared to be just a one-off encounter, with no follow-up. Manafort was closely tied to Russian interests as well as the Trump campaign, but he wasn't talking to Mueller—yet. Still, there were two other people who were well positioned to talk about the connections between Trump and Russia—Roger Stone and Michael Cohen. So Mueller went after them.

It is an overstatement, but not much of one, to say that Roger Stone created Donald Trump the politician. Indeed, Stone's legacy was even broader than that signal accomplishment. Few had contributed more than Stone to the ruthless state of contemporary politics. It was therefore notable, almost poignant, that at the moment of Stone's apotheosis—the success of Trump's campaign for president—Stone himself was almost entirely on the sidelines.

American politics has only a handful of living legends, but Stone was one. Over a career that stretched decades, he became famous more for action than ideology. He proudly wore the label of dirty trickster, and he learned from, and idolized, the master—Richard Nixon. Like Trump himself, Stone possessed in his political DNA more Nixonian ruthlessness than Reaganite optimism. He gave himself a physical manifestation of this lineage—a large tattoo of Nixon's face on his back. In 1972, when he was twenty, Stone dropped out of George Washington University to do his first tricks for Nixon. It was modest misbehavior—things like making a contribution to a Nixon rival in the name of the "Young Socialist Alliance" and then leaking the receipt to the Manchester *Union Leader*. Stone in those years acquired a taste for political skulduggery, as well as a lifelong friendship with Paul Manafort, and both men latched onto Ronald Reagan's campaign at the end of the decade. In 1979, Stone was assigned by Reagan's aide Michael Deaver to start fund-raising for Reagan in New York. To that end, he showed up in the brownstone of Roy Cohn, who was holding court in his bathrobe with one of his longtime clients—Anthony "Fat Tony" Salerno, the boss of the Genovese crime family. ("Roy, here, says we're going with Ree-gun this time," Salerno said.)

At that point, as Salerno noted, Cohn was already a Reagan supporter, and he had a piece of advice for Stone's local finance committee. "You need Donald and Fred Trump," Cohn said, adding that Fred, Donald's father, had been big for Goldwater in 1964. Cohn had represented Fred Trump's interests since the early 1970s, when he helped Fred defend a Justice Department lawsuit charging him with racial discrimination in his apartment rental practices. (The case settled.) At the time, Fred was bringing on Donald as his deputy and heir to the business, and Cohn became a mentor to Donald. On behalf of Reagan, Stone went to see Donald, who was then in his early thirties, and the real estate heir helped Stone arrange office space in Manhattan for the campaign, and the two men became friends.

In the 1980s, Stone prospered as a lobbyist at Black, Manafort & Stone, but with the splintering of that firm he went off in a different direction from Manafort. Stone lacked Manafort's fixation on wringing the last dollar out of every account, and in any event he had a shorter attention span and a greater desire for public attention and mischief. In this way, he and Donald Trump were kindred spirits, and

Trump tapped Stone to choreograph his quadrennial flirtations with running for president. In 1988, Stone arranged for Trump to speak at the Portsmouth, New Hampshire, Chamber of Commerce, the first explicitly political appearance Trump had ever made. But Trump pulled back from making a full-fledged run.

In the meantime, Stone bounced from one thing to another. He did some consulting, often for gambling interests, but he never made the money that Manafort did. His louche personal life limited his rise. "I'm a libertarian and a libertine," he often said. "I'm trysexual. I've tried everything." Shortly after Stone signed on with Bob Dole's 1996 campaign, the *National Enquirer,* in a story headlined "Top Dole Aide Caught in Group-Sex Ring," reported that Stone had apparently run personal ads in a magazine called *Local Swing Fever* and on a website that had been set up with his wife Nydia's credit card. "Hot, insatiable lady and her handsome body builder husband, experienced swingers, seek similar couples or exceptional muscular . . . single men," the ad on the website stated. The ads sought athletes and military men, while discouraging overweight candidates, and included photographs of the Stones. Implausibly, Stone claimed that "a sinister force" had placed the ads, but he resigned from the Dole effort.

Stone was at Trump's side when he nearly declared for president in 2000. After Ross Perot made his runs in 1992 and 1996, Trump considered declaring on the Reform Party line in the following campaign, largely because he would have received federal funding. (Stone quickly learned how reluctant Trump was to part with his own cash; for example, he rarely paid Stone for his services.) But again, in 2000, Trump held off declaring at the last minute. In the recount in Florida after the election that year, Stone claimed to have played a leading role in organizing the "Brooks Brothers riot," which shut down the recount in Miami-Dade County. But Stone had no formal affiliation with the Bush campaign and little steady work in the new decade. He turned himself into a brand of sorts—writing conspiracy-theorizing books, giving speeches, contributing to right-wing websites, and eking out a living on the fringes of modern political life.

When Trump announced his first actual campaign for president, in mid-2015, Stone was part of the staff but in a nebulous role. Predictably, however, since neither man had many stable long-term relationships of any kind, they had a falling-out. In August 2015, Trump dueled with Megyn Kelly of Fox News at the first Republican debate and then called her a bimbo, among other insults. Demonstrating that he had lesser political instincts than his candidate, Stone thought the imbroglio was a disaster for Trump. He told Trump as much, and he was fired in return. (Stone said he quit.) Stone saw Trump's political potential before almost anyone else did, but once Trump finally decided to run, Stone was gone before the campaign was barely under way.

But no one ever disappeared entirely from Trump's orbit, including Stone, who had been a guest in Trump's world for so long. Trump's frenetic use of his phone often included calls to those, like Stone, he had exiled. For his part, Stone longed to be part of the campaign that he did so much to create, and he recognized that the way to stay in Trump's good graces, especially from a distance, was to provide good gossip or intelligence, the more scabrous and sinister the better. Stone knew his own reputation for dealing in the political dark arts, and he figured correctly that that's what Trump would want to hear about from him. So Stone picked a subject on which he could add his own distinctive form of value—WikiLeaks.

Stone was as surprised as anyone by WikiLeaks' initial release of DNC emails, on the eve of the party convention in the summer of 2016. He also knew that Julian Assange, the founder and guiding spirit of WikiLeaks, nursed a profound loathing for Hillary Clinton. In light of that, Stone suspected that Assange might have more surprises in store for her. Through the final months of the campaign, Stone made frantic efforts to find out what more Assange had on Clinton and to expedite its release. The key question for the Mueller team was what the Trump campaign, and especially the candidate himself, knew about Stone's efforts with WikiLeaks and what, if anything, they did to encourage or help him.

To accomplish his WikiLeaks mission, Stone found an island of misfit toys—a collection of eccentrics who reflected Stone's journey away from the mainstream. His chief ally in this project was Jerome Corsi, who never let anyone forget that he earned a doctorate in political science from Harvard in 1972. (He made sure that the abbreviation PhD always appeared after his name.) In fact, notwithstanding the degree, Corsi had spent most of his life as a marginal academic and nomadic businessman. His work drew little notice until 2004, when he teamed up with John O'Neill, who served with John Kerry in Vietnam, and they rushed out a deeply misleading book, called *Unfit for Command,* which accused Kerry of falsifying and exaggerating his navy combat record as a commander of a swift boat. The enormous commercial success of that volume began a decade in which Corsi produced a rush of books to serve the market for right-wing fantasies. After helping to invent swift boating, he became the poet laureate of birtherism—the false and racist conjecture that Barack Obama had not been born in the United States. Corsi's books were often bestsellers.

In early 2016, Stone and Corsi met for dinner at the Harvard Club in New York to discuss their shared interest in the fulcrum of modern conspiracy theories—the Kennedy assassination. (Both wrote books on the subject.) On the surface, they had little else in common. Stone sought Dionysian thrills at his home in Fort Lauderdale, while Corsi dwelled in exurban serenity at his McMansion in New Jersey. Still, at the dinner, the two men discovered their shared enthusiasm for Donald Trump's candidacy and contemplated how they might join forces to help him. Once WikiLeaks released its first batch of stolen emails in July, the two men resolved to work together to extract more from Assange. To that end, Stone reached out to an old friend named Randy Credico, a sometime stand-up comedian and radio talk show host in New York City. Credico was a man of the left—a Bernie Sanders supporter—but he and Stone had bonded years earlier over their shared interest in marijuana legalization.

Assange had called in to Credico's radio show in the summer of 2016, and Stone began badgering Credico to get more information from Assange, who was holed up in the Ecuadorian embassy in London. Corsi worked his contacts in London for the same kind of information. He emailed Stone on August 2, "Word is friend in embassy plans 2 more dumps. . . . Impact planned to be very damaging." For his part, Stone began taunting Podesta on Twitter, comparing him to his beleaguered old friend Manafort. On August 15, he posted, "@JohnPodesta makes @PaulManafort look like St. Thomas Aquinas." Then, on August 21, Stone issued the most scrutinized tweet of the entire Mueller investigation. It read, "Trust me, it will soon the Podesta's time in the barrel. #CrookedHillary." On October 7, WikiLeaks began releasing an enormous tranche of John Podesta's emails. Stone's tweet suggested that he predicted WikiLeaks' release of the Podesta hack more than six weeks earlier.

For prosecutors, it was easy enough to track down Stone and Corsi's emails. The challenge was to determine what they meant. Did Stone really have advance knowledge that WikiLeaks was going to release Podesta's emails? Were the two men in direct contact with Assange or others at WikiLeaks? Was Stone in touch with Trump—as he had been for decades? What, if anything, did Stone tell Trump about the email hacking initiative? What, in other words, did Trump know and when did he know it?

The three men—Stone, Corsi, and Credico—responded to the Mueller inquiries in characteristic ways. Credico, the least involved in the story, had mostly just fended off Stone's frantic demands for information about WikiLeaks. Credico was emotionally fragile in the best of circumstances, and Stone traumatized him with threats to deter him from cooperating with investigators. Stone sent him menacing emails, including one that said, "Prepare to die, cocksucker," and others that included vows to steal Credico's constant companion—his thirteen-year-old therapy dog, a Coton de Tulear named Bianca.

Corsi, on the other hand, regaled prosecutors with an improbable tale of his own brilliance. He said he did not have an inside source at WikiLeaks, but rather had used his powers of deduction to figure out that WikiLeaks would be leaking Podesta's emails in October. Corsi, as he later recounted, had examined the June–July email dump. "I started with each e-mail and said, 'Who sent them and who did they send them to?' And I mapped these all out, and I started developing a tree—who was contacting who and where the lines of communication were. And suddenly it hit me. There were about ten officials that were handling ninety per cent of these e-mails. And none of them were John Podesta. Now, I knew John Podesta's e-mails had to be in that server." Prosecutors knew that Corsi's story made no sense—and was literally impossible—but they had no specific means to disprove it.

Later, Corsi spun his own bizarre tale of conspiratorial intrigue about his dealings with the Mueller office. He said a woman prosecutor on Mueller's staff attempted to intimidate him with her choice of clothing during his grand jury testimony. "I was shocked to see that [the prosecutor] was wearing what appeared to be an expensive, possibly designer-made see-through blouse," Corsi later wrote. "Maybe my seventy-two years were showing but I had never imagined any woman would appear before a grand jury exposing her breasts to public view through a see-through blouse." This, to put it simply, was madness, and Corsi's conjecture said more about his own obsessions than the prosecutor's couture.

That left Stone, who was always the most important figure to Mueller, because Stone was the one with the relationship with Trump. It turned out that Stone gave prosecutors a gift. Rather than avoiding testifying, notably by taking the Fifth Amendment, Stone had exercised his customary bravado by agreeing to speak to the House Permanent Select Committee on Intelligence on September 26, 2017. And he had lied. He was asked, "So you have no emails to anyone concerning the allegations of hacked documents . . . or any discussions you have had with third parties about [Assange]? You have no emails, no texts, no documents whatsoever, any kind of that nature?" Stone answered, "That is correct. Not to my knowledge." This was false—and foolish. Stone had discussed Assange many times on email with Corsi and Credico. (Later in his testimony, he lied further by saying he had never emailed with Credico.) Stone also lied to the committee about his dealings with the Trump campaign. At that point, prosecutors didn't have proof that he spoke to Trump, but they did have records of his contacts with Steve Bannon. To cite just one example, on October 4, 2016, just three days before WikiLeaks dropped the Podesta emails, Stone emailed Bannon that Assange had a "serious security concern" but would release "a load every week going forward."

Certainly the strangest part of the Stone investigation concerned his dealings with his friend Credico. The two men had a bantering relationship, mostly by text, full of buffoonery and bluster and pop culture references. It was clear from the texts that Stone didn't want Credico to testify about their relationship, but it wasn't clear how much Stone was actually trying to intimidate Credico and how much he was just engaging in their private, tough-guy shtick. Was "Prepare to die, cocksucker" an actual death threat? What did this one mean? "You are a rat. A stoolie. You backstab your friends-run your mouth my lawyers are dying Rip you to shreds." Or: "I'm not talking to the FBI and if your smart you won't either." Sometimes the texts became meta in the extreme, as when Stone quoted his hero Nixon, from the White House tapes, to Credico: "'Stonewall it. Plead the fifth. Anything to save the plan' . . . Richard Nixon."

Throughout Stone's career, there was always some mystery about whether he really was a gangster or he just liked to be perceived as one. The Mueller investigation took that question a step further. Prosecutors had to decide whether Stone's invocation of a *movie* gangster meant that he was trying to behave like a real one. Stone repeatedly told Credico that when he spoke to investigators, he should do a "Frank Pentangeli" to avoid contradicting Stone's testimony. As an unnamed film buff in Mueller's office later explained in a stilted but accurate court filing, "Frank Pentangeli is a character in the film *The Godfather: Part II,* which both STONE and [Credico] had discussed, who testifies before a congressional committee and in that testimony claims not to know critical information that he does in fact know."

The close textual analysis of Stone's texts had a serious purpose. Mueller had few witnesses who actually interacted with Trump, and Stone was one of them. To Mueller's team (as well as those who knew Stone's history), it seemed likely that Stone did discuss WikiLeaks with the candidate during the 2016 campaign. But Stone insisted in public, and to the House Intelligence Committee, that he had never discussed the subject with Trump. So Mueller's team wanted to lean on Stone to prompt him to tell the truth. Stone's false testimony to Congress gave the prosecutors leverage. If they filed a case against Stone, the theory went, they could convict him and trust that, facing the prospect of prison, he would flip.

The problem was, the case against Stone didn't look overly promising. Prosecutors usually bring false statement cases when the lies concern illegal activity. Here prosecutors had not found proof that Stone had engaged in illegal hacking with WikiLeaks or even had direct contact with the hackers. He had simply lied about his emails with his friends. That's a crime, too, but it doesn't have a lot of appeal for a jury. And could prosecutors really charge Stone with witness intimidation regarding his dealings with Credico? Wasn't it all just too weird? Would a jury believe Credico or care about Stone's loony texts? Would they have to screen *The Godfather: Part II* for the jury?

Mueller's answer was clear. He himself was a rule follower when it came to Justice Department policy, but he was just as much of a hard-ass with others who didn't follow the rules. Stone lied to Congress, and he was holding back valuable information. Charge him, Mueller said.

13

Flipping Rick Gates

Everyone who joined Mueller's staff expected long hours, intense pressure, and public scrutiny, but Mueller's insistence on total secrecy exacted the greatest personal toll. Staff members couldn't even tell family members about their work. This isolation added to the stress and, not incidentally, helped produce the weight gain that became known—among prosecutors, FBI personnel, and support staff—as the "Mueller 15." The claustrophobic environment also contributed to close friendships among the prosecutors—like the one between Jeannie Rhee, the head of the Russia team, and Andrew Weissmann, who led the Manafort investigation. They had adjoining offices in the special counsel's work space at Patriots Plaza and similar obsessions with their work.

With a diet that appeared to consist mostly of caffeine and candy, Rhee seemed to have a metabolism that allowed her to process calories through speaking—usually directed, often at high volume, at Weissmann. She talked nonstop—great torrents of outrage or joy, depending on the circumstances. Weissmann affected exasperation at the constant interruptions, but he was grateful for the company. Still, he liked to tease Rhee about her volubility. Weissmann swiped a sign from Amtrak during one of his journeys to New York and posted it between their offices. "Quiet Car," the sign said. "Please refrain from loud talking or using cell phones in this car." (Not long afterward, Mueller pointed to the pilfered sign and said gravely to Weissmann and Rhee, "I believe that a federal crime has been committed here.")

The tie between the two prosecutors went beyond office banter. By the end of 2017, Rhee and Weissmann had emerged as the most aggressive and productive prosecutors on Mueller's staff, and their moves hinted at the beginning of a split in the office. At that point, Rhee's team had won the guilty plea from Papadopoulos, run the investigation of Roger Stone and another into the Trump Tower meeting, and was preparing to file a pair of indictments against the Russians—in the social media investigation of the Internet Research Agency and in the Russian military intelligence hacking case. Weissmann had taken the Manafort investigation from a standing start to the execution of the search warrant and then to the indictment of Manafort and Gates in October. In that time, there had been only one other visible sign of progress from the Mueller office. On December 1, 2017, Zainab Ahmad finally completed the torturous negotiations that produced a guilty plea from Michael Flynn, Trump's former national security adviser, for lying to the FBI.

Still, for all the progress, the special counsel's office had a long way to go. Who could tell Mueller's team what Trump knew, if anything, about his campaign's connections to Russia? Stone wasn't talking. Flynn agreed to cooperate, but he was a peripheral figure in the campaign and was gone from the administration almost as soon as it began. Donald Trump Jr.? Not a realistic possibility. That left Manafort, above all.

Weissmann operated at only one speed—all out—and he approached all targets in the same way that he had gone after gangsters in Brooklyn. That included Manafort and Gates. At the arraignment after their indictment in Washington, the special counsel's office didn't object to either man being released on bail, but prosecutors insisted that both remain under house arrest, with ankle monitors to make sure they didn't flee. The judge agreed, and Manafort was confined to his town house in Alexandria. But with his trademark arrogance, Manafort more or less tried to pick up where he left off before he was arrested—still servicing his Ukrainian clients. Apparently not realizing that his communications were being monitored while he was on bail, Manafort stayed in contact with Konstantin Kilimnik, his longtime associate and alleged Russian intelligence asset, who had delivered the Russian-backed peace plan to Manafort at the cigar bar summit while he was still running the Trump campaign. Together, Manafort and

Kilimnik ghostwrote an op-ed piece for the *Kyiv Post,* the English-language newspaper in Ukraine, for Oleg Voloshin, who had served in government when Manafort's allies were in charge. Voloshin's article, as published, celebrated the good judgment of Paul Manafort. Notably, and typically, the story was fundamentally false—claiming that Manafort and his clients in Ukraine had tilted toward Europe, not Russia. Manafort was aware that he, and the president, were being portrayed as tools of Putin, and this op-ed piece was a small attempt to muddy the record. In a characteristically aggressive move, Weissmann used the article as an excuse to ask the court to revoke Manafort's bail and have him locked up pending trial. Weissmann asserted that the article was a violation of the gag order imposed on the parties.

The judge in Manafort's Washington case was Amy Berman Jackson. She had been a prosecutor early in her career but spent most of her years as a lawyer as a successful defense attorney in D.C. Barack Obama nominated her to the bench in 2010, and she quickly emerged as one of the finest judges in the country—knowledgeable, fair, and swift. Cleverness apparently ran in her family. Her son Matt Jackson was a thirteen-time champion on *Jeopardy!,* and while the Manafort case was pending, he played in the game show's all-star reunion tournament. "My mother is white, liberal, and Jewish, and my dad is black, Christian, and conservative," Matt told Alex Trebek during the show. (Matt's father was a Commerce Department official under George W. Bush.)

Judge Jackson, in so many words, told Weissmann to calm down. Ghostwriting an article in a Kyiv-based publication was an arguable violation of the gag order, but the story was unlikely to prejudice either side's chances of obtaining a fair trial in Washington. True, Jackson said, with "the power of retweeting," the story could be read by locals, but Manafort's actions did not deserve revocation of his bail. Still, the judge had a clear warning for Manafort. "I'm inclined to view such conduct in the future to be an effort to circumvent and evade the requirements of my order as it's been clarified this morning," the judge said. In other words, don't do it again. Weissmann lost this round before the judge, but he had put Manafort and his lawyer on notice that he was going to press every lever against him.

—

It had been clear for some time that the route to Manafort went through Rick Gates, Manafort's junior colleague who was now his co-defendant. Weissmann used a classic technique that had been pioneered in organized crime cases. Find the vulnerable, less culpable defendant and squeeze him until he pleads guilty and flips. Gates was an especially ripe target. An army brat, he had gone to work at Black, Manafort, Stone & Kelly shortly after he graduated from William & Mary in 1994. He had originally apprenticed with two of the more establishment figures in the company—Charlie Black (the firm patriarch, who had worked for every Republican presidential campaign since 1972) and Rick Davis (who went on to be John McCain's campaign manager in 2008). Gates then drifted into Manafort's orbit and later became his deputy on the Ukraine work. But while Manafort was making millions and buying mansions and horse farms, he was paying Gates, at most, several hundred thousand dollars a year. They weren't poverty wages by any means, but the contrast to Manafort's riches bred a resentment that a prosecutor could exploit. And since being indicted, of course, Gates was earning nothing. He and his wife were raising four young children in Richmond. After paying an initial round of legal fees, Gates, now in his mid-forties, was nearly destitute and clearly desperate.

In the days following the indictment of Manafort and Gates, in October 2017, their few public statements promised defiance of Mueller and solidarity with each other. Their lawyers shared information in a joint defense agreement, as is common in conspiracy cases. But as the reality of Gates's situation began to sink in over the holidays, he became restless. He started expressing misgivings about his team's legal strategy to various friends, and a familiar ritual in multi-defendant prosecutions began to unfold. One of Gates's friends, Rick Davis, his former colleague at Black, Manafort, reached out to Tom Green, a veteran Washington defense lawyer, to ask if he would help out with Gates's defense. Green was interested, but he wasn't going to play backup to Gates's current lawyers. More to the point, he knew that Gates was close to tapped out already, and Green didn't want to commit to a major defense engagement if he knew he wasn't going to be paid. A trial (if there was one) would have cost Gates at least seven figures, which he didn't have.

Green didn't go to court for Gates's pretrial proceedings, but he agreed to make an evaluation of the evidence against him. Was this a winnable case for Gates at trial? So Green called up Weissmann and asked to see the evidence. By this point, Weissmann had been joined on Mueller's Manafort team by Greg Andres, another alumnus of the Brooklyn U.S. Attorney's office. Like Weissmann, Andres had won a series of mob cases—the Bonanno family once put out a contract on him for his trouble—but Andres gave off a very different vibe, both in the courtroom and in the office. A graduate of Notre Dame and the University of Chicago Law School, and still a triathlete at fifty, Andres projected all-American earnestness rather than sneering intensity. The plan was for Weissmann and Andres to try Manafort and Gates together.

Many prosecutors, especially new ones, try to hoard and hide their evidence from defendants until they are legally obliged to disclose it. Weissmann and Andres did the opposite. When Green came to their offices in Patriots Plaza, they showed him notebooks full of documents implicating Gates and, not incidentally, Manafort as well. The case, especially for tax evasion, was a slam dunk against both of them. Gates had handled the mechanics of transferring the money from their clients in Ukraine to the bank accounts in Cyprus and then into the United States. Most of that money went to finance Manafort's princely lifestyle—the multiple homes, the bizarrely extravagant clothing purchases. But Gates had also used some of that laundered money to cover his own personal expenses—his mortgage, tuitions for his children, the interior decorating of his house. The amount Gates received paled in comparison to Manafort's take, which was at least $15.5 million, but it was also true that Gates never paid taxes on the money that he spent on himself. In addition, the evidence showed that Manafort and Gates had both clearly advocated in the United States for the Ukrainian government without registering as foreign lobbyists, as required by the Foreign Agents Registration Act (FARA). As the prosecutors intended, Green recognized that it would be futile for Gates to go to trial on any of these issues. Plus, as a veteran of Washington scandals, Green knew that Manafort, with his connections to Trump, was the one prosecutors really wanted. If he cooperated against Manafort, Gates could look forward to a generous plea for leniency from the special counsel's office and a kindly reception for those arguments from Judge Jackson.

As a first step toward a plea bargain, Green brought Gates in for a series of proffer sessions—a Queen for a Day—where he would tell everything he knew in hopes of being allowed to plea to lesser charges than those in the indictment. At one proffer session, Gates made a typical mistake for aspiring cooperators. He lied to Weissmann and Andres about a relatively minor matter—the agenda for a meeting back in 2013. In those circumstances, prosecutors usually confront the witness with his falsehood and allow him to correct the record. But Weissmann and Andres, demonstrating their hard-ass credentials, demanded that Gates plead guilty to lying in his proffer as part of his plea bargain. Still, Green put the deal together with the prosecutors, and Gates agreed to plead guilty to conspiracy as well as making a false statement. The arrangement, which was finalized during the first two weeks in February 2018, meant that prosecutors now had a star witness against Manafort.

And Weissmann and Andres weren't finished leaning on Manafort. The previous October, Manafort had been charged in Washington, D.C., federal court in a thirty-one-page, twelve-count indictment. The series of crimes included conspiracy, money laundering, and failure to file with the government as a foreign lobbyist under FARA. This was, of course, a very serious set of charges. But in a typical example of Weissmann's sledgehammer approach, on February 22, 2018, he obtained an additional indictment against Manafort, this one charging him over thirty-seven pages with thirty-two counts, including bank fraud, tax fraud, and failure to report foreign bank accounts. This second case was filed in federal court in Alexandria, Virginia, just across the Potomac River from Washington. (The case had to be filed there because Manafort's criminal behavior took place in this part of Virginia.) It's not terribly unusual for a prosecutor to charge a single defendant in two federal jurisdictions—in Manafort's case, Washington, D.C., and the Eastern District of Virginia. But this is where things got complicated.

Kevin Downing, Manafort's lead lawyer, followed a familiar career trajectory in Washington. He spent fifteen years at the Justice Department, eventually becoming the nation's top expert on piercing Swiss bank secrecy laws. His work yielded an extraordinary bonanza for the

U.S. Treasury—a billion dollars in back taxes from formerly secret Swiss accounts. Then, like so many before him, having come to Washington to do good, Downing stayed to do well. As a successful defense lawyer, he came almost to resemble Manafort—two beefy guys with thick, meticulously barbered heads of hair. Downing's suits, on the other hand, cost a great deal less than Manafort's.

Defense lawyers whose clients are indicted in two jurisdictions have to make a choice. They can insist on separate trials, or they can "waive venue" and agree to a single combined trial on both sets of charges in the jurisdiction that prosecutors select. Defense lawyers almost always choose to waive venue and have one trial instead of two. In the federal system, where prosecutors win roughly 90 percent of jury trials, it generally makes little sense to give them two chances to obtain convictions. In addition, trials are extremely expensive for defendants with retained lawyers; most individual clients have trouble paying for one trial, much less two. Still, Downing defied convention and insisted on two trials for Manafort—one in Virginia and one in Washington.

His reasons were rooted in the unique circumstances of the Mueller investigation and the Manafort prosecution. The first involved the judges in the two cases, who were assigned in each case by random draw. The Alexandria courthouse is known as the rocket docket, where judges move cases quickly from indictment to trial; so Downing knew that Manafort would be tried first in Virginia, even though he was indicted first in Washington. And this was appealing to Downing because of the judge who was assigned in Alexandria—T. S. Ellis III, one of the worst judges in the federal system, the polar opposite of Judge Jackson in nearly every respect. Some bad judges are lazy and inept but politically unbiased; other bad judges are competent but partisan. Ellis, who was nominated by Ronald Reagan in 1987 and was now pushing eighty, managed to display both withered judicial skills and right-wing bias. Downing would get a fair trial from Judge Jackson in Washington, which, in light of the strength of the case against Manafort, was the last thing he wanted. Ellis, perhaps with his thumb on the scale for Manafort, was the better bet.

The demographic makeup of the two communities also steered Downing toward northern Virginia. The District of Columbia is about half African American, with a jury pool to match. In light of

Donald Trump's unpopularity among black Americans, his former campaign chairman could expect a frosty reception in Washington. Northern Virginia had become more diverse, and more Democratic, in recent years, but the jury pool still looked more sympathetic to a rich white Republican like Manafort. Regardless of specific charges and evidence in the two cases, the thinking went, Manafort stood a better chance of winning in Virginia.

Then there was another factor, related even more specifically to Manafort's unique circumstances. In keeping with his disregard for the norms that previous presidents had observed, Trump had dangled the possibility of pardons since the beginning of the Mueller investigation. By not ruling them out, he had distinctly raised the chances. After *The Washington Post* reported in July 2017 that Trump had discussed pardons with his staff, he tweeted, "While all agree the U. S. President has the complete power to pardon, why think of that when only crime so far is LEAKS against us. FAKE NEWS." Just a few days after Flynn pleaded guilty in December 2017, Trump was asked about a pardon for him, and the president hardly rejected the idea. "I don't want to talk about pardons with Michael Flynn yet," he said. "We'll see what happens. Let's see." If Manafort could win the case in Virginia, in front of Judge Ellis, he might never have to face a D.C. jury and Judge Jackson. The backlash against a failure of this magnitude by Mueller's staff—a flat-out acquittal in its first trial—might give Trump the excuse he needed to use a pardon to prevent a second trial from taking place. That, in any event, was the theory. So two trials it would be for Manafort.

That prompted a change of plans, too, in Mueller's office. Instead of trying Manafort together, Andres and Weissmann would split the trials as lead counsels. Andres would take the first one, in Virginia, and Weissmann the second, in Washington. The stakes in both were enormous.

For all the good news in late 2017 for Mueller and his staff—the Flynn and Papadopoulos guilty pleas, the progress in the Manafort investigation, the near completion of the indictments against the Russians—there was one negative development. News broke that Peter Strzok, who had been the lead FBI agent on Mueller's investigation, had exchanged anti-Trump text messages with a colleague during 2015 and 2016. Mueller had removed him from the investigation when he learned about the texts during the summer of 2017, but the public revelation of the texts in December prompted a new level of scrutiny of the backgrounds and political views of Mueller's staff.

Raised in upper Michigan in a military family, Strzok had joined the army after graduating from Georgetown in 1991. He was hired by the FBI in 1996 and enjoyed a meteoric career in counterintelligence. After several years investigating the remains of Soviet intelligence efforts in the United States, he moved to the criminal side. There, he was assigned to be the lead agent on the examination of Hillary Clinton's emails. Given the intense political controversy on the subject, this was a dubious privilege. By all accounts, Strzok did an honorable job in the Clinton investigation. However, during that time, he began an extramarital affair with an FBI lawyer named Lisa Page. They exchanged thousands of text messages on their FBI devices, and the bureau discovered the texts as part of a follow-up investigation. Most of the messages had nothing to do with politics, but a handful disparaged various public figures, including Eric Holder, Chelsea Clinton, Bernie Sanders, and Donald Trump. For example, in early August 2016, after Page asked Strzok, "[Trump's] not ever going to become president, right? Right?!" Strzok responded, "No. No he won't. We'll stop it."

No evidence ever surfaced that Strzok behaved improperly during his brief tenure with the special counsel, but the stories about him raised a legitimate issue about the political motivations of Mueller's team. Since the civil service reforms of the early twentieth century, there has been widespread agreement that all government action, and especially criminal prosecutions, should be conducted in a nonpartisan manner. As long as local prosecutors have been elected in partisan contests, and U.S. Attorneys nominated by sitting presidents, this goal has sometimes been elusive, but the principle has endured. In light of the vast power of the FBI and other national investigatory agencies, the independence of federal prosecutions in particular has been seen as especially important. This is why in the Watergate era and afterward, there have been attempts to insulate politically sensitive investigations of the executive branch from partisan manipulation.

The idea behind naming special prosecutors, independent counsels, or special counsels has been to place these investigations in the hands of people with unquestioned integrity and clear nonpartisanship.

But who chooses to work *for* the prosecutors in these politically charged cases? What if the boss is nonpartisan, but his staff has an ideological agenda? The subject of an investigation by a U.S. Attorney has legitimate expectation that the line prosecutors will be civil servants drawn from a politically diverse pool of lawyers. What kinds of lawyers go to work for a special counsel, and why? The disclosures about Strzok set journalists to looking at the backgrounds of Mueller's staff. What they found was not surprising. Thirteen of the seventeen lawyers were Democrats. Quarles, Rhee, and Weissmann—three of Mueller's team leaders—had contributed thousands of dollars to Clinton's campaigns over the years. Six other lawyers also contributed to candidates, all Democrats. (Quarles occasionally gave to Republicans as well.)

Of course, Mueller himself was a Republican who had served as a political appointee in the last two Republican administrations. But there was no denying that his staff had a clear Democratic orientation. Not surprisingly, the alleged partisanship of the staffs of outside prosecutors in presidential scandals has been a recurring issue over the years. Starr's tenure in the Clinton years was the most dramatic example of this phenomenon because Starr himself was a partisan Republican as were most of the lawyers on his staff. Many years before his appointment as independent counsel, Lawrence Walsh had been part of Dwight Eisenhower's administration, and he led an investigation of another Republican president, but his staff had a clear Democratic lean.* To some extent, these problems are inevitable in outside investigations. Political supporters of the president are unlikely to want to investigate him. At the same time, it's unfair to conclude that prosecutors who belong to the opposite party of the president are on a political mission to bring him down. Experienced prosecutors (like virtually everyone on Mueller's staff) know that they must wield their

---

* I was a junior prosecutor on Walsh's staff. I never conducted a formal survey of my colleagues, but my sense was that there was a substantial Democratic majority among the lawyers.

power with restraint, and to bring only cases that have a strong probability of success before juries. For good prosecutors, professionalism will always trump partisanship.

Still, the Strzok revelations opened the door to a great deal more scrutiny of Mueller's staff. Weissmann, who had the highest (and most controversial) public profile, bore the brunt. As soon as he emerged as a public target, Weissmann went to Mueller and offered to resign, to spare the office the critical attention. "Don't worry about my feelings," he told Mueller. "I can just leave."

"You shouldn't ever worry that I care about your feelings," Mueller responded. "Just get back to work." As usual with Mueller, his needling indicated that the recipient was still in his good graces.

Even though much of the criticism was just noise on social media, there were also more thoughtful critiques. On December 13, 2017, Andrew McCarthy, a former prosecutor turned right-wing writer, wrote an op-ed piece for *The Washington Post* headlined "Mueller Needs to Make a Change." The article observed that Weissmann had emailed support to Sally Yates, the acting attorney general whom Trump had fired for refusing to defend his initial Muslim ban on immigration. This, to McCarthy, was an overt sign of Weissmann's bias against Trump, and he concluded, "Removing Weissmann, just as Mueller removed Strzok, would be a reassuring course correction." Again, in light of this article, Weissmann was prepared to offer his resignation.

But when Weissmann arrived at work on the day the story ran, he found Mueller waiting by his office door. Before Weissmann had a chance to say anything, Mueller said, "Your last day in this office is going to be my last day in the office."

Weissmann went into his office, closed the door, and wept in gratitude.

14

"Cut the Bullshit, Bob"

The most important event for the Mueller investigation at the end of 2017 took place in total secrecy, and it involved a person who was, at that point, completely unknown to the public. Annie Donaldson was a soft-spoken young southerner, a native of Kentucky, and a graduate of the University of Alabama who went on to Harvard Law School. After getting her law degree in 2011, she alternated between working for Republican political campaigns and working for Washington law firms. Then Don McGahn, Trump's White House counsel, hired her as his chief of staff. Donaldson came to Patriots Plaza for an interview with the Mueller team on November 6, and what she delivered was, from a prosecutor's perspective, pure gold.

Donaldson operated as McGahn's amanuensis. In addition to managing the operations of the counsel's office, especially with regard to judicial nominations, Donaldson sometimes accompanied McGahn to meetings as his note taker. And often when she did not attend, including after meetings between McGahn and the president, Donaldson would debrief McGahn and write down his recollections on legal pads. The notes were mostly straightforward summaries, but Donaldson made occasional deadpan interjections, like "Just in the middle of another Russia Fiasco." Thanks to her notes, Mueller's prosecutors had a guide to the central issue in the investigation of the White House—obstruction of justice.

A few weeks later, on November 30, McGahn himself made his

first visit to Mueller's office. Improbably, given McGahn's toxic relationship with the president, he was still White House counsel at the time. McGahn didn't try very hard to hide his contempt for Trump—for the president's ignorance, his impatience, his failure to appreciate what McGahn was doing for him. (Not incidentally, McGahn and Jared Kushner, Trump's son-in-law, also loathed each other because of conflicts over Kushner's security clearance.) Working with Mitch McConnell, the Senate majority leader, who cared as much about judges as McGahn did, the White House counsel was setting in motion an unprecedented pace of judicial confirmations. Trump's conservative supporters understood the importance of this achievement, even if the president did not. For McGahn, at least for the time being, creating this legacy was worth the aggravation of dealing with Trump.

But McGahn wasn't going to protect Trump from himself. McGahn was a good enough student of history, and a smart enough lawyer, to know how much trouble people in his position had found themselves in by trying to take one for the team. He was going to tell the special counsel the truth. If McGahn's testimony turned out to be incriminating for Trump, that was the president's problem. Still, any witness, even one committed to telling the truth, is not going to remember the details of every conversation from months earlier. That's why Donaldson's notes mattered so much. Prompted with the notes, McGahn was able to tell a story that was rich in detail and devastating to Trump.

So a rotating cast of prosecutors started taking McGahn through his recollections. Jim Quarles, the former Watergate prosecutor who was head of the White House team, and Andrew Goldstein, the former Manhattan Assistant U.S. Attorney, were the fixtures in the room, but several other prosecutors and FBI agents participated as well. They proceeded in chronological order. First, they asked McGahn about his conversations with Michael Flynn, during the early days of the administration, in the series of events that led up to Flynn's lies to the FBI. Next they covered the president's interactions with Comey and then the president's decision to fire the FBI director. McGahn's testimony was relevant in these areas, but he was mostly filling in blanks in stories that prosecutors already knew by this point.

Then McGahn turned to the subject of his interactions with the president about Mueller's own investigation—specifically, Trump's demands that McGahn initiate the firing of the special counsel in June 2017. McGahn laid out in spellbinding detail the president's calls to his home, demanding that he produce Mueller's scalp. He talked about his weekend journey to pack up his office in the White House, in preparation for his resignation, which he vowed to give rather than participate in another "Saturday Night Massacre." True, McGahn pulled back from the brink and stayed in his job when Trump did not pursue the issue further, but the counsel's testimony was highly incriminating nonetheless.

This was new. And this was big. It was the clearest evidence so far, according to many in the Mueller office, that the president had committed a crime in office—obstruction of justice.

Even by the standards of the special counsel's office, the White House team operated in secrecy. Sometimes Quarles said little or nothing at the daily meetings of the investigative team leads and shared the results of his inquiries only with Mueller himself. Such was Quarles's paranoia about leaks—in an office that produced exactly zero leaks—that he didn't even trust his colleagues with some of what he knew. Not for Quarles the high-volume byplay between Rhee and Weissmann. McGahn's testimony, backed by Donaldson's notes, raised a question that had hovered in the background of the Mueller investigation from the beginning. Until these interviews, it had been a theoretical question—an abstraction, not grounded in the facts of the investigation. But now there was evidence to make the issue real: Could Mueller—could any federal prosecutor—indict a sitting president of the United States?

The Constitution itself was silent on the question. Article II defines the procedure by which Congress may remove a president—for impeachment and conviction of "Treason, Bribery, or other high Crimes and Misdemeanors." The Constitution also makes clear that Congress, in the impeachment process, may not levy *additional* punishments on the president. Article I states, "Judgment in Cases of Impeachment shall not extend further than to removal from Office" and disqualification from additional federal service. At other points in the Constitution, notably the Bill of Rights, the Framers defined the rights of criminal defendants, including the right to due process of law, to bail, and to be free from double jeopardy and cruel and unusual punishment. But nowhere does the Constitution address whether a president can also be a criminal defendant. That gap in the law had been addressed twice in the modern era by the Justice Department's Office of Legal Counsel, which operates as a kind of internal rule maker for the executive branch.

The timing of these OLC opinions—in 1973 and 2000—was no coincidence. The first came as the Watergate scandal was gathering around Richard Nixon, and the second was issued after the impeachment and Senate acquittal of Bill Clinton. The issue of a presidential indictment arises only at times of major scandal. But for most of American history, including the time of the Framers, no one seems to have considered whether a sitting president could be indicted. Alexander Hamilton, in Federalist No. 69, wrote, "The President of the United States would be liable to be impeached, tried, and upon conviction . . . removed from office, and would afterwards be liable to prosecution and punishment in the ordinary course of law." The use of the word "afterwards" suggested that Hamilton believed that the president could not be prosecuted during his term in office, but that implication was hardly definitive or binding.

The analysis in the two OLC opinions dug deeply into the history of the Constitution and the texts of Supreme Court opinions, but ultimately they reached the same commonsense judgment. Two branches of the federal government, the legislative and judicial, are collections of people, and thus no single person in either branch is irreplaceable. The executive branch is a person—the president. Accordingly, as the 2000 opinion put it, "the President occupies a unique position within our constitutional order." As such, he deserves some protection from the burdens imposed on other citizens, because "criminal litigation uniquely requires the President's *personal* time and energy, and will inevitably entail a considerable if not overwhelming degree of mental preoccupation." Imposing this kind of obligation on a president "would have a dramatically destabilizing effect upon the ability of a coordinate branch of government to function." To put it another way, the president cannot do his job to protect the nation if he is sitting in court all day and then worrying at night about his fate in the hands of jurors.

The OLC opinion has sometimes been criticized as putting the president "above the law." But that's not exactly true. As Hamilton noted, the president can always be removed from office and then prosecuted, like any other citizen. At worst, a lawbreaking president might suffer a delayed criminal reckoning, but he would not receive indefinite immunity. (The OLC opinion recognized the possibility that the statute of limitations might lapse on certain offenses while the president is in office but decided that this remote risk was worth taking.) This, then, was the state of the law as Mueller was weighing Trump's fate. In the straightforward words of the second OLC opinion, "We believe that the Constitution requires recognition of a presidential immunity from indictment and criminal prosecution while the President is in office."

Still, an OLC opinion is not enforceable in the same way that a law is. Mueller was a Justice Department employee and thus presumably bound by the OLC opinion, but his anomalous status as a special counsel at least raised the question of whether he would feel compelled to honor the policy. (Kenneth Starr, who was an independent counsel and thus less subject to Justice Department supervision, conducted his own legal analysis of the question. His staff disagreed with the OLC opinions and concluded that a sitting president could be indicted, but Starr never authorized such a charge against Clinton.) In any event, Trump's lawyers wanted to know if Mueller felt bound by the OLC opinion. So they decided to ask him.

John Dowd was still Trump's lead defense lawyer as 2017 ended, and Ty Cobb was still representing the interests of the White House with Mueller. They were both still advocates of cooperation with the special counsel, and they felt that their approach had been more or less vindicated at that point. Document production from the White House to Mueller was almost complete, and the office interviews of administration staffers were proceeding without incident. True, Flynn had pleaded guilty, and Manafort was under indictment, but Dowd and Cobb took comfort in the fact that Mueller appeared to have nothing on Trump. The president seethed about Mueller, but still mostly in private. He had promised Cobb that he wouldn't attack the special counsel, and he was still keeping his word. In light of all this, both Dowd and Cobb fell victim to the curse of excessive optimism.

They told reporters—and Trump—that they thought Mueller might be wrapping up his investigation by the end of 2017. Mueller had only been appointed in May; the idea that he might finish a complex white-collar investigation by the end of the year was unrealistic in the extreme, even if he was ultimately going to clear the president.

Dowd had an open channel of communication with Mueller, and they kept in touch, mostly about logistical matters. But one major issue remained unresolved—whether Trump would agree to speak to Mueller's prosecutors, and whether Mueller would subpoena Trump if he refused. This was, in part, a constitutional question, so Dowd brought in the lawyer who became, in effect, his deputy, Jay Sekulow. In the end, Sekulow would turn out to be the longest-tenured member of Trump's team—the only one who lasted from the days of Marc Kasowitz (Trump's first lawyer after Mueller was hired) through the final vote on impeachment in the Senate. In a way, this was fitting, because Sekulow had led one of the most significant, and most unlikely, legal careers of his generation.

Even as he passed his sixtieth birthday, Sekulow still looked like what he was—a nice Jewish boy from Long Island. He still wore the sharply tailored suits of a garment district executive, and he still flavored his speech with Yiddishisms. His family had moved from Long Island to Atlanta when he was a teenager, and as an indifferent student in those days Jay drifted into a local college, Atlanta Baptist. His father, a moderately observant Jew, had no complaint about his choice of schools. "Baptist-shmaptist," he told his son. "Go ahead. Get yourself a good education."

Most of the other students were Christian, of course, and one day a fellow student challenged Sekulow to read the book of Isaiah. Sekulow knew that Jews were supposed to believe that someday the Messiah would come but that he had not yet done so. But in reading the passages about the Messiah, Sekulow thought he recognized the description: it was Jesus Christ. In time, he learned that there were other Jews who shared his belief, and they were called Jews for Jesus. At a ceremony in February 1976, just before his twentieth birthday, Sekulow rose at a Jews for Jesus church service and announced that he had dedicated his life to Jesus Christ.

After college, Sekulow decided to go to law school, at Mercer University, also in Georgia. In his first years out of school, a business venture soared, then soured. He also started a law firm, which went bankrupt. He had, in essence, just a single client left—his own Jews for Jesus church, which he had agreed to represent as their general legal counsel. From that unpromising start, Sekulow changed American constitutional law, virtually single-handedly.

Jews for Jesus adherents are famous (and notorious) for proselytizing, often in public places like airports. When they were banned from doing so, as they often were, the church members usually claimed that their behavior was protected under the "free exercise" of religion clause of the First Amendment. But when the Los Angeles International Airport authorities evicted Jews for Jesus proselytizers in 1984, Sekulow tried a new defense. He said the airport was punishing free speech, not just religion. The Supreme Court had a long history of defending obnoxious speech, and Sekulow wanted to put his case in line with those decisions. His LAX case went to the Supreme Court in 1987, and he won a unanimous victory that the airport authorities violated the free speech rights of his Jews for Jesus clients. Then he won another Supreme Court case on similar grounds, then another. Thanks to Sekulow's arguments, religious groups won all sorts of new opportunities to use government property because their actions were protected under the Constitution as free speech.

Pat Robertson, the evangelical leader and proprietor of the *700 Club* television show, noticed Sekulow's success, and he asked him to join forces in a group they decided to call the American Center for Law and Justice. The initials—ACLJ—were meant as a challenge to the American Civil Liberties Union, because Robertson and Sekulow wanted to start a conservative counterpart to the liberal legal mainstay. And like the ACLU, Sekulow's ACLJ began representing all sorts of conservative legal causes—against abortion, for school prayer, against gay rights.

For Sekulow, the Robertson connection had another crucial advantage. The preacher's direct-mail prowess allowed Sekulow to turn the ACLJ into a cash machine—indeed, something closer to a grift. Over the next three decades, Sekulow transformed his nominally nonprofit operations into vehicles to finance a princely lifestyle for his entire family. In Washington, he lived and worked in a meticulously renovated row house a few steps from the Supreme Court. There, servants proffered drinks on crystal coasters in an anteroom featuring a trompe l'oeil mural. For years, journalists investigated the way Sekulow has parlayed the contributions of evangelicals into tens of millions of dollars for his family. As *The Guardian* put it, Sekulow came up with a plan, at the height of the recession, that pushed "poor and jobless people to donate money to his Christian nonprofit, which since 2000 has steered more than $60 million to Sekulow, his family and their businesses." The money has gone to companies controlled by his wife, sons, brother, sister-in-law, niece, and nephew. Again courtesy of his nonprofit, Sekulow frequently travels by private jet among homes, also paid for by others, in Washington, Tennessee, and France. None of these investigations have uncovered violations of law by Sekulow or his family.

As part of Sekulow's growing empire, he became a fixture on radio and television. He long had a daily radio show on syndicated Christian radio, and his Christian television empire has included such shows as *Jay Sekulow Live!, Jay Sekulow Weekend, ACLJ This Week, Law and Justice Feature, The Jordan Sekulow Show,* featuring his son, and *The Messianic Hour,* featuring Rabbi Scott Sekulow, Jay Sekulow's brother. Jay Sekulow was also a regular guest on Fox News, as well as occasionally on CNN, and that was how he came to Trump's attention.

Sekulow was, indeed, a rare bird—a lawyer who could perform effectively on television but who also displayed a real understanding of the law. Marc Kasowitz (with support from Steve Bannon) originally brought him into the Trump camp, but Dowd quickly recognized his value to the team and kept him on. Sekulow's original duties on the defense team were limited to constitutional issues; he had next to no experience as a criminal defense lawyer. But he was a fast study and had good legal judgment and the trust of the client because Trump liked the way Sekulow defended him on television.

By late 2017, the two sides had already gone back and forth on the issue of Trump's testimony a number of times. Sekulow, as the constitutional authority, had made the case that the courts would not enforce a grand jury subpoena against the president. He argued that the prosecutors' two strongest precedents did not apply. In *United States v. Nixon,* in 1974, the Supreme Court ordered President Nixon to turn over White House tapes for use in the Watergate conspiracy trial against his former aides. But Sekulow argued that the case of a grand jury subpoena against Trump would be different. The tapes already existed; Nixon himself didn't have to testify at all. He would not have had to take time away from his duties to prepare to give testimony. In addition, one reason the Court ruled against Nixon was that the tapes would be evidence in a pending criminal trial, which should be decided with all available evidence. Trump was not a witness in any pending case, so Sekulow asserted that the courts would believe Mueller, in seeking to talk to Trump, was just fishing. In *Clinton v. Jones,* from 1997, the Court ordered Bill Clinton to give a deposition in Paula Jones's sexual harassment civil case against him. Sekulow asserted that the Jones case concerned only Clinton's behavior before he took office, so there was no way that the questioning would risk disclosure of matters relevant to his presidency. In the Jones case, the Supreme Court did not have to address the issue of whether the substance of Clinton's testimony would include any privileged, executive branch matters. In light of that, Sekulow asserted, the Jones case had little bearing on how a court would address a grand jury subpoena to Trump to talk about his actions as president.

Mueller's legal team, led by Michael Dreeben, had answers for these arguments. There was nothing in the Nixon case that would necessarily limit its holding to just tapes or just criminal trials; the principle upheld in *Nixon* was that the president has to comply with criminal process, and that would include a grand jury subpoena. As for the Jones case, Mueller's team pointed out that the courts have always held that there is a greater public interest in forcing compliance with criminal matters, like a grand jury subpoena, than in civil cases. The fact that the Court directed the president to give a deposition in a civil case was powerful evidence that the justices would uphold a grand jury subpoena, where the public interest was greater. And Mueller was looking to examine Trump about matters that took place before he became president as well as after; so the Jones precedent, which concerned Clinton's prepresidential conduct, was squarely relevant on that score. (Starr issued a grand jury subpoena to Clinton, but the president ultimately agreed to testify voluntarily rather than test the issue in the courts.)

So which side was right? Who had the better argument? Who would win if Trump challenged a Mueller subpoena in federal court? What would happen if the case went all the way to the Supreme Court? The truth was, no one knew. The question of whether the courts would uphold a grand jury subpoena to the president was a difficult, unresolved legal issue. Trump himself often told his lawyers that he was ready and willing to testify. (He said versions of this in public as well.) Dowd and Sekulow never knew how much stock to put in Trump's statements. Like everyone else, they knew that Trump said a lot of things. But Trump was the client, and it seemed as though he wanted to testify, so they started planning for an examination to take place. Dowd went back and forth on whether Trump should talk—he was nearly as erratic as his client—but he agreed to pursue the issue with Mueller.

But first, Trump's lawyers demanded an agenda. What questions did Mueller want to ask? This demand ate up several more weeks, but Mueller eventually did come up with a list of subject areas. By and large, Trump's legal team was encouraged by the list, all of which covered familiar territory. Mueller had clearly not discovered some smoking gun that Trump's lawyers had never seen. Mueller wanted to know what Trump knew about Flynn's contacts with Russians; about his decision to fire Comey; about his demeaning of Jeff Sessions, the attorney general. There were also questions about the campaign—about what Trump knew about the Trump Tower meeting; about his knowledge of WikiLeaks' efforts; about his contacts with Michael Cohen and plans to build a Trump Tower in Moscow. Dowd and Cobb felt Trump could deal with all these issues, with the right amount of preparation. They even made a tentative deal with Mueller for a time and place for Trump to testify. It would take place on Saturday, January 27, 2018, at Camp David. The amount of time was unsettled—somewhere between two and six hours—but Mueller promised time for bathroom breaks. But the most important issue—the scope of the questioning—was still up in the air.

Sekulow thought the deal was madness. He didn't want Trump to answer Mueller's questions—at all, under any circumstances. He recalled for his colleagues Cobb's original philosophy regarding cooperation with Mueller. The reason Cobb had agreed to produce all the administration documents, and allow the interviews with White

House staffers, was so he could argue against the enforcement of a subpoena to Trump in court. Under the D.C. Circuit's Espy decision, the courts would uphold a subpoena to the president only if the information sought from him could not come from "alternative sources." Under Cobb, the White House had provided thousands of pages of documents and dozens of interviews. Those were the alternative sources. Why give Mueller a Trump interview too?

Even after the Camp David session was tentatively set, Trump's lawyers and Mueller's team kept meeting at Patriots Plaza to see if they could settle the outstanding issues. As the date grew closer, the negotiations grew more tense. Dowd had a blustering style, and he used these face-to-face encounters to berate Mueller about the entire basis for the investigation. Dowd and Mueller had known each other for years—this was a big reason why Trump hired Dowd—and the defense lawyer played on this familiarity.

"Cut the bullshit, Bob," Dowd said. "You know you have nothing on him."

Dowd knew that obstruction of justice would be the key accusation against Trump, if any were to be made. "What's your theory, Bob? What law did the president violate? You're seriously going to claim that firing the FBI director is a criminal act? You know he can fire the director for any damn reasons he wants." Mueller greeted most of these sallies with silence.

Sekulow played the scholar to Dowd's pugilist. Sekulow was against any kind of interview, but in order to avoid undercutting Dowd, he concentrated on trying to narrow the scope of any interview rather than stopping it altogether. He told Mueller that he thought Trump might be able to answer some questions about his actions during the campaign—that is, before he became president—but anything about his presidency should be off-limits. Those actions were covered by executive privilege, and Trump wouldn't waive it. (This was a highly debatable assertion by Sekulow—that everything Trump did as president was covered by executive privilege. Clinton, of course, had answered many questions about his presidency during his grand jury testimony. Mueller greeted this argument, too, with silence.)

But Sekulow really got to the heart of the issue when he asked Mueller why he needed any interview at all. His prosecutors had the documents and the testimony of others. They knew the facts—that Trump fired Comey, that he tweeted insults at Sessions. What more did he need?

For once, Mueller answered, and his words, in a way, defined his entire investigation. "We need to know his state of mind," Mueller said. In one sense, this was a narrowly legalistic response. Most crimes, like obstruction of justice, had an intent requirement; in order to obtain a conviction, prosecutors had to prove that the defendant had bad or corrupt intent. As Sekulow pointed out, Mueller already knew that Trump fired Comey, but Mueller said he needed to know why.

We need to know his state of mind. Mueller repeated the phrase several times—"state of mind."

Throughout his presidency, even throughout his life, Trump had been surrounded by enablers, many of them lawyers. They contrived to come up with legitimate explanations for his behavior. The Comey firing was a classic example. Those around Trump tried to use Rod Rosenstein to assert that Trump fired the FBI director because of his ill-treatment of Hillary Clinton rather than because he wanted to forestall the Russia investigation. Later, Trump's supporters invented an explanation for why Trump withheld military aid from Ukraine. They said the president did so because he wanted to fight corruption rather than because he wanted to embarrass Joseph Biden, a political rival. The facts were not in dispute in either case. Trump fired Comey, and he withheld the aid to Ukraine. The question in both was why. Was his intent legitimate or corrupt? What was his state of mind?

By the time Trump's lawyers were negotiating with Mueller, the president had pretty much stopped taking questions except in friendly interviews with Fox News and brief question-and-answer sessions with reporters as his helicopter blasted noise in the background. Even then, as everyone knew, he often lied or otherwise stepped into trouble. Still, too, whether out of arrogance or ignorance, Trump had a habit of blurting out the truth about controversial matters. He admitted to NBC's Lester Holt and to the Russian foreign minister that he had fired Comey because of the Russia investigation. Later, after the Ukraine scandal broke, he acknowledged, in public statements, that he wanted foreign governments to investigate the Biden family.

As president, Trump had never subjected himself to the kind of sustained, orderly questioning that an interview with Mueller's team would entail. To be sure, in such a session, Trump would filibuster and dodge, but it would still be the only opportunity to confront him with the fundamental issue in the case: why he did what he did. As Mueller said, the prosecutors wanted to know his state of mind.

In reply, Sekulow provided a moment of real candor. "Bob," he said, "why would I allow you to do that? If you were me, would you allow him to do that?"

Sekulow was not posing a rhetorical question. He really wanted to know: What was in it for Trump in answering Mueller's questions?

Mueller struggled to answer. He was wise enough in the ways of the criminal justice system to know that no lawyer would ever want a client like Trump—much less a client who was president of the United States—to answer questions in a grand jury setting. Let a congenital liar testify? Why would Sekulow—any lawyer—allow such a thing to happen?

Mueller managed to say something about "the best interests of the country." That's why Trump should testify. But Sekulow had made his point, and the meeting soon ended. A few days later, about two weeks before the scheduled Camp David session, Dowd called Mueller to pull the plug on the whole idea. Trump was not going to sit for an interview.

This, then, presented Mueller with the most consequential decision of his tenure as special counsel. Should he issue a grand jury subpoena for Trump to testify? To do so would be to invite a court fight with an uncertain outcome. But if he issued the subpoena at that moment, in January 2018, there was a chance it would receive expedited review in the Supreme Court by the end of June. At that point, Mueller's own tenure would be just a year old. A resolution in June would still allow Mueller to complete his investigation with reasonable dispatch. No one could fairly accuse him of using the fight over the subpoena to extend his own investigation. Mueller had every reason to pursue what certainly would have been the single most important piece of evidence in this investigation.

Mueller didn't. He backed down. He couldn't bring himself to launch a direct legal attack against the president of the United States. He decided to continue negotiating. Maybe Trump would agree, as

198 TRUE CRIMES _and_ MISDEMEANORS

Sekulow suggested, to answer questions about the campaign, if not the presidency. Maybe the president would answer written questions, if not oral ones. In this critical moment, Mueller showed weakness. Compared with his retreat on the subpoena to Trump, Rhee's sprawling dragnet and Weissmann's ferocious attack on Manafort paled. Trump noticed that Mueller, after all this talk about the president's testimony, backed off when confronted. The president's behavior— and Mueller's investigation—were never the same again.

PART FOUR

15

Michael Avenatti's Campaign for President

Don McGahn came to Patriots Plaza for his first debriefing with Mueller's prosecutors on November 30, 2017, and he returned twice more in the next two weeks, on December 12 and 14. In all, he would spend more than thirty hours with Mueller's team, and when prosecutors came to write their report, they would cite McGahn 157 times, more than any other witness. It wasn't just that Mueller's team referred to McGahn frequently; it's that his testimony was the most incriminating to Trump. McGahn vividly and directly implicated Trump in the effort to fire Mueller, which was the heart of the obstruction of justice evidence against the president. Of course, McGahn's interviews with Mueller's White House team in November and December were conducted under the strict rules of secrecy that Jim Quarles demanded.

So it was a particular shock to prosecutors when, on January 25, 2018, *The New York Times* published an enormous scoop about McGahn's statements to Mueller. The story, by Michael S. Schmidt and Maggie Haberman, reported, "President Trump ordered the firing last June of Robert S. Mueller III, the special counsel overseeing the Russia investigation, . . . but ultimately backed down after the White House counsel threatened to resign rather than carry out the directive." The *Times* story, which was accurate in every detail about McGahn's allegations, electrified Washington because it confirmed the long-standing rumors that Trump tried to have Mueller fired and raised the prospect that Trump's own White House lawyer would be the lead witness against him for obstruction of justice. The story broke when Trump was at a conference in Switzerland. Questioned by reporters, he dismissed the story, saying, "Fake news, folks. Fake news. A typical *New York Times* fake story."

Trump was obsessed with *The New York Times,* which was, after all, his hometown newspaper. Throughout Trump's career, he had longed for its approval, and he was especially bitter when he didn't get it. He had a surprisingly detailed familiarity with the *Times* reporters and their beats. Notably, he was especially enraged about the *Times*'s McGahn scoop because of the byline of Michael Schmidt. Trump knew that Schmidt had already written several stories that reflected positively on McGahn, and the president attributed this latest one to McGahn's effort to ingratiate himself with the reporter and make himself look good to the public, at Trump's expense. The president's reaction to the story also showed how he lied to and about his staff as much as he lied to and about others. The president told his aide Hope Hicks that John Kelly, his chief of staff, had told him that McGahn completely repudiated the *Times* story. But Kelly later said that he had not even spoken to McGahn about the story and had told Trump no such thing. Trump told similar lies to Rob Porter, his staff secretary. Trump's thrashing with his aides was designed to persuade McGahn to repudiate the story, so he simply lied and informed his staff that McGahn had already done so—which he hadn't, and wouldn't.

Trump wouldn't let go of the issue of the *Times* story about McGahn's statements to Mueller. The president instructed his lawyer John Dowd to arrange for McGahn to ask the *Times* for a retraction. Dowd called William Burck, the well-wired Republican attorney who was representing McGahn, and asked him to get his client to object to the story. McGahn told his lawyer, who told Dowd, that he wouldn't ask for a correction, because the story was accurate.

If Trump had ceased his efforts at this point, his actions might have been inconsequential as a legal matter. It's not unlawful for presidents, or anyone else, to complain about news stories or to lie to their own lawyers or their subordinates. But what happened on February 5 changed the legal calculus. Trump went back to Porter and again told him the *Times* story was "bullshit"—that he never told McGahn to fire the special counsel. He then told Porter that he needed to get McGahn to "create a record" that the *Times* story was false and that he never tried to fire Mueller. Trump told Porter that his White House counsel was "a lying bastard," adding, "If he doesn't write a letter, then maybe I'll have to get rid of him." (When Porter passed along Trump's demand to McGahn, he said the same thing he had told everyone else—that he wouldn't write the letter, because the *Times* story was accurate.)

From a prosecutorial perspective, the key moment took place the next day, when Trump approached McGahn directly in the Oval Office. The president instructed the White House counsel to "correct" the *Times* story. This was different from the president's previous actions. This wasn't mere venting. Now Trump was asking a subordinate to create a false record about the subject of a pending grand jury investigation. In his conversation with McGahn, Trump quibbled over the use of the word "fire." He said he never used the word. McGahn responded, "What you said is, 'Call Rod [Rosenstein], tell Rod that Mueller has conflicts and can't be the Special Counsel.'" When McGahn stood by his recollection, Trump went on a tirade about note taking. "Why do you take notes? Lawyers don't take notes. I never had a lawyer who took notes." McGahn responded that he was a "real lawyer" and real lawyers took notes. (This is true.) Then, inevitably, Trump tried to settle the argument by invoking his Platonic ideal of a lawyer: "I've had a lot of great lawyers, like Roy Cohn. He did not take notes."

McGahn was in a surreal position. He was still White House counsel—one of the president's closest advisers—and he had already offered incriminating testimony against the president when he went to the prosecutors' offices in November and December. But as 2018 began, McGahn could at least feel as if he were finished with that unpleasant duty. But now, in February, Trump had just behaved as badly as he had done the previous summer, when he tried to arrange Mueller's dismissal. Trump was now asking—demanding—that McGahn lie. So after consulting with Burck, his lawyer, McGahn returned to Mueller's office on March 8 and told Quarles's team about the president's latest improper overture.

Even then, though, McGahn returned to work at the White House because he wanted to see if Anthony Kennedy was going to retire from the Supreme Court in 2018. For McGahn, the chance to engineer the confirmation of a second justice was worth the continuing ordeal of dealing with Trump. Kennedy did retire, and in July, Trump nominated McGahn's old friend Brett Kavanaugh to the Court. Still, the poisonous relationship between Trump and McGahn remained. On August 29, McGahn was surprised to see the following tweet from Trump: "White House Counsel Don McGahn will be leaving his position in the fall, shortly after the confirmation (hopefully) of Judge Brett Kavanaugh to the United States Supreme Court. I have worked with Don for a long time and truly appreciate his service!" This was news to McGahn, and he did leave in the fall. McGahn made what he called an "Irish exit"—a farewell without saying goodbye to practically anyone, including his boss.

Trump's obsessive campaign to discredit the *Times*'s accurate story about McGahn and the special counsel reflected a broader change in the president's behavior as 2018 began. During 2017, Trump had more or less kept his word to Ty Cobb, the White House liaison with Mueller, that he wouldn't attack the special counsel. At the same time, the president had allowed Cobb to cooperate with Mueller by giving the prosecutor's team access to White House witnesses and documents. But what, Trump came to wonder, had his accommodating posture gotten him? Flynn had pleaded guilty. Manafort was awaiting trial, with Gates as the star witness against him. Jeannie Rhee's indictment in the Internet Research Agency social media case had come down too. Mueller was obviously still going full steam, despite Ty Cobb's prediction that he would be finished by the end of the year. It was not Trump's style to suffer in silence, so he started looking for targets for his rage.

First, Trump turned on his own people, starting with his lawyers. Their defenestration came with what became a familiar ritual in this White House. First, there were news leaks, citing anonymous sources, that Trump was unhappy with his lawyers. Ty Cobb, who never wanted to stay more than a year anyway, began easing himself out in early 2018. John Dowd's departure was uglier. Dowd was a reluctant and unpolished television performer, which soured Trump on him from the beginning. He also had an unsteady grip on new technology and even the facts of the case. After Flynn pleaded guilty in December, Dowd wrote a tweet for Trump's account saying that the president had fired Flynn for lying to the FBI. But Trump's position had long been that he fired Flynn just for lying to the vice president. Trump had never acknowledged that he believed Flynn lied to the FBI; indeed, Trump asked Comey to drop the FBI's investigation of Flynn. Dowd had to apologize for the tweet. The failed negotiations about the possible Camp David interview in January left Trump unhappy too. (Trump should have been grateful that his lawyers spared him the chance to lie to Mueller's prosecutors, but the president, characteristically, didn't see it that way.) Trump was glad to see Mueller back down on the subpoena, but he still wanted a lawyer who could tell him how the Mueller probe was going to end—probably an impossible request—and Dowd didn't have an answer. At the end of March, Dowd "resigned," but his departure resembled one once described by baseball's Casey Stengel: "We call it discharged because there is no question I had to leave."

Trump needed a new lead lawyer. He appeared at one point to be close to hiring the husband-and-wife team of Joseph diGenova and Victoria Toensing. DiGenova had been U.S. Attorney in Washington during the Reagan administration, and he became famous for his pursuit of the city's mayor, Marion Barry, who had a drug-fueled lifestyle in those days. At the same time, Toensing had worked for the Justice Department in national security. Ever since the 1990s, the pair had been reliable talking heads supporting Republican causes, and Trump was drawn to their television personas. But diGenova was seventy-three and Toensing seventy-six; neither one had the stamina or the recent experience for defending a case of this magnitude. They never even started work.

At that point, in March, Sekulow was essentially alone on the defense team. He had a healthy regard for his own skills, but he was also realistic enough to know that he had next to no experience in criminal defense. He needed help—and soon. His first move was unexpected but wound up looking smart. He hired a different husband-and-wife team, Jane and Marty Raskin, former prosecutors who practiced with great success in Miami, though they were largely unknown in the snobby and insular world of white-collar defense lawyers in Washington. Sekulow arranged for the Raskins to meet with Trump at Mar-a-Lago on a Monday, when the club was closed, and their hour-long session with the client made the deal. (Trump, who always cared about personal connections more than legal argument, liked that Jane Raskin had once worked in the Organized Crime Strike Force in Boston at the same time that Mueller was a senior prosecutor there.)

The hiring of the Raskins relieved some of Sekulow's burden, but he knew that he needed someone else, too. The Raskins were behind-the-scenes operators; they had neither the experience nor the inclination to represent the president in the news media. Sekulow could do some of that advocacy work, but he knew, too, that he lacked the stature to be the lead defense lawyer. Besides, there was a new problem on the horizon, in a forum that mattered a great deal to the president—cable news.

Ever since Mueller was appointed in May 2017, covering his investigation was a journalistic challenge. As a visual medium, television in particular needs strong personalities to represent all sides. Trump, of course, was a constant and forceful presence on the airwaves, but there was no comparable figure among his adversaries. Mueller and his team decided to be invisible. (Kenneth Starr, during his time as independent counsel, made a different choice.) Republicans controlled both houses of Congress in this period, so they used their power to limit investigations of Trump almost to nonexistence. That meant congressional Democrats had little ability to produce new evidence against the president. Adam Schiff, the ranking Democrat on the Intelligence Committee, emerged as a kind of unofficial spokesman for his party, but he didn't have a lot of raw material. All of which left a vacuum—which a hitherto little-known lawyer named Michael Avenatti hastened to fill.

In addition to the Flynn guilty plea and the Manafort indictment, there was another reason for Trump's dark turn of mind in early 2018. On January 12, *The Wall Street Journal* reported that Trump had paid a pornographic film actress named Stormy Daniels $130,000 in October 2016 to sign a "hush agreement" that would require her to keep their affair secret. This was, at one level, a peculiar expenditure, because in 2011 a website called TheDirty.com had already published a story about the tryst. Still, the frantic effort to silence Daniels at that time made sense because it came right after the disclosure of the *Access Hollywood* tape, on October 7, 2016, when Trump and his allies were desperate to avoid further attention to his personal life a few weeks before the presidential election. (The "affair" between Trump and Daniels—whose real name is Stephanie Clifford—consisted of a single one-night stand at a celebrity golf tournament in Lake Tahoe, in 2006, shortly after the birth of Trump's son Barron.) The *Journal* story included a quotation from Michael Cohen, Trump's personal attorney, who said, "President Trump once again vehemently denies any such occurrence as has Ms. Daniels."

Avenatti became part of the story the following month, in February 2018. Referred by another lawyer, he met with Daniels in the lobby of the Waldorf Astoria Beverly Hills. There, he agreed to represent the actress and to file a lawsuit on her behalf, which he did on March 8. Daniels sued Trump, arguing that their agreement was invalid, because only Cohen, not Trump himself, had signed the document. As a result, Daniels sought the right to talk publicly about her relationship with Trump. As a technical legal matter, the lawsuit was absurd. Daniels had no basis to overturn the agreement with Trump. She had made a knowing decision to take the money in return for her silence; a deal was a deal. In addition, the agreement plainly stated that any disputes should go to private arbitration, not a public courtroom. (Not surprisingly, a judge tossed out the case promptly.)

But from Avenatti's perspective, the lawsuit was an act of genius, notwithstanding its legal defects. Avenatti was a kind of doppelgänger for the president—egomaniacal, self-obsessed, dishonest, but with an intuitive understanding of the modern news media. At forty-seven, he was a plaintiff's personal injury lawyer, based near Los Angeles, who had experienced the booms and busts that are common to that line of work. He had worked for years on cases that produced no fee, but he also won massive contingency fees on multimillion-dollar victories. He lived at high speed—literally. His hobby was driving Ferraris in road races. As it turned out, the money to fund such an extravagant hobby wasn't necessarily his own, and Avenatti was plagued with business disputes and lawsuits (as Trump was). Avenatti's personal and business lives were filled with carnage—a bitter, ongoing divorce, a failed coffee chain investment in Seattle, a string of disputes with clients over payments and former partners over fees. But Avenatti was an answer to the prayers of cable news. (In the two months after he filed the Daniels lawsuit, he appeared on CNN and MSNBC 108 times.)

What Avenatti understood was that the legal merits of his lawsuit were not the point. No one particularly cared what or whether a judge ruled about the validity of Daniels's "hush agreement." This was fortunate for Avenatti because as he became increasingly besotted with the spotlight, his legal judgment, which was never acute to start with, deteriorated. When Trump denied having an affair with Daniels, Avenatti sued him for defamation, on Daniels's behalf. The lawsuit was so meritless that the judge not only dismissed the case but ordered Daniels herself to pay $293,000 in Trump's legal fees. Notwithstanding the legal fiascoes, and drunk on the attention, Avenatti gave nonstop interviews, including one to *Vanity Fair* about his "style and skincare routine." ("I've worn a lot of designers and never found a suit like Tom Ford," Avenatti told the author. "The cut, the silhouette, is really extraordinary—his eye toward aesthetics is unsurpassed." The story continued, "He does moisturize twice a day, but shuns complicated skincare products such as eye creams and 40-minute masks.") In a crowning act of lunacy, Avenatti announced he was considering running for the Democratic presidential nomination in 2020, and he made preliminary campaign appearances in Iowa and New Hampshire.

Still, for all his excesses, Avenatti understood one important point. The lawsuits didn't matter as much as Trump's underlying conduct—especially to a cable news audience. In part, of course, there was the value, in sheer salaciousness, of the president of the United States sleeping with a porn star. This was always the core of the appeal of the Stormy Daniels story. At some level, Trump understood this, too, and it rattled him. He started lashing out at his enemies, including, for the first time, Mueller by name. Just a few days after Avenatti filed his first case against Trump, the president tweeted, "Why does the Mueller team have 13 hardened Democrats, some big Crooked Hillary supporters, and Zero Republicans? Another Dem recently added . . . does anyone think this is fair? And yet, there is NO COLLUSION!" (Trump was correct about the ideological orientation of the special counsel's staff at Patriots Plaza, but the president always declined to mention that one Republican also worked there—Mueller himself.)

What made the Stormy Daniels situation worse for Trump was that it wasn't just an embarrassment. There was an important legal issue embedded in the tawdry facts. Why was the president party to an agreement to pay Daniels $130,000? And why did the money change hands on the eve of the election? What was the propriety, even the legality, of that?

And thanks to Avenatti's provocations, the story became even weirder. Perhaps the most obvious question raised by the peculiar "hush agreement," which identified Trump as "David Dennison," related to the source of the $130,000. Who put up the money that went to Daniels? In a brief statement to *The New York Times,* Michael Cohen said he paid the money out of his own pocket. "Neither the Trump Organization nor the Trump campaign was a party to the transaction with Ms. Clifford, and neither reimbursed me for the payment, either directly or indirectly," Cohen said. (Notably, though few noticed at the time, Cohen did not deny that Trump *himself* reimbursed him.) "The payment to Ms. Clifford was lawful, and was not a campaign contribution or a campaign expenditure by anyone." Cohen's story was self-evidently ridiculous—that he, as an attorney, would pay out of his own pocket for the silence of a woman who had slept with his client. In the United States, attorneys do not pay their clients' settlements; clients do.

Yet when Trump himself was asked about the $130,000 payment to Daniels, he backed up Cohen's preposterous version of events. While speaking with reporters in the rear of Air Force One, Trump was asked why Cohen would have paid Daniels if the allegations of the affair were untrue, and he said, "You'll have to ask Michael Cohen. Michael's my attorney." Asked if he knew about the payment to Daniels at the time it was made, Trump said, "No." Asked if he knew where the money came from to pay Daniels, Trump told reporters, "No, I don't know."

Like any prosecutor, like any *person,* Mueller wanted to know what the hell was going on here. Less than a month before the election, Cohen asserted that he paid out of his own pocket to silence a porn star who slept with the candidate? And the candidate—Trump—asserted that he knew nothing about it at all? Was that plausible? The only person who was in a position to answer those questions was Michael Cohen. As it turned out, Mueller had been trying to figure out Cohen's role since almost the first day of his investigation. On July 18, 2017, well before Mueller had even fully staffed the office, his team obtained a secret search warrant to examine Cohen's Gmail account. It was no wonder that Mueller looked hard at Cohen. No one knew more of Trump's secrets than Cohen, the self-proclaimed "fixer" to the president.

For many years, Michael Cohen's life amounted to a realization of the American dream: personal happiness and financial success on a grand scale. His father, Maurice, escaped from Poland during the Holocaust and found his way to Canada, where he went to medical school. A head-and-neck surgeon, he moved to New York, met Sondra, a nurse, whom he married, and settled with her in Lawrence, one of the Five Towns, on Long Island. There, the couple raised four children, all of whom became lawyers. Michael graduated from American University in 1988 and from Thomas M. Cooley Law School in Michigan in 1991. In New York, he worked at a negligence-and-malpractice law firm for five years, until his fortunes turned when he became acquainted with the Shusterman family.

Fima Shusterman and his family immigrated to the United States from Ukraine in the early 1970s, and in New York he first made ends meet by driving a cab. He did a stint in the garment business and started buying taxi medallions when they were rapidly appreciating in value. (New York City requires operators of yellow taxis to possess government-issued medallions, and the number of medallions has remained unchanged for decades.) Shusterman's rise was only slightly slowed when he pleaded guilty, in 1993, to participating in a tax-evasion scheme. After he testified against his accountant, in Brooklyn federal court, he received a sentence of probation. Around this time, Cohen met Laura Shusterman, Fima's daughter, and the two were married. Cohen ultimately joined forces with the Shusterman family in the medallion business.

Cohen prospered during the post-9/11 recession, which particularly affected the New York City taxi industry. Many Sikh drivers, who wore turbans and beards, felt threatened by anti-Muslim sentiment and left the business. Cohen picked up more medallions at depressed prices, and he and his father-in-law came to control almost three hundred of them. In time, Cohen was worth some $90 million on paper. In the early years of the twenty-first century, he and his in-laws bought apartments in Trump World Tower, at 845 United Nations Plaza. The families later bought other Trump apartments as investments, and Cohen met and became friendly with Donald Trump Jr.

In 2006, the Trump Organization was dealing with a rebellion of the condominium board at Trump World Tower—some residents wanted to remove Trump's name from the building—and Don junior suggested to his father that Cohen, who was still practicing law, might help to resolve it. Cohen engineered a coup d'état on the building's board, installing a new group favorable to Trump. His partner in the effort to keep the Trump name on the building was another resident, a young corporate lawyer named George Conway. In order to protect their majority on the board, Conway proposed that his wife, Kellyanne, join the board with Cohen, and they served together for several years. Characteristically, Trump did not pay Cohen for his good deed at Trump World Tower, but he hired the lawyer for the Trump Organization in 2007. Cohen's title—executive vice president and special counsel—reflected his unique position at the company. As Cohen later said, "My role was specifically for him, as his special counsel—anything that came up, that upset him, that related to him, that others wouldn't be able to deal with or needed special handling." He was to take care of any matters, personal or professional, that Mr. Trump, as Cohen always referred to him, wanted him to address.

In the decade before Trump became president, Cohen used intimidation, threats, and bluster to do his bidding. He frequently dealt with the press. On one oft-recounted occasion, Tim Mak, then a reporter for *The Daily Beast*, asked Cohen about the allegation by Trump's first wife, Ivana, which she later recanted, that Trump had raped her. Cohen told Mak, "I'm warning you, tread very fucking lightly, because what I'm going to do to you is going to be fucking disgusting." Cohen earned a reputation for extreme devotion, even sycophancy, toward Trump, who repaid him, on occasion, with disdain. In 2009, when Trump was dissatisfied with Cohen's performance, he cut his salary from $400,000 per year to $200,000. (Two years later, he restored the salary.) Notwithstanding the slights, Cohen remained loyal to Trump. As he told me, "I actually enjoyed him, interestingly enough. When he's good, he's great. When he's horrible, he's the worst human being on the planet. I mean it. He has no heart and no soul when he's mean."

Cohen's aggression with Trump's adversaries contrasted with his hang-dog timidity around Trump himself. Cohen's neediness seemed to prompt Trump's contempt, and he relished humiliating his devoted aide. Despite his later denials, Cohen wanted to serve in the new Trump administration, and the president-elect dangled the possibility of a job but never offered one. As an alternative to government service, Cohen made a brazen effort to exploit his connection to Trump, and this prompted his first round of scrutiny from Mueller.

When Trump became president, Cohen left the Trump Organization and set up shop at a law firm, where he put himself on the market as a consultant to large corporations. In short order, he took in more than $4 million from clients like Novartis and AT&T as well as foreign companies controlled in Russia, South Korea, and Kazakhstan. In addition, Cohen signed on as an adviser to Columbus Nova, a firm that invested money for Viktor Vekselberg, a Russian oligarch with ties to the Kremlin. Cohen had no expertise in any of these fields, but his business card summed up his only qualification: "Personal attorney to Donald Trump." It was an especially transparent attempt to cash in, and the news reports about his business dealings prompted Mueller's prosecutors to obtain the search warrant for Cohen's emails on July 18. Later, Mueller's team obtained Cohen's financial records as well. The corporations had hired Cohen as a consultant, rather than as a lobbyist, but the outsized fees raised the question of whether Cohen was lobbying without registering with the government to do so.

The prosecutors also started looking at Cohen's behavior before Trump became president, not after. Did he engage in any behavior that was relevant to Mueller's mandate—specifically regarding Trump's financial relationship with the Russians? Cohen had been Trump's point person on the last iteration of the Trump Tower Moscow project. Working with Felix Sater, another longtime Trump associate, Cohen had arranged for Trump to sign the nonbinding letter of intent to build a multipurpose tower in Moscow. Trump made the deal in October 2015, and Sater celebrated with Cohen. Still, as provocative as these events were, it was also clear that no money changed hands in the Moscow deal, and it went no further than the letter. Of course, Trump's signature on the letter of intent proved that he lied throughout the campaign, when he said he had no business dealings with Russians. But it's no crime to lie to the public.

Cohen had also given Mueller's prosecutors a gift. On August 28, 2017, he had written a letter to the House and Senate Intelligence Committees describing his role in the negotiations over Trump Tower Moscow. (On October 25, he testified before the Senate Intelligence Committee.) In those statements, Cohen did his best to back up the story that Trump had been telling about the Moscow project—that it never amounted to anything, that the project was over by the time of the 2016 Iowa caucuses, and that Trump himself knew nothing about it. But once Mueller obtained Cohen's emails, he could tell that Cohen had lied to the congressional committees. In fact, Cohen had kept Trump regularly updated on the project, including about his conversations with Russian government officials, and the negotiations about the project continued well after January 2016. In other words, Cohen had made the same mistake as Roger Stone. He might not have committed an underlying crime, but he lied to Congress, which was a criminal offense.

As with Stone, then, the false statements gave Mueller important leverage. He could use the threat of prosecution to force Cohen to come clean about all his dealings with Trump and all his criminal activity. Cohen's complex and potentially incriminating financial dealings also gave prosecutors another point of potential leverage. In light of all this, Mueller went to Rod Rosenstein in October 2017 and asked for and received permission to investigate Cohen. Cohen was actually a far more important figure than Stone, because Cohen was much closer to Trump. Mueller also had leverage on Cohen because of the Stormy Daniels case. By his own public account, Cohen delivered $130,000 to Daniels on the eve of the 2016 election, to keep her quiet and thus to help Donald Trump win. It would not be a stretch to describe that money as a campaign contribution, and an illegal one.

The amount greatly exceeded what any individual could donate to a single campaign. Mueller could also use the threat of a prosecution for campaign finance charges to squeeze Cohen and find out what else he knew.

But that's not what the special counsel did. Instead, after receiving permission to investigate Cohen, Mueller gave the case away.

16

"A TOTAL WITCH HUNT!!!"

I t was a tough call—whether Mueller should keep or give away the investigation of Michael Cohen. It was obviously appropriate for *someone* to investigate whether Cohen had participated in an unlawful campaign contribution scheme to pay off Stormy Daniels. But which prosecutor? Was the case within Mueller's jurisdiction? Rosenstein had said Mueller could examine "any links and/or coordination between the Russian government and individuals associated with the campaign of President Donald Trump." Clearly, Daniels had nothing to do with Russia. But Rosenstein also said Mueller had the right to examine "any matters that arose or may arise directly from the investigation." Cohen's false statements to Congress about Trump's plans in Moscow plainly fell within Mueller's jurisdiction. But did the Daniels matter arise "directly" from Mueller's other work? As it happened, the Daniels story arose from the report in *The Wall Street Journal*. Would Rosenstein view a follow-up on a news report as a legitimate basis for expanding Mueller's jurisdiction? In addition, when Mueller's team reviewed Cohen's phone records and emails, they found evidence of possible financial misconduct, relating to his outside business interests. Who should investigate those matters? What if prosecutors could extract a guilty plea from Cohen on financial crimes and induce him to cooperate? Would Rosenstein find it relevant that pressure on Cohen, even on an unrelated matter, could help Mueller's Russia investigation?

As ever, Mueller's caution prevailed. The special counsel never

found out if Rosenstein would approve the expansion of his jurisdiction to include Cohen's financial misconduct and his preelection
payoff to Stormy Daniels, because Mueller never asked. Instead, with
the approval of his staff, the special counsel turned the Cohen investigation over to the Southern District of New York, the federal prosecutors based in Manhattan. They, in turn, went after Cohen with gusto,
uncovering a variety of misconduct, some involving Trump and some
unrelated to him.

It turned out that Cohen's assignment to protect Trump from bad
press went beyond his overture to Stormy Daniels. Indeed, Trump
had an entire network in place to prevent bad stories about his personal life from coming to light, and Cohen served as the facilitator
of the operation. In June 2016, Karen McDougal, the 1998 Playboy
Playmate of the Year, began shopping to tabloids the story of her relationship with Trump, which also began in 2006. Unlike the one-night
stand with Daniels, Trump and McDougal saw each other several
times over the course of about ten months. In the effort to keep the
stories under wraps, Cohen and Trump had an important ally, David
Pecker, who was the chief executive of American Media Inc. (AMI),
the parent company of the *National Enquirer.*

Pecker was like a more senior and successful version of Cohen, and
he somewhat resembled a friend of Trump's, rather than just a supplicant, but also one willing to do his bidding. Pecker and Trump met in
the early 1990s, when Pecker was in charge of the Hachette Filipacchi
magazine company. Pecker had created a custom-publishing division
at Hachette, producing magazines for clients who would dictate the
content and then distribute them to customers. He came up with the
idea of doing one about Donald Trump. Pecker had a home in Palm
Beach, not far from Mar-a-Lago, and a neighbor there introduced
him to Trump, who agreed to the project. The result was a magazine
called *Trump Style,* which today looks like a glossy preview of the
fawning coverage Pecker later gave Trump in his tabloids. Representative samples include "Trump Tower, with its bronze façade and swaths
of rose marble, combines New York City's most glittering destina-
tion with shops both popular and posh"; "40 and Fabulous: Donald
Trump's latest real estate venture, a landmark office building at 40
Wall Street, could not be in a better location"; "A weekend at Trump

Taj Mahal can't help but be an exhilarating exercise in glamour and fun."

In 1999, Pecker led an investment group that took control of the *Enquirer* and later the *Star* and virtually every other supermarket tabloid. By the time Trump ran for president, the circulation of the *Enquirer* was only around 300,000, down 90 percent from its heyday in the 1970s, but it remained a visible presence in American life, if only for the millions of people who saw the covers at the checkout counter. Throughout the 2016 campaign, the *Enquirer* embraced Trump with sycophantic fervor. The magazine made its first political endorsement ever, of Trump, in the spring of 2016. Cover headlines promised, "Donald Trump's Revenge on Hillary & Her Puppets" and "Top Secret Plan Inside: How Trump Will Win Debate!" The publication trashed Trump's rivals, running a dubious cover story on Ted Cruz that described him as a philanderer and another highly questionable piece that linked Cruz's father to the assassination of John F. Kennedy. Pecker later said that the *Enquirer*'s embrace of Trump was a business decision; pro-Trump covers sold well. But it was true, too, that Pecker wanted to help his friend become president.

Indeed, Pecker showed just how much he wanted to boost Trump in the summer of 2016, when McDougal put her story up for auction. Cohen urged Pecker to buy her account and then bury it—a practice known in the argot of tabloids as catch and kill. Cohen promised Pecker that Trump would reimburse AMI for the cost of McDougal's silence. According to Cohen's audio recording of a conversation with Trump, the deal was negotiated with input from Allen Weisselberg, the long-tenured chief financial officer of the Trump Organization. On the recording, Cohen says to Trump, "I've spoken to Allen Weisselberg about how to set the whole thing up with—" Trump interrupts: "So, what do we got to pay for this? One-fifty?" Cohen answers, "Yes."

In August 2016, AMI did buy McDougal's story for $150,000. True to his word, Pecker made sure that McDougal's relationship with Trump was never disclosed in the *Enquirer*. True to Trump's reputation, he never reimbursed Pecker; he never covered any of the fee paid to McDougal. At this point, Pecker and AMI became just another contractor whom Trump stiffed. Cohen received furious phone calls from Pecker about Trump's failure to pay the McDougal fee. He recalled that he would say to Pecker, "David, why are you yelling at me? Go yell at Trump." Still, Cohen had accomplished his mission of keeping Trump's relationship with McDougal out of the tabloids before the election. Two months later, even closer to Election Day, he accomplished the same goal with respect to Stormy Daniels.

The Southern District prosecutors took hold of the Cohen investigation in early 2018, and they quickly discovered, as Mueller's team had sensed, that Cohen had legal problems well beyond possibly illegal campaign contributions. Cohen's financial empire was still mostly based on taxi medallions, and their values had plummeted in recent years, thanks to the rise of Uber and other ride-sharing services. In response, Cohen made the classic mistakes of people in financial extremis: he lied to banks about his financial condition, and he didn't pay his taxes. The prosecutors took an especially aggressive tack, planning to obtain search warrants for Cohen's new law office, his apartment, and the hotel suite where his family was staying while the home was being renovated. As the FBI agent's affidavit stated, "The United States Attorney's Office for the Southern District of New York and FBI are investigating, among other things, schemes by Target Subject Michael Cohen (a) to defraud multiple banks from in or about 2016 up to and including the present, and (b) to make an illegal campaign contribution in October 2016 to then-presidential candidate Donald Trump."

The affidavit was both monumental—268 pages—and devastating. It revealed that Cohen owed $22 million to banks on loans related to his medallions, and it cataloged the myriad ways he had hidden his true financial condition. Through false statements to the banks, the affidavit stated, "Cohen avoided making monthly payments on his loans, and attempted to fraudulently induce the banks to relieve him of certain repayment obligations and personal guarantees that Cohen and his wife had signed." The affidavit's several references to Cohen's wife were especially ominous, because they raised the prospect of possible charges against her as well.

Using evidence from his emails and texts, the affidavit provided a nearly minute-by-minute reconstruction of how Cohen engineered the $130,000 payment to Stormy Daniels/Stephanie Clifford. At this point in the FBI's investigation, in early 2018, Cohen was still taking the position in public that he, and not Trump, had funded the deal with her. As the affidavit noted, there was some evidence to support that version of the facts. On October 26, Cohen transferred $131,000 from his own home equity line of credit to Essential Consultants, the shell company he had just created. The next day, the affidavit continued, Cohen wired $130,000 to Daniels's attorney, "with the funds intended for Clifford—for the purpose of securing her ongoing silence with respect to the allegations that she had an extramarital affair with Trump." In sum, according to the FBI agent, there was probable cause to believe that "Cohen made this payment to Clifford for the purpose of influencing the presidential election, and therefore that the payment was an excessive in-kind contribution to the Trump campaign."

At the time, Jay Sekulow was by default the stopgap lead defense counsel for Trump, and as such he represented the president in all dealings with Mueller. In that capacity, on April 9, Sekulow was heading to a meeting at Patriots Plaza, when his phone buzzed with major breaking news: the FBI had just executed search warrants at the home and business of Michael Cohen. To handle the fallout, and especially his client's reaction, Sekulow canceled the meeting with Mueller.

The comprehensive search of Cohen's home and office was an extraordinarily aggressive move on the part of the Southern District prosecutors. Searches of attorneys' offices are rare; when investigators rummage among lawyers' possessions, they risk seeing material that should be protected by attorney-client privilege. Accordingly, Justice Department policy calls for U.S. Attorney's offices to obtain permission from Main Justice in Washington before seeking search warrants for attorneys. The prosecutors in Manhattan followed the rule, and the criminal division gave permission for the Cohen raids. The Southern District justified initiating a search of Cohen's properties, as opposed to issuing grand jury subpoenas to him, on the ground that Cohen would destroy documents if he was alerted to the investigation. Rosenstein was given a heads-up that the criminal division had approved the search, and he, in turn, alerted Jeff Sessions on the morning of April 9. Anticipating Trump's reaction, Rosenstein told his boss, "Monday's going to be a bad day."

Rosenstein was right. More than any other event—more than Mueller's appointment, Flynn's guilty plea, or Manafort's indictment—the execution of the Cohen search warrants ignited Trump's paranoia and rage. His initial reaction came, of course, on Twitter. "Attorney-client privilege is dead!" . . . "A TOTAL WITCH HUNT!!!" . . . "Attorney Client privilege is now a thing of the past. I have many (too many!) lawyers and they are probably wondering when their offices, and even homes, are going to be raided with everything, including their phones and computers, taken. All lawyers are deflated and concerned!" After the *Times* ran a profile of Cohen, following the raid, Trump unleashed a three-part Twitter epic that underlined his anger about the situation. "The New York Times and a third rate reporter named Maggie Habberman [*sic*], known as a Crooked H flunkie who I don't speak to and have nothing to do with, are going out of their way to destroy Michael Cohen and his relationship with me in the hope that he will 'flip.' They use . . . non-existent 'sources' and a drunk/drugged up loser who hates Michael, a fine person with a wonderful family. Michael is a businessman for his own account/lawyer who I have always liked & respected. Most people will flip if the Government lets them out of trouble, even if . . . it means lying or making up stories. Sorry, I don't see Michael doing that despite the horrible Witch Hunt and the dishonest media!" Trump knew enough about the criminal justice system to recognize the Cohen raid for what it was—a massive show of force designed to convince Cohen that resistance was futile and that pleading guilty was his only option. Trump's first public comment, other than on Twitter, underscored his concern that Cohen might flip. "I just heard they broke into the office of one of my personal attorneys, a good man, and it's a disgraceful situation," he said.

Still, what Trump didn't know, and what the breathless news coverage of the Cohen raid didn't recognize, was that the Southern District's investigation of Michael Cohen . . . was an investigation of Michael Cohen. It was not, and never would be, an investigation of Donald Trump. The prosecutors in New York showed the same caution and restraint that Mueller's team displayed in Washington. It's almost part of the DNA of experienced prosecutors to tread carefully beyond areas where they can identify specific criminal behavior. This was why Trump's repeated invocations of the Democratic affiliations of Mueller's staff, while understandable, missed the point.

More important than the political inclinations of Mueller's team was their professional training as prosecutors, and those honed instincts limited their ambitions. The same was true for the prosecutors in New York. Notwithstanding the rumors (and the hopes of Trump's political opponents), the Southern District prosecutors never sought or obtained Trump's tax returns or subpoenaed his financial records, at Deutsche Bank or anywhere else. Their reluctance to delve into Trump's behavior or finances was heightened, too, by the Office of Legal Counsel opinions barring prosecution of a sitting president. If the Southern District couldn't bring charges against Trump anyway, the thinking went, there was no point in examining his behavior—especially since none of it, on the surface, looked criminal.

Trump himself, on the other hand, saw the Cohen raid as more than just another unfair attack on him, but rather as part of a continuum of harassment that he had experienced since he won the election. The president believed that the deep state—or, as he sometimes called it, the "Crooked and Demented Deep State"—had mobilized against him from day one. Comey of the FBI turned on him even before the inauguration. John Brennan, Obama's director of the CIA, became a harsh critic on MSNBC. ("Deep state henchman," Trump called Brennan.) Sessions's recusal opened the door for Rosenstein to appoint Mueller, who in turn set the "13 angry Democrats" against him. As for Don McGahn, the "lying bastard" who was his White House counsel, he was McConnell's man, an establishment figure, a favorite of *The New York Times;* all that, in Trump's view, was why McGahn turned against him.

Now, with the Cohen case, Trump thought that the Southern District was also revealing itself to be a deep state outpost. Trump had fired Preet Bharara, the previous U.S. Attorney there, after promising to keep him on. As president, Trump then took the unusual step of interviewing the man who became his replacement, Geoffrey Berman. (Presidents rarely interview U.S. Attorney candidates.) But Berman recused himself from the Cohen investigation (for still-unexplained reasons), which meant that the case was supervised by his deputy, Robert Khuzami, who had been an Obama-era appointee to a top job at the Securities and Exchange Commission. In other words, as the president saw it, the two Trump appointees who should have been protecting him—Sessions and Berman—had recused themselves and left him to the mercies of the deep state. Of course, implicit in Trump's theory of the deep state was that he had never done anything to deserve the scrutiny of the FBI, the CIA, or the Justice Department. For Trump, his own blamelessness was a given.

The Cohen search was a kind of last straw for the president. Under the guidance of Cobb and Dowd, the president had tried accommodation. The two lawyers believed that their strategy reflected confidence in their client. Cobb and Dowd thought Trump had done nothing wrong, and thus had nothing to hide. That's why they preached cooperation; they trusted Mueller to reach the same conclusion. But Trump was both temperamentally and politically unsuited to that kind of strategy, which he thought only encouraged ever more aggressive attacks from his enemies. His entire philosophy of government— indeed, his approach to life—was to answer every slight, respond to every provocation, with even greater ferocity. Throughout the campaign, and in his first year in office, many people around Trump had advised him to dial back his aggression, take the high road, be more "presidential." He never did.

And when Trump was told to behave in a more conventionally palatable manner, he was also instructed to surround himself with more "grown-ups," more Washington insiders. He did, at first—people like Reince Priebus, his first chief of staff; Rex Tillerson, his first secretary of state; and H. R. McMaster, who succeeded Michael Flynn as national security adviser. The story of Trump's first year in office was, in many ways, how he liberated himself from the need to follow this advice. He would act as he pleased and hire whom he wanted. After the Cohen searches, Trump thought it was time, at last, for a lawyer who shared his instincts. So Dowd was out; Cobb was heading that way. Trump hated weakness, and his lawyers were weak. They didn't fight back. No one ever answered the question he asked all the time. Where's my Roy Cohn? *Where's my Roy Cohn?*

Finally, on April 19, 2018, ten days after the FBI swarmed into Michael Cohen's office and home, Trump answered his own question. He hired Rudolph Giuliani as his lead defense attorney.

17

"Truth Isn't Truth"

Rudy Giuliani remembered with clarity the first time he took notice of Donald Trump. It was 1986, and the City of New York had spent years trying, without success, to renovate Wollman Skating Rink in Central Park. Trump, who had started to draw public notice as a developer, volunteered to complete the project in just four months, at a lower price than the city was proposing to pay. The forty-year-old real estate scion was as good as his word, and his success with the project embarrassed Ed Koch, the city's mayor. Still, Koch had to invite Trump to the rink's reopening ceremony. Giuliani was the U.S. Attorney for the Southern District at the time and planning his own run for mayor. At the event, Trump announced that he thought the rink should be renamed in his honor, which blindsided and enraged Koch and led to an enduring feud between the two men. Giuliani, on the other hand, loved Trump's bravado and enlisted him as a major supporter in his runs for mayor—a defeat in 1989 and victories in 1993 and 1997.

The two men had much in common. They were peers and New Yorkers, both born on the cusp of the baby boom: Giuliani in 1944, Trump in 1946. Giuliani grew up in a working-class family in Brooklyn, and Trump was raised in rarefied splendor in Queens, but the city shaped them both. Their shared formative era was the 1980s, when New York was recovering its verve and prosperity after near bankruptcy in the 1970s. Both men thrived under the scrutiny of the city's tabloids, which chronicled Giuliani's crime fighting and Trump's

tower building. Both men had complicated personal lives, each, ultimately, with three marriages. They were also both so immersed in
their careers and public roles that they had little inclination for what
others would call friendships; they had alliances, including one with
each other. In one way, though, there was an authentically intimate
bond between them. Giuliani announced his second divorce at a press
conference toward the end of his mayoralty, without first informing
his wife. The ugliness of that split soured relations between Giuliani
and his teenage son, Andrew. After the divorce, Trump made Andrew
a kind of surrogate son, as well as a frequent golf partner, and he
encouraged him to resume contact with his father—earning enduring
gratitude from Rudy. Andrew later went to work for Trump in the
White House.

The closest link between Trump and Giuliani was stylistic; both
men made aggression and attention seeking their hallmarks. As U.S.
Attorney, Giuliani won plaudits for prosecuting insider trading on
Wall Street and for his relentless pursuit of the Mafia. He racked up
more than four thousand convictions, including those of Ivan Boesky
and of four of the five heads of the New York Mafia families. But he
was also criticized for his practice of "perp walking"—marching white-
collar criminals, in handcuffs, through the financial district, often in
front of reporters who had been alerted in advance. He sometimes
arrested people in their workplaces and then dropped the charges,
seemingly as a way to intimidate them and send a message to associates. He drew ridicule for donning a leather jacket to make a supposedly undercover drug purchase in Washington Heights. Giuliani's
obsession with self-promotion, and his skill at it, rivaled Trump's.

After Giuliani became mayor, his performance in office served in
some ways as a prototype for Trump's during his presidency. Giuliani
radiated belligerence, racial animus, and cultural grievance. His overtures to outer-borough white people anticipated Trump's appeals
to their midwestern counterparts. Giuliani made the fight against
street crime and disorder (especially the "squeegee men" who offered
unsought window washes at intersections) the touchstones of his tenure. He oversaw a police crackdown that was associated with plunging
crime rates, and was reelected in a landslide, in 1997. Giuliani defi-
antly stood up for New York cops accused of killing unarmed black

men, as Trump would during his presidency. In a city that values free expression, he had little appreciation for the First Amendment, and courts repeatedly slapped him down. Outraged by a painting at the Brooklyn Museum by Chris Ofili, which depicted a black Virgin Mary and incorporated lumps of dried elephant dung, he began withholding the museum's city subsidies and threatening to terminate its lease, remove its board, and possibly seize the property. Trump's denunciations of the press as "enemies of the people" and his ridicule of football players who kneeled for the national anthem tracked the ideological grooves that Giuliani laid down.

Trump's and Giuliani's careers moved in a sort of counterpoint to each other. During Giuliani's two terms as mayor in the 1990s, Trump endured his first rounds of bankruptcy, after the failures of his casinos in Atlantic City. Later in the decade, though, Trump's fortunes revived when he began licensing his name for various consumer products. At the same time, Giuliani was unpopular, even discredited in the city, before September 11, 2001. Then, however, his resolute leadership in the aftermath of the attacks made him a worldwide symbol of resistance to terrorism. He arrived at the World Trade Center just after the second plane hit and was nearly trapped at the site. Afterward, while President George W. Bush was largely silent, he reassured the rattled country. "Tomorrow New York is going to be here," Giuliani said. "And we're going to rebuild, and we're going to be stronger than we were before." *Time* named him Person of the Year, and Queen Elizabeth II bestowed an honorary knighthood on him. Trump's fortunes declined again, in the post-9/11 downturn, while Giuliani parlayed his fame into prosperity. In 2001, Giuliani claimed that he had just $7,000 in assets. In 2002, he set up a security-consulting business and began giving speeches around the world. By the time he embarked on his presidential run, in 2007, he estimated his wealth at more than $30 million. But Giuliani's campaign was an abject failure, and by that point Trump had begun starring in *The Apprentice* and his celebrity and fortune were restored.

The final turn came in 2016. Giuliani threw himself into Trump's campaign for president, traveling on the candidate's plane and serving as his warm-up act on the campaign trail. When the *Access Hollywood* story broke, and several campaign aides wanted Trump to withdraw, Giuliani was the only top official who agreed to defend the candidate on the Sunday shows. (With typical ingratitude, Trump denounced Giuliani's performance, telling him, "Man, Rudy, you sucked. You were weak. Low energy.") Nevertheless, at his election night celebration, Trump thanked Giuliani by name. Giuliani's service on the campaign failed to persuade Trump to give him what he really wanted—the position of secretary of state. Giuliani asserted that he turned down Trump's offers of the leadership of the Justice Department and the Department of Homeland Security—others disputed that the offers were made—but one thing was clear: when Trump took office, Giuliani was on the outside.

In fact, Giuliani spent the first year of Trump's presidency at loose ends. He maintained his security-consulting business but took a leave from his affiliation with his law firm. He began divorce proceedings with his third wife, Judith Nathan, and the split proved to be as contentious as the second one. Increasingly, Giuliani didn't go to an office at all, but instead held court at the Grand Havana Room, the cigar bar located on the top floor of Jared Kushner's 666 Fifth Avenue, the one also favored by Paul Manafort. On those days, Giuliani sat with soft drinks or cocktails amid the overstuffed armchairs, the oversized ashtrays, and the persistent haze of smoke. He would sink into a chair, pull the knot of his tie down to his chest, and remove a Padrón fiftieth-anniversary cigar (retail price: $40) from a carrying case. At seventy-four, Giuliani looked weary. He limped. He surrendered his comb-over to full-on baldness, and as his torso thickened, his neck disappeared. He lit the Padróns with a high-tech flame lighter—"good for the golf course," he said. (He was a member of eleven country clubs.)

What Giuliani was really doing in the clouds of cigar smoke was waiting for the call, which he finally received from the president in April 2018. Giuliani not only agreed to serve as Trump's defense attorney but said he would do it for no fee. This generosity might have been due, at least in part, to his desire to lower his current income so that he would have to pay less following his latest divorce. (Always happy to save money, Trump had no objection to being a pro bono client.) But it was true, too, that Giuliani worked for free because he was so hungry to return to the action.

—

At times, in the months after Giuliani took over Trump's defense, it looked as if he had no plan at all. He made wild and intemperate statements. He made mistakes, or to put it less charitably, he lied. He appeared on television frequently, usually with Sean Hannity of Fox News, but also occasionally on CNN. Giuliani's television performances were so bizarre that they prompted some observers to ask whether he had been drinking. "I'm not drinking for lunch," Giuliani said in an interview with *Politico*. "I may have a drink for dinner. I like to drink with cigars."

Giuliani set the tone in one of his first television appearances as Trump's lawyer, on Hannity's show. In a rambling interview, in language that was anything but lawyerly, he said that Hillary Clinton was a "criminal," Comey was a "very perverted man," and Jared Kushner was "disposable." He asserted that if Mueller tried to interview Ivanka Trump—"a fine woman"—the country would turn against him. Giuliani also made some real news about the Stormy Daniels matter during the Hannity appearance. At the time, Trump's position was the one he had expressed in the interview on Air Force One; he was denying any knowledge of Michael Cohen's $130,000 payment to the porn actress. Likewise, Cohen's position was still that he had paid Daniels out of his own pocket and was never reimbursed by anyone. But in this interview, Giuliani completely changed Trump's version of what happened. "I'm giving you a fact now that you don't know. It's not campaign money. No campaign finance violation. . . . They funneled through a law firm, and the president repaid it." *The president repaid it?*

Hannity gulped in astonishment and sputtered, "Oh. I didn't know that. He did?" The Fox News stalwart was never one for tough questions to Trump allies like Giuliani, but even he had to ask, didn't the president just say that he didn't know about the payment to Daniels? And now you're saying that he reimbursed Cohen for the full $130,000?

"Ah, he didn't know about the specifics of it, as far as I know," Giuliani answered. "But he did know about the general arrangement, that Michael would take care of things like this. Like, I take care of this with my clients. I don't burden them with every single thing that comes along. These are busy people. The settlement payment . . . is a very regular thing for lawyers to do."

This was, at one level, madness. Giuliani just blithely changed the president's position on a critical factual issue. He exposed that the president lied on Air Force One when he was asked about the payments to Daniels. As later became clear, Trump had reimbursed Cohen in a series of checks that he signed after he became president. (Even though Trump repaid Cohen from his own personal funds, the negotiations about the payment took place between Cohen and Allen Weisselberg, the longtime chief financial officer of the Trump Organization. In keeping with the general ethical tenor of the parties, Cohen lied about his expenses in order to extract an additional $50,000 from Trump.) Even more bizarrely, Giuliani told Hannity that Trump's payments to Cohen were "a very regular thing." Giuliani said he had handled similar matters for clients himself. But it is not normal, or even permissible, for lawyers to pay their clients' judgments out of their own pockets. (This assertion prompted Giuliani's law firm to cut its remaining ties to him.)

But there was a kind of method to Giuliani's approach. He understood, as Dowd and Cobb did not, that the struggle between Trump and Mueller was essentially political, not legal. In the current, polarized political environment, Giuliani could make any claim he wanted on Trump's behalf, and it would be embraced by the president's supporters, like Hannity. It made sense, then, to get the real story of the Stormy Daniels payments out in public. Giuliani had to get the truth out because he knew that Cohen might flip, and Trump's checks to Cohen reimbursing him for the money paid to Daniels might be revealed at some point (as they were). In light of this, Giuliani thought he should get ahead of the story. He never had to worry about Trump's supporters criticizing the president for flip-flopping, or lying, because his supporters never criticized him for anything.

As Trump's lead attorney, Giuliani was responsible for defending him in a complex series of overlapping investigations—of his campaign's connections to Russia, of possible obstruction of justice in the White House, and of the hush money payments to Daniels and McDougal. But Giuliani never even bothered to learn the facts of the cases, preferring instead to bluster off the top of his head. One of the key questions in the obstruction of justice inquiry was whether Trump encouraged Comey to go easy on Michael Flynn when the national security adviser was under investigation for lying to the FBI. At first, Giuliani acknowledged that Trump had asked Comey to give Flynn "a break." Later, he denied that Trump even discussed Flynn with Comey. Giuliani's comments about the Trump Tower meeting in June 2016, between campaign officials and the Russian attorney Natalia Veselnitskaya, similarly devolved into falsehoods. In an appearance on *Meet the Press,* Giuliani asserted that the campaign officials, including Kushner and Donald Trump Jr., "didn't know she was a representative of the Russian government, and, indeed, she's not a representative of the Russian government, so this is much ado about nothing." The email that led to the meeting, sent to Trump junior, explicitly said that the gathering was "part of Russia and its government's support for Mr. Trump."

For Giuliani, these details, otherwise known as facts, were not the point; aggression was. Giuliani thought (as did Trump) that the most important objective was always to stay on offense against their enemies. On Hannity and elsewhere, Giuliani adopted the president's characterization of the Mueller investigation as a "witch hunt." He denounced the president's pursuers as "thugs" and worse. As for the FBI agents who searched Cohen's home and office, Giuliani called them "storm troopers," comparing federal law enforcement officials to Nazis—a remarkable statement coming from a former U.S. Attorney. (Cohen said that the agents were "extremely professional, courteous, and respectful.") With no evidence, Giuliani accused Mueller of leaking to the press. He argued, again on no evidence, that Attorney General Sessions should appoint a special counsel to investigate Mueller. "Investigate the 'investigation and investigators,'" he tweeted. "Unlike the illegal Mueller appointment you will be able to cite, as law requires, alleged crimes." As ever, Mueller responded to these attacks with silence.

Giuliani turned representation of Trump into identification with him. This was, perhaps, unsurprising in light of the long ties between the two men. But Giuliani recognized what worked for Trump—insults, diversions, lies—could work for him as well. And it did work. Giuliani, in a very determined way, sought to turn Mueller into just another Trump enemy, just another Democrat (even though Mueller is a Republican). When Mueller was appointed, polls showed bipartisan support for him, but after Giuliani's attacks public opinion about the special counsel divided along the same partisan lines as on any other issue. Giuliani brought Mueller down to his level—and Trump's. Giuliani's apotheosis—the moment that best summed up his service to the president—came on *Meet the Press*. Giuliani had said that one reason Trump might not do an interview with Mueller was that the prosecutor might set a "perjury trap." But Chuck Todd, the host, asked Giuliani whether a perjury trap could even exist, since a witness who told the truth couldn't be trapped. Giuliani responded, "When you tell me that, you know, he should testify because he's going to tell the truth and he shouldn't worry, well that's so silly because it's somebody's version of the truth. Not the truth."

Todd responded, "Truth is truth."

"No, it isn't truth," Giuliani said. "Truth isn't truth."

Indeed, starting in the spring of 2018, when Giuliani took over, he and Trump fed on each other. With Cobb on his way out, Trump viewed his promise to refrain from attacking Mueller as no longer operative. After not mentioning Mueller on Twitter for nearly a year, Trump started going after him daily. He added Mueller to his other favorite targets, including Sessions and Rosenstein, who remained in the Trump administration and also silent in the face of his repeated attacks. The president's solicitude for Putin's Russia remained a constant, as in this tweet: "Much of the bad blood with Russia is caused by the Fake & Corrupt Russia Investigation, headed up by the all Democrat loyalists, or people that worked for Obama. Mueller is most conflicted of all (except Rosenstein who signed FISA & Comey letter). No Collusion, so they go crazy!" Another regular Trump theme was that Mueller had conflicts of interest (which he didn't) and should actually investigate Hillary Clinton (which he couldn't): "No Collusion and No Obstruction, except by Crooked Hillary and the Democrats. All of the resignations and corruption, yet heavily conflicted Bob Mueller refuses to even look in that direction. What about the Brennan, Comey, McCabe, Strzok lies to Congress, or Crooked's Emails!"

Still another Trump obsession, perhaps his greatest, was the extramarital relationship between the FBI agent Peter Strzok and Lisa Page, the bureau lawyer. It was back in the summer of 2017 that Mueller removed Strzok from his investigation after his text messages, some critical of Trump, were revealed to the public. But not only months later but *years* later, Trump was still mocking them in lewd and cruel ways. In campaign speeches, he did breathless reenactments of sexual encounters between the two "lovers," as he always referred to them. But in this first spasm of partisanship, in mid-2018, Trump contented himself with tweets, like this one: "Universities will someday study what highly conflicted (and NOT Senate approved) Bob Mueller and his gang of Democrat thugs have done to destroy people. Why is he protecting Crooked Hillary, Comey, McCabe, Lisa Page & her lover, Peter S, and all of his friends on the other side? . . . care how many lives the [*sic*] ruin. These are Angry People, including the highly conflicted Bob Mueller, who worked for Obama for 8 years. They won't even look at all of the bad acts and crimes on the other side. A TOTAL WITCH HUNT LIKE NO OTHER IN AMERICAN HISTORY!" Mueller, though, became Trump's main target: "Bob Mueller (who is a much different man than people think) and his out of control band of Angry Democrats, don't want the truth, they only want lies. The truth is very bad for their mission!"

Inside Patriots Plaza, Mueller and his staff did their best to ignore the onslaught from the president. No one enjoyed the assaults, but there was a fatalistic understanding that nothing could be done about them. To the extent there was any reaction at all, black humor predominated. Mueller never issued a formal edict banning his staff members from socializing with outsiders, but in light of all the attention, and their obligation to keep quiet about their work, some prosecutors found it easier to relax together. Jeannie Rhee hosted occasional small groups for beers on the weekends, and for one her husband tried to lighten the mood by printing up baseball caps for Jeannie and Andrew Weissmann: "Angry Dem #1" and "Angry Dem #2." Because of his greater notoriety, Weissmann received the cap marked number one.

But Trump's open hostility toward Mueller started to have real effects. For starters, as liaison with Mueller, Trump replaced Ty Cobb with Emmet Flood, a partner at the Williams & Connolly law firm. Flood welcomed the assignment of ending Cobb's era of cooperation with Mueller. Flood's law firm was famous for presenting uncompromising defenses, as well as making repeated, and sometimes unfounded, accusations of prosecutorial misconduct. By the middle of 2018, Cobb had already completed document production from the White House, and most administration officials had given interviews to Mueller's team. So Flood had a limited ability to interfere with Mueller's investigation. Flood had a decorous and buttoned-up personality and style, and he didn't give interviews or go on Twitter tirades. But the message to Mueller of Flood's appointment was as clear as one of Trump's tweets: the special counsel would never again receive any cooperation from the White House.

Another change in the Giuliani era was harder to measure but even more important. It's a myth that defendants plead guilty, agree to cooperate, or even just start to tell the truth because they have attacks of conscience or religious awakenings. They do so because they believe the alternatives would be worse for them. To cite the most obvious example, defendants plead guilty and cooperate because they think that going to trial will result in a conviction and a longer sentence. For this reason, prosecutors thrive on fear. Without fear, defendants—even ordinary witnesses—feel emboldened to challenge and defy prosecutors. However, a president who is under investigation has a unique ability to remove the element of fear for those who might be witnesses against him. A president can issue pardons.

In all modern Washington scandals, no president ever dared even hint in public that he would pardon prospective witnesses against him. In one of the most notorious Nixon White House tapes, the president and John Dean weighed the possibility of a pardon for E. Howard Hunt, one of the Watergate burglars. "Hunt's now demanding clemency or he's going to blow. And politically, it'd be impossible for you to do it," Dean said. ("Clemency" is another word for pardon.) Nixon agreed: "That's right." Dean continued, "I'm not sure that you'll ever be able to deliver on clemency. It may be just too hot." Nixon then replied, "You can't do it until after the [1974] elections, that's for sure." In other words, even Nixon and Dean understood that the prospect of a pardon for a figure in a White House scandal violated every political, legal, and moral norm.

Here, again, Trump and Giuliani revised the unwritten rules governing presidential conduct. Soon after he began representing the president, Giuliani began telling reporters that Trump was considering pardons for people involved in the Russia scandal. "When the whole thing is over, things might get cleaned up with some presidential pardons," Giuliani said in one interview. Around the same time, Trump started talking about pardons, including for himself, as in this tweet: "As has been stated by numerous legal scholars, I have the absolute right to PARDON myself, but why would I do that when I have done nothing wrong? In the meantime, the never ending Witch Hunt, led by 13 very Angry and Conflicted Democrats (& others) continues into the mid-terms!" Even before Giuliani came on board, Trump had dangled the possibility of a pardon for Michael Flynn, too: "I don't want to talk about pardons for Michael Flynn yet. We'll see what happens. Let's see. I can say this: When you look at what's gone on with the FBI and with the Justice Department, people are very, very angry." In a similar comment, Trump opened the door to a pardon for Paul Manafort as well.

Prosecutors in complex white-collar investigations make progress in one way—by persuading targets to plead guilty and cooperate against higher-ups. The plea by Rick Gates, Manafort's deputy, was an important step for Mueller in that vein. But the special counsel's team needed more people to flip—among them, Manafort himself, Flynn, Cohen, and Roger Stone. But after Trump and Giuliani started talking about pardons, their discussions of cooperating stalled, or never started in the first place. In all, then, Giuliani might have sometimes looked silly on television, but he delivered real accomplishments for his client: he set loose the president to turn the Republican base against Mueller; he used pardon talk to shut down the pipeline of cooperators; he cleaned up the facts of the Stormy Daniels situation so the president was not continuing to defend a false version of what transpired. As 2018 began, Mueller's investigation was soaring as indictments and guilty pleas mounted. Just a couple of months after Giuliani took charge, Mueller's work was stalled, and it never recovered its momentum. For this, Giuliani deserves a large measure of credit or blame, depending on one's perspective.

By May 2018, when Mueller completed his first year on the job, he was no longer perceived as the hero, with bipartisan acclaim, that he had been when Rosenstein named him. Trump and Giuliani had gone to war against Mueller, and that opened the way for attacks from every corner of the Republican universe. Some of the criticism of Mueller even came from his old friends, like William Barr.

Nearly three decades earlier, Barr had been the attorney general for the last year or so of George H. W. Bush's term, and Bob Mueller was the assistant attorney general in charge of the criminal division—one of his top advisers. They met daily, and became friends, but they were always very different personalities, and they came at issues in different ways. Barr came from the Office of Legal Counsel—the constitutional voice of the department—and he was focused on big conservative ideas, especially about the need to protect the prerogatives of the president against congressional encroachment. Barr focused on the big picture, and he was more enmeshed in political combat with Democrats than was Mueller. As a Republican political appointee, Mueller was a member of Barr's team, but he was more comfortable discussing the details of his investigations than engaging in partisan conflict with Democrats. His prosecutions rarely had an obvious political dimension. Barr, who began his legal career at the CIA, twitted the former marine about his dour earnestness. After Bush lost, the two men went their separate ways. Mueller stayed in law enforcement, first as a line prosecutor in Washington and then as Bill Clinton's U.S. Attorney in San Francisco and ultimately as FBI director. Barr went into corporate law, first as general counsel to GTE, the telephone company, which became Verizon; he left in 2008 with about $28 million in deferred compensation. Barr mostly just dabbled at that point, serving on corporate boards, supporting Catholic charities, working part time at Kirkland & Ellis, an elite stronghold for conservative lawyers, and joining the rightward drift of the Republican Party. He and Mueller stayed friends, if not close ones. They went to the same Christmas parties, and their wives attended the same Bible study class. While Mueller was leading the FBI and then the special counsel's office, Barr was mostly at home, stewing about the immoral, disorderly drift of American government and society.

For those who knew Barr, especially in recent years, his letter of June 8, 2018, was not a great surprise. On that day, he delivered a nineteen-page single-spaced memorandum of roughly eight thousand words to Rosenstein and Steven Engel, who had Barr's old job, leading the Justice Department's Office of Legal Counsel. Even the subject line—"Mueller's 'Obstruction' Theory"—dripped with contempt for his old friend. It was the work, first of all, of a man with a lot of time on his hands, but also one who had deep and fundamental disagreements with how the special counsel was doing his job. "I am writing as a former official deeply concerned with the institutions of the Presidency and the Department of Justice. I realize that I am in the dark about many facts, but I hope my views may be useful," it began. The gist was that much of Mueller's investigation was illegitimate. Barr said that Trump's decision to fire Comey—for any reason, or no reason—was within his power as president, and it should not be the basis for an obstruction of justice investigation. Barr said Mueller's possible attempt to subpoena testimony from Trump was similarly unconstitutional. Mueller's approach to the investigation, Barr wrote, "would have grave consequences far beyond the immediate confines of this case and would do lasting damage to the Presidency and to the administration of law within the Executive branch."

Barr's memorandum drew polite acknowledgments from its two recipients, who knew Barr only as a respected figure from the distant past of the Justice Department. As Barr acknowledged in the document, he had no inside knowledge of Mueller's investigation, either about the facts he had uncovered or about the legal theories he was pursuing. Accordingly, Barr's memorandum was mostly useful as an insight into the former attorney general's own state of mind and the growing hostility to Mueller within Republican circles. When Trump ran for president, many formerly high-ranking Republican officials identified themselves as "never Trumpers." Barr traveled in never-Trump circles; in 2016, he gave more than $400,000 to super PACs supporting Jeb Bush before he made a token contribution to Trump. But like the Republican Party as a whole, once Trump became president, Barr became an enthusiastic convert to his cause—not least because Trump and Giuliani succeeded in making Mueller's investigation the defining partisan issue of the moment.

Despite his sometimes cartoonish television appearances, Giuliani had the stature to command a room, which he did on his first visit to Patriots Plaza. After Dowd's departure from Trump's defense team, Sekulow asked Quarles for a time-out in all negotiations, including over the prosecutors' demand for an interview with Trump. Sekulow said he wanted to get a new lead lawyer on board before any major decisions were made. Giuliani came on in April, and it took several more weeks to arrange a meeting. At last the summit was arranged, on May 5, and the lawyers filled both sides of a long conference table in Mueller's suite. Mueller was flanked by Quarles, Dreeben, and Andrew Goldstein. Giuliani faced him, with Sekulow and Jane and Marty Raskin by his side. There was no doubt who led each team—Mueller and Giuliani.

Trump's team had requested the meeting as a get-acquainted session for Giuliani as the new lead counsel. Giuliani wanted to nail down Mueller's commitment that he would follow the OLC policy barring indictments of sitting presidents. Aaron Zebley volunteered that Mueller would.

The subject, as ever, returned to Mueller's request for an interview with Trump. The issue had remained on hold since Dowd canceled the planned Camp David session in January. Then there was another delay when Dowd left and Giuliani came on board.

Perhaps, Giuliani offered, their team might agree to allow the president to answer written questions, but maybe only about his actions during the campaign. Trump's behavior as president would remain off-limits, Giuliani said. Everything he did as president was covered by executive privilege. Not so, said Mueller. They went back and forth.

Finally, Giuliani called the question. *What are you going to do? Are you going to subpoena the president?*

It was the most important decision of Mueller's tenure as special counsel—and maybe of his entire career. The legal fate of a subpoena was uncertain. The Supreme Court could say he had no right to question Trump. But the Court might say that Mueller did have the right to question Trump under oath. And given the president's track record, it was close to certain that he would lie—about big and small things. The Trump examination would certainly be the climax of his investigation, just as Clinton's testimony was the high point of Starr's. But Mueller didn't want to be Starr, and he didn't want to wait around anywhere as long as Starr did to conclude his investigation. Mueller had pondered the question for months. His legal team had analyzed the issue from every angle. Their memos ran to dozens of pages. But the decision was his. So what was his answer to Giuliani about the subpoena?

"We'll get back to you," Mueller said. More weeks passed.

18

"There's Tears in Your Eyes"

I n addition to the constant stream of attacks from Trump and Giuliani, as well as the looming threat of pardons, the Mueller team faced another major challenge in the spring of 2018—an actual trial, perhaps two of them. The special counsel had indicted Paul Manafort for a series of related crimes—bank fraud, money laundering, tax evasion, illegal lobbying—in Washington and Virginia. Because Manafort's lawyers refused to waive venue and agree to a single trial, he would have two. Manafort was indicted first in Washington, but in keeping with the speedy customs of the "rocket docket" in Arlington, the first trial would be there—in the courtroom of Judge T. S. Ellis III, a seventy-eight-year-old Ronald Reagan appointee.

For Mueller, the stakes were enormous. He had won guilty pleas from Flynn and Papadopoulos, and he had indicted more than a score of Russians (who were unlikely ever to appear in an American courtroom) in the social media and hacking cases, but the office of the special counsel had never before tried a case to a jury. An acquittal would both shatter Mueller's image and lead to calls to shut down his investigation altogether. A conviction, on the other hand, represented his best chance to break open the case. If Manafort were to be convicted in either Virginia or Washington, or especially both, he would be looking at a great deal of time in prison. At that point, cooperation might be Manafort's only route out of an effective life sentence. As his team prepared for trial, Mueller did have one important advantage. Rick Gates, Manafort's deputy, had pleaded guilty and decided to cooperate against his former boss. With a star witness in place, Mueller had even less reason to lose, which made the prospect of a not-guilty verdict even more calamitous.

Both indictments against Manafort related to his lobbying and consulting work in Ukraine, starting in 2005. In a nutshell, the cases were based on accusations that Manafort earned millions of dollars in Ukraine and hid the transactions from U.S. tax and banking authorities. He was also charged with lobbying in the United States for the government of Ukraine and failing to register as a lobbyist. Framed in this way, the cases had nothing to do with Manafort's work for the Trump campaign. In fact, the charges were intimately bound up with the rest of Mueller's investigation. For starters, the indictments charged that Manafort continued to commit these crimes while he was chairing Trump's campaign. More important, the cases raised the fundamental question of which side Manafort was really on. Manafort made his millions from pro-Putin forces within the Ukrainian political system. What did they want from him in the Trump campaign? What did they get from him—and from Trump? The trials might begin to provide the answers.

In the trial in Virginia, Mueller's team faced a formidable obstacle— the partisanship and incompetence of Judge Ellis. This was evident from the first moments Mueller's prosecutors appeared in Ellis's courtroom. Michael Dreeben, who ran Mueller's legal team, had spent the last several decades arguing cases before the Supreme Court. He had won and lost before the justices, but he had always been treated with respect, if not deference, in his appearances there. Not so, however, when Dreeben crossed the Potomac to argue a motion before Judge Ellis.

Manafort's lawyers had moved to dismiss the indictment on the ground that Mueller had no right to bring it. According to Rod Rosenstein's appointment form, the special counsel was directed to investigate "any links and/or coordination" between the Russian government and the Trump campaign. Because the indictment charged Manafort with frauds that began long before 2016, his lawyers argued that the case was outside Mueller's jurisdiction.

Ellis's contempt for Dreeben—and thus Mueller—was obvious from practically the judge's first remark. "Let me ask the government—or not the government—the Special Counsel, a few questions," the judge said. Of course, the special counsel was "the government"—that is, the prosecution—but Ellis didn't see it that way. The judge apparently regarded Mueller's prosecutors as freelance mercenaries rather than what they were—employees of the U.S. Department of Justice. Trump had been tweeting about Mueller's "angry Democrats," and Ellis's questions, as well as his entire attitude in court, amounted to a judicial ratification of the president's view. To begin his questioning of Dreeben, Ellis pointed out that the investigation of Manafort must have been under way before Mueller was appointed. "Did they turn over their file on their investigation of Mr. Manafort to you all?" he asked.

"Essentially, Your Honor, the Special Counsel was appointed to conduct an investigation—"

Ellis cut him off, saying, "I'm sorry. Answer my question. Did you remember what my question was? . . . I don't see what relation this indictment has with anything the special prosecutor is authorized to investigate."

Dreeben had a simple answer. "Your Honor," he said, "our investigatory scope does cover the activities that led to the indictment in this case." Dreeben explained that Rosenstein's appointment order authorized the special counsel to investigate more than just the campaign period; it said Mueller could examine matters that "arose" from the Russia investigation. In addition, Mueller had gone back to Rosenstein in August 2017 to obtain specific authorization to investigate Manafort's possible financial crimes. In other words, far from being an unguided missile, Mueller had received express approval from his superior in the Justice Department for what he had done.

But Ellis brushed off Dreeben's answer. "What is really going on," the judge said, "is that this indictment is used as a means of exerting pressure on the defendant to give you information that really is in your appointment, but it itself has nothing whatever to do with it." In other words, was Mueller trying to put pressure on Manafort to cooperate? The answer to that question was *of course*. That's what prosecutors do. Or, as Dreeben explained, Manafort had business interests in Russia and Ukraine. "Investigators want to understand the full scope of his relationship, how he was paid, with whom he was associated, what happened to the money, and that leads to the activities that are at issue in this indictment," he said. In other words, the special counsel would not apologize for doing his job.

Apparently frustrated with this line of inquiry, Ellis turned to subjects that reflected the obsessions of right-wing talk radio—the expense and the length of the Mueller probe, even though neither had any relevance to the issue before him. The judge demanded to know the budget of the special counsel's office. "I think you were given $10 million to begin with," he said. Dreeben demurred. "Are you in a position to tell me when the investigation will be over?" Ellis asked.

"I am not, Your Honor," Dreeben answered.

At last, Ellis reached the heart of his objections to Mueller's investigation. As far as the judge was concerned, the Department of Justice had launched a legitimate probe of Manafort's finances at some point in the past, but Mueller had turned it into a crusade, and an illegitimate one. "This was an ongoing investigation," Ellis said. "You all got it from the Department of Justice. You're pursuing it. Now I had speculated about why you're really interested in this case. You don't really care about Mr. Manafort's bank fraud. Well, the government does." Again, Ellis was referring to the original prosecutors as "the government" and Mueller's team as some sort of trespasser. Warming to this theme, Ellis went on, "You really care about what information Mr. Manafort can give you that would reflect on Mr. Trump or lead to his prosecution or impeachment or whatever. That's what you're really interested in." Again, this was the routine business of federal prosecution—whether of a drug ring or the White House. Prosecutors convicted lower-level figures and then persuaded them to testify against higher-ups. That Ellis would turn this practice into an attack on the special counsel revealed more about his own biases than Mueller's tactics. Still, by the time Ellis issued his opinion, he was compelled to recognize that Dreeben was right. It was not a close issue. Mueller did have the authority to charge Manafort. Ellis dismissed Manafort's motion and set the start date for his trial for July 31, 2018.

Because Manafort was indicted first in Washington, Judge Amy Berman Jackson set his original bail conditions, which Ellis more or less ratified for the Virginia proceedings. Greg Andres took over the trial before Judge Ellis in Virginia, and Andrew Weissmann ran the case in Washington, and he did so with his trademark aggression.

Back in the early part of the decade, Manafort created what he called the Hapsburg group—a group of former senior European politicians (including former Italian prime minister Romano Prodi) to lobby on behalf of the Ukrainian government, both in Europe and in the United States. Manafort had managed the Hapsburg group with the assistance of his old friend and colleague Konstantin Kilimnik, the alleged Russian intelligence operative. Because the money for the Hapsburg project came from Manafort's Ukrainian clients, he was required to register as a lobbyist, but he didn't do so. So on February 23, 2018, Mueller's prosecutors filed a superseding indictment with a new charge against him—that Manafort had failed to register as a foreign lobbyist.

Manafort responded to this new charge in characteristic fashion—by committing more crimes. His bail conditions allowed him to remain under house arrest at his Arlington, Virginia, condominium, but he had to wear an ankle bracelet with GPS monitoring to make sure that he didn't flee. Also, apparently, Manafort still did not realize that his phone and email were being monitored. Immediately after he was hit with the new charges, he started contacting members of the Hapsburg group and trying to line up a story that they had lobbied only in Europe, not in the United States. As Manafort texted to one person involved, "We should talk. I have made clear that they worked in Europe." (In fact, to cite just one example, Manafort had arranged for Prodi to lobby Congress on behalf of Ukraine in 2013.) So in other words, after Manafort was indicted for illegal lobbying in February 2018, he promptly tried to tamper with the witnesses.

Upon learning of Manafort's post-indictment outreach, Weissmann added still another charge against him—this one for witness tampering, which is another name for suborning perjury. But Weissmann did something even more consequential: he filed a motion to revoke Manafort's bail in Washington and lock him up before his trial in Virginia. It was inconvenient for Manafort to be confined to his multimillion-dollar condo, but he could still live a relatively normal and comfortable life. Jail is an entirely different universe, especially in the crowded conditions facing defendants who are awaiting trial. For a man who had led a life of ostentatious luxury, as Manafort had, the prospect of incarceration was even more perilous. Of course, Weissmann's effort to revoke bail was more than just a response to Manafort's new crimes; it was another way he tried to show Manafort what awaited him if he didn't plead guilty and cooperate. If Manafort didn't flip, in other words, this was the life he could expect. With two trials ahead of him, Manafort knew that a bail revocation would mean at least many months in jail and, with the likelihood of conviction, many years in prison to follow.

So the stakes were especially high on the morning of June 15, 2018, when Manafort appeared before Judge Jackson for his bail revocation hearing in Washington. When he arrived at the courthouse that morning, this sixty-nine-year-old onetime confidant of presidents and potentates didn't know whether he had spent the last night in his own bed for the foreseeable future. As the world would soon learn, in embarrassing detail, Manafort took great care with his appearance, and he wore a precisely tailored pin-striped suit for his day in court. His thick head of hair was precisely barbered and immaculate. With his barrel chest and short legs, Manafort slightly resembled a penguin as he paced outside the courtroom. He said little to his lawyers or to his wife; he was never a big talker. The courtroom filled to capacity before Judge Jackson took the bench precisely on time.

With two pending trials, and a variety of similar charges in each jurisdiction, Manafort's legal situation was complicated. So was the law relating to the revocation of bail, which required a judge to weigh evidence according to varying standards of proof. But Jackson, in an opening monologue, aptly summarized the situation, demonstrating an enviable ability to communicate, in plain English, the issue before her. She recounted the government's evidence for witness tampering and Manafort's defense—"he argues that he wasn't advancing a false story; the Hapsburg group work was about Europe and not about the United States," the judge said. Greg Andres summed up the government's position. "Judge, the danger here is not a physical danger or a danger of violence," he said. "The danger is that Mr. Manafort will continue to commit crimes. The danger to the community is that if Mr. Manafort is released, that there have to be conditions that prevent him from continuing to commit crimes, and it's on that point that we don't think there are conditions."

Richard Westling, one of Manafort's lawyers, made some good

points for him. He noted that Manafort's bail requirements did not include a total prohibition on contact with possible witnesses. And Manafort had no notice that the individuals he contacted were witnesses. "I don't see any evidence that suggests that there was any kind of threat, any kind of promise, any kind of the traditional things that you see in cases involving an effort to tamper with or undermine witness testimony," Westling said. All that was necessary at this point, according to Manafort's lawyer, was a clear order saying no contact with any possible witness, and his client would be happy to abide by it. Jackson acknowledged that there were good arguments on both sides, and she took a fifteen-minute break to organize her thoughts. At counsel table, Manafort appeared immobile, frozen, as he waited.

When she returned to the bench, Jackson offered a rare note of candor from a judge. "I have struggled with this decision," she said. Still, she undertook a careful review of the precedents, which included a rejection of one of Manafort's best arguments—that he never threatened anyone with violence. "Any kind of witness tampering affects the integrity of the court and invokes the public concern of encouraging individuals to serve as witnesses," she said. But still, Jackson continued, she was obliged to consider whether there were any conditions she could impose to ensure Manafort's appearance at trial and the safety of the community. The case was unusual, Jackson went on, because the special counsel was arguing that Manafort represented an unusual kind of threat to the community. "We don't have what one would consider the typical sort of harm to the community at large—dangerous substances being peddled on the corner, unlawful possession of firearms," she said. "The harm in this case is the harm to the administration of justice. It is the harm to the integrity of the court system."

But how was the judge supposed to protect the community from the kind of threat that Manafort presented? "This is not middle school. I can't take his cell phone," she said. Manafort had access to any number of communication devices. She turned directly to the defendant. "I thought about this long and hard, Mr. Manafort. I have no appetite for this. But in the end, I cannot turn a blind eye to these allegations. Given the number of contacts, the persistence of the contacts and their obvious intent and import, it is how they were perceived and received by the person to whom they were made. And this witness tampering occurred while the defendant was already on bond and already under an order by another judge not to do this." She went on, displaying considerable insight into Manafort's character, "I am concerned that you seem inclined to treat these proceedings as just another marketing exercise and not a criminal case brought by a duly appointed federal prosecutor in a federal court." She exhaled and concluded. "You have abused the trust placed in you six months ago. And, therefore, the government's motion will be granted. And the defendant will be detained pending trial as of today."

For courtroom spectators, white-collar criminal cases often look like civil cases. It's hard to tell the lawyers from their clients, and everyone comes and goes from the courtroom as they please. But the proceedings before Judge Jackson served as a sobering reminder of the stakes before her. As soon as she left the courtroom, a pair of deputy marshals steered Manafort to the door behind the judge's bench, the one that led to the courthouse lockup. A couple of minutes later, one of the marshals returned with Manafort's belt, wallet, and silk tie, which he handed to the defendant's wife.

Manafort's trial in Virginia began the following month. It took about three minutes for Judge Ellis to go to war against Mueller's prosecutors.

"A man in this courtroom believed the law did not apply to him— not tax law, not banking law," Uzo Asonye began his opening statement for the prosecution. (Asonye was an Assistant U.S. Attorney based in the northern Virginia courthouse. At Judge Ellis's insistence, Mueller had recruited a local prosecutor to try the case with Greg Andres.) "This man collected over $60 million for his work in a European country called Ukraine. But this man didn't want to report all his income, so he used shell companies and foreign bank accounts to funnel—"

Ellis interrupted him. "The evidence, you contend, will show this?" he said.

"Yes, Your Honor," Asonye answered.

"Then that's the way I would put it, Mr. Asonye."

"Yes, Your Honor."

"All right," the judge said. "Do it that way, please."

Asonye was offering a perfectly routine and appropriate opening statement, but Ellis was harassing him from the start.

The prosecutor resumed, "The evidence will show that he used shell companies and foreign bank accounts to funnel millions of dollars of untaxed income into the United States, concealing it from U.S. authorities and bankrolling his extravagant lifestyle. The evidence will show that from 2010 to 2014 he spent this secret income on luxury items. He purchased over $6 million of real estate in cash, an apartment in Manhattan, a town house in Brooklyn, a $2 million house just a stone's throw away from this very courthouse in Arlington, Virginia.

"The evidence will show he spent millions of dollars renovating his house in Florida, and a ten-bedroom/twelve-bathroom house in the Hamptons. And with those funds, he bought himself more than a half million dollars in fancy clothes, a half million dollars in rugs. He drove high-end vehicles. He got whatever he wanted."

Ellis interrupted again. "Mr. Asonye, you might focus on the elements of the offense. It isn't a crime to have a lot of money."

Asonye struggled through Ellis's interruptions to complete his opening statement, explaining how Manafort used the foreign bank accounts to pay his suppliers directly so the income would never be reported to the IRS. When Manafort's funding in Ukraine dried up in 2015, he started lying to banks to get loans. He lied to his accountants when they asked him if he had any foreign bank accounts. He lied to his bookkeeper, too. He also used shell companies in Cyprus to create "loans" that were really income, on which he paid no income tax.

The opening statement showed what the evidence would soon reveal: the case, with its eighteen counts, was a slam dunk. Manafort received the income, and he didn't pay taxes on it. The loan applications to the banks were full of lies. There was little more to the story. The damning facts provided a challenge to Manafort's lawyers, which they answered in the customary way—by attacking the cooperator, Rick Gates. "You're going to learn that Mr. Gates will tell untruths about Mr. Manafort and about anyone and anything to save himself from prison time, from huge criminal fines, to save himself from having to pay his back taxes, and all the penalties that are associated with those taxes that are owes because of his own personal misdeeds," Thomas Zehnle, another Manafort lawyer, said in his opening. It was true that Gates was intimately involved in executing the frauds that were the basis of the case against Manafort, but the problem was that these frauds overwhelmingly benefited Manafort, not Gates. As is often the case in criminal trials, defense attorneys did not have an abundance of effective arguments to choose from; blaming Gates was probably the best one they had, but it wasn't very good. The money trail, which was proved more by documents than by Gates's testimony, was irrefutable.

Manafort got the jury he wanted—nearly all white—and, even better for the defendant, Judge Ellis took an immediate dislike to Greg Andres. Ellis hurried the prosecutors along, especially when Andres introduced evidence relating to the lavishness of Manafort's lifestyle. No prosecutor could have resisted detailing the bizarre excesses of Manafort's expenditures. For example, he spent $520,000 at the House of Bijan, the famous appointment-only boutique in Beverly Hills, where he bought such items as a $12,000 pink pin-striped suit and a $48,000 blue lizard jacket. The infamous $15,000 ostrich jacket came from a New York boutique. After the opening statement, Ellis mostly gave a pass to Asonye, who was a familiar figure to him, since he practiced in the Arlington courthouse. But Ellis took Andres for a northern interloper who disdained the lowly locals. Everything Andres did seemed to irritate the judge, starting with the presentation of Manafort's spending, which the prosecutor had every right to introduce. Still, Andres's very presence—even the way he stood in silence—infuriated the judge. This led to surreal exchanges like this one:

"Look at me when you're talking to me," Ellis said to Andres (fortunately outside the presence of the jury).

"I'm sorry, Judge, I was," Andres replied.

"No, you weren't. You were looking down."

"Because I don't want to get in trouble for some facial expression," Andres said. "I don't want to get yelled at again by the Court for having some facial expression when I'm not doing anything wrong, but trying my case."

At another point, Ellis said to Andres, "Well, I understand how frustrated you are. In fact, there's tears in your eyes right now."

"There are not tears in my eyes, Judge," he answered.

Always insistent on having the last word in his courtroom, Ellis shot back, "Well, they're watery."

Still, the main drama of the trial was the defense's cross-examination of Gates, Manafort's longtime deputy and now the principal witness against him. Like a lot of men, Gates had grown a beard in apparent compensation for the hair disappearing from the top of his head. Even with the facial hair, he still looked more like the William & Mary preppy he was rather than the mountain man he apparently aspired to be. Andres had prepared him well, and his direct examination was fluid and clear, though he was a problematic witness. He admitted his own culpability in Manafort's scheme—he too had failed to pay his taxes—and he acknowledged that he had stolen some of Manafort's money as well. The exact amount was never clear, though Gates admitted to a skim of "several hundred thousand dollars." Gates also acknowledged, grudgingly, that he had lied in one of his office interviews with the special counsel, which led Mueller's office to demand that he plead guilty to an additional false statement crime as well.

But Gates's bad actions hardly served to show that Manafort was innocent. This is why cooperators are often such effective witnesses, because they show the kind of company that the defendant keeps. Kevin Downing, Manafort's lead lawyer, did a skillful job of forcing Gates to recount his misdeeds, especially his unauthorized dips into the foreign bank accounts that belonged to Manafort. Still, by focusing on this issue, Downing implicitly admitted that the money belonged to Manafort, and his failure to pay taxes on that cash was the heart of the government's case. In short, Gates worked for Manafort, who profited a great deal more from Gates's misdeeds than Gates himself did.

Andres drove that point home during his re-direct. He asked Gates whether he had reported those foreign bank accounts to the IRS, as the law required him to do, and when Gates said no, Andres asked why.

"Paul Manafort directed me not to," Gates said.

Ellis did succeed in hustling the trial to a swift conclusion—after just ten days of testimony. (The defense called no witnesses.) The summations followed predictable themes. For Manafort, Westling deployed a venerable strategy in white-collar crime cases, employing the jujitsu move of turning the mountain of evidence against the defendant into proof of his innocence. "Mr. Manafort involved his bookkeeper, his accountant, Mr. Gates, and others in the way that he communicated with bankers and other people," the defense lawyer told the jury. "That's not consistent with someone who is attempting to commit a fraud. Fraud is about secrecy at its very core." (The answer, of course, is that Manafort acted that way because he was a criminal who hadn't yet been caught.) And, of course, Westling tried to blame the whole thing on Gates: "He was orchestrating a multimillion-dollar embezzlement scheme and he was trying to keep it outside of the purview of the accountants."

Manafort's lawyers made one argument that was tailored to the unique political circumstances of the case. The courtroom rules wouldn't allow Westling to argue directly that Mueller was targeting Manafort because he was a Republican. But the lawyer still made the point by implication. Westling recounted Manafort's service for such candidates as Ronald Reagan, Gerald Ford, and George W. Bush. And then he said Mueller's team was "going through each piece of paper and finding anything that doesn't match up to add to the weight of evidence against Mr. Manafort." As evidence of the excessive prosecutorial zeal, the lawyer pointed out that Manafort was even charged with fraudulent statements in an application for a loan that was never granted.

"What would be the motivation?" Westling asked. "I'll leave you to determine what was behind that."

The defense strategy almost worked. Four days passed without a verdict. As it turned out, eleven jurors had quickly agreed that Manafort was guilty of all eighteen counts, which charged both bank fraud and tax fraud. But a single juror held out. In the end, the juror relented on the bank fraud counts but wouldn't yield on the tax counts. So on August 21, Judge Ellis accepted a partial verdict—guilty on eight counts and a hung jury on the other ten. In later interviews with reporters, one juror, who described herself as a strong supporter of President Trump, said she shared the skepticism of the defense team for Mueller's motives. She agreed that Mueller had targeted Manafort in an effort to get evidence on Trump. But the juror said that the evidence against him "was overwhelming." She added, "I did not want

Paul Manafort to be guilty, but he was." As for the holdout, she said the juror wouldn't listen to reason. Thus, the partial deadlock.

Mueller's prosecutors hadn't exactly triumphed, but they had survived, overcoming both a hostile judge and a holdout juror. Under the federal sentencing guidelines, it almost didn't matter that the jury failed to reach verdicts on some counts; on the charges for which he was convicted, Manafort was still looking at an enormous amount of prison time. But notwithstanding the dire implications for Manafort himself, the result looked to the public like a mixed verdict— something less than a convincing show of strength for Mueller. Not surprisingly, Trump tried to reinforce this impression, tweeting after the verdict, "A large number of counts, ten, could not even be decided in the Paul Manafort case. Witch Hunt!"

But the verdict in the Manafort trial didn't even turn out to be the biggest news of the day on August 21. At almost the same time as Judge Ellis accepted the verdict in Virginia, Michael Cohen pleaded guilty in New York to charges filed in the Southern District. The president's fixer had flipped—or so it seemed.

19

Friends in High Places

B y 2018, the world had become largely inured to Trump's tweets—even with their racism and misogyny, their mindless belligerence, norm-shattering impropriety, and constant lies. The news media had neither the time nor the inclination to analyze the daily barrage of tweets, and Trump's supporters found it convenient to ignore them, or to dismiss them with a shrug—"That's just Trump." But for better or worse, the tweets offered a window into the president's soul; they were the best way to learn what he was really thinking. And as he approached the midterm elections, with the Republican Party in clear trouble, the president's thoughts turned especially brittle and troubled.

For example, not long before the midterms, the Justice Department filed criminal charges against two Republican congressmen, Duncan Hunter and Chris Collins, in unrelated corruption cases. In response, Trump tweeted, "Two long running, Obama era, investigations of two very popular Republican Congressmen were brought to a well publicized charge, just ahead of the Mid-Terms, by the Jeff Sessions Justice Department. Two easy wins now in doubt because there is not enough time. Good job Jeff." If there was any bedrock principle at the Justice Department, it was that criminal investigations, especially of public figures, should be conducted without regard to party or to electoral consequences. (Comey's violation of this principle, in October 2016, was one reason why so many Justice Department veterans were appalled by his behavior.) The crude political calculus of Trump's tweet—that his Justice Department should protect Republican officeholders—was shocking in its vulgar indecency. The tweet was so bad, in fact, that Rod Rosenstein felt compelled to give a pep talk to his subordinates to remind them that the values of the department remained intact, regardless of what the president said. (To be sure, though, neither Rosenstein nor anyone else at the Justice Department offered a public repudiation of the president for the tweet.)

Trump's response to the twin blows of August 21—Manafort's conviction and Cohen's guilty plea—displayed the same twisted values. At 8:21 the following morning, he tweeted, "I feel very badly for Paul Manafort and his wonderful family. 'Justice' took a 12 year old tax case, among other things, applied tremendous pressure on him and, unlike Michael Cohen, he refused to 'break'—make up stories in order to get a 'deal.' Such respect for a brave man!" The levels of pathology on display in this single tweet were remarkable. To begin, the president felt "very badly" for the "brave man" who had just been convicted of multiple serious felonies, which Trump did not even acknowledge. Rather, he put "Justice" in scare quotes, even though the department was part of his own administration. But the clear focus of the tweet, and of Trump's mind, was the issue of who would flip and cooperate with the government—who would "break," in the president's parlance. Of course, the issue of Cohen's and Manafort's possible cooperation was hardly of just academic concern to Trump. The clear subtext of the tweet was that Trump was worried that both might turn on him. So he used the power of the presidency, which includes the power to pardon, to encourage Manafort to continue to stonewall—against the efforts of his "Justice" Department. Still, the point remained: Would Cohen or Manafort turn on Trump?

Ever since the FBI searched his home, hotel room, and office on April 9, Cohen had engaged in quasi-public agonizing about whether to plead guilty and cooperate. This manifested itself in a panicked roundelay of changing lawyers, switching positions, and making conflicting statements. He appeared, in a way, to be trying to channel Trump, at whose knee he learned the art of damage control. But Cohen had neither Trump's resources, nor his intelligence, nor his deep reservoir of street smarts. As a result, over the next several months, Michael Cohen made every mistake a criminal suspect could make. He did everything wrong. The main victim was Cohen himself; the principal beneficiary was Donald Trump.

In the days immediately after the raid, Cohen remained what he had always been—a Trump acolyte hungering for the approval and support of the boss. He got it, briefly. Trump called Cohen a couple of days after the searches, saying he wanted to "check in" and urging Cohen to "hang in there" and "stay strong." The call was an artful demonstration of how Trump skated close to the line of impropriety and illegality. Even in Cohen's account, Trump did not specifically urge Cohen to lie to protect him or to do anything illegal. But as Comey had recognized more than a year earlier, the gangsterish subtexts to Trump's communications could scarcely be clearer. *Hang in there. Stay strong. Take care of me and I'll take care of you.*

In one way, Cohen showed what he had learned from Trump by auditioning a series of lawyers and persuading them to work for him without actually retaining or paying them. The first was Robert Costello, a former Southern District prosecutor who was an old associate of Giuliani's. Costello reached out to Giuliani, who had just taken over Trump's defense, and the former mayor reassured Costello that the president was anxious to keep his former fixer on the team. "Michael," Costello emailed Cohen on April 21, "I just spoke to Rudy Giuliani and told him I was on your team. Rudy was thrilled and said this could not be a better situation for the President or you. He asked me if it was ok to call the President and Jay Sekelow [*sic*] and I said fine." The next day, Costello emailed Cohen another encouraging message: "I spoke with Rudy. Very, Very Positive. You are 'loved.' . . . Sleep well tonight, you have friends in high places." On the same day, Trump issued his supportive tweet, calling Cohen "a fine person with a wonderful family."

But Cohen quickly came to recognize what he knew in the back of his mind—that loyalty for Trump was always a one-way street. The signs that Trump was abandoning Cohen came quickly. In May, Giuliani admitted to Sean Hannity that Trump had reimbursed Cohen for the $130,000 payment to Stormy Daniels. This was true, of course, but the president and Giuliani began to put their spin on the story—specifically, that Cohen alone came up with the idea of paying off the porn actress and he alone orchestrated it. It was clear by this point that the Southern District was weighing whether to charge Cohen with making an unlawful campaign contribution by paying Daniels on the eve of the 2016 election. In light of this, Trump and Giuliani had to figure out a way to separate the president from Cohen's actions.

Their first effort came on May 3, when Trump tweeted a series of icy legalisms about the Daniels agreement: "Mr. Cohen, an attorney, received a monthly retainer, not from the campaign and having nothing to do with the campaign, from which he entered into, through reimbursement, a private contract between two parties, known as a non-disclosure agreement, or NDA. These agreements are . . . very common among celebrities and people of wealth. . . . The agreement was used to stop the false and extortionist accusations made by her." (This tweet, of course, was false at several levels. First, unbeknownst to Trump at that point, Cohen recorded his conversation where he gained Trump's approval for the payment to Daniels. Second, the transaction had everything to do with the campaign, since it took place a few days before the election. Third, arrangements like the one between Cohen and Daniels were not "very common." Fourth, the notion that Daniels's account of their encounter was "false" was itself preposterous.)

Failing to pick up the signs from these tweets, Cohen's lawyers approached Giuliani about obtaining a presidential pardon for Cohen. Not at this time, Giuliani told them. The stiff arm to Cohen was delivered in another way when the Trump Organization stopped paying his legal bills. The unkindest cut, from Cohen's perspective, was when Giuliani put out the word that Cohen no longer represented Trump, and thus Cohen lost his treasured designation of "personal attorney to the president."

Spurning Costello (without paying him), Cohen turned to Guy Petrillo, another Southern District alum, who belonged to a younger generation than the Giuliani era. Unlike Cohen and Costello, Petrillo focused on the actual evidence in the case, and he recognized that his client was in a great deal of trouble, not only because of the payment to Stormy Daniels, which was a possible unlawful campaign contribution, but also because of Cohen's tangled business interests. Petrillo also recognized that Cohen's hopes of a pardon were fanciful. In the meantime, Cohen had recruited yet another (unpaid) lawyer,

Lanny Davis, who earned some renown two decades earlier as a vocal defender of Clinton's during the Starr investigation. Unlike Petrillo, Davis advocated a public campaign by Cohen, though to what end was unclear. Guided by Davis, Cohen gave an interview to George Stephanopoulos on July 2, asserting that he was willing to cooperate with both Mueller's office and the Southern District. This sealed his breach with Trump, but it didn't get Cohen any closer to a resolution of his legal troubles. The television interviews also poisoned relations between Davis and Petrillo, who regarded publicity for publicity's sake as a hindrance to making a favorable deal.

At this point the consequences of Mueller's decision to hand the Cohen case to the Southern District came into play. Petrillo wanted to resolve Cohen's legal troubles, but with whom? Mueller had given the Southern District the investigations of the illegal campaign contributions and Cohen's personal financial dealings. But Mueller had kept the investigation of Cohen's false statement to the Senate Judiciary Committee, when he testified that negotiations over Trump's plan to build a tower in Moscow had ended in January 2016, when in fact they continued until June. Petrillo offered to meet with the Southern District prosecutors, and he was rebuffed. This was unusual, because prosecutors usually like to meet with defense lawyers—to obtain information, to test the chances for a guilty plea, to listen rather than to make any commitments. But the Southern District prosecutors were investigating the facts so quickly that they didn't want to tip their hands about what they knew. Mueller's office, in contrast, agreed to meet with Petrillo and hear what Cohen had to say. Unable to resolve matters until both prosecution offices were aligned, Petrillo stewed for much of the summer.

All through July, Cohen, with the help of Lanny Davis, was putting out the word that he was ready to turn on Trump. On Chris Cuomo's CNN program, they released the audio that Cohen had secretly recorded of the phone call where Trump agreed to the Stormy Daniels payoff. Trump replied by tweet: "Inconceivable that a lawyer would tape a client-totally unheard of & perhaps illegal. The good news is that your favorite President did nothing wrong!" Thanks to Davis, Cohen was becoming almost a hero of the anti-Trump resistance, but the attention brought him no closer to resolving his legal difficulties.

Then, suddenly, Petrillo received an ultimatum from the Southern

District prosecutors: they would indict Cohen on a range of crimes by mid-August unless he immediately agreed to plead guilty and, just as important, to tell everything he knew. Only then would the Manhattan prosecutors agree to Cohen's request for a reduced sentence. The demand for full cooperation was a particular obsession in the U.S. Attorney's office in Manhattan. In some other jurisdictions, prosecutors would agree to accept partial cooperation from defendants; they would allow defendants to put some subjects off-limits in their discussions. But in the Southern District, as Petrillo well knew, cooperation was an all-or-nothing proposition. Cohen, though, thought he could finagle his way out of the policy. He never explained to anyone what subjects he wouldn't talk about or why; he certainly was willing to tell everything he knew about Trump. But Cohen would not sign a cooperation agreement that promised a full spill of what he knew.

Drunk on the attention he was receiving from the news media, Cohen thought he could engage in brinksmanship with the Southern District. In light of his celebrity, he thought he could get a deal with partial cooperation. As Petrillo (and others) tried to tell him, this was insanity. Then, at the last minute, Cohen became so frustrated with the process that he just decided to plead guilty to get it all over with. Petrillo managed to talk the Southern District out of a bank fraud charge—which would have increased Cohen's sentencing exposure considerably—but the prosecutors still drove a hard bargain. Cohen had to plead guilty to eight felonies—five counts of tax evasion, one of making a false statement on a bank loan application, and two of illegal campaign contributions, in relation to the Daniels payment. At his guilty plea hearing, on August 21, Cohen said he worked "in coordination with and at the direction of the candidate in making those payments." It was this statement incriminating Trump that prompted the president to lash out at Cohen in a tweet the next day.

Cohen had managed to choose the worst of all possible worlds. He pleaded guilty, thus losing the chance for an acquittal on charges that were at least plausibly defensible. But by refusing to cooperate fully with the Southern District, he also gave up the opportunity to reduce his sentence. When he did meet with prosecutors from the Southern District, his haughty defiance compounded his problems. He did nothing but alienate the prosecutors who, to a great extent, held his fate in their hands. Ironically, when Cohen started talking to Mueller's prosecutors, after his guilty plea in Manhattan, they found him trust-worthy and forthcoming. He gave them full accounts of the Trump Tower Moscow negotiations and other important details. Cohen said Donald Trump Jr. told his father in advance about the June 2016 Trump Tower meeting with the Russian lawyer. He also said he knew that Roger Stone gave Trump advance notice about the WikiLeaks disclosures. In addition, Cohen agreed to plead guilty to Mueller's prosecutors for making a false statement to the Senate Judiciary Com-mittee in 2017. But Cohen's poisonous relationship with the Southern District alongside his positive dealings with Mueller meant little when he was sentenced; the main charges against him were in the Southern District, and the judges there listened to their local prosecutors.

Cohen's botched handling of his legal predicament also shredded his public credibility. Yes, he turned into a principal Trump accuser, but for most of his claims he had no proof besides his own word. (No one knew better than Cohen why Trump eschewed emailing and texting.) Cohen could and did explain that he made his false state-ment to Congress in order to protect Trump's account of the Moscow Trump Tower deal, but his guilty plea offered a plump target for his critics: Cohen was now a "convicted liar." And unlike for many defen-dants who flip, Cohen's prosecutors wouldn't vouch for him. Before he was sentenced, the Southern District prosecutors sent the judge a scathing assessment of Cohen's cooperation and his character. "Cohen repeatedly declined to provide full information about the scope of any additional criminal conduct in which he may have engaged or had knowledge," the Manhattan prosecutors wrote. "Cohen managed to commit a panoply of serious crimes, all while holding himself out as a licensed attorney and upstanding member of the bar," they wrote. "Cohen's years-long pattern of deception, and his attempts to mini-mize certain of that conduct even now, make it evident that a lengthy custodial sentence is necessary to specifically deter him from further fraudulent conduct, whether out of greed or for power, in the future."

Trump turned on Cohen even more vindictively. The president inveighed against Cohen for recording him (which was indeed outra-geous), and he dismissed what his former lawyer said about the Dan-iels payoff (which was undoubtedly true). As for Cohen's statements about the Trump Tower meeting, and Stone's report on WikiLeaks, Trump simply branded his former attorney a liar. Indeed, Cohen turned into a favorite Trump target, as in this tweet: "'Michael Cohen asks judge for no Prison Time.' You mean he can do all of the TERRIBLE, unrelated to Trump, things having to do with fraud, big loans, Taxis, etc., and not serve a long prison term? He makes up stories to get a GREAT & ALREADY reduced deal for himself." There was also this tweet, which combined several of Trump's obsessions: "Remember, Michael Cohen only became a 'Rat' after the FBI did something which was absolutely unthinkable & unheard of until the Witch Hunt was illegally started. They BROKE INTO AN ATTORNEY'S OFFICE! Why didn't they break into the DNC to get the Server, or Crooked's office?" The president also all but invited prosecutors to investigate Cohen's family: "Cohen claimed his shady father-in-law's 'in the clothing business' when in fact he's loan shark in same taxicab medallion." Cohen's misjudgments and Trump's assault neutralized Cohen as a witness against the president. So the first of the two threats to Trump that emerged on August 21 fizzled. That left Manafort.

Jail aged Manafort in a hurry. Even though he had been locked up only since June, he looked transformed by the time he was convicted on August 21. His hair dye faded. His skin took on a pasty pallor. Worst of all, his gout flared, and he was left to hobble in and out of court with a walker. Manafort had become an old man. Notwithstanding the partial verdict in his case, the Federal Sentencing Guidelines told a dismal story about his future. Based on the counts for which he was convicted, the range of his likely sentence was nineteen to twenty-four years. Those recommendations were not binding, but most judges, including Ellis, usually followed the guidelines. And Manafort was still looking at another trial, and thus another possible prison sentence, before Judge Jackson in Washington. Manafort was financially and physically depleted, so he did what defendants in that position usually do. He began to consider pleading guilty to the outstanding charges and cooperating. He told his lawyers to explore the possibility of a deal with Mueller's office.

The first step toward a cooperation agreement came together quickly. Manafort's lawyers and Weissmann agreed that Manafort would give a proffer—an audition of sorts. He would submit to questioning, and if the prosecutors found him believable, they would offer him a deal. The agreement would require him to plead guilty and provide evidence and testimony, and if Mueller's prosecutors continued to find him credible, they would advocate for a reduction in sentence. On September 11, 2018, barely three weeks after the verdict in his trial before Judge Ellis, Manafort came in for his proffer—or, as courthouse slang had it, his Queen for a Day.

Weissmann and his lead FBI agent presided over the questioning. In office interviews for white-collar investigations, prosecutors usually lead the discussion. Sometimes the agents do little more than take notes in order to produce the official summaries of interviews, known as 302s. But more experienced prosecutors know to make their agents into partners, both in questioning suspects and in evaluating the credibility of the answers. In that first session, Weissmann led Manafort through a first rough draft of his story—his work in Ukraine, his duties for the Trump campaign. In such settings, the contrast between Cohen and Manafort was striking. Cohen jabbered constantly, alternating between hangdog self-pity and boiling rage. Manafort exuded taciturn menace. He said little, paused often, and answered questions narrowly, or barely. Weissmann liked and trusted the agent, who was soft-spoken and experienced. After several hours, Weissmann sent Manafort back to his cell.

"So?" Weissmann asked the agent when Manafort was gone.

"That man is evil," the agent said.

Still, a deal came together quickly. Neither side wanted to admit it, but they needed each other. Manafort was looking at essentially a life sentence; he had to do something—anything—to avoid that fate. There was a measure of desperation on Mueller's team as well, though that's not the word they would have preferred to use. By September, the special counsel had been in operation for well more than a year. After the early burst of activity in late 2017 and early 2018—the Flynn guilty plea, the two indictments against the Russians, the Gates plea, and the Manafort indictment—there had been fewer signs of progress. The obstruction of justice investigation, with Don McGahn's testimony, was nearly wrapped up, but the results were not yet public. Giuliani and Sekulow had successfully strung out the negotiations about how, or whether, the president would answer questions. The Manafort trial was a victory, but it had not yet produced any new disclosures about Mueller's core assignment—determining the relationship between the Trump campaign and Russia. Who besides Manafort might have useful information on that subject?

In ordinary circumstances, Weissmann might not recommend a cooperation agreement for Manafort, because his performance in the proffer sessions had been grudging and incomplete. If this were a typical case, Weissmann might just forge ahead and proceed to the second trial in Washington. But this was not an ordinary case, and more to the point this was not an ordinary schedule. U.S. Attorney's offices exist in perpetuity; there are always prosecutors around to try a case. Mueller was fixated on *not* existing in perpetuity. So the question arose of what, if anything, a second trial would accomplish? Sure, Manafort was likely to be convicted, especially in front of a D.C. jury. But he would probably not get an appreciably longer sentence than the one he was already facing in Virginia. Would his second conviction evoke more candor from him than the first? Probably not. For this reason, it made sense to make a deal now and hope that Manafort came clean, or at least cleaner.

So on September 14, 2018, just three weeks after his conviction in Virginia, Manafort pleaded guilty in Washington to conspiracy to defraud the United States and conspiracy to obstruct justice. He also admitted to all the other crimes Mueller accused him of in both cases—from money laundering and bank fraud to foreign lobbying violations related to his work for the pro-Putin Ukrainians. Weissmann told Judge Jackson that under Manafort's plea agreement the other charges would be dropped after he was sentenced in both jurisdictions "or at the agreement of successful cooperation." There was no Trump tweet in response, but Giuliani issued a statement that said, "Once again an investigation has concluded with a plea having nothing to do with President Trump or the Trump campaign. The reason: the President did nothing wrong."

After the guilty plea, Weissmann led Manafort in an intensive round of debriefings—five additional meetings in September, and four more in October, followed by two appearances before the grand jury. And predictably, Manafort lied. In part, he lied about financial matters, insisting that he had not taken in as much money from his

Ukraine operation as the documents indicated that he did. The more consequential lies involved his associate Konstantin Kilimnik, the Russian with whom Manafort ran his Ukrainian operation. Kilimnik was charged in the witness tampering case along with Manafort in February 2018, but he had never come to the United States and was likely never to be within the jurisdiction of the American courts. But even after Manafort left the Trump campaign, Kilimnik continued working with him on a plan to restore their old client Viktor Yanukovych to power in Ukraine. (Yanukovych, who led the pro-Putin Party of Regions, was forced out of office and into exile in Russia in 2014.) In his debriefings with Mueller's team, Manafort continued to lie about his dealings with Kilimnik and his plans for Ukraine.

Why did this matter? Not long after the initial rounds of questioning, Weissmann petitioned Judge Jackson to void the cooperation agreement because Manafort "had lied in multiple ways and on multiple occasions." If the judge granted Weissmann's motion, the Office of Special Counsel would no longer be obligated to move the court for a lower sentence than the one suggested by the guidelines. This was bad news for Manafort, of course, because it meant he appeared to be losing his best chance to avoid a long prison sentence. But it was bad news, too, for Mueller and his team. By publicly condemning Manafort as a liar, they were giving up on their best chance to learn what, if anything, went on between Russia and the Trump campaign. White-collar crime cases are invariably made with the testimony of insider witnesses who cooperate. In the Russia investigation, only Rick Gates had made a meaningful and sincere switch in allegiances, but he was a secondary figure. On August 21, it appeared that both Michael Cohen and Paul Manafort might become the cooperators who made the case against the president. That was why the president sent such a panicked tweet the following day. But Cohen and Manafort, each for different reasons, blew up as possible witnesses.

Still, in the wreckage of Manafort's failed cooperation, there was, largely unnoticed at the time, the kernel of future disaster for the president. In the fall and winter of 2018, few Americans knew or cared anything about Ukraine, much less about the internal struggles for power in the former Soviet republic. But the contest between pro-Russian and pro-Western forces in Ukraine was inching closer to the surface of American politics. Manafort's deal with the special counsel's office blew up because of the intensity of his commitment to the pro-Putin cause in Ukraine. He was willing to lie, and thus face extra prison time, to tend to this alliance. This, it turned out, was a widely shared sentiment within the president's orbit. It was a kind of proxy and supplement to Trump's long-standing affection for Vladimir Putin. When it came to Ukraine, everyone who cared to look knew which side Donald Trump was on.

20

"There's Nothing Ambiguous About Crosshairs"

The isolated, even claustrophobic, nature of work for the Office of Special Counsel kept the prosecutors largely oblivious to events in what they called the outside world. Whether it was their own birthdays and anniversaries or the Oscars and the World Series, the prosecutors and their colleagues, preoccupied with their all-consuming work, barely noticed. So, too, for the midterm elections. But on December 22, 2018, there was an event that jolted the office. Because President Trump and Congress could not agree on a budget, the federal government shut down.

Under the peculiar rules of government shutdowns, some employees are deemed essential and continue to be paid, while others receive nothing and still keep working. The lawyers on Mueller's staff were designated essential and received their salaries, while everyone else—notably the FBI agents, analysts, and support staff—did not. This was irrational as well as unfair. Most of the lawyers came from law firms, or had professional spouses, which meant that they had other funds to cushion the loss of pay. In contrast, most of the FBI employees lived paycheck to paycheck, which meant that the shutdown created real hardship for many of them. Days passed without a resolution to the shutdown, then weeks. The FBI personnel didn't let up on their work, but they struggled to make ends meet. One junior FBI analyst took up dog-walking assignments at 11:00 p.m. and on weekends. Others drove for Uber. The shutdown, the longest in history, finally ended after thirty-five days, on January 25, 2019.

What made the shutdown especially unnerving was that it came during the final investigative push in the office—to charge Roger Stone. The case against Stone was a marginal one, and he was a dubious target as well. Stone had lied in testimony before the House Intelligence Committee, so there was an actual crime for the special counsel to investigate. But he lied about a fairly peripheral matter— his contacts with his eccentric friend Randy Credico. Stone had also made bombastic if perhaps not entirely serious threats against Credico and his beloved dog. ("I'm going to take that dog away from you. Not a fucking thing you can do about it either because you are a weak piece of shit," Stone wrote to Credico in one email.) It was clear that during the 2016 campaign Stone had been curious about WikiLeaks and its releases of damaging information about Democrats. But there was never any proof that he had been in direct touch with WikiLeaks, much less that he participated in their disclosures. What's more, Mueller's team had interviewed enough people on the 2016 campaign to know that Stone was a marginal figure in Trump's effort. Much to Stone's dismay, he was basically an outcast from Trump's world in 2016. During the campaign, he talked now and then on the phone with Trump, as he had done for years, but even if Stone decided to flip (which was unlikely), he probably wouldn't have much inside information to provide.

But Mueller gave the go-ahead not just for the filing of charges against Stone but for a dramatic show of force—a dawn raid on his home in Fort Lauderdale, for the execution of search and arrest warrants. The reasoning was much the same as the Southern District's justification for the takedown of Michael Cohen. The prosecutors were afraid that Stone would destroy documents and records if he knew the government was seeking them. This was not how prosecutors acted in routine white-collar crime cases. In most circumstances, defense lawyers, when they knew their clients were targets, agreed in advance to bring in their clients voluntarily after they were charged. (For example, Manafort was allowed to surrender that way.) Stone's lawyers would certainly have made the same deal. But a dawn arrest is a form of prosecutorial shock and awe, designed both to seize evidence and to rattle a target into cooperating.

A group of CNN journalists had been conducting a sophisticated form of surveillance of Mueller's operation for more than a year. From the hallways of the Washington courthouse, they monitored the comings and goings in the grand jury; from the lobby at Patriots Plaza, they noted visitors to Mueller's floor. By the grand jury, the CNN journalists saw that a number of witnesses related to the Stone investigation had testified in late 2018. During the third week in January, they saw prosecutors spend more than an hour with the grand jurors without any witnesses, which is what the government does when it is seeking an indictment. Then, on January 24, 2019, they saw Aaron Zelinsky, one of Mueller's prosecutors in the Stone investigation, wheeling a suitcase in and then out of the Patriots Plaza office building. The CNN journalists figured he might be traveling to Florida that day. In light of these clues, CNN decided to send a camera crew to stake out Stone's house the following morning.

Stone lived in an unpretentious rented house in a comfortable but not luxurious neighborhood in Fort Lauderdale. The house fronted on a quiet street and backed against one of the city's many canals. (Fort Lauderdale and Venice are sister cities.) The CNN crew arrived shortly after five in the morning, and the journalists' vigil was quickly rewarded when they saw half a dozen police vehicles arrive with lights flashing but no sirens. About a dozen agents in FBI windbreakers and tactical vests, several bearing large weapons, surrounded the house. One agent pounded on the door.

"FBI—open the door!" he shouted.

No response.

"FBI—warrant!"

A light went on in the second floor. A few seconds later, Stone, in pajamas, opened the front door. Within a few minutes, he was whisked away in handcuffs to be booked, his wife was seated in the kitchen, and the agents began swarming through the house, looking for evidence. (At the same time, FBI agents searched the apartment in Harlem that Stone used to share with Kristin Davis, who was a former madam and onetime New York gubernatorial candidate and thus someone about as notorious as Stone was.)

Stone didn't have much for the agents to find. They took his phones and his computers, but the search mostly revealed that he led a modest existence, especially compared with his onetime partner Manafort. Even before Stone's arrest, his income had dipped to almost nothing—a few speeches, some fees from writing for fringe right-wing websites and publishers. Once Stone knew he was under investigation from Mueller, he'd started a website to raise money for his legal defense. The agents chose not to seize one of his fund-raising gimmicks—a box of polished rocks that Stone had signed with a Sharpie. He marketed the rocks for $10 each and called them "Roger stones." Sales were slow.

In recent years, Stone had resembled a performance artist as much as a political figure, which made his entry into the criminal justice system more peculiar than most. His standard mode of expression was, to put it charitably, hyperbole; another way to describe it was that he lied a lot. For example, shortly after he was arrested, Stone told me, "Those who think the Mueller investigation will die out with a whimper are dreaming. This is a pretext to allow them to remove both Trump and Pence and replace them with Leather Face—I mean, Nancy Pelosi—and then she can appoint Hillary Clinton as VP. That's been the agenda from the beginning." It wasn't clear whether Stone believed what he was saying, but his comments were legally harmless in the context of a conversation with a journalist.

This kind of behavior was more problematic, of course, in more formal settings, like in congressional or courtroom testimony. Leaving the Washington courthouse after his first appearances as a defendant, Stone would raise his arms and make V-for-victory signs—an homage to his hero Richard Nixon. Even as a criminal defendant, Stone appeared to believe that he could behave as if nothing in his life had changed. In particular, he kept up his online columns and social media posts, with no change in tone or content, as if he were not out on bail. Mueller's prosecutors had declared the Stone case related to the Manafort prosecution, which meant that it would also be tried by Judge Amy Berman Jackson. (Prosecutors are known to game the related-case rules to keep cases in front of favored judges.) In Stone's initial appearance, the judge issued a limited gag order, prohibiting Stone from talking about the case while he was in or near the Washington courthouse but otherwise allowing him to continue his outspoken ways. Stone immediately abused this privilege by posting on Instagram a photograph of Judge Jackson next to a crosshairs target. A caption described the judge as "an Obama appointed Judge who dismissed the Benghazi charges against Hillary Clinton and incarcerated Paul Manafort prior to his conviction for any crime." Unamused,

Jackson summoned Stone for a hearing to explain why she shouldn't revoke his bail.

At the hearing, Stone took the stand to apologize—sort of. "I am kicking myself over my own stupidity, though not more than my wife was kicking me. I offer no excuse for it, no justification," Stone told the judge. "This is just a stupid lack of judgment." But instead of simply apologizing, he went on to explain and make his problems worse. He told the judge that the image had been selected by a volunteer assistant, and it wasn't really crosshairs anyway. Stone said the design was a "Celtic symbol," which it wasn't. In any event, Jackson was having none of it. "The post had a more sinister message," she said. "Roger Stone fully understands the power of words and the power of symbols, and there's nothing ambiguous about crosshairs." She gave Stone a break by declining to revoke his bail, but she did impose a sweeping gag order on him.

In an effort to clean up this corner of the investigation, the Mueller team also tried to make a case against Jerome Corsi, the seventy-two-year-old right-wing author who worked with Stone in the unsuccessful attempt to obtain advance information about the WikiLeaks disclosures. Corsi had not testified before Congress, but he did give a series of office interviews to the Office of Special Counsel in the fall. He took a more bizarre tack in responding to Mueller than Stone did. Even before he had been charged with anything, Corsi sued Mueller for $350 million, saying that the special counsel had engaged in prosecutorial misconduct and illegal surveillance, among other misdeeds. Corsi was represented by Larry Klayman, an eccentric Washington lawyer best known for filing multiple lawsuits against Bill Clinton's administration (and one against his own mother). Corsi also published an e-book, *Silent No More: How I Became a Political Prisoner of Mueller's "Witch Hunt,"* which recounted his experiences with Mueller's team and what he called being "mentally tortured by Mueller's Deep State prosecutors." Corsi also said his interviews with the prosecutors were "worthy of the Gestapo, the KGB, or the Red Guard under Mao. Increasingly, I felt like I was a U.S. soldier captured during the Korean War being interrogated by the Communist Chinese. All this lacked was the sleep deprivation, the torture beatings, and the blinding white interrogation lights that blocked me from seeing my inquisitors." (In other words, all the Mueller interviews lacked was any resemblance to those Korean War interrogations.)

Perhaps not surprisingly, in light of their garrulous crankiness, Stone and Corsi also had a falling-out with each other. Though it was not directly relevant to the charges against him, Stone was still believed by many to have had an inside source at WikiLeaks. According to this theory, the source gave Stone the information that led to his infamous tweet on August 21, 2016: "Trust me, it will soon the Podesta's time in the barrel. #CrookedHillary." (WikiLeaks released John Podesta's emails in October.) Corsi said that Stone asked him to come up with a cover story about how Stone came to write that tweet; Stone denied asking Corsi for any such thing. When I spoke to Stone, he denied having asked Corsi to come up with a cover story and said that his explanation for the tweet has been consistent from the beginning— that it was really about future revelations about the business dealings of the brothers John and Tony Podesta, not about WikiLeaks. Stone told me, of Corsi, "He's certifiably insane, and he has told multiple provable lies." Corsi sued Stone for defamation, arguing that Stone's public statements about him were designed to intimidate him and to coerce him into giving false testimony at Stone's criminal trial. Corsi sought damages "in excess of $25,000,000." (Judges quickly dismissed both of Corsi's lawsuits.)

Mueller's lawyers thought they could wrap up Corsi's case quickly, much as they did with Michael Flynn and George Papadopoulos. The prosecutors believed that Corsi had lied to them (and to the FBI agents present) during his first office interview in September. As with Flynn and Papadopoulos, the prosecutors thought they could obtain a quick guilty plea from Corsi to the crime of making a false statement in an official investigation, which is a felony. The statement itself was somewhat convoluted. In the interview, Corsi acknowledged that Stone had asked him to reach out to WikiLeaks in 2016, to find out what the group might be planning to disclose about the Democrats. But Corsi told Mueller's people that he had not done so. By the time of the interview with Corsi, Mueller's team had obtained his emails, which showed that he had forwarded Stone's email to Ted Malloch, a conservative writer based in England, with a request to learn what he could about WikiLeaks' plans. He also sent several follow-up requests to Malloch on the subject. So that was the lie that Mueller's team wanted to charge: that Corsi had falsely denied following up on Stone's request to learn more about WikiLeaks' plans to release more documents.

At first, Jeannie Rhee's Russia team took an aggressive tack with Corsi. On November 14, they sent Corsi's lawyer a draft information, which is the kind of document used when a defendant waives indictment and decides to plead guilty. The information said Corsi "knowingly and intentionally made . . . materially false statements during the interview" with Mueller's investigators on September 6, 2018. Corsi came back to the prosecutors and protested his innocence. He said he had forgotten about the exchanges with Malloch, which in any event had not produced any information about WikiLeaks. He said he had not had access to his emails when he prepared for his interview, because he had accidentally deleted them. No dice, said the prosecutors. Corsi still had to plead guilty, and the prosecutors gave him a deadline of November 20. If Corsi didn't plead guilty by that time, Mueller would indict him. Corsi said no. He would not plead guilty—to anything.

And Mueller's office did . . . nothing. Corsi stared them down, and the prosecutors blinked. They filed no charges at all against him. This was, at one level, an understandable decision. Corsi was an older man, and a fringe figure in the case, and the case against him was not particularly strong. A jury in the District of Columbia might have convicted him, but it was not a sure thing. Jurors might have believed that Corsi forgot about the relevant emails and thus did not lie to the prosecutors on September 6. And Corsi did correct the record in five subsequent interviews with the special counsel's office. More to the point, from Mueller's perspective, was that a new indictment, with months of pretrial proceedings to follow, as well as a trial, would extend the investigation, which was something the special counsel himself did not want to do.

Still, it's an understatement to say that it's rare for federal prosecutors to threaten an indictment, send a draft of guilty plea papers to defense counsel, set a deadline for compliance, and then just walk away. Mueller had never announced that he was close to closing up shop and ending his investigation; he never said anything about his activities, except in court filings. But as 2019 began, there was a great deal of speculation that Mueller was winding down. The surrender on Corsi made Mueller's plans clearer than any announcement: he was finished.

There was never a single moment when Mueller told his staff that it was time to wrap things up. It was more a gradual process of recognition. But some conclusions were apparent by the end of 2018. There was a strong case against President Trump for obstruction of justice—on a variety of bases. This had originally been an almost minor part of the investigation, based exclusively on Trump's decision to fire James Comey. But it had metastasized as the president made repeated efforts to interfere with Mueller's own efforts, mostly through Don McGahn.

But the core of the investigation—the examination of the relationship between the Trump campaign and Russia—had not revealed any criminal conduct on the president's part. It was always a source of frustration to Mueller—and a sign of his obliviousness to the realities of American politics—that his two cases against the Russians did not receive more attention. He had uncovered a genuinely massive conspiracy in Russia, stretching from the military to the private sector, and from Moscow to St. Petersburg, to interfere in the most solemn right of our democracy. As the nation's chief counterintelligence officer for a dozen years, Mueller was chilled and appalled by this discovery. But the social media and hacking cases about Russia fell into a news vacuum, because there was no proof, indeed no evidence, that the Trump campaign had anything to do with them.

So as to the central question the nation asked of Mueller—was there collusion between the Trump campaign and Russia?—the answer was clear: no. This was true in both the legal and the colloquial sense of the word. There is no such crime as "collusion," but a knowing partnership between an American political campaign and a foreign power could easily qualify as any number of criminal offenses. No one on the Trump campaign, including the candidate himself, committed any such crime. Nor did anyone on the campaign collude with Russia in the more colloquial sense of the word. There was much irony in this conclusion, because it was clear that Trump himself and his closest associates *wanted* to collude with Russia. Trump's son wanted dirt from the Russians in the Trump Tower meeting. Trump wanted Russia to hack Hillary Clinton's emails, and he "loved" WikiLeaks' efforts to distribute property stolen from Democrats. But there was never an agreement, a meeting of the minds, between the Trump campaign and Russia. Mueller's cheering section in the political world might have wished that the facts were otherwise—indeed, some on his own staff felt this frustration—but Mueller himself would not stray from what his investigation revealed, for better or worse.

The conclusions about obstruction and collusion left only one piece of unfinished investigatory business for the special counsel and his staff: their wish to interview the president of the United States.

21

"The Immense Burden the Process Imposed on the President and His Office"

On the issue of whether and how Donald Trump would submit to questioning, Mueller caved. He did so in the manner that a character in Ernest Hemingway's *The Sun Also Rises* describes going bankrupt: "Gradually, then suddenly."

Mueller raised the issue of a Trump interview almost as soon as he was appointed, in May 2017. He discussed it in early meetings with John Dowd, during Dowd's tenure as lead defense attorney, and the special counsel made his first formal request to speak to the president in December 2017. There was the very tentative deal for an interview at Camp David the following month, but Dowd pulled the plug before it took place. Still, negotiations continued.

There were desultory exchanges between Mueller's deputies and Trump's lawyers on the subject throughout most of 2018. With Giuliani in charge, and with Sekulow's strong endorsement, they put up a harder line than Dowd and Ty Cobb had done the previous year. They effectively dared Mueller to try to subpoena Trump. The Trump lawyers had several lines of defense. They knew that Mueller would have to get permission from Rosenstein to subpoena Trump. Giuliani and Sekulow planned to lobby the deputy attorney general hard to decline the request. If Rosenstein approved a subpoena, the Trump team was increasingly confident that they would win a motion to quash it in the lower courts and eventually in the Supreme Court. (This was especially true after Brett Kavanaugh, with his belief in robust executive power, was confirmed in October 2018.)

In a series of phone calls and letters, Mueller gradually retreated. First, he gave up on a grand jury subpoena. Then he decided not to press the issue of an oral interview. Trump's lawyers asserted that the president wouldn't answer any questions about his behavior in office. Every moment of Trump's life as president, they maintained, was covered by executive privilege. Finally, Trump's lawyers presented Mueller with a take-it-or-leave-it proposal. Trump would answer only written questions and only about matters that took place before he became president. Mueller took it.

This was never an easy issue for the special counsel. The legal issue of whether the courts would approve his subpoena to the president was unsettled. Mueller might well have lost in the Supreme Court, or even in the lower courts, if he tried to enforce a subpoena for the president's testimony. As for written questions and answers, Mueller knew (as any competent lawyer would know) that Trump's answers would be sanitized by his lawyers and designed more to avoid a perjury charge than to provide any real information. As Mueller wrote in his report, "We thus weighed the cost of potentially lengthy constitutional litigation with resulting delay in finishing our investigation, against the anticipated benefits for our investigation and report." But Mueller himself was responsible for much of the delay. He could have issued a subpoena after the Camp David interview blew up in January 2018; he didn't even submit the written questions until September 17, 2018, without a due date for Trump's replies.

Mueller's written questions for Trump concerned five areas: the Trump Tower meeting on June 9, 2016; Russian hacking/Russian use of social media/WikiLeaks; the Trump Organization's Moscow project; contacts with Russia during the campaign; and contacts with Russia during the transition. Sekulow and the Raskins took charge of preparing the responses, which turned out to be a maddening and vaguely comic endeavor. They were determined to protect Trump, and would draft his answers accordingly, but they still had to talk to the president to get at least some sense of what he knew. This was difficult. Trump had trouble focusing in the best of circumstances, and his anger and resentment about the Mueller investigation led him to avoid meetings with the lawyers to prepare his answers. And when the lawyers did come to the Oval Office, Trump preferred to rage about the investigation rather than to answer the questions. Plus, this president—any president—is busy. It was hard for the lawyers to get on his calendar. One session with the lawyers had to be stopped because news broke that pipe bombs had been mailed to prominent Democrats and media outlets; another was interrupted by phone calls from Turkish president Recep Tayyip Erdogan and Chinese president Xi Jinping.

But what, after all, was the hurry for Trump's lawyers? They knew that Mueller, even more than most prosecutors, wanted to move fast, if only to wrap up his investigation. The lawyers knew that Mueller might want to respond to the submission of the letters in some way, so it was safer, as always, to string out the process. And Jane and Marty Raskin were fastidious about checking Trump's verbal responses against the documentary record—videos of his campaign appearances, Trump's personal schedule, emails among his campaign subordinates. They were determined to avoid any answers that put Trump in conflict with provable facts. In the end, the answers, nominally by Trump and signed by him, were submitted to Mueller on November 20. In the answers to the various questions in the five subject areas, Trump said he failed to "recall" twenty-two times and had no "recollection" fourteen times.

Trump's answers about the Trump Tower meeting offered representative examples of his lawyers' approach:

I have no recollection of learning at the time that Donald Trump Jr., Paul Manafort, or Jared Kushner was considering participating in a meeting in June 2016 concerning potentially negative information about Hillary Clinton.

And:

At this point in time, I do not remember whether I spoke or met with Donald Trump Jr., Paul Manafort, or Jared Kushner on June 9, 2016. My desk calendar indicates I was scheduled to meet with Paul Manafort on the morning of June 9, but I do not recall if that meeting took place. It was more than two years ago, at a time when I had many calls and interactions daily.

Such answers were virtually impossible to disprove, even if Mueller had specific evidence to do so (which he didn't). As for advance knowledge of the WikiLeaks dump in October 2016, Trump answered,

> I have no recollection of being told that WikiLeaks possessed or might possess emails related to John Podesta before the release of Mr. Podesta's emails was reported by the media. Likewise, I have no recollection of being told that Roger Stone, anyone acting as an intermediary for Roger Stone, or anyone associated with my campaign had communicated with WikiLeaks on October 7, 2016.

When Trump answered this question, he and his lawyers did not yet know that both Michael Cohen and Rick Gates had told Mueller that they knew Trump discussed WikiLeaks with Roger Stone before the Podesta documents were released. Still, neither Cohen nor Gates had corroboration of his assertions, and both men were at that point convicted felons. To the extent that their stories conflicted with Trump's, the president and his supporters could and did dismiss the two men as liars.

Mueller's team had low expectations for Trump's answers, but the president didn't even live up to them. The prosecutors felt that Trump's lawyers were almost taunting them with their misuse of the format. So Mueller's prosecutors did what they could at that late date. They wrote a letter.

Opposing lawyers write each other a lot of letters. Sending letters is a lot cheaper, and less risky, than filing lawsuits. Lawyers usually justify the practice by saying they are "making a record"—that is, laying the groundwork to prove their case in the event that a dispute ever winds up in court. But most disputes do not end up in court, and the letters have no afterlife except as a reminder of past contentiousness. To put it another way, the letters are pointless—displays of aggression that may give the lawyers, or their clients, a momentary rush of satisfaction.

From May 2017 to December 2018, Mueller's prosecutors and Trump's lawyers exchanged many letters—about document produc-

tion, about witness interviews, but mostly about the special counsel's desire to interview the president. By the end of this period, there
was really little left to discuss. Mueller had decided to forgo issuing a
grand jury subpoena for oral testimony from Trump and taking his
chances in the court battle that was certain to follow. Instead, Mueller had submitted his written questions, and Trump had answered
them, more or less. Still, there was one final exchange of letters on the
subject—one that captured, in microcosm, the contest between the
prosecutor and the president.

Quarles, who handled much of the negotiating over the interview,
initiated this round with a letter on December 3, 2018, about Trump's
written answers. "We said that we would assess the responses in good
faith and determine to what extent additional testimony would be
necessary. We have done so," Quarles wrote, before praising the special counsel's own efforts. "The questions are easy to understand,
call for straightforward responses and are sufficiently detailed to
make clear what is being asked." Nevertheless, Trump avoided giving
straight answers and said he didn't recall or recollect more than thirty
times. The answers, Quarles wrote, "demonstrate the inadequacy of
the written format, as we have had no opportunity to ask follow-up
questions that would ensure complete answers and potentially refresh
your client's recollections or clarify the extent or nature of his lack of
recollection."

Quarles offered a potential solution—that the president grant
Mueller an in-person interview on ten areas relevant to his investigation. "This is the President's opportunity to voluntarily provide us
with information to evaluate in the context of all of the evidence we
have gathered," he wrote. "They also involve matters of your client's
knowledge and intent that can only be effectively explored through
the opportunity for contemporaneous follow up and clarification."
Quarles's letter was either a masterpiece of passive aggression or a
study in self-delusion. Trump's lawyers had just spent a year and a
half maneuvering their way out of an in-person interview where their
client, as was his practice, would have lied constantly and egregiously;
instead, the lawyers had managed to substitute their own banal non-
answers to Mueller's written questions. As Quarles knew, the letter
had no chance of achieving its goal. In the name of sounding tough,
the letter only underlined the weakness of the special counsel.

Trump's lawyers took a leisurely nine days to answer Quarles's letter, and when they did, all four on the defense team—Giuliani, Sekulow, Jane and Marty Raskin—signed it, because it represented a summation of their efforts. Their letter of December 12, which ran to three single-spaced pages, was an aria of disdain and triumph. "The White House has provided unprecedented and virtually limitless cooperation with your investigation, and the President has supplied written answers to your questions on the central subject of your mandate," they wrote. "The President answered the questions despite the additional hardship caused by the confusing and substantial deficiencies of the form we articulated to you in our transmittal letter. And he did so in spite of the fact that, eighteen months into the special counsel's investigation, you had failed to specify any potential offense under investigation, let alone any theory of liability, as to which the President's provision of direct information regarding his various 'Russia-related matters' was sufficiently important and necessary to justify the immense burden the process imposed on the President and his Office. You still have not done so."

The conclusion of their letter was preordained. "When we embarked on the written question and answer procedure, we agreed to engage in a good faith assessment of any asserted need for additional questioning after you had an opportunity to consider the President's answers," they wrote. "Your letter has provided us no basis upon which to recommend that our client provide additional information on the Russia-related topics as to which he has already provided written answers."

In plain English, Trump's lawyers told the special counsel to pound sand. Mueller did.

PART FIVE

22

"Thank You to My New Friend Rudy Giuliani for Your . . ."

The infant on Rudy Giuliani's lap howled, and for good reason. The mohel had just completed the ritual circumcision at Nathan Parnas's bris. As the boy's godfather, Giuliani had the honor of comforting Nathan following this trauma. Two dozen or so guests, sheltered from the late-summer Florida sunshine, circulated around the platters of bagels and smoked fish. Nathan was Lev Parnas's sixth child, and his mother was Lev's third wife. Lev had a gift for good times and an infectiously joyous personality, which had somehow survived a lifetime of business calamity—a string of financial failures, and lawsuits from aggrieved creditors, that stretched the length of the Florida peninsula. His best friend was the president's lawyer, who came with his girlfriend, Maria Ryan, to the bris of his son in September 2018.

They were the unlikeliest of intimates, even if, oddly enough, they kind of resembled each other. Parnas was in his mid-forties, more than two decades younger than Giuliani, but his many cares took a toll on his appearance, if not his demeanor. Giuliani had surrendered to encroaching baldness, but Parnas battled hair loss with a greasy straight-ahead comb-over, which made it look like a small serpent had landed on his forehead. Both men grew up in Brooklyn, but in different worlds. Giuliani was raised in a heavily Italian part of Flatbush, but his own family was a generation removed from Italy, and his accent bore no traces of the old country. Parnas was three years old when he arrived from what was then the Soviet Republic of Ukraine.

His family eventually settled in an enclave of Brighton Beach that was so heavily Russian that decades later Parnas's accent still sounded as if he had just arrived from Odessa. Giuliani was a world-famous politician, still revered in many circles for his leadership of New York City after the attacks of September 11, 2001. Parnas, in contrast, was a serial failure, always on the make without making it. Somehow, in 2018 and 2019, they became inseparable.

Parnas displayed early hustle. When he was just sixteen, he started as a real estate agent, selling apartments in the towers that Fred Trump built for the middle class in Brooklyn. Parnas made it through high school and a year or so of college before moving to Florida, where he entered the world of boiler-room finance. He used the name Larry Parnell—better for cold-calling—at firms named Euro-Atlantic Securities, Mammoth Bullion, Monolith Bullion, and eventually Parnas Holdings, which apparently did not hold very much and soon dissolved. Still, there were moments of prosperity for Parnas, and he at one point drove a Rolls-Royce and lived in a $15,000-per-month house in Boca Raton. (He was evicted for nonpayment of rent.) Along the way, Parnas became a regular at a club in Miami called Lique ("Our sophisticated and stately lounge is the ideal space for any sized entourage"), where he met a fellow émigré named Igor Fruman. Taciturn where Parnas was voluble, Fruman maintained social ties and business interests in Ukraine, where his holdings included the nightclubs Mafia Rave and Buddha Bar. (Paul Manafort went to Buddha Bar.) Thanks to more pedestrian ventures, like canned milk, Fruman became at one point, according to a local magazine, the 195th richest person in Ukraine, with a net worth of $29 million.

Parnas believed that life worked like a slot machine, which is what led him to the world of political fund-raising. He put money in so he could get money out. He had no strong political views, but he figured out that big-dollar political events were good places to meet rich people who might fund his ventures. Shortly before the 2016 election, he somehow found the wherewithal to attend a $50,000-a-head fund-raiser for Trump and the Republican National Committee in south Florida. (Parnas arrived after sundown, because it was Yom Kippur.) There Parnas met the host, a local billionaire named Robert Pereira; Giuliani, who attended to support Trump; and the guest of honor, Trump himself. Parnas was inspired to host his own "Russians for Trump" fund-raiser (at Lique) shortly thereafter, and as a result Trump invited him to his final debate with Hillary Clinton, in Las Vegas. Parnas hitched a ride there on Pereira's private plane, and he also found his way to Trump's victory party in New York and then, with his family, to the inauguration in Washington. (Fruman and Parnas had a brief falling-out, because Parnas, as was his custom, stiffed Fruman on the hotel bills from the inauguration.)

Once Trump became president, Parnas bought his way into more rarefied circles. In May 2018, he and Fruman paid $325,000 to a pro-Trump super PAC called America First Action, which earned the pair an invitation to dine with the president in a private room at the Trump International Hotel in Washington. Against all decorum (and rules), Fruman secretly recorded the dinner on his phone, including all conversation with the president. Parnas made a pitch for marijuana legalization—a favorite cause and possible business interest—but the others at the table, including Donald Trump Jr. and Jack Nicklaus III, expressed no interest. ("It does cause an IQ problem," the president said of marijuana.)

As it happened, President Petro Poroshenko of Ukraine had just acknowledged receipt of American anti-tank missiles called Javelins, to use in the low-grade war it was fighting on its eastern border with Russia. A discussion on this subject prompted Parnas to introduce his (literally) silent partner, Igor Fruman, to the president, and to tell Trump that Fruman also came from Ukraine. Parnas knew how Trump valued fawning. "They love you, though," Parnas told Trump about Ukrainians. "I can tell you that much. They love you."

"Great," the president replied. "I'll tell you, they're great fighters."

"They're great fighters. They love you," Parnas said.

At the time, one of Fruman and Parnas's business pipe dreams was to sell American natural gas to Ukraine, which would help wean the former Soviet satellite from its dependence on Russia. Parnas had good things to say to Trump about Ukraine's president—"Poroshenko is a good guy. He wants the right thing for it"—but Parnas informed Trump that he had a problem in Ukraine.

"A lot of the European countries—they're backstabbing us basically, and dealing with Russia," Parnas said. "That's why you're having such difficulty. I think if you take a look, the biggest problem there I think where you need to start is, we've got to get rid of the ambassador. She's still left over from the Clinton administration." (Presumably, Parnas meant the Obama administration.)

"Where? The ambassador where? Ukraine?" Trump asked.

"Yeah," Parnas answered. "She's basically walking around telling everybody, 'Wait, he's going to get impeached. Just wait.'"

"Really?" said Trump.

"It's incredible," Parnas replied.

Trump asked the ambassador's name, and Parnas said he couldn't remember it. What happened next stunned Parnas. Trump turned to the White House aide who was present and said, "Get rid of her. Get her out tomorrow. I don't care, get her out tomorrow. Take her out, okay? Do it."

Parnas had basically been riffing throughout the conversation with the president. He knew little about Ukraine, even less about its politics, and he was just repeating complaints that he had heard from Fruman, who still did business there. Still, the lesson stuck. The president wanted intelligence on his adversaries within his own government, and one of them, it appeared, was his ambassador to Ukraine. Notwithstanding Trump's order at the dinner table, the ambassador, whose name was Marie Yovanovitch, was not fired the next day. But an idea had been planted.

At the time, in mid-2018, Giuliani still held the title of lead defense counsel for President Trump in the Mueller investigation, but he left the day-to-day work to Sekulow and the Raskins. They were the ones who did most of the haggling with Mueller's team about the written questions to the president, and they tried to pin Trump down to produce the answers. This freed up Giuliani to pursue his far-flung business interests. One of his higher-profile endeavors was to star in infomercials for LifeLock, a company that helped individuals protect against identity theft. By this point, Parnas and Giuliani had met several times at various Trump events, so it wasn't surprising that Parnas sought out the former mayor's advice for another one of his business interests—a company called, improbably, Fraud Guarantee.

The venture was born out of a failed real estate deal where Parnas's partner went to prison. Parnas then reconstituted the planned company around the concept of fraud insurance; for a fee, Fraud

Guarantee would examine possible business partners and determine if they were likely to commit fraud. Parnas selected the name to game the Google search engine; he thought that when people googled his name, they would find his new company rather than links to his sketchy business history. In any event, Parnas thought Giuliani would make an ideal pitchman for Fraud Guarantee, so he set up a meeting in New York with Giuliani and several of his lawyers and advisers. After the meeting, where Parnas laid out the concept, Giuliani's colleagues were unanimous. The business idea was dubious, rife with regulatory problems, and a cursory review of Parnas's history raised a host of red flags. Stay away, they counseled.

Giuliani himself felt differently, which was probably based more on his personal situation at the time than on the business prospects of Fraud Guarantee. Giuliani was working pro bono for the president. His law firm, Greenberg Traurig, cut ties with him after his statements to Sean Hannity that Michael Cohen's payment to Stormy Daniels was a routine matter and that Giuliani himself did the same kinds of things for his clients. Judith Nathan, Giuliani's third wife, had just filed for divorce. In that litigation, Giuliani would soon assert that he had assets of $30 million but very little cash flow. He even had to borrow $100,000 from Marc Mukasey, his longtime law partner and friend (and another attendee at the Parnas meeting), to make tax payments. Giuliani's high profile as Trump's lawyer and his eccentric behavior in that role had scared away clients for his law and security businesses. All of which made Giuliani favorably disposed toward Parnas—or anyone—as a client. It was never exactly clear what Giuliani would do for the money. At this point, Fraud Guarantee had no actual business or clients (and never would), so Giuliani had nothing to endorse as a pitchman. But he agreed to serve as a general adviser to Parnas—for a fee of $500,000. Parnas, in turn, began hunting for an investor to come up with the money to pay Giuliani since he had almost none of his own. Parnas found one in Charles Gucciardo, a successful personal injury attorney on Long Island, who invested $250,000 in return for a piece of the as-yet-nonexistent company.

Giuliani and Parnas were now business partners, after a fashion, and Giuliani began to regard the younger man with considerable affection. They spent much of the summer and fall of 2018 together as Parnas tagged along on Republican contributors' private planes when

Giuliani campaigned for congressional candidates in the midterm elections. And when they weren't out on the stump, Parnas sat with Giuliani as he held court in either of the dual unofficial headquarters of Trump world—the lobby bar of the Trump hotel in Washington or the Grand Havana cigar bar in New York. Cementing their relationship, Giuliani came to Parnas's home in Florida, in September, for the bris of Nathan. Giuliani's visit paid dividends in another way. Charles Gucciardo, who also attended, was so impressed by Giuliani's closeness to Parnas that he agreed to invest the second half of the $500,000 that Fraud Guarantee needed for Giuliani's fee.

Parnas became nearly a constant companion for Giuliani, almost like a mascot. They crossed paths with the president several more times in 2018, including at a fund-raiser in upstate New York for Congresswoman Claudia Tenney. Parnas was an assiduous user of social media, and he documented at least eight occasions when he was present with Trump. (Presidents take countless grip-and-grin photos, but the number and frequency of Trump's contacts with Parnas were well beyond the norm.) After the midterms, in December, Giuliani demonstrated his closeness with Parnas when he took him as his plus-one to George H. W. Bush's state funeral in Washington.

After Trump won the presidency, he dashed Giuliani's hope to become secretary of state. This failure rankled Giuliani, who fancied himself an expert on international relations after running his security-consulting business since 9/11. Throughout Trump's presidency, Giuliani took on diplomatic projects, largely on his own initiative, but always keeping Trump informed. The State Department and the president's national security advisers generally regarded Giuliani's forays with disdain, if not alarm. On the other hand, the president saw the national security establishment—especially the State Department's Foreign Service—as a hostile outpost of the deep state, so he liked to hear reports from an outside loyalist like Giuliani. All through the fall, as he was traveling around the country with Parnas, Giuliani was focused on Venezuela, working connections with the resistance to the socialist government there. During that period, Parnas listened to Giuliani's side of several conversations with the president about Venezuela.

After the midterms, though, a new subject came up for Giuliani—Ukraine. Giuliani was an old acquaintance of Kevin Downing, who was still Paul Manafort's lead defense lawyer. Manafort had been convicted by this point, but Downing went to Giuliani with the claim that Manafort had been set up by his enemies in Ukraine. He had the idea that somehow Giuliani could scare up information that would help Manafort overturn his conviction. To this end, Downing introduced Giuliani to Manafort's network in Ukraine—the pro-Putin forces associated with his longtime client Viktor Yanukovych. In November, Giuliani started talking to these people and sharing his excitement about what he heard with Parnas and also with the president. Sometimes, it seemed to Parnas, Giuliani had become obsessed with Ukraine. Giuliani said he was onto an earthshaking story. According to his sources, the American people had been fed a completely fictional story about Russian meddling in the 2016 election. It was nothing but fake news. The real meddler, according to Giuliani's sources, was Ukraine.

As it happened, President Bush's funeral was the day before the White House Hanukkah Party, and Parnas and Fruman had been invited since they were now major Trump campaign contributors. (The source of their funds would be a subject of continuing controversy.) For this trip to the White House, Parnas, Fruman, and Giuliani were joined by a different woman friend of the former mayor's, Ashley Hutson, who traveled between Paris and Florida as an internet influencer on fashion. (Hutson's mother also came.) After the group arrived, Giuliani went to the residence to confer privately with Trump for about half an hour. As Parnas understood it, this was so Giuliani could update Trump on his Ukraine discoveries.

After the main reception, Secret Service agents brought Parnas and his party to join a much smaller group in the Red Room at the White House. There he found Vice President Pence and his wife, Karen, Jared Kushner, and Giuliani and Hutson. The president and first lady arrived a few minutes later, and Trump immediately walked up to Hutson, ogled her up and down, and said to Giuliani, "Great job, Rudy!" (Melania Trump, disgusted by her husband's leering, walked off and refused to pose for photographs.) Hutson clearly enjoyed the visit to the White House, tweeting afterward, "What an epic visit to

Washington DC yes my mom and I played dress up DC Barbie LOL It really was a once in a lifetime experience! Thank you to my new friend Rudy Giuliani for your . . ."

Later in the evening, the president pulled Parnas aside for a brief, private word. In the manner that Trump interlocutors like Comey had long recognized, Trump said nothing direct. He didn't even mention Ukraine. But he thanked Parnas for the work he was doing with Rudy. It was important and he was grateful. Keep it up, the president said.

Parnas did.

23

Fraud Guaranteed

The midterms had gone poorly for the president and his party, and Trump was stewing. On the day after the elections, Trump finally dismissed Jeff Sessions as attorney general, after humiliating him on Twitter and elsewhere for most of the previous two years. Trump soon replaced him with William Barr, who had proved his anti-Mueller bonafides with his unsolicited memo about obstruction of justice. But Giuliani had what Trump really wanted—a counternarrative to the Russia scandal that still plagued him. The former mayor could not have come up with a better story—*Ukraine Helped Hillary in 2016*—for a more receptive audience. As it happened, Trump had already given considerable thought to Ukraine.

Trump was never one for acknowledging failure or accepting responsibility, and that was true for this political setback in the midterms, too. In his reckoning, he had been blamed for things that weren't his fault—like the Mueller "witch hunt"—and he had received insufficient credit for his accomplishments like the booming economy. It wasn't *fair.* Trump had an almost childlike fixation on the word, which he used all the time. The fake news media. The deep state. They had been collaborating against him since the early days of his campaign. Not *fair.* But even as he complained about the forces arrayed against him, the president hated being a victim, and he loved to fight back.

Trump's main resentment was against Mueller. Though he knew

at this point that he was likely to survive anything Mueller would disclose in his report, the president hated everything about the investigation—starting with its premise. He believed that the assertion that Russia helped him win election in 2016 diminished his achievement. It was bad enough that he was accused of colluding with Russia—which he didn't do—but Trump was also offended by the idea that he received assistance from Putin's minions, which he did. Trump wanted it known that he won the presidency entirely on the strength of his own efforts, without help from anyone else, especially a foreign country. So how could he prove that he *didn't* owe his victory to Vladimir Putin?

The president, a master of projection, came up with a characteristic answer to this dilemma. He wasn't the candidate who benefited from foreign assistance; it was his opponent. And Russia was not the country that meddled; it was Ukraine. By this point, in late 2018, Trump had been obsessing about Ukraine for more than two years, since the regime there leaked the "black ledger," which forced the departure of Paul Manafort from Trump's 2016 campaign. Manafort had vented to Trump about the perfidy and corruption of his enemies within the Ukrainian regime. A little while later, Trump embraced the CrowdStrike conspiracy, which posited that this Ukrainian-owned company had covered up Ukraine's role in the hacking of the DNC. Then, when the Trump Tower story broke in July 2017, Sean Hannity had asserted that the Ukrainian embassy in Washington had assisted Clinton's campaign. With Trump, these grievances against Ukraine were never far from the surface.

Trump raised the CrowdStrike server conspiracy again the following year, during his notorious news conference with President Putin in Helsinki, when the president dismissed the evidence that Russia had interfered in the 2016 election. "You have groups that are wondering why the FBI never took the server," Trump said, as Putin listened. "Why haven't they taken the server? Why was the FBI told to leave the office of the Democratic National Committee? I've been wondering that. I've been asking that for months and months, and I've been tweeting it out and calling it out on social media. Where is the server?" As Trump and others refined the theory, they claimed that the DNC disposed of the evidence of the hack by turning over its servers to CrowdStrike, which then spirited the hardware back to its base in Ukraine so the FBI couldn't examine it. In other words, CrowdStrike was a Ukrainian asset, and the company was complicit in covering up Ukraine's role in the DNC hack.

Even by Trump's standards, the CrowdStrike theory was madness—false in every respect. CrowdStrike was never a Ukrainian company; it was American. The DNC servers never went to Ukraine; they remained in Washington. And the FBI had all the access to the servers that it needed. Moreover, the blame-Ukraine hypothesis never even made any sense. For starters, why would Ukraine, in an effort to help Clinton, hack and release emails that damaged her campaign? It wouldn't, and it didn't. Later, of course, the intelligence agencies unanimously concluded that Russia was behind the hacking, and then Mueller brought a detailed indictment showing how Russian military intelligence pulled off the data intrusion inside the United States. As with the mainstream news reports, the fact that the deep state intelligence agencies, and Mueller himself, pinned the intervention on the Russians amounted to proof, for Trump's supporters, that the opposite was true. So the CrowdStrike lie endured.

But there was an even more sinister element to Trump's embrace of the blame-Ukraine theory. This wasn't just a convenient story that Trump and his supporters embraced. It was disinformation created by, and for the benefit of, Vladimir Putin's Russia; in other words, Trump was repeating Russian propaganda. Russia was only too happy to stoke the blame-Ukraine theory, to remove its own fingerprints from its attack against the U.S. political system. Russia's emissaries and assets injected the story into Trump's world. Not surprisingly, then, according to Rick Gates, one advocate for the blame-Ukraine idea was Manafort's old friend and colleague Konstantin Kilimnik, the alleged Russian intelligence asset. Giuliani, in turn, was led down this road by Downing, Manafort's lawyer, who plugged Giuliani in to the network of pro-Russian Ukrainian politicians whom Manafort had nurtured in Kyiv. Much later, in the impeachment proceedings against President Trump, Fiona Hill, the former National Security Council (NSC) staffer, dismissed the idea that Ukraine, not Russia, interfered in the 2016 elections. "This is a fictional narrative that has been perpetrated and propagated by the Russian security services themselves," she said. American intelligence officials said Russian operatives had begun pushing the false blame-Ukraine theory "starting at least in 2017"—at exactly the time that Trump himself began using his enormous platform to tell this false story to the world.

In all, then, when Giuliani started telling Trump, in late 2018, that he had evidence that Ukraine meddled in the 2016 election, the president welcomed the news. But there was another reason Giuliani and Trump were thinking about Ukraine, and it involved former vice president Joseph Biden and his son Hunter.

As the next presidential contest began, Biden appeared to be Trump's most formidable Democratic rival. Early polls showed him leading Trump, often by substantial margins. But the president had an instinct for the political jugular, and he knew that Biden had a potential vulnerability. The story wasn't a secret—the basic outlines had been known for years—but Trump understood how he and a compliant news media could convert a minor problem into a mortal threat. What had worked with Hillary Clinton's emails could work with Joe Biden's son.

Trump built on an insight that Republicans had discovered years earlier—that the best way to attack an opponent was to go after what appeared to be his greatest strength. When John Kerry ran for president in 2004, Democrats thought that his experience as a Vietnam War hero would be a major political asset, until Republicans manufactured a phony controversy over his military record as a swift boat commander. Kerry never recovered. For Biden, the story of his family had always cast him in a sympathetic glow. In 1972, a few weeks after he was first elected to the Senate, Biden's wife and daughter were killed, and his sons, Beau and Hunter, seriously injured, in an automobile accident. Biden was sworn in by the boys' hospital bedside, and he then commuted from Washington to Wilmington daily, to raise them as a single father. Later, he remarried, to Jill Biden, and they had a daughter together.

Beau Biden grew up to resemble a new-and-improved version of his father. He was a prosecutor and an army officer who served in Iraq, and in 2006 he was elected attorney general of Delaware. His political future appeared unlimited. But while his father was vice president, Beau was struck by a virulent form of brain cancer. He died in 2015, at the age of forty-six. For a second time, Joe Biden's life had been upended by premature death in his family. Even political opponents mourned with him.

Hunter Biden had a much rockier passage through life. He was nearly fifty years old as his father contemplated running against Donald Trump, and his biography included long struggles with alcohol addiction and drug abuse. He'd gone through a rancorous divorce, and he was being pressed for child support by an Arkansas woman who was a brief acquaintance. Hunter had graduated from Yale Law School in 1996, spent several years working for MBNA America, a bank holding company in Delaware, and then joined the Clinton administration. He then became a lobbyist and a private equity investor, never with great success. Then, in 2014, he was named to the board of Burisma, one of the largest natural gas producers in Ukraine. Hunter had no apparent qualifications in the field or the region, other than his relationship to his father, whom President Obama had assigned to oversee relations with the government of Ukraine. Hunter's position at Burisma had at least the potential for conflict of interest with his father. At a minimum, the situation looked seedy; at worst, corrupt.

Giuliani told Trump that Hunter Biden's work in Ukraine represented a potential gold mine of opposition research. It was the same story with the information about the Ukrainian role in the 2016 election. All this political dirt was waiting to be discovered on the ground in Ukraine. Giuliani said he had Parnas and Fruman, natives of the region, who could help him make contacts on the ground. Should Giuliani mobilize his troops and start a Ukraine project?

This moment, on the night of the White House Hanukkah Party in 2018, was a crucial turning point in the Trump presidency, though surely it did not seem that way at the time. It was just another conversation between lawyer and client in the White House residence, something Giuliani and Trump had done any number of times. And there is no indication that either man agonized about what they were considering, even though the action they took would turn out to be of momentous importance. At that moment, Giuliani had a great deal to be proud of about his legal work for the president. His methods had been unconventional, to be sure, but his public advocacy for Trump had transformed Robert Mueller's image from that of a revered public servant into that of just another partisan actor. Under Giuliani's leadership, Trump's defense team had dodged a subpoena from Mueller and negotiated a nearly risk-free substitute of written questions and answers, only about the campaign period. True, Mueller's report would soon be released, but Giuliani's team had already assembled a "prebuttal," which would immediately respond to all of Mueller's likely claims. In light of this, Giuliani had every reason to expect that the likely reaction to Mueller's report would break along the same partisan divide as every other issue in the Trump era, with no lasting damage to the president or the presidency. In other words, if Giuliani had ceased his representation of Trump on this day, he could have, with justification, retired a hero to the president and his supporters.

Instead, Giuliani pressed ahead, with Trump's encouragement, to begin a full-scale investigation about Joe and Hunter Biden in Ukraine. If Giuliani had done anything else, Donald Trump would not have been impeached. For this reason, Giuliani's work must rank among the most disastrous pieces of advocacy in the history of American lawyering. Giuliani was as toxic in the Ukraine phase of the investigation as he was successful in the Russia period. The efforts were related, of course, but it was easier to trash an investigation than to run one. Giuliani's bumptious, improvisational media takedowns of Mueller worked, so he tried the same kind of seat-of-the-pants operations in Ukraine. Giuliani proceeded without a plan or any real knowledge of Ukraine or its politics. It was never clear whether he represented Trump as an individual, or whether he represented the presidency, or whether he represented the U.S. government. At times, Giuliani behaved as if he represented all three. In addition, his staff for this venture consisted of Parnas and Fruman—Lev and Igor, the proprietor of Fraud Guarantee and his partner—who were almost comically unfit for the assignment, lacking the knowledge, wisdom, and values to undertake a project of this magnitude. Their motives, as they scraped for cash at home and abroad, even as they worked for the president of the United States, were dubious, and obviously so. Failure, even fiasco, was preordained.

Above all, though, Giuliani failed in the most basic obligation of a lawyer—to tell his client no. In 2018, Trump saw potential in Ukraine for what seemed only dimly possible in Russia in 2016. From every indication ("Russia, if you're listening . . ."), Trump would have welcomed Russian assistance—collusion—in 2016, but he had nothing yet to trade in return. That was different in 2018, when he was president. He now had an abundance of tools to use as leverage to get what he wanted from Ukraine, starting with the ability to grant or withhold direct military aid. To make that trade of U.S. government assistance for dirt on his political opponents was at least immoral. It was the job of Trump's lawyer to tell him not to do it. But that's not what Giuliani did. To the contrary, Trump sent Giuliani to Ukraine, and he went. Together, the two men didn't just advocate for collusion with Ukraine; they executed it.

Parnas went to Kyiv in January 2019. His mission was easy to define, if difficult to complete. He was to find people who could provide evidence that President Trump could use against Democrats in general and Biden in particular. Parnas had a lead from Giuliani: find Viktor Shokin, the former prosecutor general of Ukraine. With his characteristic resourcefulness and moxie, Parnas did, and he arranged a Skype call between Giuliani and Shokin on January 23, 2019. By this point, Parnas was in New York with Giuliani in his Park Avenue office, and he served as the translator on the call.

Shokin was effectively the chief law enforcement officer in Ukraine in the early days of President Poroshenko's time in office. By 2015, though, he had become an international symbol of Ukraine's failure to address its corruption problems. As a result, the International Monetary Fund, the European Union, and the U.S. government all wanted Shokin fired. In December 2015, Vice President Biden visited Kyiv and delivered the verdict of the international community to Poroshenko: Shokin had to go. Indeed, the Obama administration was going to withhold $1 billion in loan guarantees if Shokin remained. In a later public appearance, Biden described what happened during his visit: "I looked at them and said, 'I'm leaving in six hours. If the prosecutor is not fired, you're not getting the money.' Well, son of a bitch!"—laughter—"He got fired. And they put in place someone who was solid at the time."

But when Giuliani and Shokin spoke by Skype, Shokin asserted he had been fired for a very different reason—the opposite, in fact, of Biden's stated justification. Shokin said that Biden arranged for his firing because Shokin was aggressively investigating corruption in Ukraine—specifically at Burisma, where Biden's son was on the board. In this version, the vice president orchestrated Shokin's firing to protect Hunter's lucrative sinecure at Burisma. Parnas made another promising connection in Kyiv. Later in January, Yuriy Lutsenko, who was Shokin's successor as prosecutor general and still in office, flew to New York to speak with Giuliani. Over the course of two days of meetings, Lutsenko told the president's lawyer what he wanted to hear—that Ukraine had aided Clinton in the 2016 election and Vice President Biden had protected his son's job at Burisma.

Through Giuliani, Shokin and Lutsenko became central figures in the story. Giuliani came to trust them completely, and he repeated their stories all over Washington, most notably to Trump. For Giuliani, the opposition research the two men provided was pure gold. Their stories were also a pack of lies, told by a pair of opportunists who were at a minimum oblivious to Ukraine's corruption and possibly complicit in it. As prosecutor general, Shokin was best known for stifling the work of David Sakvarelidze, a respected anticorruption leader, then firing him. After U.S. officials found that Shokin's allies tried to get Geoffrey Pyatt, the American ambassador to Ukraine, recalled early in Obama's presidency, U.S. law enforcement officials stopped working with Shokin. Lutsenko worked even harder than Shokin did to ingratiate himself with Giuliani. As Kurt Volker, Trump's former special envoy to Ukraine, later testified, "My opinion of Prosecutor General Lutsenko was that he was acting in a self-serving manner, frankly making things up, in order to appear important to the United States."

When Lutsenko came to New York, he brought with him financial information purportedly drawn from bank records, which, he said, proved that Burisma had paid Hunter Biden and his business partner to "lobby" Joe Biden. "Lutsenko came in with guns blazing," Parnas told *The New Yorker*'s Adam Entous. "He came in with records showing us the money trail. That's when it became real." Giuliani thought the material vindicated his hopes for the Ukraine project. The following month, in February, he went to Warsaw to speak on behalf of Mujahedin-e-Khalq, an Iranian resistance group that was on the State Department's list of terrorist sponsors until 2012. While in Poland, Giuliani met with Lutsenko again and heard more of his grievances about the Bidens' actions in Ukraine. When Giuliani returned to the

United States, he started putting the information from Shokin and Lutsenko to work for Trump.

Giuliani wanted Shokin to come to the United States so he could report his claims to the Justice Department and denounce Biden in public. (In a pattern that would recur, Giuliani just wanted accusations about Biden to be circulating in public. He didn't really care if any actual investigation of the former vice president and his family took place.) But Giuliani had a problem. In order to come to the United States, Shokin needed a visa. And the American embassy in Kyiv, which was led by Ambassador Marie Yovanovitch, denied Shokin permission to visit the United States. The reason was straightforward, as George Kent, her deputy, later testified. "We felt, under no circumstances, should a visa be issued to someone who knowingly subverted and wasted U.S. taxpayer money," Kent said, echoing the reason that Biden wanted Shokin fired in the first place. Yovanovitch, who made fighting corruption in Ukraine a cornerstone of her tenure, would not reward a facilitator of corruption with a visa.

This denial enraged Giuliani, and he blamed Yovanovitch. It had been almost a year since Parnas, on the thinnest of justifications, disparaged the ambassador to the president at the Trump hotel fundraiser. Now Giuliani's clique had a real reason to be angry at her, and Giuliani knew how to take his revenge. He and Parnas became part of a salon of sorts, with Victoria Toensing and Joe diGenova, the married couple who were briefly considered for Trump's legal team, as they schemed to put this Ukrainian information to work. They usually met in the BLT Prime steak house, on the mezzanine at the Trump International Hotel in Washington. In one initiative, Giuliani worked directly to undermine Yovanovitch. In February, Toensing asked Giuliani in a text message, "Is there absolute commitment for HER to be gone this week?" Giuliani answered, "Yes, not sure how absolute. Will get a reading in morning and call you. Pompeii [*sic*] is now aware of it. Talked to him on Friday." (Mike Pompeo was secretary of state.)

Giuliani's Ukraine initiative moved quickly. Perhaps the most extraordinary early chapter took place when Parnas and Fruman returned to Kyiv in February and obtained an audience with President Poroshenko. (Lutsenko was also present.) Here were two American businessmen, of exceedingly dubious provenance, representing the U.S. government and delivering what Parnas recalled as a "stern" message. Over three hours, Parnas told the Ukrainians that they had to announce an investigation of the Bidens if they wanted successful relations with the Trump administration. As if there were any ambiguity about the purpose of the gathering, Parnas later referred to it, in public and private, as the "quid pro quo meeting." If Poroshenko wanted anything from the United States—military aid, Oval Office meetings with Trump—he would have to deliver the announcement of an investigation of the Bidens in return. Notably, all that Parnas required was the announcement of an investigation, not an investigation itself. The announcement of a corruption investigation would damage Biden politically, which was the point of the Ukraine initiative. Whether Ukraine actually investigated corruption was of no consequence to Parnas or his patron. At the conclusion of the meeting, the Ukrainian president and his prosecutor general told Parnas that they would see what they could do.

Back in Washington, Giuliani moved ahead on yet another track. He used his contacts in the government to try to bring down Yovanovitch. Now that he had deployed Parnas to get the investigation announcement in Kyiv, it was time for a public relations offensive in Washington, because that was the best way to get the president's attention. Trump disdained briefings but inhaled Fox News. After conferring with Toensing and diGenova, Giuliani thought the best option was to launder their accusations against Yovanovitch and the Bidens through a journalist—John Solomon, a veteran conservative reporter who was then writing for *The Hill,* a small magazine with an avid readership in Washington political circles. Giuliani assigned Parnas the role of introducing Solomon to Lutsenko, the Ukrainian prosecutor general. Parnas forwarded to Lutsenko a letter from Solomon, which included a list of questions he would ask. "I sent you the questions and the invitation from the journalist, call me when you wake up," Parnas texted Lutsenko after sending him the letter. After the two men spoke, Solomon produced a column about Lutsenko on March 20 that bore the headline "Top Ukrainian Justice Official Says US Ambassador Gave Him a Do Not Prosecute List." Solomon's story concluded, "Former Rep. Pete Sessions (R-Texas), who was at the time House Rules Committee chairman, voiced concerns about Yovanovitch in a letter to the State Department last year in which he said he had proof the ambassador had spoken of her 'disdain' for the

Trump administration." (In an example of the circular nature of the information flow in this group, Sessions's "proof" in the letter came entirely from his conversations with Parnas, who actually knew nothing about Yovanovitch's feelings about the Trump administration.)

But that was just the beginning of the media cycle. On the night that his column in *The Hill* ran, Solomon went on Sean Hannity's Fox News program and repeated the charges against Yovanovitch and described Ukraine's purported advocacy for Clinton in the 2016 election. Introducing the segment, Hannity said, "Ukraine's top prosecutor has opened a criminal probe into whether senior law enforcement officials in that country tried to sway the U.S. election, influence our election, to help Hillary Clinton win." Completing the circle, President Trump then tweeted an endorsement of the Hannity segment about Solomon's column: "John Solomon: As Russia Collusion fades, Ukrainian plot to help Clinton emerges. @seanhannity @FoxNews." Two days later, Giuliani tweeted, "Hillary, Kerry, and Biden people colluding with Ukrainian operatives to make money and affect 2016 election."

So the route of the story was clear: from Lutsenko to Parnas to Giuliani, back to Parnas, to Solomon to Hannity to Trump's seventy-two million followers on Twitter. And Giuliani's team kept feeding Solomon more stories, which produced headlines like "Senior Ukrainian Official Says He's Opened Probe into US Election Interference" and "Let's Get Real: Democrats Were First to Enlist Ukraine in US Elections" and "Joe Biden's 2020 Ukrainian Nightmare: A Closed Probe Is Revived." The themes, which continued to radiate out from Solomon into the broader conservative media universe, were clear. Ukraine helped Hillary more than Russia helped Trump in 2016 . . . The disloyal deep-stater Yovanovitch was out to get the president . . . The corrupt Biden intervened to help his son fill his pockets. All of these stories were false in their entirety. Ukraine did not collude with the Clinton campaign. Yovanovitch was an apolitical career government servant. Biden's efforts in Ukraine served an international consensus against Shokin and had nothing to do with his son's job. (Lutsenko later admitted that Yovanovitch did not give him a "do not prosecute" list; that there was no evidence that Vice President Biden intervened to help his son; and that the financial records Lutsenko produced were meaningless.) All of these facts notwithstanding,

Giuliani, with the assistance of his motley assortment of friends and allies, had managed to create and circulate a full counter-narrative that served Trump's political agenda. And Giuliani was just getting started.

But on March 22, 2019, two days after the president tweeted out Hannity's take on Solomon's story, Giuliani had to take a break from his labors on the Ukraine story. On that day, Attorney General William Barr informed Congress that he had received Robert Mueller's long-awaited report, and Giuliani had to prepare to offer his reaction.

24

"Ultimate Conclusions"

The final chapter of the Mueller investigation—the delivery of what became known as the Mueller Report—began during the first week of March. Aaron Zebley, Mueller's de facto chief of staff, called Ed O'Callaghan, who was Rod Rosenstein's deputy, to give him a heads-up about the report. Rosenstein had designated O'Callaghan as his liaison with the Mueller office, and O'Callaghan had met regularly with Zebley during the investigation. The two dealt with bureaucratic issues like budgets, and Zebley also gave O'Callaghan advance notice of major developments, like indictments and now the release of the report. The two were cordial but wary of each other.

Mueller's office had started pulling together what became the report nearly a year earlier, in mid-2018. It was a massive undertaking. Each of Mueller's teams had been creating informal chronologies of events, and the lawyers began integrating and cross-referencing their efforts—drawing on hundreds of FBI interviews and grand jury examinations, thousands of pages of transcripts, and millions of documents from the executive branch and private parties. One big decision was made early—to split the report into two parts. The first would cover the Russia side of the investigation, and the second would deal with obstruction of justice in the White House.

The conclusion of part 1—about Russia—was apparent fairly early in the investigation. As the executive summary of part 1 stated,

"Although the investigation established that the Russian government perceived it would benefit from a Trump presidency and worked to secure that outcome, and that the Campaign expected it would benefit electorally from information stolen and released through Russian efforts, the investigation did not establish that members of the Trump Campaign conspired or coordinated with the Russian government in its election interference activities." When the report was released, this was taken, especially by Trump himself, as a total exoneration—"no collusion," as he said any number of times. This was more true than not, but Mueller's verdict was somewhat more nuanced. As the report stated elsewhere, "While the investigation identified numerous links between individuals with ties to the Russian government and individuals associated with the Trump Campaign, the evidence was not sufficient to support criminal charges." Certainly, Mueller found abundant evidence that Trump and his campaign *wanted* to collude and conspire with Russia, but they hadn't been able to close the deal. Moreover, witnesses such as Flynn, Papadopoulos, and Manafort never came clean with Mueller's office about the campaign's ties to Russia, which hamstrung the prosecutors' effort to discover the truth. In simple terms, the report's verdict was more *insufficient evidence* than *innocent*. But to be fair, the most inflammatory charge against Trump—that he himself conspired with Russia to help him win the 2016 election—was not borne out by Mueller's investigation.

Zebley's call to O'Callaghan concerned part 2 of the report—obstruction of justice—and it was the result of a complex and consequential internal debate within the Mueller office. Mueller had uncovered extensive evidence that Trump committed the crime of obstruction of justice—repeatedly. Trump told Comey to stop the investigation of Flynn—"let this go." He fired Comey when Comey didn't stop the Russia investigation. Trump told Corey Lewandowski to tell Jeff Sessions to limit the special counsel investigation. Most dramatically of all, Trump told Don McGahn to arrange for Mueller to be fired and then, months later, told McGahn to lie about his earlier order. These were just the most prominent examples of Trump's actions to obstruct the investigation of him. Mueller's report, if read carefully, establishes that Trump committed several acts of criminal obstruction of justice. The impeachment proceedings against both

Nixon and Clinton were rooted in charges of obstruction of justice, and Trump's offenses were even more extensive and enduring.

Moreover, Mueller's staff analyzed in detail whether each of these actions by Trump met the criteria for obstruction of justice. In the report, the special counsel spelled out that in at least these four examples—Trump's attempt to stop the Flynn investigation, his firing of Comey, his attempt to limit the scope of the Mueller investigation, and his use of McGahn to try to fire Mueller and then his attempt to tell McGahn to lie about it—Trump's conduct met every element of the crime. In other words, Mueller described Trump's actions, recounted how his behavior met the requirements for proving obstruction of justice, but stopped short of saying Trump committed the crime.

Why? Why didn't Mueller simply come out and say what his report proved? His reasoning was complicated—because Mueller made it complicated. As a Justice Department employee, Mueller was bound by the policy that banned criminal prosecution of a sitting president. So his team faced a dilemma. What should they say about evidence in a case they could never bring? This was the subject of Zebley's phone call to O'Callaghan.

"I just wanted to let you know that we are not going to reach a prosecutorial decision on obstruction," Zebley said. "We're not going to decide crime or no crime."

O'Callaghan puzzled over this, and they had a couple of calls so Zebley could clarify the office's position. "Are you saying that you would have indicted Trump except for the OLC opinion?" O'Callaghan asked.

"No, that's not what we're saying," Zebley said. "We're just not deciding one way or the other."

The report eventually spelled out Mueller's reasoning in greater detail. If Mueller had actually brought criminal charges against Trump, the president would have had the chance to defend himself in court, but in light of the OLC opinion Mueller could not charge Trump. But if Mueller said in his report that Trump was guilty of a crime, the president would have no forum to defend himself, as an ordinary criminal defendant would have. As the report stated, "A prosecutor's judgment that crimes were committed, but that no charges will be brought, affords no such adversarial opportunity for public name-clearing before an impartial adjudicator." In other words, Mueller withheld a final judgment about whether Trump committed crimes as a gesture of fairness to the president.

Still, that left Mueller with a dilemma. There was clear evidence that Trump did commit crimes. What should Mueller say about that? He decided to lay out the evidence but reach no conclusion about it. This judgment was announced in what became the most famous (and infamous) paragraph of the Mueller Report:

> Because we determined not to make a traditional prosecutorial judgment, we did not draw ultimate conclusions about the President's conduct. The evidence we obtained about the President's actions and intent presents difficult issues that would need to be resolved if we were making a traditional prosecutorial judgment. At the same time, if we had confidence after a thorough investigation of the facts that the President clearly did not commit obstruction of justice, we would so state. Based on the facts and the applicable legal standards, we are unable to reach that judgment. Accordingly, while this report does not conclude that the President committed a crime, it also does not exonerate him.

It takes multiple readings to make sense of the gnarled, legalistic prose of this paragraph. *We can investigate the President, but we can't prosecute the President. If our investigation determined that he was in the clear, we'd say that—but we're not saying that. Nor are we saying that he's guilty of anything. So we're not saying he's guilty—but we're not saying he's innocent, either. Basically.*

Nothing in Mueller's mandate required him to reach such a baffling and inconclusive conclusion about the most important issue before him. He was a prosecutor. A prosecutor's job is to determine whether the evidence is sufficient to bring cases. In this unique situation, the OLC opinion prohibited Mueller from actually bringing a case, but Mueller gave Trump an unnecessary second benefit from the OLC opinion. The first benefit was not prosecuting him; that was mandatory. But the second benefit was not even saying whether the evidence supported a prosecution; that was simply a gift to Trump. In Mueller's reasoning, a federal prosecutor could neither prosecute the president nor say whether he should be prosecuted, which in this case placed Trump effectively above the law. And Mueller expressed this tortured, overthought conclusion in such confusing language that most mortals could not understand what he had done at all. Sadly, the bewildering denouement undermined the extraordinary, meticulous, and fairminded work of his staff in building the obstruction of justice case against Trump in the first place.

Mueller's compromise had another ill effect. Because the language in the report was so complicated and difficult to parse, it opened the door for his work to be misrepresented by partisans acting in bad faith—like, for example, the attorney general of the United States.

The Zebley-O'Callaghan phone calls took place, in part, to set up a meeting between Bill Barr and his staff and Mueller and his team on March 5. Once Barr was confirmed as attorney general, in February, he took over formal control of the Mueller investigation from Rod Rosenstein, who had been in charge since the beginning because Jeff Sessions was recused. But Barr let Rosenstein more or less continue in this role, and this meeting was Barr's first chance to take stock of the Mueller investigation before the report was released.

It was a fairly relaxed meeting. Mueller made a brief introduction. Later, Barr's team made a point of telling reporters that Mueller looked tired and old, which he did and he was. Because Mueller had been the focus of so much public attention for nearly two years but said nothing in public, he had taken on an almost mythic status, even among people who once knew him well, as Barr did. To see him in the flesh, after this exhausting enterprise, a man who was not a young seventy-four, was bound to be deflating.

Zebley summarized part 1 of the report about Russia. He said the special counsel had found insufficient evidence to charge anyone affiliated with the Trump campaign with a substantive crime relating to Russia. Jim Quarles handled part 2—about obstruction. He repeated what Zebley had told O'Callaghan earlier in the week. There would be no conclusion about whether Trump committed a crime. Like O'Callaghan, Barr was puzzled. No recommendation? That's right, said Quarles. It wasn't that Mueller was unable to reach a conclusion about whether Trump committed a crime but that under the circumstances he chose not to do so. In other words, Quarles said, Mueller *could* reach a determination, but he *would* not.

As the meeting was breaking up, Barr asked a few questions about public release of the report. During his confirmation hearings, he had promised to release the report, and he was going to do so. The question was how, and when. They all knew the report was lengthy and would have to be first reviewed for classified information, grand jury material, and other matters that should not be released. What should Barr release immediately after getting the report? The Mueller team had thought of this issue. Both parts of the report had a one-page introduction and about a ten-page summary. Mueller told Barr that it would be appropriate to release those sections immediately. Barr agreed to think it over. In some back-and-forth comments over the next two weeks, the Mueller team had the impression, but not the commitment, that Barr would release the summaries as soon as he received the report.

At around noon on Friday, March 22, a courier delivered a single copy of the 448-page report to O'Callaghan at the Department of Justice. Rosenstein, O'Callaghan, and their team advised Barr of its arrival, and the attorney general wrote to Congress to advise that the report had been delivered. He also told Pat Cipollone, the White House counsel. (When they heard the news, Trump's lawyers— Giuliani, Sekulow, and the Raskins—scrambled from around the country to gather in Washington so they could ready their response.) Rosenstein's team spent all of Friday reading and digesting the report, which was more or less as advertised by Mueller in their meeting two weeks earlier. On Saturday, they prepared a draft of a letter that Barr would release the next day.

On Sunday, March 24, around noon, O'Callaghan called Zebley at home. He said that Barr was going to release a letter about the report that afternoon. Did Mueller's team want to review the letter before Barr released it? The call surprised Zebley. He was under the impression that Barr was going to release Mueller's own summaries, not Barr's gloss on the report. After conferring with Mueller and others on the team, Zebley got back to O'Callaghan and said Mueller didn't want to see the letter. Barr's letter was Barr's letter. Mueller wasn't going to vouch for it. O'Callaghan had made a clever bureaucratic gambit—to get Mueller's buy-in to Barr's interpretation—but the special counsel wasn't going to do it. This made sense at the time, but it might have been a strategic error. Zebley's refusal to read the letter deprived the Mueller team of the opportunity to dissociate itself in advance if the letter turned out to be misleading. In any event, Mueller, Zebley, and their colleagues awaited Barr's announcement like the rest of the country.

Barr released his letter, four single-spaced pages, at about 3:30 on Sunday afternoon, March 24. He said he was reporting the "principal conclusions" of Mueller's report. Like Mueller, Barr divided his letter into two parts—one about Russia, one about obstruction of justice. Regarding Russia, Barr quoted Mueller's conclusion: "The investigation did not establish that members of the Trump Campaign conspired or coordinated with the Russian government in its election interference activities." Barr did not quote the first part of that sentence in the report, which said, "The investigation established that the Russian government perceived it would benefit from a Trump presidency and worked to secure that outcome, and that the Campaign expected it would benefit electorally from information stolen and released through Russian efforts." In other words, Barr spun Mueller's conclusion about Russia in a way favorable to Trump, but his letter was not technically inaccurate on this subject.

Then Barr turned to obstruction, and he explained that Mueller "determined not to make a traditional prosecutorial judgment. The Special Counsel therefore did not draw a conclusion—one way or the other—as to whether the examined conduct constituted obstruction. Instead, for each of the relevant actions investigated, the report sets out evidence on both sides of the question and leaves unresolved what the Special Counsel views as 'difficult issues' of law and fact concerning whether the President's actions and intent could be viewed as obstruction. The Special Counsel states that 'while this report does not conclude that the President committed a crime, it also does not exonerate him.'"

This, too, was accurate as far as it went. But then Barr continued with two paragraphs of epic importance:

The Special Counsel's decision to describe the facts of his obstruction investigation without reaching any legal conclusions leaves it to the Attorney General to determine whether the conduct described in the report constitutes a crime. Over the course of the investigation, the Special Counsel's office engaged in discussions with certain Department officials regarding many of the legal and factual matters at issue in the Special Counsel's obstruction investigation. After reviewing the Special Counsel's final report on these issues; consulting with Department officials, including the Office of Legal Counsel; and applying the principles of federal prosecution that guide our charging decisions, Deputy Attorney General Rod Rosenstein and I have concluded that the evidence developed during the Special Counsel's investigation is not sufficient to establish that the President committed an obstruction-of-justice offense. Our determination was made without regard to, and is not based on, the constitutional considerations that surround the indictment and criminal prosecution of a sitting president.

In making this determination, we noted that the Special Counsel recognized that "the evidence does not establish that the President was involved in an underlying crime related to Russian election interference," and that, while not determinative, the absence of such evidence bears upon the President's intent with respect to obstruction. Generally speaking, to obtain and sustain an obstruction conviction, the government would need to prove beyond a reasonable doubt that a person, acting with corrupt intent, engaged in obstructive conduct with a sufficient nexus to a pending or contemplated proceeding. In cataloguing the President's actions, many of which took place in public view, the report identifies no actions that, in our judgment, constitute obstructive conduct, had a nexus to a pending or contemplated proceeding, and were done with corrupt intent, each of which, under the Department's principles of federal prosecution guiding charging decisions, would need to be proven beyond a reasonable doubt to establish an obstruction-of-justice offense.

In other words, Mueller didn't reach a conclusion on whether Trump committed a crime, but Barr did, and he decided that the president did not commit any crimes. In just two days, without speaking to the authors of the report about their evidence or their conclusions,

Barr and Rosenstein asserted that they had digested hundreds of pages of dense findings and found the justification to give the president, their boss, a clean bill of health. Barr did not refute, or even describe, Mueller's factual presentation or legal analysis; he simply asserted the case against Trump did not comport with "the Department's principles of federal prosecution." The portion of Barr's letter exonerating Trump was longer than his description of what Mueller found about Trump. The letter was an obvious and unjustified act of sabotage against Mueller and an extraordinary bequest to the president.

The letter represented a culmination of Barr's evolution, like that of the Republican Party, from principled conservative to Trump apologist. Contrary to what Barr said, the report did not "leave[] it to the Attorney General to determine whether the conduct described in the report constitutes a crime." Rather, Barr chose to make that determination. And he chose to do it in a slapdash, conclusory way that was impossible to refute, because the report itself was still secret. Long before, Barr had provided more than a hint of how he would come down on Mueller's conclusion about the president. His nineteen-page June 8, 2018, memo to Rosenstein, written when Barr was still a private citizen, said that "Mueller's obstruction theory is fatally misconceived. . . . If credited by the Department, it would have grave consequences far beyond the immediate confines of this case and would do lasting damage to the Presidency and to the administration of law within the Executive branch." Less than a year later, as attorney general, Barr had the opportunity to put a stake in Mueller and this "theory," and he did just that.

Trump celebrated. He was at Mar-a-Lago for the weekend, and he spoke to reporters on the tarmac in Florida on Sunday afternoon before he returned to Washington. Based on Barr's letter, Trump declared that the Mueller Report was a "complete and total exoneration." He said, "It's a shame that our country had to go through this. To be honest, it's a shame that your president had to go through this." Back in Washington, Trump's legal team gathered in the Yellow Oval Room to toast their success. They had planned for months to release a "prebuttal" of Mueller's report, but now, clearly, there was no need.

Barr had done it for them. Trump arrived in the early evening and offered thanks to everyone. He had been saying it for months—no collusion, no obstruction—and now so had the attorney general.

The following morning, on Monday, March 25, O'Callaghan called Zebley to check in. *Are we good?* Zebley said, *Uh, not so much. Barr's letter said Mueller's report had reported facts "without reaching any legal conclusions." That wasn't true. There were legal conclusions—such as we could not rule out that Trump committed a crime. That was a legal conclusion. And anyway, we thought you were going to release the executive summaries. What happened to them?* O'Callaghan was noncommittal. He'd look into it. Later that day, Zebley sent O'Callaghan the executive summaries, with all classified information and grand jury material redacted, so they could be released immediately. O'Callaghan did not respond.

Many on Mueller's team, especially at the lower levels, were incandescent with fury at Barr. He had undermined two years of work by mischaracterizing it for Trump's benefit. He had screwed Mueller and them. And with the report still secret, there was nothing to do to respond. Mueller was also aggrieved, but in his customary, rule-following fashion. On Wednesday, he wrote a letter of modest protest to Barr. "The introductions and executive summaries of our two-volume report accurately summarize this Office's work and conclusions," Mueller wrote. "The summary letter the Department sent to Congress and released to the public late in the afternoon of March 24 did not fully capture the context, nature, and substance of this Office's work and conclusions. We communicated that concern to the Department on the morning of March 25. There is now public confusion about critical aspects of the results of our investigation. This threatens to undermine a central purpose for which the Department appointed the Special Counsel: to assure full public confidence in the outcome of the investigations." (Even with its restrained language, the letter would have caused a sensation if Mueller had leaked it, which he didn't do. In fact, the letter did not become public for more than a month.)

Barr set up a call with Mueller for the next day, Thursday, March 28. It was indicative of their respective temperaments that Barr acted like the aggrieved party. "What was up with that letter, Bob?" he said. "Why didn't you just pick up the phone?" Mueller said his team had worked long and hard on the summaries, and they expected they were going to be released. Barr said he meant his letter only to be focused on Mueller's "conclusions," not his "summaries." Mueller suggested they get the summaries out right away. "We don't want to do it piecemeal," Barr said. "We just want to get the whole report out." Mueller was powerless against Barr. The ability to release some or all of the report was in the hands of the Department of Justice, not the special counsel.

At the end of the week, Barr revealed that he would be conducting a review of the full report for classified, grand jury, and other sensitive information and then releasing the full report with those redactions. In other words, the Justice Department was again refusing to release the summaries, as Mueller and his staff had been requesting for weeks. The review of the report then proceeded at a stately pace. Days, then weeks passed. In the meantime, the conventional wisdom around Mueller's report hardened. *Mueller found nothing on Trump. No big deal. A bust. No collusion, no obstruction.*

Finally, on April 18, almost a month after Mueller submitted his report, Barr announced at a news conference that he was releasing it. Barr's comments on that day were so wildly inappropriate, so grotesquely deferential to Trump, that they stand as a useful metaphor for Barr's tenure as attorney general.

Barr's comments showed, above all, that he felt Trump's pain. "It is important to bear in mind the context. President Trump faced an unprecedented situation," Barr said. "As he entered into office, and sought to perform his responsibilities as President, federal agents and prosecutors were scrutinizing his conduct before and after taking office, and the conduct of some of his associates. At the same time, there was relentless speculation in the news media about the President's personal culpability." Barr went on, "There is substantial evidence to show that the President was frustrated and angered by a sincere belief that the investigation was undermining his presidency, propelled by his political opponents, and fueled by illegal leaks." Finally, Barr said, "The President took no act that in fact deprived the Special Counsel of the documents and witnesses necessary to complete his investigation. Apart from whether the acts were obstructive, this evidence of non-corrupt motives weighs heavily against any allegation that the President had a corrupt intent to obstruct the investigation."

Giuliani and Sekulow themselves could not have given a more solicitous, even fawning, introduction to the Mueller Report than the one Barr delivered at the news conference. Barr neglected to mention that the investigation that was under way when Trump took office took place because the Russian government engaged in a systematic attempt to help Trump win the election, which Trump and his staff encouraged. It was true, as Barr said, that Trump felt sorry for himself, and he did believe the investigation was undermining him, but self-pity does not represent a defense of his efforts to interfere with the investigation. And the only reason Trump took "no act to interfere with the investigation" was that his subordinates, including McGahn, Lewandowski, and Rob Porter, refused to follow his directives.

Throughout this period, Barr took every step he could to diminish Mueller's report and dilute its impact. Trump finally had what he had wanted all along—an attorney general who put Trump's personal political well-being ahead of the national interest, the traditions of the Justice Department, and the rule of law. But Barr was able to perform his partisan dismantling of the Mueller Report only because the special counsel and his staff gave him the chance. Mueller forfeited the opportunity to speak clearly and directly about Trump's crimes, and Barr filled the void with his sycophantic, and high-volume, exoneration.

25

"Talk to Rudy, Talk to Rudy"

Barr had engineered a thunderous anticlimax for the Mueller investigation. His misleading letter, followed by weeks of waiting for the report itself, sapped momentum for further investigations, to say nothing of impeachment. Those who made the commitment to read all four-hundred-plus single-spaced pages found a devastating tale about Trump. But even though *The Washington Post's* instant paperback version of the work became a bestseller, few had the patience to wade through and absorb the details, especially in light of the Mueller team's deadpan tone. On political if not moral grounds, Trump had reason for his declaration of victory. So did Giuliani.

On Ukraine, too, Giuliani's project was making progress across the globe during the spring of 2019. Lutsenko committed to announcing an investigation of Biden and Burisma. (He more or less did so through Solomon's columns.) Giuliani poisoned the Trump appointees at the State Department against Yovanovitch. The propaganda war against her, and against Biden, conducted mostly through Solomon, was in full swing. Solomon's stories reverberated among congressional Republicans, on Fox News, and on the president's Twitter feed. But on April 21, three days after the Mueller Report was released to the public, there was a serious setback to Giuliani's plans. In Ukraine's presidential election, Poroshenko was routed by a young challenger named Volodymyr Zelensky, who became famous as a comedian and political satirist. All the connections that Giuliani's team had cultivated with Poroshenko and his subordinates were now useless. Because

Zelensky made Poroshenko's failures to rein in corruption the focus of his campaign, Lutsenko, the prosecutor general, was an especially discredited figure, who was shortly to be unemployed. Parnas confessed to Giuliani that he didn't know anyone in the new president's circle. Over the next several months, Parnas continued his frenetic travels in support of Giuliani's (and Trump's) agenda in Ukraine, but there were soon bigger guns deployed in the effort.

The election results in Ukraine called for a change in strategy. Giuliani had been pushing on an open door in Ukraine, dealing with a regime that shared political DNA with the team that Manafort had helped to install in the White House. Now that group—which included Poroshenko, Shokin, and Lutsenko—became irrelevant overnight. The new challenge was to persuade Zelensky's administration to display the same zeal as its predecessor to damage Trump's political opponents in the United States. This called for a heavier hand from Washington. So Trump himself replaced Giuliani as the leader of the project. And the president deployed something a great deal more effective than Lev Parnas. Out was a hapless ne'er-do-well from south Florida; in was the power of the U.S. government.

Trump began his personal initiative in Ukraine with his congratulatory call to Zelensky, who was even more dependent on the largesse and encouragement of the United States than Poroshenko. Zelensky came from the pro-Western, anti-Moscow faction within Ukraine, and especially given his unconventional background he had to prove that his putative allies in the United States were taking him seriously and willing to support him. Putin was likely to challenge the newcomer with an expanded military effort on Ukraine's eastern border, which meant that Zelensky had a consuming need for American military aid. The new president's vulnerabilities became clear when Trump called him from Air Force One on the day of his victory. Zelensky immediately asked for a show of support. "You are a great example for our new managers," he said. "I'd also like to invite you, if it's possible, to the inauguration. I know how busy you are, but if it's possible for you to come to the inauguration ceremony, that would be a great, great thing for you to do to be with us on that day."

Trump replied noncommittally—"I'll look into that"—and promised that if he couldn't come, he would send someone from "a very, very high level." Then Trump shifted to a more congenial subject. "When I owned Miss Universe, they always had great people. Ukraine was always very well represented," Trump said, and then he dangled a valuable but vague invitation. "When you're settled in and ready, I'd like to invite you to the White House." Zelensky jumped: "Well, thank you for the invitation. We accept the invitation and look forward to the visit." The only conclusion Trump could draw from the brief conversation was that he had Zelensky on the hook. Trump had what the Ukrainian president wanted—presidential attention and American aid. The question, then, was how to exploit the Ukrainian's desperation. (Later in the week, Zelensky spoke to Vice President Pence, who at Trump's direction accepted the Ukrainian's invitation to attend his inauguration.)

First, though, Trump had to take care of some unfinished business. On April 24, Marie Yovanovitch was told she was fired as ambassador to Ukraine, and she was instructed to return to the United States "on the next plane." She was flabbergasted, not least because just a month earlier the State Department had asked her to extend her term into 2020. When she returned to Washington, she asked John Sullivan, the deputy secretary of state, for an explanation. According to her later testimony, he said, "The President has lost confidence in me and no longer wished me to serve as his ambassador. He added that there had been a concerted campaign against me, and that the Department had been under pressure from the President to remove me since the summer of 2018. He also said that I had done nothing wrong and that this was not like other situations where he had recalled ambassadors for cause."

Trump pushed his agenda forward the next night, in the familiar venue of Sean Hannity's program on Fox. Hannity introduced Trump by saying, "Let me start with this issue of the Ukraine. I don't know if you were following the top of the show or John Solomon's new report . . ." Trump answered, "Well, I think it's incredible when you hear it. . . . It sounds like big stuff. It sounds very interesting with Ukraine."

Hannity went on: "Ukraine is offering this evidence to the United

States. Would you like the United States—with all this talk about collusion, they are saying they colluded on behalf of Hillary Clinton's campaign in 2016. Does America need to see that information, in spite of all of the attacks against you on collusion?"

"Well, I think we do," Trump replied. "And, frankly, we have a great new Attorney General [Barr] who has done an unbelievable job in a very short period of time. . . . I would imagine he would want to see this. . . . People have been saying this whole—the concept of Ukraine, they have been talking about it actually for a long time." (For good measure, Trump later repeated his customary lie about his encounter with Mueller in 2017: "And, you know, Bob Mueller, I turned him down to run the FBI, the next day, he was appointed to be this—Special Counsel, as they call it. . . . He was conflicted for that reason.") In another interview with Fox, the following week, Trump was asked about Vice President Biden's actions in Ukraine. Trump said, "I'm hearing it's a major scandal, major problem. Very bad things happened, and we'll see what that is."

In the rosy glow of the days following the release of the Mueller Report, in late April and early May, Giuliani felt emboldened. Staff members at the U.S. embassy in Kyiv began hearing reports of Giuliani's calls to people in Zelensky's inner circle as he sought to make a new set of connections. Giuliani was so brazen that he bragged to Kenneth Vogel, a reporter for the *Times,* about a trip he was planning to Ukraine. Vogel's story, headlined "Rudy Giuliani Plans Ukraine Trip to Push for Inquiries That Could Help Trump," ran on May 9. The article said the trip was "part of a monthslong effort by the former New York mayor and a small group of Trump allies working to build interest in the Ukrainian inquiries. Their motivation is to . . . undermine the case against Paul Manafort, Mr. Trump's imprisoned former campaign chairman; and potentially to damage Mr. Biden, the early front-runner for the 2020 Democratic presidential nomination." Giuliani was quoted as saying, "We're not meddling in an election, we're meddling in an investigation, which we have a right to do." The next day, Giuliani sent a personal letter to President Zelensky, writing, "In my capacity as personal counsel to President Trump and with his knowledge and consent, I request a meeting with you on this upcoming Monday, May 13th or Tuesday, May 14th."

For two years, in response to the Mueller probe of foreign involvement in the 2016 election, Trump had made his mantra "no collusion." And here was his personal attorney heading overseas to collude with Ukraine to help Trump in the 2020 election. On the day the *Times* story appeared, Giuliani went on Laura Ingraham's Fox News program and said of his Ukraine inquiries, "It's a big story. It's a dramatic story. And I guarantee you, Joe Biden will not get to election day without this being investigated." Giuliani's hypocrisy was brazen, even by the standards of the Trump administration. As Adam Schiff, the Democrat who was now chairman of the House Intelligence Committee, said in a tweet, "Today, Giuliani admitted to seeking political help from a foreign power. Again." This was, Schiff said, "immoral, unethical, unpatriotic and, now, standard procedure." Republicans were silent, which passed for criticism in the Trump era. In any event, in a rare concession to Trump's adversaries, Giuliani canceled his trip to Ukraine while still asserting that it would have been appropriate to go. The *Times*'s story—and Giuliani's reaction to it—put the Trump administration's relationship with the new government in Ukraine on the radar of the president's adversaries in Congress. Schiff and his colleagues didn't start formal investigations at this point, but they recognized that something was up and vowed to keep an eye on it.

The canceled trip hardly deterred Giuliani from further efforts on Ukraine, but it did lead to a change in emphasis. After a series of phone calls with the White House, Giuliani turned his ire against Ukraine and its new leader. Despite his initial kind words with Zelensky (and praise for Ukraine's Miss Universe competitors), Trump always regarded Ukraine as an unreliable and corrupt nation—a lesson that he absorbed from Manafort years earlier. In May, Giuliani turned sour on Zelensky, and he and the president apparently decided that their relationship with him would be defined more by the stick than the carrot. Giuliani told Fox News, "I'm not going to go" to Ukraine, "because I think I'm walking into a group of people that are enemies of the President." In a text message to *Politico,* he asserted that he canceled the trip because Zelensky "is in [the] hands of avowed enemies of Pres Trump." As it happened, Trump was hearing a similar message in May from two kindred spirits and trusted sources of advice—Vladimir Putin himself and Hungarian prime minister Viktor Orbán. In a phone call with Putin on May 3 and a meeting with Orbán on May 13, both authoritarians dismissed Ukraine as corrupt, unreliable, and not even a real nation. (This, of course, was the long-held view of Russian nationalists like Putin and the reason his troops were violating Ukrainian sovereignty in the east.) In the first specific manifestation of his harder line with Ukraine, Trump directed Pence to cancel his plans to attend Zelensky's inauguration, which was scheduled for later in May.

The real turning point in American government policy toward Ukraine took place on May 23, when Trump held a meeting about Ukraine in the Oval Office with the three men he had selected to represent the United States at Zelensky's inauguration: Rick Perry, the secretary of energy; Gordon Sondland, the ambassador to the European Union; and Kurt Volker, Trump's special representative for Ukraine negotiations. The president had selected a malleable group. Perry, the dutiful former Texas governor, had survived in the cabinet through abject deference to Trump. Sondland, who owned boutique hotels in the Northwest, was a veteran Republican activist who switched loyalties to Trump late in the campaign and purchased his ambassadorship with a $1 million contribution to his inauguration. Volker was a longtime survivor in the Washington foreign policy establishment, sometimes as an aide to Senator John McCain, sometimes as an independent businessman. Volker was working without a salary, but he was also making business contacts in Ukraine. The three men opened their meeting on an optimistic note about Ukraine. They said that Zelensky was an impressive new leader and the country could become an important bulwark against Russian expansion in Europe. They counseled that Trump should hold the Oval Office meeting with Zelensky that he had promised in his phone call with the new Ukrainian president.

Trump wanted none of it. The president said Ukraine was "a terrible place, all corrupt, terrible people." Still worse, he said, Ukraine "tried to take me down" in the 2016 election. (He didn't elaborate.) Trump rejected the group's positive assessment of Zelensky, explaining "that's not what I hear" from Giuliani. As for Trump's marching orders for the group, the president defaulted to the elliptical, mobboss style he often used when discussing legally dubious assignments. He said the Oval Office meeting with Zelensky was off the table. So what should they do instead with Ukraine? The president wouldn't specify. "Talk to Rudy," Trump said. "Talk to Rudy."

The three visitors to the Oval Office arrived believing that one policy was appropriate for Ukraine and left with instructions to implement an entirely different one. But they understood that Trump expected sycophancy from his aides, so they resolved to follow his hard line. Indeed, they took to the task with such enthusiasm that Perry, Sondland, and Volker dubbed themselves "the Three Amigos," and, as directed, they did talk to Rudy. With Yovanovitch out of the way, the Three Amigos were now driving U.S. government policy in Ukraine, and they were to take their orders from Rudy and implement his agenda. His priority—for Zelensky to announce an investigation of the Bidens—became that of the Three Amigos.

The U.S. government is, however, a multifaceted beast. When a president orders something to be done, that does not mean it just happens. A directive from a president is important, of course, but the forces of law, custom, and bureaucratic inertia, as well as internal opposition, may also be in play. The story of American policy in Ukraine over the next four months, from May to September 2019, demonstrated this tectonic struggle in action. Trump and Giuliani's goal in this period was straightforward—to use every lever of government policy to force Ukraine to help Trump win reelection. At the same time, there were a number of officials, including several inside Trump's White House, who recognized (correctly) that Trump's initiative in Ukraine was legally, morally, and strategically disastrous. The tension between the president and his internal adversaries defined the period.

The most important issue was military aid. The assistance began flowing after Paul Manafort's pro-Putin client, Viktor Yanukovych, was forced out of the presidency in 2014 and into exile in Russia. At that point, Putin ordered a military offensive that cost thirteen thousand Ukrainian lives and counting. In response to this Russian aggression, Congress appropriated $391 million in military assistance to Ukraine for 2019, and President Trump signed the bills in September 2018 and January 2019. Because of Ukraine's history of corruption, the law required that the secretary of defense certify that the country was making progress on that score before all the funds would be released. The secretary's designee certified Ukraine's acceptable performance on corruption on May 23, 2019—by coincidence, the day that Trump met with the Three Amigos in the Oval Office. Military aid to Ukraine represented a rare point of bipartisan consensus in Trump's Washington—supported by liberals who disdained Putin's reactionary authoritarianism and by conservatives who wanted to check, as in Soviet days, Russian expansionism. Trump saw the military aid in a different way—as the most compelling form of leverage to use on Zelensky.

The Three Amigos embraced their assignment to work with Giuliani. Perry reached out to him first, because they knew each other from their mutual forays into national politics. Perry then turned over the details to Volker and Sondland. They sent word to William Taylor, the diplomat who took over the Kyiv embassy from Yovanovitch, that Trump's meeting with Zelensky was on hold because Trump "wanted to hear from Zelensky before scheduling the meeting in the Oval Office." Sondland, the hotelier, took a special pleasure in lording his new insider status over those in the customary chain of command. On June 18, Fiona Hill met with Sondland at the White House, where he informed her that "he was in charge of Ukraine." The British-born Hill, who possessed a regal temperament of her own, demanded, "Who put you in charge of Ukraine?" As she later testified, "I'll admit, I was a bit rude. And that's when he told me the President, which shut me up." For his part, Giuliani made sure no one missed his real priority. On June 21, he tweeted, "New Pres of Ukraine still silent on investigation of Ukrainian interference in 2016 election and alleged Biden bribery of Pres Poroshenko. Time for leadership and investigate both if you want to purge how Ukraine was abused by Hillary and Obama people." What was extraordinary about the Trump-Giuliani Ukraine offensive of 2019 was its resolute singlemindedness. American relations with Ukraine existed in a complex matrix of multiple issues: East-West relations in the post-Soviet era; America's demands on its Western allies to share the burdens of support for Ukraine; American efforts to reduce corruption in Ukraine. For Trump, none of those issues mattered or even merited a mention. All the president cared about was using Ukraine—this battered, vulnerable, embattled nation—to help him get reelected.

The president's principal internal adversary in this struggle worked just down the hall from the Oval Office—John Bolton, the national security adviser. A veteran cold warrior and neoconservative, he had a long-held hostility to Russia and resolved to keep the aid to Ukraine flowing. As a veteran of Washington's bureaucratic wars, Bolton quickly sized up the situation. He saw Trump outsource Ukraine policy to Giuliani, and he knew why, and he thought it was a disgrace. At first Bolton tried to stop Giuliani. He passed the word to his subordinates that "nobody should be meeting with Giuliani." But once he learned that Trump himself wanted Giuliani in charge of the Ukraine account, Bolton tried to do the politic thing—keep his own hands, and those of his staff, clean. According to Fiona Hill, Bolton's aide for Russian matters, he repeatedly referred to Giuliani as a "hand grenade that was going to blow everybody up." After a meeting with Sondland, where the ambassador described his efforts in Ukraine with Giuliani and Mick Mulvaney, Trump's acting chief of staff, Bolton tried to remove himself from the whole matter. He told Fiona Hill to report them to White House lawyers, saying, "I am not part of whatever drug deal Sondland and Mulvaney are cooking up."

The president, in contrast, was. There was an almost manic quality to Trump's Ukraine obsession in this period. On June 18, the Defense Department issued a routine press release announcing the forthcoming delivery of $250 million in military aid to Ukraine. This came to the president's attention, and he demanded that the word go down through the bureaucracy that the money be placed on hold. (Later, a series of career officials in the Defense Department and the Office of Management and Budget, or OMB, testified that they were bewildered by this unprecedented, and possibly illegal, cessation of congressionally mandated spending.) The next day, Trump returned to Sean Hannity's program on Fox News and raised the CrowdStrike fantasy again: "How come the FBI didn't take the server from the DNC? Think about that one, Sean. Think about that one." (As always, Trump's conjecture was based on two false ideas—that the Ukrainians owned CrowdStrike and that the DNC servers were spirited to Ukraine after the hacking was discovered.) By July 12, the freeze on aid was official. On that date, a deputy to Mick Mulvaney sent an email to OMB stating, "The President is directing a hold on military support funding for Ukraine."

Events converged in July—Zelensky's hopes for an Oval Office meeting, the withheld military aid, and plans for a telephone call between Trump and Zelensky. Volker met up with Zelensky and his top aide at a conference in Toronto and gave them a heads-up about Trump's priorities. As Volker recounted in a text to Taylor, in Kyiv, he "pulled the two of them aside at the end and explained the Giuliani factor." Specifically, Volker told Zelensky that President Trump "would like to hear about the investigations . . . thinking of Burisma and 2016." In another text to Taylor, Volker said, "The key thing is to tee up a phone call w potus and then get visit nailed down." In other words, by early July, Zelensky knew the price for continuation of American military aid to his country: the announcement of a Ukrainian investigation of Trump's political rivals.

The new regime in Ukraine was learning how the game was played in Trump's Washington. When Andriy Yermak, Zelensky's top adviser, visited Washington in early July, he chose to stay at the Trump International Hotel, where he had breakfast with Volker. At a meeting in the White House the same day, Sondland told Yermak explicitly that Zelensky would not get a meeting with Trump unless he announced an investigation of "Bidens and Burisma." Sondland then told Timothy Morrison, who was replacing Fiona Hill in her job at the NSC, the "sole purpose" of a presidential call was for President Zelensky to assure President Trump that "any hampered investigations will be allowed to move forward transparently." The key was "transparently," of course; Trump wanted Zelensky to announce the investigations because of the political damage they would inflict on Biden. Trump had no interest in whether any investigation actually took place.

A few days later, on July 18, Volker texted Giuliani, "Can I buy you breakfast tomorrow?" They met the next morning—where else?—at the Trump hotel, and Lev Parnas joined them. There, Giuliani gave Volker the same talk he had been peddling on Fox and Twitter—that former vice president Biden had engaged in a corrupt alliance with his son to forestall investigations of Burisma. Volker knew this wasn't true, but he was a wily bureaucratic survivor. He knew better than to challenge the president's lawyer and, he realized, the real architect of American policy toward Ukraine. So later that day, Volker texted Giuliani, "Mr Mayor—really enjoyed breakfast this morning. As discussed, connecting you here with Andrey Yermak, who is very close to President Zelensky." Clearly, Giuliani had made the president's priorities clear to Volker, who promptly texted Sondland, "Had breakfast with Rudy this morning-teeing up call w Yermak Monday. Must have helped. Most impt is for Zelensky to say that he will help investigation." On Monday, July 22, Giuliani, Volker, and Yermak had a three-way call for thirty-eight minutes where Giuliani received assurance from Yermak that Zelensky understood what was expected of him in a phone call with Trump. The investigation of the Bidens—not burden sharing with the West, not corruption in Ukraine, not saving lives from Russian bullets and bombs—was all that mattered.

Final preparations accelerated for the call between Trump and Zelensky, which was finally scheduled, after much back-and-forth, for July 25. Sondland called the Ukrainian president and reminded him that he needed to make a public commitment to an investigation of the Bidens. Volker traveled to Kyiv and had lunch with Yermak, Zelensky's aide. Afterward, with the call scheduled for the next day, he texted Yermak: "Heard from White House—assuming President Z convinces trump he will investigate / 'get to the bottom of what happened' in 2016, we will nail down date for visit to Washington. Good luck!"

All was in readiness, except that the attention of the political world, and of President Trump, was sidetracked for a day, because Robert Mueller was going to testify before two congressional committees on July 24.

Mueller handed in his report in March, which was just after Democrats assumed control of the House of Representatives, following their victories in the midterm elections. Not surprisingly, then, several House committees wanted Mueller to testify because they regarded his report as a road map for impeachment. Their interest was especially intense because of the controversial way Barr engineered the rollout of the report. Democrats in the House felt that Barr misled the public about the contents of the report and worked to downplay its impact. How better to revive interest, and clarify the facts, than to have Mueller himself testify in public?

Mueller didn't want to do it. He had an old-fashioned idea about the work of prosecutors—that they should speak in the courtroom or not at all. This was once generally true, but no longer. In major investigations, especially regarding the president of the United States, prosecutors have sometimes elaborated on their findings before Congress and elsewhere. This happened, in varying degrees, with Archibald Cox and Leon Jaworski (regarding Watergate), Lawrence Walsh (about Iran-contra), and Kenneth Starr (on Whitewater and Lewinsky). But Mueller was, to the end, old-school. He stood by the report. He didn't have anything to add.

Mueller recognized political reality. He knew that Democrats wanted to use his testimony about his report to renew their attacks on President Trump and build a movement for impeachment. Many Democrats said so explicitly. Being part of any political crusade was anathema to Mueller. He wanted no part of it. The heated political context of the House in 2019 made him even more reluctant to testify. Various congressional staffers reached out to Aaron Zebley and Jim Quarles throughout the spring asking for Mueller's cooperation. They got none. Over and over the answer came back from Mueller's camp: the report is his testimony.

Mueller made one formal attempt to forestall a congressional appearance. He gave a short speech at the Justice Department on May 29, announcing the closure of his office. "Beyond these few remarks it is important that the office's written work speak for itself," he said. He summarized the cases the office had brought; his pride in the two Russian cases—the social media case and the hacking case—was evident.

He said the Russian efforts were designed "to damage a presidential candidate." This was as close as Mueller came to saying, on this occasion, that the Russians hurt Clinton and helped Trump. He explained his decision not to determine whether Trump committed a crime: "It would be unfair to potentially accuse somebody of a crime when there can be no court resolution of the actual charge." Finally, he said, "I hope and expect this to be the only time that I will speak to you in this manner."

No dice, said his pursuers in Congress. They still wanted his testimony. Congressional staffers engaged in long, frustrating talks with Zebley and Quarles. The Mueller deputies suggested private, closed-door testimony. *No.* They said Mueller would testify for a short period of time so that there wouldn't be enough time for each member to ask questions. *Out of the question.* Finally, the congressional staffers just said the committees would subpoena Mueller. In that case, the word came back, Mueller would show up. He wasn't going to end his career in law enforcement by defying a subpoena. Finally, negotiations led to a pair of appearances on July 24—before the Judiciary Committee in the morning and the Intelligence Committee in the afternoon.

The entire event was set up for failure. Mueller didn't want to be there. He told the Judiciary Committee that his answers would hew closely to the report. Partisan dysfunction affected the proceedings in bizarre ways. When the Democrats took over the committee in January, they learned that the Republicans had some peculiar rules—like no cameras allowed in the well between the witness table and the first row of members. Democrats obtained a temporary waiver of that rule for major witnesses like Mueller, but access to the well was controlled by representatives of the congressional Radio Television Correspondents' Gallery, who had no interest in limiting the number of photographers. So, in the absence of real rules agreed to by both the Democrats and the Republicans, that meant that a swarm of photographers, with their shutters clicking loud, were present throughout Mueller's testimony.

Jerry Nadler, the Judiciary Committee's new chairman, went first. "Did you actually totally exonerate the president?"

"No," Mueller said.

"Now, in fact, your report expressly states that it does not exonerate the president."

"It does."

"And your investigation actually found, quote, 'multiple acts by the president that were capable of exerting undue influence over law enforcement investigations, including the Russian interference and obstruction investigations.' Is that correct?"

"Correct."

"Now, Director Mueller, can you explain in plain terms what that finding means so the American people can understand it?"

"Well, the finding indicates that the president was not exculpated for the acts that he allegedly committed."

This was as good as it got for the Democrats—which was not very—and for Mueller.

Soon enough, Mueller's associates were getting texts from friends. *What's wrong with him? What's going on?* The sound was perfect for listeners at home—no clicking of the cameras—so viewers wondered why Mueller was having such a hard time hearing. But over and over again, Mueller asked for questions to be repeated. Also, the committee members did not proceed in the order in which they sat, so it wasn't always clear who would be asking the next questions. And because each member's turn lasted only five minutes, there was a frequently changing cast of questioners. Mueller was often searching the room for the right person . . . failing to hear the questions . . . asking for repetitions . . . offering brief, dismissive answers . . . "No" . . . "Yes" . . . "I will leave the answer to our report." Before too long, the hearing settled into a desultory pattern. Democrats read excerpts from Mueller's report, and Mueller acknowledged the quotation was accurate; Republicans used their five minutes to give speeches defending the president, while Mueller, and the television audience, listened.

It was an unfortunate spectacle. Even allowing for the loudness of the cameras and the shifting locations of the questioners, Mueller did not look good. The grind, the pressure, the criticism of the previous two years had taken their toll. The seventy-four-year-old who testified in 2019 was a different, diminished man from the seventy-two-year-old who became special counsel in 2017. Mueller looked somewhat better in the afternoon, largely because the Intelligence Committee had only fifteen members, compared with forty-one on Judiciary. Mueller could see and hear the questioners, but he proved no more voluble in his answers.

Mueller kept his word. He made no news before Congress. Instead, unfortunately, *he* was the news—his performance. As Donald Trump knew better than anyone, television is about appearance at least as much as substance, and Mueller had failed at both levels. He looked bad and said little. Mueller had come of age at a different era in American justice and American life, when modesty and self-effacement were ascendant values. There was something admirable in his embrace of this vanishing world. Then and always, he kept to his code of personal honor. But some people can maintain their code and adapt to the demands of a changing world; Mueller couldn't. In the investigation and before Congress, Mueller could not be other than who he was, and that was both his greatest strength and his greatest weakness.

Mueller knew that the Democrats planned to use his appearance to propel their flagging momentum for impeaching the president. It wasn't his intention to help or hurt that effort—that was precisely the kind of role he abjured—but his appearance had the opposite effect from the one the Democrats intended. By adding nothing to the existing weight of evidence against Trump, Mueller implicitly suggested that there was nothing more to be found. By the time he completed his testimony in the early evening of July 24, the prospect of Donald Trump's impeachment had gone from unlikely to unthinkable. The president's ordeal was over.

PART SIX

26

"I Would Like You to Do Us a Favor Though"

Judging by his Twitter feed, Donald Trump awoke in good spirits on the morning of July 25, 2019. Nothing pleased him more than the distress of his enemies, so he reveled in the dismal reviews Mueller received for his performance before Congress the previous day. At 6:06 a.m., he tweeted, "'Yesterday changed everything, it really did clear the President. He wins.' @ainsleyearhardt," citing one of the hosts of *Fox & Friends*. A few minutes later, Trump tweeted, "'It turns out Mueller didn't know what was in his Report.' @Steve Doocy @foxandfriends." A few minutes after that, Trump issued a more mysterious tweet, not clearly apropos of anything: "TRUTH IS A FORCE OF NATURE!"

During his presidency, Trump endured some mockery for his habit of arriving late at the Oval Office, but he did often begin his workday in the White House residence. This was true on this steamy Thursday in July. Shortly after eight, he spoke to Gordon Sondland, for a final review of the plans for Trump's conversation with Zelensky. At 9:03 a.m., Trump was patched through to the Ukrainian president. As is common in conversations between heads of state, about a dozen U.S. government staffers listened and took notes. Several of them later collaborated on a transcript of the exchanges between Trump and Zelensky; it was not an exact rendition of what was said, but those who listened to the call found the record generally accurate. The staffers on the line also agreed on the demeanor of the two men. Zelensky was nervous, jumpy, eager to please, flitting back and forth between

English and Ukrainian. The cheerful Trump of the early-morning tweets was gone. He sounded dour; Zelensky's attempts at humor fell flat.

Zelensky had been well briefed on Trump's hunger for praise. After Trump congratulated him again on his victory, Zelensky responded, "I would like to confess to you that I had an opportunity to learn from you. We used quite a few of your skills and knowledge and were able to use it as an example for our elections." After Zelensky thanked Trump for American support, Trump went off on a tangent: "We do a lot for Ukraine, we spend a lot of effort and time, much more than the European countries are doing. Germany does almost nothing for you." This was false. By that point, the United States had given approximately $1 billion in aid to Ukraine since 2014; the European Union, led by Germany, had given more than $16 billion. Still, Zelensky tried to humor his patron, saying, "Yes, you are absolutely right, not only 100 percent, but actually 1000 percent!"

Zelensky then tried to turn the conversation to his continuing need to purchase more missiles. "We are ready to cooperate for the next steps—specifically we are almost ready to buy more Javelins from the United States for defense purposes," he said.

But Trump had a very different idea about the next steps in the U.S.-Ukraine relationship. What followed became the most notorious utterance of his presidency. After Zelensky mentioned his need for military equipment to assure Ukraine's survival, Trump changed the subject to his own needs. "I would like you to do us a favor though," he said, "because our country has been through a lot and Ukraine knows a lot about it. I would like you to find out what happened with this whole situation with Ukraine, they say CrowdStrike . . . I guess you have one of your wealthy people . . . The server, they say Ukraine has it." Almost unbelievably, the president was still pushing the conspiracy theories about CrowdStrike and Hillary Clinton that had been repeatedly proven false over the previous three years. (The ellipses in the partial transcript do not appear to refer to omitted words, but rather reflect Trump's habit of meandering from one subject to another.) Moving on, he said, "As you saw yesterday, that whole nonsense ended with a very poor performance by a man named Robert Mueller, an incompetent performance, but they say a lot of it started with Ukraine. Whatever you can do, it's very important that you do it, if that's possible."

Zelensky replied to Trump's disjointed monologue with immediate agreement and a recognition of the key intermediary in the relationship between the nations. "We are ready to open a new page on cooperation in relations between the United States and Ukraine," he said. "One of my assistants spoke with Mr. Giuliani just recently, and we are hoping very much that Mr. Giuliani will travel to Ukraine, and we will meet once he comes to Ukraine."

Trump continued in a negative vein. "I heard you had a prosecutor who was very good, and he was shut down"—this was Giuliani's friend Lutsenko, who was part of the corrupt prior regime in Ukraine—"and that's really unfair. A lot of people are talking about that, the way they shut your very good prosecutor down and you had some very bad people involved." Trump went on, "Mr. Giuliani is a highly respected man. He was the mayor of New York City, a great mayor, and I would like him to call you. I will ask him to call you along with the Attorney General. Rudy very much knows what's happening and he is a very capable guy. If you could speak to him, that would be great." (Barr later said that he had no idea that Trump invoked his name to Zelensky.) Trump then turned to another of his obsessions—the perfidy of Marie Yovanovitch. "The former ambassador from the United States, the woman, was bad news, and the people she was dealing with in the Ukraine were bad news, so I just want to let you know that," he said.

Then, finally, Trump turned to the most important subject of all: "The other thing, there's a lot of talk about Biden's son, that Biden stopped the prosecution, and a lot of people want to find out about that, so whatever you can do with the Attorney General would be great. Biden went around bragging that he stopped the prosecution so if you can look into it . . . It sounds horrible to me." It was notable, in light of subsequent defenses of Trump's behavior on the call, that he made only two demands of Ukraine: to investigate CrowdStrike and the Bidens. Trump said nothing about the need for Zelensky to fight corruption in Ukraine or to defend his country against Russia. All Trump cared about was extorting this vulnerable nation for his personal electoral advantage.

Zelensky, still trying to agree with everything Trump said, expressed the view that Yovanovitch wasn't too good to him either. Trump replied darkly, again in a mob-boss phrasing, "Well, she's going to go through some things." Wrapping up, Trump said, "I will have Mr. Giuliani give you a call, and I am also going to have Attorney General Barr call, and we will get to the bottom of it."

Trump's behavior was so wildly and obviously inappropriate—pressuring a foreign leader to help the president's reelection—that two listeners that very morning went to John Eisenberg, the National Security Council lawyer, to complain. Lieutenant Colonel Alexander Vindman, the NSC's Ukraine expert, and Tim Morrison, Vindman's boss (and Fiona Hill's replacement), told Eisenberg the call wasn't just a departure from the planned talking points for the conversation but a misuse of presidential power. Jennifer Williams, an NSC aide to Vice President Pence, thought the same thing. But Eisenberg put them off, saying he'd look into it. In the small circle of experts on Ukraine within the U.S. government, the story of Trump's behavior on the call generated disgust and anger. In particular, one analyst at the CIA, who was quickly informed about the call, simmered with fury.

Trump's plan was being put into operation. He'd made his demands clear to Zelensky. The military aid to Ukraine had been cut off. On the afternoon of July 25, top staffers at the Pentagon received panicked contacts from Ukrainian officials about the freeze on military aid. Where was the money? Why had it been withheld? Bewildered themselves about the reasons, the military officials promised to look into it. Without explanation to career officials, the budget office confirmed that evening that the aid was not to be released. This was an order of the president, passed on by his acting chief of staff, Mick Mulvaney.

Trump ended the momentous day of July 25 the same way he began it—gloating about Robert Mueller's failure. He called in to Sean Hannity's program in prime time. In light of Mueller's failure before Congress, Hannity told the president, the Democrats' fantasies about impeachment had been "totally completely flushed down the drain."

Gordon Sondland, the most ebullient of the Three Amigos, was euphoric that the long-gestating phone call between Trump and Zelensky had finally taken place. Sondland happened to be in Kyiv on the day after the call, and he decided to host three staffers from the American embassy at a celebratory lunch. He took the group to a restaurant called SHO, which means "what" in Ukrainian and offers a modern take on such Ukrainian specialties as *varenyky,* the national dumpling. The ambassador was in such a good mood that he ordered a bottle of wine for his guests, which was unusual for government officials at lunch. The quartet basked in the warmth at an outdoor table.

But the meal took a surreal turn when Sondland, apparently trying to show off for the group, placed a phone call to the president of the United States, who promptly came on the line. Trump's booming voice was so loud that Sondland winced a couple of times, and he held the device a little away from his ear. This allowed the staffers to eavesdrop. (Kyiv is notorious for infiltration by Russian intelligence services, so others were probably also listening on Sondland's unsecure line.) Trump first mentioned a matter related to Sondland's duties as ambassador to the European Union. A rapper named A$AP Rocky had been arrested in Sweden after a street brawl the previous month, and his cause had been taken up by Kanye West and Kim Kardashian West. Trump wanted to know what Sondland was doing to help Rocky. "He's kind of fucked," Sondland explained. If Rocky had just pleaded guilty, he would have been released by now. Bantering with the president, Sondland said that Trump should let Rocky "get sentenced, play the racism card, and give him a ticker-tape when he comes home." On the bright side, Sondland added, "At least you can tell the Kardashians that you tried." (David Holmes, the counselor for political affairs at the embassy and a guest at the lunch, later testified, with wry understatement, that listening to the call "was an extremely distinctive experience in my Foreign Service career.")

Next, the conversation turned to the real purpose of Sondland's call—to hear the president's take on his conversation with Zelensky the previous day. Sondland told Trump that the Ukrainian president "loves your ass." Trump then said, "So he's going to do the investigation?" Sondland reassured Trump: "He's going to do it. He'll do anything you ask him to."

The moments that followed this phone call were among the most revealing of the entire U.S.-Ukraine saga. The staffers were understandably agog to be privy to such a conversation, more for the

content of the call than for the casual vulgarity. These career Foreign Service officers had, of course, devoted their lives to advancing
American foreign policy, and in Kyiv their assignment was to assist a
struggling democracy survive in an especially dangerous corner of the
world. But here they had a vivid demonstration of the real priorities
of their president. Holmes testified that after Sondland hung up, "I
then took the opportunity to ask Ambassador Sondland for his candid
impression of the President's views on Ukraine. In particular, I asked
Ambassador Sondland if it was true that the President did not give a
shit about Ukraine. Ambassador Sondland agreed that the President
did not give a shit about Ukraine.

"I asked why not, and Ambassador Sondland stated, the President only cares about 'big stuff,'" Holmes continued. "I noted that
there was 'big stuff' going on in Ukraine, like a war with Russia. And
Ambassador Sondland replied that he meant 'big stuff' that benefits
the President, like the Biden investigation that Trump's personal attorney Rudy Giuliani was pushing." Without apology or explanation,
Sondland gave Holmes an accurate distillation of Trump's motivation
and character. In personal and political terms, Trump was incapable of
empathy. Dirt on his political opponents was "big stuff"; the American national interest, as well as the lives of Ukrainians at war, was not.
There was no need for a more complicated explanation for the root of
the scandal that would soon engulf the president.

The Three Amigos, plus Giuliani, now had to close the deal—that is,
obtain Zelensky's announcement of the investigation of Biden. As a
measure of the Ukrainians' determination to open the spigot of aid
again, Andriy Yermak, Zelensky's aide, traveled all the way to Madrid
on August 2 to meet with Giuliani, as they had planned in their
phone call the previous month. As always, Giuliani was accompanied
by his shadow in this matter, Lev Parnas. Giuliani's demand was clear,
as it had been for months. The Ukrainians had to announce an investigation of CrowdStrike and the Bidens in order to get a firm date for
an Oval Office meeting with the president. (In Madrid, Giuliani and
Parnas found time to take in a bullfight, and Parnas took a video of
Giuliani greeting the matadors and holding a red cape.)

At last, or so it seemed, it looked as if the deal were coming together. Kurt Volker texted Giuliani that it "would be good" if he updated "the boss"—that is, Trump—about his meeting with Yermak so the White House meeting with Zelensky could finally be put on the calendar. Volker then texted Sondland and Giuliani to suggest they have a phone call "to make sure I advise Z correctly as to what he should be saying." The president, as ever, was impatient for Ukraine's announcement of the Biden investigation. Sondland responded to Volker, "I think potus really wants the deliverable." The president— POTUS—told Bolton the same thing. Trump was tired of discussing the issue. He'd made up his mind about what he wanted from Ukraine.

Still, just beneath the surface, there was a ripple in the quiet bureaucratic earth. A CIA analyst, who was an expert on Ukraine, had not listened to the call in real time, but received a briefing on it later on July 25. It was the analyst's job to follow events with Ukraine closely, and he had been growing more and more outraged. The story in the *Times* in May confirmed that Giuliani saw himself as some kind of hybrid investigator and policy maker with regard to Ukraine. True, he had canceled his trip to Kyiv at that time, but on Twitter and elsewhere he kept agitating for the Zelensky government to do Trump's political bidding. From both public and private sources, the analyst saw how Giuliani was effectively running the show. The call between the two presidents, with Trump's instruction to Zelensky to talk to Giuliani, was a final straw.

On Friday, July 26, the CIA analyst contacted a lawyer at the agency's general counsel's office to express his dismay about the president's behavior with regard to Ukraine, notably on the phone call with Zelensky. The lawyer quickly shared the report with the general counsel of the CIA, who over the weekend informed John Eisenberg, the NSC lawyer, about the complaint. It was all vague and general at that point, but Eisenberg was now aware of considerable disquiet in the ranks about Trump and Ukraine. Within seventy-two hours of the phone call between the two presidents, Eisenberg had heard complaints from his colleagues Vindman and Morrison and from a CIA employee, who was now a possible whistle-blower.

On Monday, July 29, the CIA lawyer told the analyst that his concerns had been shared with the White House. It had been proper for the CIA to inform Eisenberg of the issue, but the involvement of the White House unnerved the CIA analyst. He didn't think that the issue would be aired properly, especially not to Congress, if the White House was in charge of the response. So the analyst began looking for other options, and he chose the obvious one—Congress itself. The analyst had a former CIA colleague who was on the staff of the House Intelligence Committee, now chaired by Adam Schiff. (It's common for staffers to move between working for the intelligence agencies and working for Congress on intelligence issues.) The analyst arranged to meet up with the staffer away from Capitol Hill on July 30. There, he gave a very general sense of his complaint and asked for advice. This kind of approach was not especially unusual for the Intelligence Committee, which received approaches from about half a dozen would-be whistle-blowers a year. They usually had the same question as this one did. How could he get the full story to Congress? The Intelligence Committee staffer replied cautiously, telling the analyst that he should get a private lawyer who could give him specific, accurate advice. The staffer then also told Schiff what little he knew—that there was a CIA analyst with concerns about Ukraine policy. This news, of course, came on top of Schiff's existing concerns about Giuliani and Ukraine, which had been highlighted by the *Times*'s story in May. But the staffer did not tell Schiff the CIA analyst's name. Schiff and his staff waited to hear more.

A friend referred the analyst to a lawyer named Andrew Bakaj, a Ukrainian American who had himself been a whistle-blower during an earlier stint in government, first in the Defense Department and then at the CIA. Bakaj was on the golf course when he received the first call from the analyst, and it took a few days for them to connect. The analyst signed a retainer agreement with Bakaj on Monday, August 5. Bakaj gave the analyst a tutorial on the whistle-blower laws and told him to start preparing a letter, to outline his concerns. The analyst, like many in his position at the CIA, was a meticulous student and observer, and he took to the assignment with alacrity and determination. Bakaj never saw the letter; he just told the analyst the requirements for such a document and where to send it. Over the last generation or so, a considerable body of law had arisen around the protection of whistle-blowers. They can avoid disclosure and retaliation, but only if they follow certain specific guidelines, which Bakaj described for the CIA analyst.

The analyst completed the letter on August 12. It was addressed to Richard Burr, the chairman of the Senate Intelligence Committee, as well as Schiff, the House committee chairman, but Bakaj told the analyst to deliver the letter initially to Michael Atkinson, the inspector general of the intelligence community, who had the authority to pass it to the congressional leaders. The letter is an extraordinary document—four thousand words over nine single-spaced pages, written in a restrained, factual style but still seething with outrage. Following Bakaj's directions, the letter began with an invocation of the whistle-blower law: "I am reporting an 'urgent concern' in accordance with the procedures outlined in 50 U.S.C. §3033(k)(5)(A). This letter is UNCLASSIFIED when separated from the attachment." But the second sentence told the story: "In the course of my official duties, I have received information from multiple U.S. Government officials that the President of the United States is using the power of his office to solicit interference from a foreign country in the 2020 U.S. election." He went on, "This interference includes, among other things, pressuring a foreign country to investigate one of the President's main domestic political rivals. The President's personal lawyer, Mr. Rudolph Giuliani, is a central figure in this effort."

The letter made clear that the author was not the only person concerned about the president's actions. "Multiple White House officials with direct knowledge of the call informed me that, after an initial exchange of pleasantries, the President used the remainder of the call to advance his personal interests," he wrote. "The White House officials who told me this information were deeply disturbed [that they] witnessed the President abuse his office for personal gain." It was clear, too, that the letter could not be written off as the work of a malcontent or a crank. The letter displayed a mastery of Ukrainian politics down to below the ministerial level. (CIA veterans recognized the tone, and even the format and citation style, as that of an experienced CIA analyst.) In the next few days, Atkinson, the inspector general, followed the letter of the law and concluded that the information in the letter was "urgent" and "credible" and merited disclosure to Congress.

At this point, in late August, events began converging quickly. The

Three Amigos continued final negotiations with Zelensky's people about how and when he was going to announce the investigations of the Bidens. They discussed the possibility that Zelensky might announce the probe in an interview with CNN. Increasingly desperate for the aid, the Ukrainians were prepared to agree to almost anything. Then, on August 28, *Politico* made public that the Trump administration had secretly put a hold on the military assistance to Ukraine. Suddenly there was bipartisan outrage and demands to the White House for explanation. None was publicly forthcoming.

In Kyiv, William Taylor, the veteran diplomat placed in charge of the embassy, was increasingly apoplectic about the distortion of American foreign policy and values. He was in touch with John Bolton at the White House, who felt similarly about what was going on. Bolton encouraged Taylor to use a special State Department channel to send a cable directly to Secretary of State Pompeo to protest the hold on military aid. On August 29, for the first time in his thirty-year career, Taylor used the channel to send such a cable to Pompeo. He received no response.

On September 1, President Trump was supposed to meet with Zelensky at a World War II memorial conference in Warsaw. At the last minute, Trump canceled his trip to remain in Washington to monitor a hurricane that was threatening the southern United States. Vice President Pence went instead and met with the Ukrainian president. At the conference, Sondland again told Zelensky's aide Yermak that the aid would not flow until Zelensky announced the investigations. When this conversation was repeated to Taylor, he texted Sondland, "Are we now saying that security assistance and WH meeting are conditioned on investigations?" (Sondland demurred on leaving a record of his answer, texting back, "Call me.") Taylor was still pressuring Sondland the next week, texting, "As I said on the phone, I think it's crazy to withhold security assistance for help with a political campaign."

The link between the military aid and the announcement of the Biden investigation was starting to leak into the press. In Warsaw, Pence refused to answer reporters' questions about Trump's dealings with Ukraine. On September 5 in *The Washington Post*, an unsigned editorial (an unusual venue for a scoop) stated about the cutoff in military aid to Ukraine, "Some suspect Mr. Trump is once again catering to Mr. Putin, who is dedicated to undermining Ukrainian democracy and independence. But we're reliably told that the president has a second and more venal agenda: He is attempting to force Mr. Zelensky to intervene in the 2020 U.S. presidential election by launching an investigation of the leading Democratic candidate, Joe Biden." Four days later, three committees in the House of Representatives—Intelligence, Oversight, and Foreign Affairs—announced that they would investigate Giuliani's role in Ukraine policy. Also on September 9, Atkinson, the inspector general, officially informed the Intelligence Committee of the existence (though not the content) of the whistle-blower's letter.

The next day, September 10, John Bolton quit (or was fired) as national security adviser, and the White House finally ordered the release of the military aid to Ukraine. The White House released the military aid to Ukraine *after* allegations of the link to the Biden investigation became public. In other words, the Trump administration released the aid only because it was caught linking the aid to the quest for political dirt. Also on September 10, the House Intelligence Committee voted to issue a subpoena for the whistle-blower's letter. Over the next week, bits and pieces of the whistle-blower's complaint began to leak out into the news media. Calls for impeachment among congressional Democrats, which had largely come to a halt after Mueller's testimony, resumed. On September 18, Trump tweeted, "All Polls, and some brand new Polls, show very little support for impeachment. Such a waste of time, especially with sooo much good that could be done, including prescription drug price reduction, healthcare, infrastructure etc."

Three days later, on Saturday night, September 21, Representative Abigail Spanberger put her three daughters to bed at her home in Glen Allen, Virginia, outside Richmond, and prepared to get on the telephone.

27

"The Times Have Found Us"

On July 20, 1787, Benjamin Franklin rose from his seat at the Constitutional Convention in Philadelphia to make a plea to his fellow delegates. At that point in their deliberations, they had agreed that the new structure for the American government would include a head of state—a president of the United States. The Articles of Confederation had failed in significant part because of the absence of a single chief executive for the new nation. But Franklin pointed out that the creation of a presidency carried a risk—that the person chosen would prove to be unfit. The Constitution needed a legal mechanism for his removal, or the only remedy between elections for a president's misbehavior would be assassination. A better alternative, Franklin argued, would be "to provide in the Constitution for the regular punishment of the Executive when his misconduct should deserve it, and for his honorable acquittal when he should be unjustly accused."

Franklin's invitation to his colleagues set off one of the most consequential debates at the convention. There came to be wide agreement that there should be a process for removal of a president. But how? And, even more important, on what grounds? The issue was especially relevant because the young republic was so vulnerable to foreign influence. The European nations were vastly richer and more powerful than the former colonies. What if European monarchs tried to influence the president, as they importuned one another, with gifts and pensions? The draft of the Constitution already prohibited federal officeholders from receiving "any present, Emolument, Office or Title" from a foreign state. But what could be done if a president received such ill-gotten bounty? The answer, the Framers decided, lay in an English doctrine of law that dated to 1376—impeachment.

A couple of delegates—Charles Pinckney and Gouverneur Morris—argued at first that the possibility of impeachment would unduly limit the power of the president. But a clear majority thought otherwise. Without the possibility of impeachment, William Davie asserted, a president might seek to escape punishment for wrongdoing by sparing "no efforts or means whatever to get himself re-elected." As George Mason put it, the Constitution needed to establish a check on the president precisely because his powers were so great. "Shall any man be above Justice?" Mason asked. "Above all shall that man be above it, who can commit the most extensive injustice?"

But the consensus in favor of giving Congress the power to impeach did not settle the issue of the grounds for its use. In light of the Framers' fear of foreign influence, it was no surprise that they agreed that presidents could be removed if they committed treason and bribery. What else? On this subject, there was a brief but consequential exchange between two of the most formidable Framers, George Mason and James Madison. Mason suggested that "maladministration" should also be an impeachable offense. Madison disagreed, winning over his colleagues with the argument that "so vague a term will be equivalent to a tenure during the pleasure of the Senate." The delegates then moved quickly to a vote on the final language. They agreed that it would take a majority in the House of Representatives and two-thirds of the Senate to remove a president for "Treason, Bribery, or other high Crimes and Misdemeanors."

The Framers, thus, left few clues about the meaning of these now-famous words. The short exchange between Mason and Madison did give a rough shape to the debates to come. Ours would not be a parliamentary system, where legislators could remove the head of government because he was an unsuccessful leader if he merely engaged in "maladministration." It would take something more to justify impeachment. But what? That was the question to which Abigail Spanberger, hoping to channel the Framers, turned her attention after she put her kids to bed on September 21, 2019.

—

Spanberger was a "frontliner"—one of the group of Democratic members of Congress who flipped Republican seats in the election of 2018. Their victories allowed the Democrats to retake control of the House of Representatives for the first time since 2010. Though she had just turned forty years old, Spanberger had a dream biography for a modern politician. After graduating from the University of Virginia and earning an MBA, she spent several years in law enforcement and then was hired as a case officer for the CIA. After returning to Virginia, she ran for a House seat in central Virginia that had been in Republican hands for thirty-eight years. It had been held by Eric Cantor, the former majority leader, and then Dave Brat, who had upset Cantor in a Republican primary in 2014 for not being conservative enough. Running on her national security credentials and moderate Democratic views, Spanberger narrowly defeated Brat in 2018. (The new congresswoman was no great liberal; she even voted against Nancy Pelosi for Speaker, believing that it was time for new leadership in the House.) As Trump's scandals multiplied during Spanberger's first months in office, she stuck to her focus on bread-and-butter issues and resisted calls for impeachment.

Spanberger bonded with a handful of her new colleagues, all frontliner Democrats, all with backgrounds in national security, all who also won Republican seats in 2018. They set up a group text on Signal called G-9 (short for "Gang of 9"), where they traded information and gossip and kept one another informed about political developments, or crises, on the horizon. They were all skeptics about impeachment, mostly because they wanted to focus on substantive legislative accomplishments to tout when they ran for reelection. In addition, Trump had won virtually all of their districts in 2016, so support for impeachment offered the prospect of political peril.

But the group—all of G-9—was starting to evolve on the issue of impeachment. Like everyone else in Congress, they were paying close attention as the stories about Trump and Ukraine multiplied in September. What if Trump really did withhold aid to Ukraine in order to get dirt on Joe Biden? If that wasn't an impeachable offense, what was? The little they knew about the whistle-blower made him sound like one of them—a conscientious and patriotic national security professional who simply couldn't take it anymore. One other issue in particular, not necessarily an obvious one, also troubled them. Once the Democrats took over the House at the beginning of the year, several committees began investigations of the Trump administration. They issued subpoenas for testimony of administration officials and for documents. Trump's White House responded with a stone wall. Virtually no documents. Almost no witnesses. The administration even interposed objections to prevent the testimony of *former* officials, like Don McGahn. If the White House wouldn't even let Congress investigate, how would anyone ever learn what was going on? It was starting to feel as if the Trump administration were gaslighting them, making them feel as if they were crazy for just trying to do their jobs.

The G-9 group wanted to talk about next steps, and that was the purpose of the conference call on Saturday night. The frontliners included Spanberger, Gil Cisneros of California, Jason Crow of Colorado, Chrissy Houlahan of Pennsylvania, Elaine Luria of Virginia, Mikie Sherrill of New Jersey, and Elissa Slotkin of Michigan, and most were on the call. They agreed that something had changed in the last couple of weeks; Trump's behavior appeared increasingly unhinged, indefensible. The group decided to write a joint article, an op-ed piece, expressing their views. They knew that given their backgrounds their voices carried a certain weight and they would be taken more seriously if they spoke together. That weekend several in the group also touched base with Adam Schiff, who had become a mentor to some of them. (Houlahan called Schiff her "spirit animal.") On Sunday morning, Spanberger had an appearance in Culpeper, about an hour and a half away from her home in Virginia. She took her laptop and pounded out some thoughts in the car. Over the course of the day, the group traded drafts of a Google document. On Monday, as they all returned to Washington from their districts, they agreed to meet in Houlahan's office, in the Longworth House Office Building, to discuss the article. Houlahan projected the draft on a screen, and the authors, both in person and long-distance, contributed final edits.

"Our lives have been defined by national service. We are not career politicians," the final version began. "We have sworn oaths to defend the Constitution of the United States many times over." Now, it appeared, the president himself was threatening the constitutional system. The authors summarized the apparent facts about Trump's pressure on Ukraine to investigate his political adversaries. "If these allegations are true, we believe these actions represent an impeachable offense," they wrote. "These new allegations are a threat to all we have sworn to protect. We must preserve the checks and balances envisioned by the Founders and restore the trust of the American people in our government. And that is what we intend to do." (Two members of the Gang, Jared Golden of Maine, and Max Rose of New York, declined to sign.) One thing the frontliners learned in their military training was that superior officers hate surprises, so they arranged a group call to Nancy Pelosi at 5:30 p.m. so the Speaker knew what they were about to do. They weren't asking for permission, but they were letting her know what was coming.

The frontliners remained somewhat naive about the ways of Washington and its media outlets, so they weren't sure if anyone would want to publish their work, which ran just 427 words. They chatted with one another about possibly posting the article at Medium.com, which more or less accepts everything. Spanberger's press secretary, on the other hand, recognized the newsworthiness of the article and shopped it to *The Washington Post,* which posted it that same day—on the evening of Monday, September 23.

It hit like a bomb.

Donald Trump almost had a point when he said that Democrats had been trying to impeach him since he became president. Congressman Al Green, who represented a district in Houston, was the primary early architect of the effort. Green and Brad Sherman, whose district was in Los Angeles, introduced the first article of impeachment on June 12, 2017, charging Trump with obstruction of justice, largely based on Comey's testimony about his interactions with the president. On December 6, the House rejected Green's initiative to bring impeachment up for debate by a vote of 364–58. The following month, the House rejected a similar attempt by Green, this time by a vote of 355–66.

Al Green cut a distinctive figure on the House floor. He was, for one thing, the only male member of Congress with a ponytail, and he spoke to everyone with elaborate courtesy. To the daily pleasantry "How are you?," he always replied, "Better than I deserve."

(Elaborating, if asked, he called himself "a recovering sinner.") Green was also typical of early supporters of impeachment in the House. He was very liberal, came from a safe Democratic district, and opposed Trump to the depths of his soul. Notwithstanding the lopsided results, Green placed copies of each of the impeachment resolutions in portfolios embossed with the gold seal of the House. The December resolution was paired with a list of the members who voted for it—what he called "the first 58." The January resolution faced a page containing the names of its supporters, who were called "the historic 66." Green sent portfolios to all the members of Congress who voted with him. His celebration of his failures revealed something about the nature of congressional opposition to Trump—that it was passionate and enduring. For Trump's adversaries, even defeat was a badge of honor.

While the House was in Republican hands, advocacy for impeachment was always an academic exercise, but the most important impeachment opponent in the new Congress was a Democrat— Nancy Pelosi. Of course, as a committed liberal, Pelosi shared many of the policy views of the impeachment supporters in her caucus—she even felt much the same way about Trump's character—but she was ever aware of the experience of 1998. In that year, Republicans had forced through an unpopular impeachment of President Clinton and then suffered unexpected losses in the midterm elections. (It was true that two years later George W. Bush used Clinton's impeachment to help win the presidency, but the conventional wisdom, which Pelosi shared, was that the impeachment of Clinton was a political loser for House Republicans.)

So for the first two years of Trump's term, Pelosi opposed impeachment almost as fervently as did the president's supporters. "I don't like to talk about impeachment," she told me in May 2018 as the midterms were approaching. "Impeachment is not a political tool. It has to be based on just the law and the facts. When I was Speaker, people wanted me to impeach George Bush for the war in Iraq because it was based on false information, but you can't just go from one impeachment to the next. When we are in the majority, we are going to try to be unifying, and there is no way to do impeachment in a bipartisan way right now." In the campaign of 2018, most Democrats, especially the frontliners, took Pelosi's advice and largely avoided the subject of impeachment and concentrated on issues like health care, which voters said they cared about most. The strategy was a resounding success, and the Democrats achieved a net gain of forty-one seats and won the House majority.

With the Democrats in control, impeachment suddenly entered the realm of possibility, and this created complications. The public release of Mueller's report, in April, might not have galvanized sentiment in favor of impeachment around the country, but it did prompt more congressional Democrats to announce their support. By summer, about 100 Democrats (out of 235) wanted to impeach Trump. Notably, one of them was Jerry Nadler, who had just taken over the chairmanship of the Judiciary Committee, which traditionally led the impeachment process in the House. Pelosi and Nadler had much in common. She was first elected in 1986, he in 1992; her district in San Francisco was just about as liberal as his on Manhattan's West Side. But their responsibilities and priorities differed. Pelosi was a national figure whose main responsibility was to preserve her politically diverse majority. Nadler had spent decades as a frustrated member of the minority on Judiciary, which traditionally attracted the most partisan members of both parties. Among Democrats, the committee was a hotbed of support for impeachment. In addition, in his home district Nadler was looking at a potential primary challenge from the left— the kind of race that Alexandria Ocasio-Cortez had just won over Nadler's longtime New York colleague Joe Crowley. In other words, Pelosi had to protect her right flank, Nadler his left. Conflict was inevitable.

Trump's own behavior raised the stakes. When the Democrats took over the House, it was widely anticipated that they would conduct major investigations of the Trump administration. But to a degree unprecedented in American history, Trump simply refused to cooperate—denying permission for administration witnesses to testify and documents to be produced. At the time, few realized how successful this tactic could be. Some committees began the cumbersome process of voting to find witnesses in contempt and then seeking to enforce subpoenas in court, but that effort took months, as Nadler discovered when his committee tried to force Don McGahn to testify. Using brute force, Trump stymied congressional oversight.

Through the summer of 2019, Nadler pressed to open impeachment hearings, and Pelosi resisted, and she didn't appreciate the pressure from her own caucus. The lead balloon of Mueller's testimony, in July, hardened Pelosi's resolve to keep impeachment under wraps. She was resolute in her desire to protect the moderates in her caucus from taking a politically risky vote in support of impeachment. On the other hand, Nadler continued to hold hearings in the summer, which created further tension between the Speaker and the committee chairman. Their staffs played semantic games about how to describe Nadler's hearings, so they were seen as something short of actual impeachment proceedings. Eventually, they agreed on compromise language in a deal brokered by a longtime aide to Pelosi named Dick Meltzer: "The Committee is conducting hearings to determine whether to recommend articles of impeachment." (Internally, in honor of Meltzer, this would become known as "The Magic Dick Language"; this passed for congressional humor.) Still, even when Nadler managed to corral administration witnesses, his hearings produced little. When Trump allies did deign to testify, they treated Nadler's committee like a petty annoyance, picking and choosing which questions to answer. Corey Lewandowski, Trump's erstwhile campaign manager, testified on September 17, and the result was a fiasco. He treated the committee with smug contempt. Pelosi was furious, asserting later that Lewandowski should have been held in contempt on the spot.

By that point, of course, the Ukraine allegations were tumbling forth daily, and so were the calls for impeachment. But still Pelosi held the line, refusing to jeopardize the political fate of the frontliner Democrats. But she was also recalculating the politics daily, based in part on regular phone calls with Schiff, who was keeping her up to date on the progress of his investigation. It was a rough period for Pelosi, who was haunted by death. Her friend Cokie Roberts, the journalist, died on the day that Lewandowski testified. Elijah Cummings, the congressman from Baltimore who chaired the Oversight Committee, had to step away because of health problems. (He died on October 17, just before Pelosi's older brother Thomas D'Alesandro III, the former mayor of Baltimore, also died.) On Saturday, September 21, Pelosi gave a eulogy at Roberts's funeral in Washington and then flew to South Carolina, where she spoke on Sunday at the funeral of Dr. Emily Clyburn, the wife of Congressman James E. Clyburn, the third-ranking House Democrat. On Monday, September 23, Pelosi flew to

New York for a conference on the sidelines of the United Nations General Assembly. At the St. Regis hotel that afternoon, she took the call from the frontliners who had written the article about impeachment. They gave her the heads-up about what they were going to say.

Pelosi absorbed the message from Spanberger and the others without much comment, and the Speaker read their article that evening as she flew back to Washington. She understood its significance—and its magnitude—immediately. The article meant that the frontliners no longer needed or wanted Pelosi's protection from a vote on impeachment. They were ready to go. Pelosi recognized, too, that the rest of her caucus—which was mostly liberal, and mostly with safe seats—was already restless to proceed on impeachment. She exercised a measure of control over her fellow Democrats, but the House members were still independent actors. Even if she wanted to keep holding back on impeachment at this point, it wasn't clear whether she could stop a stampede of Democrats. It was true that she had often spoken of the need for impeachment to be a bipartisan process; this was her lesson from 1998. And she recognized, too, that there was little likelihood that many, or any, House Republicans were going to support the impeachment of Trump. But the public—her public—was moving, and she didn't want to be left behind. (Public opinion polls, which had barely moved during Trump's entire presidency, showed a modest but real movement toward favoring impeachment during this period.) Pelosi often quoted Lincoln: "In this age, in this country, public sentiment is everything. With it, nothing can fail; against it, nothing can succeed." In Pelosi's view, on impeachment, she now had public sentiment—or enough of it, anyway.

The next morning, Tuesday, September 24, Pelosi informed the full Democratic caucus that she would be moving forward on impeachment. One of the charms of the House of Representatives is that the members, even the Speaker, generally circulate in the Capitol among reporters and ordinary citizens. Press availabilities often take place on the run. But on this day, Speaker Pelosi arranged for an unusually formal setting for her announcement. She stood at a lectern on the Speaker's balcony, in front of a wall of American flags, and addressed the American people. Characteristically, once she committed to impeachment, she was all-in. Like the frontliners in their article, Pelosi briefly summarized the growing case against Trump—that he had tried to enlist a foreign power to help his reelection. After a brief nod to the wisdom of the Framers, Pelosi said, "Today I'm announcing the House of Representatives is moving forward with an official impeachment inquiry and directing our six committees to proceed with their investigation under that umbrella of an impeachment inquiry. . . . No one is above the law. Getting back to our founders, in the darkest days of the American Revolution, Thomas Paine wrote, 'The times have found us.'"

The frontliners' article had set off a cascade of events that had an almost irresistible momentum. Pelosi knew what her endorsement of an impeachment process meant, because she knew how to count votes. She knew that her announcement on September 24 would end in the third impeachment of a president in American history. In the space of a weekend, even less, impeachment went from nearly inconceivable to virtually certain. But Pelosi had a condition for her endorsement of impeachment, and she made it clear in private, if not in public. She wanted the entire process completed before the House took its Christmas recess in 2019. She did not want her precious frontliners to spend all of 2020 on impeachment; she wanted them to run for reelection with substantive legislative accomplishments, especially since Pelosi knew that the Senate would never vote to convict Trump.

Remarkably, the rush to impeachment took place before either Congress or the public had even seen the whistle-blower's complaint or the partial transcript of the July 25 phone call.

As the White House prepared for a new investigatory onslaught— about Ukraine instead of Russia—the cast of lawyers had changed. Emmet Flood, the White House official who succeeded Ty Cobb as the point of contact with Mueller, left the administration. Flood wasn't even replaced, because with Mueller's probe winding down, there didn't appear to be any need.

Flood's duties were absorbed by Pat Cipollone, who took over from Don McGahn as White House counsel. Like Flood, Cipollone had long practiced at a firm in D.C., and he too earned a reputation for quiet excellence as a litigator. But unlike Flood, who brought his firm's hired-gun mentality to his work, Cipollone had a distinctive ideological profile. Not only was he a devout Catholic, and the father of ten children, but he was steeped in Washington's Catholic legal sub-culture, where advocating against abortion and gay rights had been as much a part of his professional development as representing large corporations. His only legal service outside Washington was as the top lawyer for the Knights of Columbus, the Catholic fraternal group. Back in Washington, he helped create the National Catholic Prayer Breakfast and led the Catholic Information Center. His friends and allies in these endeavors included Bill Barr, now the attorney general, Rick Santorum, the former senator, and Leonard Leo, the Federalist Society leader who had helped Trump reshape the federal judiciary.

As the Ukraine crisis heated up, Cipollone needed to address two immediate challenges—the whistle-blower complaint and the July 25 partial transcript. Should these documents be released or kept secret? Under the whistle-blower statute, once the inspector general found that the complaint was "urgent" and "credible"—and the inspector general promptly did so—the complaint was supposed to be released to Congress. But the Trump political appointees at the Justice Depart-ment had raised questions about whether the complaint should be released, given that it included matters possibly covered by executive privilege. The legal position was tenuous, but it was a means to keep the whistle-blower's complaint secret, at least for the time being. As for the transcript, there was no obligation at all to release it to the public; indeed, such transcripts of presidential calls with foreign lead-ers are almost never released. If Emmet Flood were still at the White House, it was clear what his advice would have been. Release nothing. Say nothing. That was the Williams & Connolly way.

But Cipollone had to deal with Trump on a daily basis, and the president was agitating for disclosure. He was convinced that he had done nothing wrong on the July 25 call with Zelensky; he insisted he had nothing to hide. In tweets during this period, Trump said the conversation with the Ukrainian president was "perfectly fine and appropriate" and "there was nothing said wrong. It was pitch perfect!" The president's advocacy for himself turned into a curious recapitulation of the White House reaction to the start of the Muel-ler investigation in mid-2017. At that time, Trump insisted there was no collusion with Russia, so he allowed Ty Cobb to share documents and permitted White House staffers to speak with Mueller's investi-gators. Here, in September 2019, Trump urged the same course on

Cipollone. Release the "perfect" transcript. Trump believed he could shape reality; if he said the transcript was "perfect," millions of his supporters would agree, just because he said it. There was some logic in this view. Trump's hold on his party, and his media outlets, especially Fox News, was such that he could be assured of support no matter how outrageous his behavior.

But it was Cipollone's job to see outside Trump's bubble of protection. The July 25 transcript—obviously—displayed very far from perfect behavior by the president. A stronger White House counsel, or one with criminal defense experience, might have pushed back against the president. At a minimum, the transcript was problematic for Trump; at worst, it was smoking-gun evidence of abuse of presidential power. After a year in which the Trump administration refused to release even the most innocuous documents to Congress and the public, Cipollone could have contrived any number of reasons to withhold the transcript. But he didn't. Instead, he released it, voluntarily no less. This was folly, almost a dereliction of duty by Cipollone. But Trump was a persuasive man, and an intimidating client, and Cipollone did what the president wanted him to do.

First, though, Cipollone did a measure of presumptive damage control. He invited a group of close congressional allies to the White House to review the transcript in advance and line up their defense of it. The group included Senators David Perdue, Ron Johnson, and Shelley Moore Capito, as well as Representatives Jim Jordan, Devin Nunes, John Ratcliffe, Matt Gaetz, and Mark Meadows. This was hardly the group to provide an objective assessment of anything Trump did; they were his most ardent supporters on Capitol Hill. As such, they did their duty and agreed that the transcript was no big deal. At the same time, the whistle-blower's lawyer was threatening to take his complaint directly to the Intelligence Committees, regardless of what the administration ordered him to do. So Trump and Cipollone decided to preempt that effort as well. They would release both the complaint and the transcript—to show they had nothing to hide.

Trump chose to release the partial transcript on September 25— the day he was finally going to meet face-to-face with Zelensky at the United Nations. The two presidents had a joint press conference, and it was awkward, to say the least. "Well, thank you very much, everybody," Trump opened. "We're with the President of Ukraine, and he's made me more famous, and I've made him more famous." With typical bravado, Trump announced, while sitting beside Zelensky, that he would be releasing the record of their July 25 conversation. "We spoke a couple of times, as you probably remember," Trump said. "And they'd like to hear every single word, and we give them every single word." Trump took the opportunity to recite his favorite fact about Zelensky's homeland. "I know a lot of people from Ukraine. They're great people. And I owned something called the Miss Universe pageants years ago, and I sold it to IMG," he said. "And we had a winner from Ukraine." (Trump's surreal invocation of the pageant wasn't even correct. The best finish for a Miss Ukraine in Trump's era at Miss Universe was as second runner-up, in 2014.)

At right around the same time as the Trump-Zelensky news conference, the White House released to the public the partial transcript (or call record, as it came to be called) of their conversation on July 25. There was no more interested audience for this document than the staff of the House Intelligence Committee, which was housed in a Sensitive Compartmented Information Facility in the basement of the Capitol. This was the headquarters for the Democratic investigation of Trump's dealings with Ukraine, and they had been at it since Giuliani boasted about his plans to go to Kyiv in May. They had even hired a researcher fluent in Ukrainian to scour the local press for clues about the American role there. But dots in the story remained unconnected until the office printers in the Capitol basement began turning out multiple copies of the July 25 call record.

As the group read the handful of pages, the only sounds were occasional exclamations.

"Oh, shit."

"You gotta be kidding."

"Why did they ever release this?"

"This is a total mob shakedown."

But these reactions were never intended to leave the SCIF. For a public response to the disclosure, the staff awaited the thoughts of their boss, the chairman of the Intelligence Committee, Adam Schiff.

"It Reads Like a Classic Organized Crime Shakedown"

Donald Trump's nicknames always displayed a kind of primal insight, and so it was for "Little" Adam Schiff. As it happens, the congressman is not short or frail, and he is, rather, an accomplished athlete. He met his wife, Eve (yes, Adam and Eve), on the tennis court, and he took up triathlons in his fifties. (Likewise, he became a vegan in this period, not out of political conviction but to reduce his cholesterol.) But Schiff's bland countenance, vanishing hairline, and boyish cheeks signaled diminutive nonentity, not strapping jock. Trump saw that, and put it to work, when he started to recognize Schiff as a threat.

Trump's message was that Schiff was a nerd, which wasn't entirely wrong. Schiff had always been smart, which he established during an undergraduate education at Stanford and at law school at Harvard. He moved to Los Angeles after graduation and soon landed a coveted post as an Assistant U.S. Attorney. Like many young lawyers, he regarded his time there as a dream job, where he had a chance to run his own investigations and conduct his own trials. Schiff distinguished himself, notably when he led the prosecution of Richard Miller, who was the first FBI agent in history to be prosecuted for espionage against the United States, in his case on behalf of the Soviet Union.

But Schiff's real goal was politics, and after he left the U.S. Attorney's office, he ran for the state assembly from a district in Venice, where he then lived. He was, by his own later admission, a pretty awful candidate—awkward, pompous, long-winded, and lacking a gift for the sound bite, all of which was rendered somehow worse because he was just barely more than thirty years old. Schiff finished tenth in a fourteen-candidate field. Determined to try again, he schemed with a political consultant to find a locale in Southern California that was less crowded with politically ambitious young Democrats. They settled on Burbank, in the San Fernando Valley, and in 1994 Schiff took a run at a different seat in the state assembly, this one occupied by a Republican named James Rogan. Schiff lost again but did better as a candidate. Two years later, when a nearby seat in the state senate opened up, he was recruited to run, and he finally won. (Like many lawyers in Los Angeles, he also filed away several unproduced screenplays during this period.)

Schiff's political career might have stalled there, if not for the impeachment of Bill Clinton and the rage of David Geffen, the entertainment mogul. Geffen was appalled by the impeachment and especially by the conduct of the House managers—including James Rogan, who had since moved on to a Burbank-based seat in Congress. Geffen made it a mission to recruit and finance a challenge to Rogan, and he found Adam Schiff in the state senate. Thanks to Geffen's interest, Schiff raised a fortune, and so, in response, did Rogan. The race became the most high-profile, and most expensive, contest for Congress in the 2000 cycle. Notwithstanding the origin of his campaign, Schiff rarely talked about impeachment during the race but instead stuck to substantive issues, like health care. In keeping with the leftward shift of the California electorate, Schiff won by 9 percent and never faced a serious challenge again. Over time, he became so confident about his standing in his California district that he moved his principal residence with his wife and two children to the Washington area. This used to be common for members of Congress but is now seen as carrying political risk. (Schiff kept an apartment in Burbank.)

Schiff was a favorite of Nancy Pelosi's from the beginning of his career. His victory was a key building block of Pelosi's plan to transform California into a near monolith of Democrats in the House. Schiff also followed a piece of advice the Speaker had long given to new members of Congress—know your subject. Do your homework. By necessity, senators are generalists; members of the House, on the other hand, can develop real expertise. Schiff decided to do national security and foreign policy. In his early days in the House, he served on the Judiciary and International Relations Committees, where junior members have little influence. But Pelosi, as the Democratic leader, started giving Schiff plum assignments. She promoted him to a seat on the Appropriations Committee, where he served on one sub-committee that supervised the State Department budget and another that funded NASA, which runs the Jet Propulsion Laboratory, in Pasadena, in his district. (Perhaps not surprisingly, Schiff is a space geek.)

Pelosi served for twenty-five years on the Intelligence Committee, and she held the panel in special regard. It's a "select" committee, which means Pelosi and her leadership team have free rein to appoint any members they want. Members with vulnerable seats avoid the Intelligence Committee; as a rule, it's not an assignment that gen-erates much public attention or many campaign contributions. (In normal times, most of its hearings are conducted in secret.) But it's a place to assert real influence during a career in the House. Pelosi put Schiff on Intelligence in 2008, and he began working his way up the committee ladder in seniority. The committee, and Schiff him-self, operated in a fairly bipartisan fashion in those days. On election night in 2010, when Republicans retook control of the House, Lamar Smith, the incoming Republican chairman of the Intelligence Com-mittee, called Schiff and asked him to stay on the committee, because they had worked so successfully together.

At the same time, Schiff ingratiated himself with the Democratic leadership by taking on unglamorous tasks that offered no apparent political benefits. In 2010, for example, he agreed to serve as co-lead manager (with a Republican) in the impeachment trial of Thomas Porteous, a federal district judge from Louisiana who was accused of bribery and perjury. The Senate convicted Porteous, and he was removed from office. At the time, of course, Schiff's work as a House manager in an impeachment trial seemed like little more than a pecu-liar novelty in the course of his career. When Trump took office, Schiff was a respected member of Congress who had the trust of Nancy Pelosi and a future, in all likelihood, of continued obscurity.

Trump tweeted about Schiff for the first time on July 24, 2017: "Sleazy Adam Schiff the totally biased Congressman looking into 'Russia,' spends all of his time on television pushing the Dem loss excuse!" Trump would eventually tweet about Schiff more than four hundred times, but the experience of being attacked by the president of the United States—by anyone, really—was a new one for Schiff. The congressman felt obligated to prepare his family for the onslaught. Not long after that first tweet, Schiff went to pick up his son at summer camp, where electronic devices were banned. As they drove home, Adam Schiff told his son, "I just want you to know that the president called me 'sleazy' the other day." Thirteen-year-old Eli Schiff pondered this news for a moment and then asked, "Does that mean I can call you sleazy?"

As usual with the president, his tweets were revealing in unintentional ways. Trump's firing of Comey and the subsequent appointment of Mueller created a simultaneous problem and opportunity for Democrats. The news media, especially cable television, quickly developed an insatiable appetite for the Russia investigation, and Mueller and his team immediately made clear that they would not contribute to the coverage. The Republicans who were in charge of the House and Senate at the time were interested only in defending Trump and discrediting any inquiries about him. Ever mindful of what happened to House Republicans during the Clinton investigation, Pelosi did not want her party to be consumed with investigatory fever about Trump. She wanted most of her members, and all of her candidates in 2018, to do what Schiff did in 2000—focus on pocketbook issues, not presidential scandal. But someone had to speak for the Democrats in the Russia investigation. Pelosi picked Schiff, then the ranking Democrat on the Intelligence Committee, which meant there was a kind of basis for Trump's tweet. Schiff was suddenly on television a great deal. (It helped that unlike most members of Congress he lived in Washington and thus was often available to be an in-studio guest on the Sunday shows.)

Trump resented Schiff for another reason. Though the congressman had appeared on national television rarely in previous years, it turned out he was good at it—clear, concise, and above all knowledgeable. At that point, he had been in Congress for almost two decades, and he'd really participated in only one investigation, regarding the impeachment of the judge. But the Russia investigation gave

Schiff the chance to use muscles that he had developed as a federal prosecutor—to learn complicated, detailed facts and present them in an understandable way, as to a jury. Schiff did more than just talk like a lawyer. He was an unapologetic Democratic partisan, and he leveraged his legal expertise against Trump—nightly, on the news, and on Twitter. Schiff's skill, as well as his ubiquity, unnerved Trump, who bestowed his nickname on the congressman in February 2018: "Little Adam Schiff, who is desperate to run for higher office, is one of the biggest liars and leakers in Washington, right up there with Comey, Warner, Brennan and Clapper! Adam leaves closed committee hearings to illegally leak confidential information. Must be stopped!" Even by Trump's standards, he seemed malignly obsessed with "lyin', cheatin', liddle' Adam 'Shifty' Schiff," as he once called him. The tweets even verged on threats: "Shifty Adam Schiff is a CORRUPT POLITICIAN, and probably a very sick man. He has not paid the price, yet, for what he has done to our Country!"

Most of these attacks took place even before Schiff had any real power. (In Trump's view, just being on television amounted to being powerful.) Still, as the ranking member on Intelligence, he had just two full-time investigators at his disposal and no access to subpoena power. For this reason, few politicians had a bigger stake in the midterm elections than Schiff. With the Democrats' victory, he became chairman of the Intelligence Committee and Trump's chief pursuer in Congress.

When Schiff took over the Intelligence Committee, in January 2019, he had a clear plan. He would take on a subject that Mueller had avoided—Trump's financial ties to Russia and other foreign entities. This was crucial to the committee's mission—to determine threats to American national security. Mueller investigated whether anyone connected to Trump committed criminal offenses. But Schiff took on a broader question—whether Trump's ties to Russia represented a counterintelligence risk to the nation. Schiff hired Daniel Goldman, a veteran prosecutor from the Southern District of New York, to be his lead investigator, and he issued a subpoena to Deutsche Bank, which financed most of Trump's overseas transactions. Trump once told an interviewer that if Mueller investigated his personal finances, that would represent crossing a "red line." Schiff planned, as his first order of business, to trample Trump's red line.

And then . . . nothing. Like many people inside and outside Congress, Schiff underestimated the president's ability to frustrate congressional oversight. The administration would not produce witnesses or documents. No president had ever stymied congressional oversight in such a comprehensive way. Most relevantly to Schiff's probe, Trump's lawyers went to court to challenge the Intelligence Committee's subpoena to Deutsche Bank. A federal court in New York ordered the bank to comply, and the appeals court agreed that the bank had to turn over Trump's records. But the Supreme Court agreed to accept a further appeal, and Schiff's committee still had nothing from the bank at the end of 2019. In short, Schiff's financial investigation of Trump was a bust. Then came Ukraine.

Like Pelosi, Schiff was long an impeachment skeptic. Of all people, he knew the political price to be paid for a failed impeachment, since he owed his seat in Congress to one. Even after Mueller's report pushed the number of impeachment supporters in the House to more than a hundred, Schiff was not among them. At that point, there wasn't even a consensus in the Democratic Party, much less the country, in favor of impeachment. The issue created subtle but real tension between the Judiciary Committee, with its roster of firebrands, starting with Jerry Nadler, and Schiff's Intelligence Committee, with its more measured and restrained Pelosi acolytes. Schiff didn't like Trump any more than Nadler did, but they had different views of the political realities. Still, Schiff's tolerance had a limit, too, and he reached it with Ukraine.

Trump's role in Ukraine came on Schiff's radar in May 2019, when Giuliani announced plans to visit Kyiv and then withdrew them after criticism, including from Schiff. But even without going to Ukraine, Giuliani kept pushing the Hunter Biden issue, on Twitter and on Fox News. Over the summer, Schiff hired Diana Pilipenko, a Russian and Ukrainian speaker, as one of his investigators. She noticed a curious thing after the phone call between Trump and Zelensky on July 25. The White House issued no public "readout," or brief summary, of the call, even though such reports are customary after conversations between heads of state. But Zelensky's office did release a readout, and it made a strange, vague reference to corruption, which seemed related to the issues that Giuliani had been pushing. The discrepancy wasn't proof of anything in and of itself, but it was peculiar. Then the would-be whistle-blower approached the Schiff staffer a few days after the Trump-Zelensky call. Again, the appearance of a possible whistle-blower was not in itself earthshaking or unusual, but it was another vague hint about something untoward going on in relation to Ukraine. On August 28, *Politico* reported that the military aid to Ukraine was put on hold—for unknown reasons. On September 9, Atkinson, the inspector general, reported to the Intelligence Committee that he had received a whistle-blower complaint, and it was "urgent" and "credible." But the inspector general said he had been directed by the White House not to turn it over to Congress. Again, nothing was yet proven, but it seemed clear to Schiff by this point that the Trump administration was hiding something about Ukraine, maybe a lot. On September 10, Schiff issued a committee subpoena to obtain the whistle-blower's complaint.

In the following two weeks, more dribs and drabs came out in the press about Trump and Ukraine. There were suggestions that the president was leaning on his Ukrainian counterpart to provide information about Hunter and Joe Biden—but no proof. Schiff concentrated on getting his hands on the whistle-blower's complaint but made no progress. As for the record of the July 25 call, Schiff and his staff felt they were probably in for a long legal fight to get access to it, like the battle over Richard Nixon's White House tapes in 1974.

On September 23, the frontliners' article appeared in *The Washington Post,* and Pelosi announced the impeachment investigation the next day. On the twenty-fifth came the release of the partial transcript of the July 25 phone call between Trump and Zelensky. Schiff's staff was, of course, shocked to have the chance to review it, since they figured the White House would fight to keep it secret. As Schiff reviewed the record of the call, he was just as appalled as his staff was. He had a chance to express it the next day, when he conducted a public hearing to examine the director of national intelligence. The most dramatic moment that day was Schiff's first public reaction to the July 25 call record. When his staff received the document the previous day, they had been struck by how it sounded like a mob boss talking to a victim. That idea stuck with Schiff, and he went with it, in public, the next day.

"It reads like a classic organized crime shakedown," Schiff said from the chairman's position in the hearing room. "Shorn of its rambling character and in not so many words, this is the essence of what the president communicates. 'We've been very good to your country, very good. No other country has done as much as we have. But you know what? I don't see much reciprocity here. I hear what you want. I have a favor I want from you though. And I'm going to say this only seven times so you better listen good. I want you to make up dirt on my political opponent, understand. Lots of it.'" And so on. "This is in sum and character what the president was trying to communicate with the president of Ukraine. It would be funny if it wasn't such a graphic betrayal of the president's oath of office."

Before the hearing was even over, Republican members were attacking Schiff for his interpretation of the call. Representative Mike Turner said, "While the chairman was speaking I actually had someone text me, 'Is he just making this up?' And yes, he was." Schiff acknowledged as much and said his remarks were parody. This was obvious, since the actual call record had been released the previous day. But Turner's remarks were mild compared with those of Trump, who went off on Schiff on Twitter. The president said Schiff should be "questioned at the highest level for Fraud & Treason," and he charged Schiff with "lying to Congress." A day later, Trump asked, "Arrest for Treason?" It was worth noting that the president, who was in charge of the Department of Justice, had just accused a member of Congress, and a political opponent, of treason, a crime punishable by death. But by this point, for better or worse, Trump's tweets passed almost without notice, even when they were at their most reckless and irresponsible.

At one level, the controversy about Schiff's "parody" was silly, because no one could have thought that Schiff was reading the real transcript. On another, though, this was a real blunder on the congressman's part. Schiff should have been aware of how his words, as chairman of the Intelligence Committee, would be parsed, and the parody was ineffective as well as misleading. (For example, Trump didn't say anything "seven times.") Mostly, though, the controversy served as a reminder of Schiff's prominence and his status as a target.

—

Now that Pelosi had committed to an impeachment investigation, how was the House going to pull it off? What would the House examine—Mueller, Ukraine, more? And who would conduct it?

In typical fashion, Pelosi was decisive on these subjects. Ultimately, the articles of impeachment would be voted on by the Judiciary Committee, as it had done with Nixon and Clinton. But the investigation—the real work—would be supervised by the Intelligence Committee, supported by the Oversight and Foreign Affairs Committees. That allowed Pelosi to put Schiff in charge, and she told him to limit his inquiry to Ukraine. By the last week in September, he had the July 25 call record and the whistle-blower complaint. Those represented a good start, but Schiff would need a lot more—like witnesses and physical evidence. Where to start?

Schiff's core Intelligence Committee staff—about a dozen people—knew since the summer that impeachment was at least a possibility, so they started doing some casual research on the subject. They all listened to Leon Neyfakh's *Slate* podcast about Watergate, which looked at the Nixon scandal against the backdrop of the Trump presidency. Someone located a copy of Jimmy Breslin's book about the Nixon impeachment investigation, *How the Good Guys Finally Won: Notes from an Impeachment Summer*. Breslin was a longtime columnist for New York City tabloids, and he followed the Judiciary Committee as it methodically built the case against Richard Nixon. According to Breslin, the key to the committee's work was facts—facts assembled on seven-ply index cards typed and retyped by a squadron of thirty typists, most of them graduates of Catholic high schools. "They were trained by nuns to believe in causes, and now they were to work on another cause, the greatest search for justice in the nation's history," Breslin wrote. "And always the paper mounted and the files grew thicker and higher and the typists typed. The paper grew, the edges becoming sharper, sharper, sharper. Soon Richard Nixon would feel the pain as the paper began to cut his life away." Breslin's book was more than four decades old, but they found copies for everyone, including Schiff.

The message was that impeachment had to be won with facts—like those the Judiciary Committee typists put on 1.5 million pieces of paper in 1974. So Schiff's assignment to his staff was to start assembling those facts, which meant, in the modern day, locating the emails and texts that the protagonists of the story sent each other. Schiff's investigators knew that like most white-collar cases in the contemporary world this would be a document-based case. The underlying facts related to the scheduling of communications between two heads of state; the granting and withholding of military aid; and contacts between American intermediaries and the Ukrainian government. These were all complex subjects, and there had to be at least hundreds of contemporaneous emails and texts about them. Even more than witness testimony (which could be shaded or simply false), the documents would reveal the story as it unfolded. So the Intelligence Committee sent letters to all the relevant government agencies—including the State and Defense Departments, as well as the White House—requesting all records about relations with Ukraine. When the letters went unanswered, the committee issued subpoenas.

The logistical challenges for Schiff's team were considerable, because Pelosi assigned three separate committees to conduct the impeachment investigation. Including Republicans, that meant that more than a hundred members of Congress—about a quarter of the full chamber—were going to be involved at some level. Intelligence would take the lead, but the other members and staff were going to have roles as well. After a quick round of talks, the Democratic leaders of the committees agreed that the investigation would begin with private depositions, open only to members and staff, in the Intelligence Committee offices in the Capitol basement. This was a common procedure for major congressional investigations; it's just common sense to want to examine witnesses first before putting them onstage in public. Plus, in a situation like this one, when so many facts were still unknown, it was important to prevent witnesses from hearing each other's testimony so they didn't decide to line up their stories in advance.

But this was all bureaucratic wrangling. Schiff knew he had to produce real evidence, and fast. There was one principal participant who was outside the government and thus, presumably, had his own records. As soon as the scandal broke, Kurt Volker quit his role as special representative for Ukraine negotiations. He was a free agent, so the committee brought him in as a first witness, and they told him to bring his texts and emails.

At this point, the committee investigators had only a rudimentary understanding of how the Ukraine initiative worked. They knew that the whistle-blower claimed that Giuliani had a central role in pressuring the Ukraine government. They knew from the July 25 call record that Trump asked Zelensky to do an investigation of the Bidens and the 2016 election. But they didn't know a lot more.

Volker agreed to testify in a private deposition on October 3, and he turned over his texts and emails the prior night. Schiff's staff hungrily tore at the package and started reading with astonishment. The texts laid out the scheme with precision. Volker had produced not just his own messages, but all the responses from almost every major figure, including Sondland and Giuliani. Making occasional appearances in the texts, like a Greek chorus, was Bill Taylor, who was in charge of the embassy in Kyiv. He was incredulous, horrified, and powerless as he watched the extortion scheme play out in front of him. September 1: "Are we now saying that security assistance and WH meeting are conditioned on investigations?" September 8: "The nightmare is they give the interview and don't get the security assistance. The Russians love it. (And I quit)." September 9: "As I said on the phone, I think it's crazy to withhold security assistance for help with a political campaign."

Schiff's staffers read the texts with amazement. *I can't believe they actually wrote all this down.* One investigator recalled a scene from *The Wire* where a group of drug dealers is planning a score. The leader notices that one of them is taking notes. "Is you taking notes on a criminal fucking conspiracy?" he says and then yanks the pad away. "What the fuck is you thinking, man?"

29

"The Deep Disappointment and Dismay I Have Felt as These Events Have Unfolded"

Volker's deposition in the Capitol basement set the pattern for the others that followed. The witness sat at the head of a long narrow table. To his right were Schiff, and Dan Goldman, the chief investigator, who usually led the initial round of questioning. To Volker's left were the Republicans who chose to attend. In theory, since three congressional committees were nominally involved, dozens of members had the right to come to each session, but it was usually fewer than twenty at any given time. As became customary, the Volker deposition was preceded by a protest from Republican members about the unfairness of the investigation process. On this occasion, it was Jim Jordan of Ohio who made the complaint, in this case about Schiff's plans to allow only committee staff, Democrats and Republicans, to ask questions. In response, Schiff said Jordan could ask questions of Volker if he thought it necessary.

In keeping with his long Washington experience, Volker tried to shade his testimony to portray himself as a dedicated public servant. (It is true that he worked without a salary.) He said he was just serving the national interest. "My efforts were entirely focused on advancing U.S. foreign policy goals with respect to Ukraine," he said. To the extent he spoke to Giuliani, Volker said he was trying to convince the former mayor that Ukraine was worthy of support. In addition he said, "At no time was I aware of or took part in an effort to urge Ukraine to investigate former Vice President Biden." In fact, Volker was deeply involved in the effort to persuade the Ukrainian government to open investigations that would benefit Trump. In later public testimony, he repudiated and corrected key parts of his October 3 deposition on this subject.

Volker might have danced around in his deposition testimony, but the real story was told in his texts—which were, of course, irrefutable as contemporaneous records. The volume and intensity of his messages with Sondland made clear why they called themselves two of the Three Amigos. (At least based on the texts, Rick Perry was less involved, despite his status as the third Amigo.) The texts were a trove of important evidence, and Intelligence Committee investigators eagerly awaited even more such bounty, when the Trump administration started to comply with subpoenas ordering them to turn over the emails and texts of government employees. In particular, the State Department passed word to the committee that it was gathering its material to produce.

The beginning of the Intelligence Committee hearings brought Trump to new heights of fury—mostly against Schiff. The president's tweets were venomous. "Schiff is a lowlife who should resign (at least!)." . . . "Schiff is a lying disaster for our Country. He should resign." . . . "Nancy Pelosi knew of all of the many Shifty Adam Schiff lies and massive frauds perpetrated upon Congress and the American people, in the form of a fraudulent speech knowingly delivered as a ruthless con, and the illegal meetings with a highly partisan 'Whistleblower' & lawyer . . . This makes Nervous Nancy every bit as guilty as Liddle' Adam Schiff for High Crimes and Misdemeanors, and even Treason." And Trump continued to push the smear against Biden that gave rise to the whole scandal: "The Biden family was PAID OFF, pure and simple!" Again, millions of people received these tweets, but the news media largely gave up parsing Trump's blunderbuss collection of accusations. Still, it is worthy of note that he told obvious and egregious lies. For example, there was nothing conceivably "illegal" about Schiff's staff member meeting with the whistle-blower. And there is no provision in the Constitution for impeachment of members of Congress.

But Trump had the power to do more than just rage at Schiff and his investigation. The president knew, as everyone knew, that Schiff needed evidence to proceed, and most of the evidence was located within the executive branch. Volker was a private citizen, but virtually every other important witness worked under the president's direct or indirect supervision. Likewise, Trump controlled access to all of the physical evidence, like emails, located within the executive branch. Schiff wanted that evidence, and Trump was going to make sure that he didn't get it.

The Constitution provides that the House of Representatives "shall have the sole Power of Impeachment." But what kind of authority to investigate goes along with that power? Does the House have the right to demand evidence from the president in deciding whether to impeach him?

To a great extent, this subject—the obligations of the executive branch to cooperate with oversight from Congress—had been governed by norms as much as laws. All presidents in the modern era recognized that Congress had the right to examine executive branch actions, and they have by and large cooperated with these inquiries, even in the most contentious circumstances. Of course, none of these presidents relished scrutiny from Congress, but they cooperated because it was expected of them and because they wanted to show that they had nothing to hide. When Congress began investigating Watergate, Richard Nixon directed his subordinates to appear and testify before Congress. "All members of the White House Staff will appear voluntarily when requested by the committee," Nixon announced. "They will testify under oath, and they will answer fully all proper questions." In other words, Nixon allowed witnesses such as John Dean, his White House counsel, to testify without objection. Ronald Reagan made and kept similar vows of cooperation during the Iran-contra investigation. President Clinton answered eighty-one written questions from the Judiciary Committee during the impeachment investigation of him. During the Benghazi investigation, the Obama administration allowed interviews with senior administration officials and produced more than 75,000 pages of documents, including 1,450 pages of White House emails. To be sure, presidents had also resisted disclosure of specific evidence—including the White House tapes under Nixon, the testimony of Secret Service agents under Clinton, and some records of the Justice Department's Fast and Furious program under Obama. But these fights between Congress and the president were narrowly focused and served as the exception rather than the rule.

This historical backdrop made the letter that Pat Cipollone sent at this point to Pelosi and the three chairs of the House committees extraordinary. Indeed, the letter from the White House counsel became instantly legendary, and not in a good way. People in Congress started referring to it in shorthand as "the October 8 letter" or "the eight-page letter," and everyone knew what they were talking about. Cipollone's claims in the letter were so unprecedented, and so legally deficient, that it was breathtaking, even in this administration, that a government official could have sent it. And the outrageousness of the claims was matched by the letter's tone of snarling hostility, of total contempt for a coordinate branch of government.

"I write on behalf of President Donald J. Trump in response to your numerous, legally unsupported demands made as part of what you have labeled—contrary to the Constitution of the United States and all past bipartisan precedent—as an 'impeachment inquiry,'" Cipollone began. "As you know, you have designed and implemented your inquiry in a manner that violates fundamental fairness and constitutionally mandated due process." After several paragraphs of invective against Congress, mostly against Schiff for his parody of the July 25 phone call, Cipollone went right to his bottom line: "In order to fulfill his duties to the American people, the Constitution, the Executive Branch, and all future occupants of the Office of the Presidency, President Trump and his Administration cannot participate in your partisan and unconstitutional inquiry under these circumstances." In other words, the entire executive branch—including the White House and every cabinet department—would refuse to provide any information at all to congressional investigators. No witnesses, no documents—nothing. (For example, in compliance with Cipollone's letter, the State Department never produced the documents it had started gathering.)

The letter then went on to spell out the administration's grievances with the impeachment process then under way in the House, even though that process was substantially similar to the ones used in 1974 and 1998. In what became a frequent Republican talking point, Cipollone accused the Democrats of attempting to "reverse the election of 2016." This was true, in a way, because impeachment, if followed by conviction in the Senate, does overturn the will of the voters in the previous election. But that's the purpose of the impeachment provision in the Constitution—as an extraordinary remedy to remove an unfit president.

But perhaps the most astonishing part of the letter dealt with the substance of the allegations against Trump, even though the House had not yet spelled out articles of impeachment. Cipollone said Trump would not cooperate with the impeachment investigation because he did nothing impeachable. He wrote that the record "clearly established that the call was completely appropriate, that the President did nothing wrong, and that there is no basis for an impeachment inquiry." This, of course, was like the defendant in a trial concluding that he was not guilty. It wasn't surprising that a defendant would feel this way, but it was not his judgment to make. The entire reason Congress was collecting evidence was to establish a basis for the members to reach a verdict. (Notably, too, the letter, and Trump himself, attempted to frame the Ukraine investigation as based entirely on "the call"—that is, the July 25 phone call between the two presidents. In fact, Congress was weighing Trump's entire course of conduct regarding Ukraine, not just the single phone call.)

As usual with Cipollone, it was clear in the October 8 letter that he was doing his client's bidding more than acting like a lawyer. The entire letter was more a hymn to Trump than a piece of advocacy. This was especially evident in the peroration. "The President cannot allow your constitutionally illegitimate proceedings to distract him and those in the Executive Branch from their work on behalf of the American people," he wrote. "The President has a country to lead. . . . He has important work that he must continue on their behalf, both at home and around the world, including continuing strong economic growth, extending historically low levels of unemployment, negotiating trade deals." Finally, he wrote, "We hope that, in light of the many deficiencies we have identified in your proceedings, you will abandon the current invalid efforts to pursue an impeachment inquiry and join the President in focusing on the many important goals that matter to the American people."

As Cipollone did in releasing the record of the July 25 phone call, he failed in the most basic obligation of a lawyer—to defend his client's interest, even if the client didn't realize it at the time. Cipollone could have denied access to Congress in any number of other ways. He could have acknowledged the role of a co-equal branch of government and offered to discuss the matter, even if he turned down most, or even all, of its requests for evidence; in other words, he could have treated Congress with a measure of respect. It was true, as many Trump supporters later noted, that prior presidents turned down some congressional demands for information; likewise, Congress usually went to court, rather than invoked impeachment, to protect its constitutional role. But before Cipollone's letter, no president had ever issued a blanket refusal to cooperate at all with a congressional investigation, especially one relating to impeachment, which is a core prerogative of the legislative branch. In responding to the committees' subpoenas, Cipollone just channeled Trump's loathing and disrespect for the Democrats. The public may not care a great deal about separation of powers, especially the preservation of congressional power. But even newcomers to Congress like the frontliners become zealous in their defense of their place in the constitutional system. Like his release of the July 25 call record, Cipollone's letter of October 8 represented a catastrophically bad piece of lawyering. It was clear at that point that the House was going to vote to impeach Trump for his behavior with regard to Ukraine. But Cipollone's letter guaranteed that there would be an additional article of impeachment for contempt of Congress.

Cipollone's complete shutdown of any cooperation presented Schiff with several dilemmas. The investigators continued to regard the Ukraine probe as a documents case; the key evidence would be in the government emails and texts, which the president had now put off-limits. So the first issue was straightforward. Should Congress go to court to try to force the administration to produce the witnesses and documents that had been subpoenaed?

Schiff's answer was no, and the reason was clear: time. If the House investigators had decided to go to court to demand compliance from the Trump administration, they would have condemned their own investigation to a delay of months—at least. They knew this from experience. In April 2019, the Judiciary Committee subpoenaed Don McGahn, the former White House counsel, for testimony. When the

White House ordered him to refuse to comply, the committee went to court as quickly as possible to enforce the subpoena. As of October, when Schiff was debating going to court, the district court had still not decided whether McGahn was required to testify.

In other words, as Schiff weighed whether to go to court in mid-October, six months after McGahn was subpoenaed by Congress, there was no resolution about whether he would have to testify and no end to the litigation in sight. (As it happened, the trial judge ordered McGahn to testify in late November, but the administration obtained a stay of that order, and a round of appeals began. The issue was still unresolved in the spring of 2020, more than a full year after McGahn was subpoenaed.) And the issue in McGahn's case was whether he was absolutely immune from having to appear and testify. If Congress won its case, and McGahn was forced to appear, the White House was vowing to litigate question by question what he was required to answer. Again, even if Congress won, that would mean more months of delay. And, of course, the McGahn litigation involved just one witness and no documents. Cipollone's letter meant that Schiff's investigators would have to go to court to obtain access to every administration witness and every document. All in all, then, the idea of going to court was a complete nonstarter. To do so, less than a year before the next presidential election, would succeed only in allowing the White House to run out the clock on Congress's impeachment investigation.

So what then? Schiff's team had to face reality. They might have believed the Ukraine investigation was a documents case—it might have *been* a documents case—but they had to reconcile themselves to the fact that they weren't going to get any documents from the administration. The documentary record would begin and end with Kurt Volker's texts. Even if Congress was right on the law, and the committees had the right to obtain all the emails and texts they sought, it would take too long to find out. The quest for more documents led to a premature but final dead end.

Witnesses, on the other hand, might be a different story. The committees could still subpoena executive branch employees, and Cipollone and his minions had already instructed them not to testify. But the ultimate decision about whether these individuals actually appeared before the committee would belong to the witnesses themselves. Cipollone could lock up documents but not human beings. Their decisions about whether to testify would rest partly on law and chain of command but also on conscience.

After Volker's testimony on October 3, Schiff and his investigators faced real trouble. They didn't know if anyone else would agree to sit for a deposition. Days passed. Then Cipollone's letter on October 8 made the prospect of further testimony even more remote. The lull in testimony began to look like a conclusion. So the investigators made one more plea, and they tried not to look as desperate as they were. The entire fate of the impeachment investigation was coming down to a single witness on a single day. Would Marie Yovanovitch show up and testify on October 11, 2019?

Marie—"Masha," to everyone—spoke Russian before she spoke English. Her parents enjoyed the dubious distinction of having fled two tyrannies, the Communists and the Nazis. They chose exile in Germany over the fallout from the Russian Revolution and then sought refuge from Hitler. They went first to Canada, where their daughter was born, and came to the United States when Masha was three. Her family landed in bucolic Kent, Connecticut, where they taught foreign languages at a boarding school and instilled in their daughter a fierce love of their adopted land. Masha graduated from Princeton in 1980, joined the Foreign Service, and spent the following decades in service to her country. Her assignments ranged the globe, from the comfortable (Ottawa and London), to the distant (Moscow), to the dangerous (Mogadishu). By the standards of the Foreign Service, she moved up the promotion ladder quickly. She became ambassador to Kyrgyzstan in 2005, to Armenia in 2008, and then after a couple of years on assignment at the State Department in Washington, she was named ambassador to Ukraine in 2016. She had a reputation for diligence and integrity. Like many State Department lifers, Yovanovitch served successfully in both Democratic and Republican administrations.

Her experience in Ukraine had been bizarre—perhaps without precedent in American diplomatic history. When Yovanovitch was sent to Kyiv, near the end of the Obama administration, she was told to use her influence to push the Ukrainian government to crack down on its endemic corruption problems. Under Trump, her official instructions remained the same, and she took the assignment seriously. Her mission brought her into conflict with Viktor Shokin, Ukraine's prosecutor general and its chief law enforcement officer, who was derelict (or worse) in addressing corruption. What Yovanovitch had no way of knowing was that Shokin was Rudy Giuliani's main source about the alleged perfidies of Hunter Biden during his tenure at Burisma. Because Shokin had been such a malign force in Ukraine and wasted American aid dollars, Yovanovitch denied him a visa to visit the United States. (She also made an enemy of Yuriy Lutsenko, Shokin's successor as prosecutor general, who was equally lackluster in fighting corruption and also a source for Giuliani.) In return for doing the job she was assigned to do, Yovanovitch drew passionate animosity from Giuliani, who told President Trump, and anyone else who would listen, that the ambassador was an Obama apparatchik who was determined to frustrate Trump's agenda. The whisper campaign against her grew into a scream, and she was ultimately recalled as ambassador and told to return to the United States "on the next plane" in April 2019.

The mistreatment of Yovanovitch featured prominently in the whistle-blower's complaint, so it was obvious that Schiff's committee would want to hear from her during its impeachment investigation. At that point, Yovanovitch was back in Washington, still a Foreign Service officer, but in a kind of exile on a fellowship at Georgetown University. Schiff's investigators reached out to her attorney, Larry Robbins, and told him they wanted her to testify in a closed session in the Capitol basement SCIF. Of course, Cipollone's letter instructed all executive branch employees, including those at the State Department, to refuse to participate in the impeachment investigation. As if the point needed reinforcement, a State Department official instructed Yovanovitch that she was not to give any "voluntary" testimony in the congressional investigation. Intentionally or not, the State Department letter appeared to leave a loophole. As Robbins saw it, if she received a subpoena from the committee, which requires compliance, then her testimony would not be the "voluntary" participation prohibited by the letter. Robbins told the committee that a subpoena might serve to compel Yovanovitch to appear.

Still, ultimately, the choice was up to Yovanovitch—to testify or not. Though she probably could not be fired outright from the Foreign Service for testifying, she knew that if she did speak to the committee, Trump's political appointees would effectively end her career. Her chances of obtaining another ambassadorship would be nil. But if she did testify, she could tell the truth about the extraordinary corruption she had seen, not just in the government of Ukraine but also in the operation of U.S. foreign policy, as it was steered by Rudy Giuliani. Yovanovitch received a subpoena, consulted her conscience, and showed up to answer questions in the Capitol basement on October 11.

Yovanovitch spoke with poise but also with pain. "I must share with you the deep disappointment and dismay I have felt as these events have unfolded," she said. "I have served this Nation honorably for more than 30 years. I have proudly promoted and served American interests as the representative of the American people and six different Presidents over the last three decades. Throughout that time, I, like my colleagues at the State Department, have always believed that we have enjoyed a sacred trust with our government." But that trust, she said, was broken. As she narrated her time in Kyiv, she reported her horror and astonishment, as she learned—in significant part from John Solomon's articles in *The Hill*—about Giuliani's campaign to defenestrate her. In many respects, though, more important than the substance of her testimony was the fact that she delivered it at all. In doing so, Yovanovitch defied the president. And her courage emboldened a stream of others—mostly other State Department employees, but also some who worked for the White House itself—to show up and testify as well. Without Yovanovitch, there might have been almost no witnesses at Donald Trump's impeachment hearing. With her, Congress was able to learn at least the core of what happened to American policy in Ukraine. Yovanovitch's testimony was an act of tremendous honor and importance.

Yovanovitch proved that executive branch employees could testify if they wanted to, and if they received a subpoena. Schiff's investigators figured out a way to game the system so as to guarantee that those who wanted to testify could actually do so. If a witness's lawyer said the person was willing to testify, the witness would be instructed to show up at the Capitol at the appointed time. But the staff would delay the actual presentation of a subpoena until the last minute. This was designed to forestall legal challenges from the White House. If a witness had a subpoena in hand days in advance, the administration could go to court and ask a judge to quash it. But if the witness didn't yet have physical possession of a subpoena, there was no live controversy for a judge to address. The point, then, was to keep to a minimum the time between the delivery of the subpoena and the commencement of testimony. In any event, the strategy worked. All the witnesses who wanted to testify did so without interference.

Gordon Sondland, the hotelier turned diplomat and the second Amigo, agreed to testify, even though the White House specifically instructed him not to appear. But neither his motives nor his testimony was especially noble. Sondland realized that he was just prominent enough to be blamed for the whole Ukraine fiasco, and he wanted to try to make sure that didn't happen. But as with Volker, Sondland gave highly misleading initial testimony during his deposition, minimizing his role and his understanding of the plan to coerce Zelensky into announcing an investigation of the Bidens. Like Volker, Sondland had to correct his initial testimony once later witnesses came forward.

The biggest crowd of members of Congress turned up on October 22 for the testimony of Bill Taylor, who was Yovanovitch's successor as head of the American embassy in Kyiv. They filled every seat at the long table and lined up along the walls. Taylor brought a great weight of moral authority to the occasion. As with Yovanovitch's long tenure with the State Department, Taylor's even longer career served as a reminder of the extraordinary range of expertise and experience in the American government. After graduating from West Point, Taylor served for six years in the army's famous 101st Airborne Division and saw combat duty in Vietnam. He joined the Foreign Service in 1985 and served in embassies around the world, including as ambassador to Ukraine from 2006 to 2009. Secretary of State Mike Pompeo asked him personally to try to stabilize the embassy in Kyiv after Yovanovitch was ousted in the spring of 2019. (Because Taylor was never formally nominated ambassador, his title in Ukraine was chargé d'affaires.) His testimony was preceded by the usual Republican complaints about process, this time by Devin Nunes, Schiff's predecessor as chairman of the Intelligence Committee. "We're here for what you're calling an impeachment inquiry, but there are no rules governing an impeachment inquiry," Nunes said, incorrectly. "There's been no organization of this impeachment inquiry, and so we're essentially operating under a lawless situation."

When the skirmishing between the members ended, Taylor was allowed to speak. "Mr. Chairman, Members," he began, and several people around the table jerked back their heads in amazement. *That voice!* It was so deep and resonant that it reminded the more senior members of Walter Cronkite. Combined with his still-military bearing, Taylor's presence gave him a unique measure of gravitas. So, of course, did his status as the top American diplomat currently on the ground in Kyiv. And as he gave his opening statement, Taylor vented his outrage about what the Trump administration had done in and to Ukraine. "In August and September of this year, I became increasingly concerned that our relationship with Ukraine was being fundamentally undermined by an irregular, informal channel of U.S. policymaking and by the withholding of vital security assistance for domestic political reasons," he said.

Like all executive branch witnesses, Taylor was prohibited from bringing his own emails to the committee, to refresh his memory about the events. But he was an inveterate note taker, in handwriting as orderly as his bearing, so he had a day-by-day account of his work in Ukraine. In 2019, as for years earlier, Taylor worked to help Ukraine establish itself as an independent nation, free from Russian domination. To that end, he had a special interest in trying to speed the flow of American military aid to Ukraine. As part of that effort, he tried to facilitate a meeting between Trump and Zelensky, and this was where the problems began. "By mid-July, it was becoming clear to me that the meeting President Zelensky wanted was conditioned on investigations of Burisma and alleged Ukrainian influence in the 2016 elections," he said. "It was also clear that this condition was driven by the irregular policy channel I had come to understand was guided by Mr. Giuliani." As Taylor recounted his narrative, some of the Republican members of the committees covered their faces in embarrassment.

But the story that Taylor told involved more sinister matters than just a withheld meeting in the Oval Office. In August, he heard something else on a large video and audio conference call. "Toward the end of this otherwise normal meeting, a voice on the call, the person who was off screen, said that she was from OMB and her boss had instructed her not to approve any additional spending of security assistance for Ukraine until further notice. I and others sat in astonishment," he said. "This was the first time I had heard that security assistance, not just the White House meeting, was conditioned on the investigations. Very concerned, on that same day, I sent Ambassador Sondland a text message asking if we are now saying that security assistance and a White House meeting are conditioned on investigations." The committee had already seen this message, because Taylor copied Volker on it. But Taylor now recounted what Sondland told him when they spoke that day: "Ambassador Sondland told me that President Trump had told him that he wants President Zelensky to state publicly that Ukraine will investigate Burisma and alleged Ukrainian interference in the 2016 U.S. election."

The story of the exchange of military aid for campaign dirt—the quid pro quo, as many called it—had never been spelled out in such detail. Nor had the stakes of the whole subject been explained with such clarity. As Taylor said in his conclusion, "There are two Ukraine stories today, Mr. Chairman. The first is the one we are discussing this morning and that you have been hearing for the past two weeks. It's a rancorous story about whistleblowers, Mr. Giuliani, side channels, quid pro quos, corruption, interference in elections. In this story, Ukraine is an object. But there's another Ukraine story—a positive, bipartisan one. In this second story, Ukraine is the subject. This one is about young people in a young nation struggling to break free of its past, hopeful their new government will finally usher in a new Ukraine, proud of its independence from Russia, eager to join Western institutions and enjoy a more secure and prosperous life."

No hearing in front of congressmen was ever going to stay secret for long. Members of Congress talk—to reporters, to the public, to each other. But the depositions were at least nominally secret, which presented a problem for the Democrats in the House. Congress lives on short-term thinking. Impeachment was ultimately going to be a public proceeding, so the people behind it had to create a momentum for it to succeed. (As Pelosi liked to say, government relied on "public sentiment.") But it was hard to keep the public engaged without releasing the specifics from each day's closed-door testimony in the Capitol basement. Leaks alone—and there were leaks—wouldn't be enough.

As it turned out, the witnesses themselves solved this problem. Most of the major witnesses—including Volker, Yovanovitch, and Taylor—prepared lengthy and detailed opening statements for their testimony. And as was their right, the witnesses released those opening statements to the public at the time of their testimony. Those narratives filled out the story of the Giuliani-led Ukraine initiative. It was in this period when the phrase "quid pro quo" became ubiquitous in news coverage of the story. It might have been a mistake to devote so much attention to a phrase from a dead language, but the point was made through the opening statements. Trump was trading military aid and a White House visit for dirt on the Bidens. This for that. Quid pro quo.

The story was starting to unnerve the president. He was tweeting at a frantic rate—more than twenty tweets a day. "The Democrats Scam goes on and on! They Do Nothing!" . . . "Adam Schiff must be held accountable for his lies." . . . "A very dishonest sleazebag." . . . "Human scum!" On October 21, Trump gave an interview to Sean Hannity where the president indulged his favorite conspiracy theories. "There was a server—the DNC server—that never went to the FBI. The FBI didn't take it. It was taken by somebody that I guess—it's CrowdStrike—that's what I've heard." As for his phone call with Zelensky, "it was a perfect transcription of a perfect conversation." And Trump more or less admitted that he demanded Ukraine's cooperation on investigations, that is, a quid pro quo: "If Ukraine would know something about the 2016 election, you'd have to give that information. I hope that they would give the information, and everybody agrees with me 100 percent."

The next day, October 22, several Republican members of Congress, among Trump's strongest supporters, came to the White House for a pep talk. As usual with Trump, it turned into an opportunity for him to air grievances about his enemies and demand more enthusiastic demonstrations of support from his allies.

"Have to get tougher and fight!" Trump told the Republican members of Congress. So they did.

30

Two Kinds of Pizza

The leaders of the major industrialized countries of the world—the Group of 7, or G7—rotate the opportunity to host their annual meeting, which draws hundreds of aides, journalists, and hangers-on, bringing an economic boomlet in its wake. At the closing news conference of the 2019 session of the G7, in Biarritz, France, President Trump announced that he knew the perfect location for the 2020 meeting, which was due to take place in the United States: the Trump Doral resort in Miami. "They love the location of the hotel, they also like the fact it is right next to the airport for convenience. And it is Miami, Doral, Miami, so it is a great area," Trump said. "We haven't had anything that could even come close to competing with it, especially when you look at the location."

Even by Trump's standards of grifting off the presidency, the idea seemed outlandish—steering all those captive customers to one of his properties, and one that had been struggling for business, no less. But on the morning of October 17, 2019, the White House announced that the G7 conference in 2020 would indeed take place at Trump's resort. The political backlash was immediate and intense. The reaction was so ugly that Trump made the rare decision to send Mick Mulvaney, his acting chief of staff, to the White House briefing room to defend the decision.

Mulvaney's political trajectory also reflected the evolution of the contemporary Republican Party. As a congressman from South Carolina, Mulvaney had been a leader in the Tea Party movement and a founder of the Freedom Caucus, the most conservative Republicans in the House. In those roles, he became famous for his warnings about the evils of deficit spending. But when Trump named him director of the Office of Management and Budget, he presided over a massive increase in the deficit. Like many in his party, he saw his job as serving Trump's agenda rather than his previous convictions. In return for Mulvaney's dutiful service, Trump named him his acting chief of staff in December 2018, but his "acting" status made his job especially precarious and imposed on him an especially intense duty of servility. Thus his assignment to defend the indefensible—holding the G7 at Trump Doral.

Mulvaney did his best. "Doral was, by far and away—far and away—the best physical facility for this meeting," he said. "In fact, I was talking to one of the advance teams when they came back, and I said, 'What was it like?' And they said, 'Mick, you're not going to believe this, but it's almost like they built this facility to host this type of event.'" He went on, "Again, anticipating your questions: How is this not an emoluments violation? Is the President going to profit from this? I think the President has pretty much made it very clear since he's got here that he doesn't profit from being here. He has no interest in profit from being here. . . . They're doing this at cost. As a result, it's actually going to be dramatically cheaper for us to do it at Doral compared to other final sites that we had." The vague promises ("at cost," "cheaper") did nothing to quiet the outrage, and Trump, in a rare surrender to existing norms of propriety, withdrew the Doral plan later that day. But reporters at the news conference, with a prominent administration figure in front of them, moved on to other subjects, like the ongoing impeachment hearings in the House of Representatives.

Mulvaney tried to affect the Trump swagger, but he lacked the president's ability to bulldoze through questions and create his own reality. When asked about why the White House held up aid to Ukraine, Mulvaney said first that it was because of concerns about corruption. Trying to explain further, he said of Trump, "Did he also mention to me in passing the corruption related to the DNC server? Absolutely. No question about that. But that's it. And that's why we held up the money."

Following up, a reporter asked, "So the demand for an investigation into the Democrats was part of the reason that he ordered to withhold funding to Ukraine?"

"Certainly . . . ," Mulvaney said.

Jonathan Karl of ABC News sought clarity. "But to be clear, what you just described is a quid pro quo. It is, funding will not flow unless the investigation into the Democratic server happens as well."

"We do that all the time with foreign policy. . . . And I have news for everybody. Get over it. There's going to be political influence in foreign policy."

Mulvaney had committed a "gaffe," which the journalist Michael Kinsley famously defined as "when a politician tells the truth—some obvious truth he isn't supposed to say." And in keeping with the customs regarding gaffes, Mulvaney promptly issued a denial that he said what he said. Mulvaney's statements—both his original remarks and then his walk back—previewed the Trump defense in the Ukraine investigation. The evidence of what really happened was overwhelming; the testimony of the witnesses was consistent. As Mulvaney acknowledged, Trump withheld military aid and the White House meeting in return for information about his political opponents. But Mulvaney, in revising his initial story, tried to graft some of Trump's *other* policy obsessions onto the Ukraine story. *He held up the aid because he was concerned that other countries weren't doing their part. He held up the aid because he didn't want to give money to a corrupt government.* Trump did hold those views—in general. But they had next to nothing to do with his actions in Ukraine.

Notwithstanding Mulvaney's forlorn efforts at damage control, his appearance at the White House on October 17 was a fiasco, and it contributed to Trump's dark mood. The president was convinced that his allies were doing a poor job of defending him, and that's what he told the group of visiting congressmen on October 22. He sent them back to the Capitol to make trouble.

A few days earlier, Matt Gaetz, an ardent Trump supporter who represented a House district in Florida, had shown up in the Intelligence Committee SCIF without authorization. The hearing was only for members of the Intelligence, Oversight, and Foreign Affairs Committees, and Gaetz didn't belong to any of them. Schiff, who was presiding, noticed his presence and said, "Mr. Gaetz, you're not permitted to be in the room. . . . Please leave."

"Mr. Chairman, really?" Jim Jordan said.

"You're not going to include Members of Congress . . . ?" Gaetz said.

"Mr. Gaetz, take your statement to the press. They do you no good here. So, please, absent yourself," Schiff said. Eventually, and sulkily, Gaetz left. But his exchange with Schiff gave the Republicans an idea.

On October 23, the day after Trump rallied his Republican troops, Laura Cooper, a Defense Department official, was scheduled to testify at 10:00 a.m. By this point, the hearings had fallen into a kind of pattern, usually with a relative handful of members present from both sides. But on this day, more than a dozen Republicans showed up—and then another dozen, and then a dozen more. The lobby outside the door to the SCIF was nearly full, and Steve Scalise, the Republican whip, approached the desk of the security officer who controlled access to the SCIF.

The officer said, correctly, that Republican members of the three committees could enter the room, but not any other congressmen—like Scalise and Gaetz.

Scalise began pounding on the security officer's desk.

"Let us in! Let us in!" His colleagues took up the chant.

With the door open, several of the Republicans stormed past the guard and into the SCIF, which is actually a suite of offices, including the one where the hearing was held and another for Schiff, as chairman of the Intelligence Committee. The SCIF had strict rules against the possession or use of cell phones, and there were cubbyholes for members to place their devices before they entered. But the Republican demonstrators refused to surrender their phones and marched into the hearing room, some of them transmitting photos of the action. This, of course, was a grievous security violation.

The protest—nominally over the failure to admit non–committee members to the hearings—was an absurd gesture. More than forty Republicans were authorized to attend the joint hearings of the three committees. (Few bothered to do so, of course.) If the protesting Republicans wanted to know what was going on in the hearings, they could have asked their colleagues to show up and tell them. Even more absurdly, some of the protesters were members of the three relevant committees, so they were demanding to be admitted to hearings that they were already welcome to attend. The whole project was street theater of an especially farcical sort.

Once the Republican interlopers entered the hearing room, there wasn't really much for them to do except tweet. ("Democrats are trying to deny Republican Members of Congress access to Schiff's secret impeachment proceedings. What are they hiding??" Scalise tweeted, and the president promptly retweeted it.) The witness went to a holding room. Schiff, unwilling to participate in the spectacle, retreated to his office nearby in the basement. Outside the hearing room, a rotating cast of Republicans denounced Schiff and the impeachment process before the television cameras, but inside the hearing room nothing much was happening. It was approaching lunchtime, so the Republican occupiers decided to order pizza. For themselves, the Republicans bought several pies from We, the Pizza, a leading artisanal provider in Washington. For the reporters and spectators waiting outside, they ordered Domino's. The pizzas presented the journalists with an ethical dilemma. If they ate the donated pizza, were they somehow sanctioning the Republicans' protest?

Mark Meadows, one of the leaders of the insurrection, left the secure room and told reporters, "Off the record, this pizza is for you. There is no quid pro quo. You can eat it." Hardly anyone did, and the pies congealed.

At around 1:30 p.m., there was a vote called on the floor of the House, and the protesters straggled out of the hearing room. The stunt pleased the president, but the hearings continued under the same rules. After a delay of about five hours, Laura Cooper took the oath and began answering questions.

Like the testimony of many witnesses, Laura Cooper's words were quietly devastating for the president's defenders. She was the career official in the Defense Department who was in charge of administering the military aid to Ukraine. She reported her bafflement as word came down from the White House for the aid to Ukraine to be frozen. Later, she also refuted a key part of the Trump defense. The president's supporters claimed that Trump did not exert any undue pressure on Zelensky because the Ukrainians never even knew that the military aid was being withheld. But Cooper testified that she received reports as early as July 25, the time of the phone call, that the Ukrainians did know the aid was being held back, and they were clamoring for its return.

Cooper's testimony also illustrated the limits of Schiff's investigation. She was a senior bureaucrat whose professional life operated by email—particularly regarding the orders she received to distribute or withhold American aid to a foreign country. But Cipollone's letter meant that the Defense Department refused to produce any of Cooper's correspondence. Cooper gave her best recollection about the course of events, but the documents would have enhanced and clarified her testimony.

In the end, seventeen witnesses provided deposition testimony during the private phase of the investigation in the Capitol basement. During that time, the committees heard some important and courageous testimony. But the list of witnesses who defied subpoenas or otherwise refused to testify was long, and probably more consequential. It became a frequent talking point for Trump's supporters that few of the Democrats' witnesses testified to direct firsthand contact with the president, but that was because his closest advisers refused to testify or provide documents. This group included Vice President Pence, Mick Mulvaney, Secretary of State Mike Pompeo, and Secretary of Energy Rick Perry. Rudy Giuliani also refused to participate in the investigation, citing attorney-client privilege. Other important witnesses who were on the next level down in the bureaucracy also declined to speak to the committees. This group included National Security Council lawyers John Eisenberg and Michael Ellis; NSC energy adviser Wells Griffith; Office of Management and Budget officials Brian McCormack, Michael Duffey, and Russell Vought; the State Department's Ulrich Brechbuhl; and Robert Blair, an aide to Mulvaney in the White House.

And then there was John Bolton. As Trump's national security adviser, he probably knew more about Trump's behavior and motivations regarding Ukraine than anyone in the government. And he was famous in the White House for the detailed notes he took in meetings. Bolton had been an ornery, arrogant, and brilliant force on the Republican political scene for decades. A protégé of Jesse Helms, the conservative Republican senator from North Carolina, Bolton made his name in the Reagan years as a Cold War hawk. As a leading neo-conservative under George W. Bush, he was an outspoken supporter of the Iraq War. His abrasive personality, as much as his right-wing politics, contributed to his failure to win Senate confirmation to be ambassador to the United Nations in 2005. Since Trump had an iso-lationist streak and criticized the Iraq War, Bolton was always an odd fit with him in the White House, but he was hired as national security adviser in April 2018. Trump and Bolton clashed repeatedly, espe-cially over the president's negotiations with North Korea, and they had a predictably ugly parting in September 2019. Trump tweeted that he told Bolton on September 9 that "his services were no lon-ger required." Bolton said that was a lie; he had resigned of his own accord.

No one knew with certainty what kind of witness Bolton would be in the impeachment investigation. He was obviously embittered toward Trump, and he was a real-time dissenter on Ukraine policy. As a veteran anti-Soviet, Bolton refused, unlike Trump, to appease Vladimir Putin in Ukraine and elsewhere. The testimony of Bolton's aide Fiona Hill revealed that Bolton thought Giuliani was a malevo-lent influence on the president. He referred to Trump's quest for dirt on Biden as a "drug deal." In theory, then, Bolton had the potential to be the John Dean of the Ukraine scandal—the insider who revealed the corruption taking place by the president inside the Oval Office. On the other hand, Bolton was a veteran Republican partisan and, not incidentally, a long-term and well-compensated contributor on Fox News. Many who knew him doubted he would throw away a lifetime of partisanship, as well as a lucrative sinecure, to help Demo-crats remove a president. At seventy-one, Bolton still wanted a future in conservative politics and media, and a leading role against Trump might jeopardize those future options. In sum, then, Bolton's inten-tions and motivations were a mystery.

In a way, though, the speculation about Bolton's testimony—about which side he would help—was beside the point. He was an impor-tant witness. He had information relevant to the committees' consid-eration. By any standard he belonged on the list of witnesses, and the chips should fall where they may.

But Bolton, as ever, was being cagey and protective of his own interests. As soon as he left the White House, he signed a multimillion-dollar book deal and began giving paid lectures. Obviously, the main appeal of his book—called *The Room Where It Happened: A White House Memoir*—would be for him to disclose what he knew about the president's behavior with respect to Ukraine. And the value of that disclosure would be compromised if he first told that story in testimony before Congress. But Bolton didn't exactly refuse to testify. Instead, he and his lawyer, an equally savvy Washington player named Charles Cooper, strung the committee along. Schiff's committee had also demanded the testimony of Charles Kupperman, who was Bolton's deputy in the White House and who was also represented by Cooper. Rather than Kupperman's agreeing to testify or refusing outright, Cooper brought a lawsuit on his behalf in federal district court in Washington asking the judge to resolve the question. *Congress wants me to testify; the president said don't testify. Please, Judge— tell me what to do.* The Kupperman case was clearly a stalking horse for Bolton's testimony as well. The idea behind the litigation was for Judge Richard Leon to determine, in effect, whether both of them were required to testify.

As a legal matter, the lawsuit was nonsense. Federal courts resolve actual disputes; they do not offer advisory opinions about what people should or should not do in the future. (There was rare agreement between the White House and the House of Representatives that Kupperman's lawsuit should be dismissed.) Given the likely duration of the litigation, Kupperman and Bolton were clearly never going to testify, but rather were just trying to look as if they were considering cooperating. And Judge Leon made a bad situation worse by doing . . . nothing. He didn't even schedule a hearing for weeks. It was irresponsible behavior by the judge, but it served Kupperman's—and Bolton's—interest. Because they went to a judge, they could portray themselves as law-abiding citizens, but they didn't have to testify and alienate their friends. And Bolton's continued silence built anticipation for his book.

As always, Pelosi was concerned with protecting her Democratic caucus, so that meant she had an overarching demand for Schiff's Intelligence Committee and Jerry Nadler's Judiciary. She wanted haste—completion of the impeachment process in the House of

Representatives as close to the end of 2019 as possible. She didn't want her vulnerable members running for reelection in 2020 in the middle of an impeachment investigation. As young Adam Schiff did in 2000 and her frontliners did in 2018, Pelosi wanted them to run on substantive issues like health care, not scandal. In a way, too, Trump made Pelosi's decision for her. By cutting off access to witnesses and documents, the president rendered a more thorough investigation impossible. By the end of October, the Democrats in the House basically had all of the information they were going to get.

But by this point, Pelosi had shed her ambivalence about impeachment itself. She was all-in. And she proved it, as always, by controlling the process in the House. The rules of the House allow the majority party, in effect, to invent its rules as it goes along. The majority can determine which issues are considered by the House, by which committee, and for how long. For impeachment, Pelosi's staff crafted House Resolution 660, which was written in dense, legalistic language but provided a road map for the next two months and revealed the Speaker's priorities.

The resolution began with an act of legislative and political sleight of hand. It directed six committees in the House—Intelligence, Judiciary, Oversight, Financial Services, Foreign Affairs, and Ways and Means—"to continue their ongoing investigations as part of the existing House of Representatives inquiry into whether sufficient grounds exist for the House of Representatives to exercise its Constitutional power to impeach Donald John Trump, President of the United States of America." The key word was "continue." Throughout the fall, Pelosi had refused to take a full vote of the House to authorize an impeachment inquiry; as always, she wanted to protect the moderates who didn't want to take a stand on the issue. But now, clearly, the House had been weighing impeachment for weeks. So Pelosi used the resolution as a sort of retroactive authorization—with the use of the word "continue."

The resolution mentioned several committees, but it placed one in charge: Schiff's Intelligence Committee, which was directed to hold open hearings on impeachment. This was the latest Pelosi endorsement of Schiff and slap at Jerry Nadler and the Judiciary Committee. (It was, in all, a terrible period for Nadler, whose wife was diagnosed with pancreatic cancer around this time.) The resolution said that

Judiciary could hold hearings on any actual articles of impeachment, but those proceedings would take place after Intelligence gathered the facts. And the resolution also corrected a flaw that was especially evident when Corey Lewandowski testified before the Judiciary Committee. In that and other hearings in the fall, the members of the committee had asked questions in alternating five-minute turns, which made the presentation disjointed and unclear. The resolution authorized committee lawyers to question witnesses for as long as forty-five minutes at a time, which would allow for a more comprehensible presentation. The House passed the resolution, mostly along party lines, on October 31. (Two Democrats voted no; no Republicans voted yes.)

That left Schiff less than two weeks to put together public hearings. His staff put up a whiteboard, and Schiff set out to structure the presentation like the prosecution's case in a trial. He was pretty much limited to the seventeen witnesses who had already testified in the closed setting, but he could now reorder their appearances and restructure their testimony. And because of the rule established in House Resolution 660, his staffer Dan Goldman could lead each witness through a coherent version of his or her story, like direct testimony in a courtroom. Schiff decided to start the hearing by addressing some questions that had hung over the Ukraine story since it broke. Why should Americans care? What difference did it all make? If Trump traded American aid for dirt on his opponents—so what?

To answer, Schiff put Bill Taylor and George Kent first, when the hearings began on November 13. Taylor had the bipartisan credibility of having been chosen by Secretary of State Pompeo to run the American embassy in Kyiv. He had a store of righteous indignation about the way Giuliani had hijacked the American relationship with Ukraine for the president's political benefit. Kent was the senior career diplomat in Washington in charge of relations with Ukraine, and he could also speak knowledgeably about the fledgling democracy in Ukraine and the need to contain Russian influence there. On the downside, Kent looked like the embodiment of every stereotype about the State Department. He wore a bow tie and a three-piece suit and spoke in a plummy diction that sounded as if he came out of Harvard a generation before 1989, when he actually graduated. But even though Kent might have looked and sounded like an aristocratic fop, he had plenty of gritty, on-the-ground experience, in places like

Poland, Uzbekistan, and Thailand as well as Ukraine. He also spoke six languages and came to illustrate a theme of the Intelligence Committee hearings—the remarkable skill and integrity on display in the senior ranks of American public servants.

There was, most notably, Alexander Vindman, who testified a couple of days later. It would be difficult to improve on the Vindmans' story as an illustration of the virtues of immigration and the power of the American dream. He and his identical twin brother, Yevgeny, were born in Ukraine in 1975, and their mother died when they were babies. In 1979, as part of the exodus of Soviet Jews, their father took them to Brooklyn, where they grew up in the same neighborhood as Lev Parnas. Alexander went to Binghamton University on an ROTC scholarship and became an Army Ranger, serving in Iraq and winning a Purple Heart. (His brother also joined the army, went to law school, and became a JAG officer. A third brother also served in the military.) At forty-three, Alexander had risen to lieutenant colonel in the army, and he had drawn the prestigious assignment of serving in the White House on the National Security Council as its Ukraine expert. (Amazingly enough, his twin brother, who went by Eugene, achieved the same rank and was also detailed to the White House as a lawyer.) Vindman served in quiet, proficient anonymity until he was one of the designated listeners to Trump's phone call with Zelensky on July 25, 2019.

Vindman cut a daunting figure at the witness table, in his dress uniform bedecked with rows of "fruit salad"—medals and commendation ribbons. His voice, though, was soft, almost apologetic. He had never sought publicity, nor picked a fight with his superiors. But what he saw in the White House stirred him to an unfamiliar level of outrage. "In the spring of 2019 I became aware of two disruptive actors, primarily Ukraine's then-prosecutor Yuriy Lutsenko and former mayor Rudolph Giuliani, the President's personal attorney, promoting false narratives that undermined the United States Ukraine policy," he said. In early July, after a White House meeting where Gordon Sondland said Zelensky should be granted an Oval Office meeting only if he agreed to investigate the Bidens, Vindman complained to John Eisenberg, the NSC's top lawyer. After listening to the July 25 phone call, he went to Eisenberg again. (Eisenberg, apparently, did nothing either time.) As for the call, Vindman said, "What

I heard was inappropriate and I reported my concerns to Mr. Eisenberg. It is improper for the President of the United States to demand a foreign government investigate a US citizen and a political opponent. . . . If Ukraine pursued investigation into the 2016 elections, the Bidens and Burisma, it would be interpreted as a partisan play. This would undoubtedly result in Ukraine losing bipartisan support, undermining US national security and advancing Russia's strategic objectives in the region." This was the best distillation of why Trump's conduct was so damaging.

Vindman concluded his opening statement with a paean to his adopted homeland, with words that transcended the seedy corruption he had exposed. "As a young man I decided I wanted to spend my life serving the nation that gave my family refuge from authoritarian repression. And for the last 20 years it has been an honor to represent and protect this great country," he said. "Next month will mark 40 years since my family arrived in the United States as refugees. When my father was 47 years old, he left behind his entire life and the only home he had ever known to start over in the United States so his three sons could have better and safer lives," he said. "I also recognize that my simple act of appearing here today, just like the courage of my colleagues who have also truthfully testified before this committee, would not be tolerated in many places around the world. In Russia, my act of expressing concern to the chain of command in an official and private channel would have severe personal and professional repercussions, and offering public testimony involving the president would surely cost me my life. I am grateful for my father's brave act of hope 40 years ago and for the privilege of being an American citizen and public servant, where I can live free of fear for mine and my family's safety." He concluded by addressing his father directly: "Dad, my sitting here today in the U.S. Capitol talking to our elected officials is proof that you made the right decision forty years ago to leave the Soviet Union, to come here to the United States of America in search of a better life for our family. Do not worry. I will be fine for telling the truth."

31

"I Refuse to Be Part of an Effort to Legitimize an Alternate Narrative"

I n light of his extraordinary personal history and aura of rectitude, Alexander Vindman was a difficult witness for Republicans
to challenge. But they did—in a way. Their efforts at cross-
examination in the Intelligence Committee public hearing gave a
revealing picture of their overall defense strategy for the president.

Devin Nunes, Schiff's predecessor as chairman of the committee,
took the lead. To begin, he used a venerable courtroom technique—
asking questions to which the answers didn't matter. He wanted to
float dubious assertions on television, even if Vindman wouldn't confirm them.

"Did you know that financial records show a Ukrainian natural
gas company, Burisma, routed more than $3 million to the American
accounts tied to Hunter Biden?" Nunes asked.

"I'm not aware of this fact," Vindman said. (In fact, Hunter Biden
made less than $3 million from Burisma.)

"Did you know that Joe Biden called Ukrainian president Poroshenko at least three times in February 2016 after the president and
owner of Burisma's home was raided on February 2nd by the state
prosecutor's office?" he went on.

Vindman did not. (Biden did call Poroshenko as part of an interna-
tionally sanctioned effort to fight corruption in Ukraine; Biden never
mentioned Burisma.)

In other words, Nunes was doing what Trump was doing—using
the hearings to spread the same misleading accusations that were at

the core of the scandal. It was a way of winning by losing. Yes, Trump was being impeached, but in the process his allies could still publicize the accusations against Biden. And that was what Nunes, and Trump, continued to do.

Later, Nunes turned to a new subject. "Lieutenant Colonel Vindman, did you discuss the July 25th phone call with anyone outside the White House on July 25th or the 26th, and if so, with whom?" he asked.

"Yes, I did," Vindman said. "My core function is to coordinate U.S. government policy, interagency policy, and I spoke to two individuals with regards to providing some sort of readout of the call."

"Two individuals that were not in the White House?"

"Not in the White House, cleared U.S. government officials with appropriate need to know," Vindman answered.

"And what agencies were these officials with?"

Vindman said one was with the State Department and the other was "an individual in the intelligence community."

Nunes pursued him, saying, "As you know, the intelligence community has 17 different agencies. What agency was this individual from?"

At this point, Schiff had had enough. He knew what Nunes was doing. He was trying to prompt Vindman to disclose the name, or even just the position, of the whistle-blower. It was obvious from the whistle-blower's complaint that he had spoken with Vindman, and there were very few people in the government with the whistle-blower's high level of expertise about Ukraine. Nunes wanted at least to narrow the suspects.

Schiff jumped in, saying, "If I could interject here, we don't want to use these proceedings . . . We need to protect the whistleblower."

Nunes, now the ranking member of the committee, ignored Schiff and resumed: "Mr. Vindman, you testified in your deposition that you did not know the whistleblower."

"Ranking member," Vindman replied icily, "it's 'Lieutenant Colonel' Vindman, please." Schiff then shut down this line of questioning.

Here, again, Nunes was doing Trump's bidding. The president began insulting the whistle-blower, on Twitter and elsewhere, as soon as his complaint came to light. "Shifty Adam Schiff wants to rest his entire case on a Whistleblower who he now says can't testify, & the reason he can't testify is that he is afraid to do so because his account of the Presidential telephone call is a fraud & totally different from the actual transcribed call," he tweeted as Schiff's hearings began. Later, the president began demanding that the whistle-blower's identity be revealed, tweeting, "Where is the Whistleblower, and why did he or she write such a fictitious and incorrect account of my phone call with the Ukrainian President?" Later, Trump began tweeting repeatedly, "Where is the whistleblower?" Worst of all, he retweeted a tweet that purported to identify the whistle-blower by name. (Some of Trump's allies, such as Jerome Corsi, had already been tweeting the name.)

Even by Trump's standards, his behavior with regard to the whistle-blower was outrageous and arguably illegal. The entire point of the many federal laws protecting whistle-blowers is to shield them from identification and retribution. As a technical matter, it was unclear if those laws applied to the president, but Trump egregiously violated at least their spirit if not their letter. Trump was also wrong about the substance of the whistle-blower's complaint. The whistle-blower's summary of the July 25 phone call was accurate, as was the rest of the complaint, especially about Giuliani's pernicious role in the Ukraine initiative. Through the power of repetition, Trump sought to demonize the whistle-blower, as he did the author of the Steele dossier. But while the dossier contained several claims that were either unproven or disproven, the whistle-blower's complaint was scrupulously accurate. Still, the whistle-blower served Trump's need for an enemy—a target for his wrath and blame. If Trump had accomplices—people like Nunes who were willing to sanction his lying and bullying—that was so much the better.

Schiff's staff presented witnesses in pairs, as part of an effort to move through the testimony more efficiently, and on November 21, Fiona Hill and David Holmes appeared together. They didn't know each other, and had never served together, but their testimony offered strange echoes of earlier witnesses. Fiona Hill's life story bore some resemblance to Alexander Vindman's, and David Holmes looked like a younger George Kent. At the same time, Hill's and Holmes's stories were unique—and uniquely devastating.

Like Vindman, Hill was an immigrant, and her tale was nearly as

remarkable as his. She grew up in a working-class family of coal min-
ers in the north of England; her father went to the mines when he was
fourteen years old. When the mines closed in the 1960s, her father
wanted to immigrate to the United States, but he stayed behind to
care for his mother and grandmother, who were crippled from their
own kind of hard labor in the region. Fiona excelled as a student,
attended the University of St. Andrews in Scotland, and was selected
for an exchange program in the Soviet Union in 1987. There she met
an American professor who encouraged her to apply for a fellowship
at Harvard, which she did. She went and stayed—to become what she
called "an American by choice."

"Years later, I can say with confidence that this country has offered
me opportunities I never would have had in England," Hill testified. "I grew up poor, with a very distinctive working-class accent.
In England, in the 1980s and 1990s, this would have impeded my
professional advancement. This background has never set me back in
America." She became a nonpartisan foreign policy expert who served
in both Democratic and Republican administrations.

But for all the similarity between Hill's and Vindman's passion for
their adopted homeland, they differed in temperament and experience. Vindman was a bureaucratic innocent, with a wounded faith in
a government he revered. Hill, who was Vindman's boss, had a more
worldly understanding of the White House and a more cynical take
on its denizens. To put it another way, Vindman was a staffer, Hill was
a player; Vindman was mournful, Hill was *pissed*.

To Americans untutored in how class differences are revealed in
British accents, Hill just sounded regal and authoritative. She was a
Russia hawk; this was why Bolton, the old cold warrior, trusted her
at the NSC and kept her by his side, including during a face-to-face
meeting with Putin himself. And she was candid in her disdain for the
effort, led by Trump, to blame Ukraine instead of Russia for interfering in the 2016 election. Fearlessly, Hill went after the committee
members directly. "Based on questions and statements I have heard,
some of you on this committee appear to believe that Russia and its
security services did not conduct a campaign against our country
and that perhaps, somehow, for some reason, Ukraine did," she said.
"This is a fictional narrative that is being perpetrated and propagated
by the Russian security services themselves. The unfortunate truth

is that Russia was the foreign power that systematically attacked our democratic institutions in 2016. . . . I refuse to be part of an effort to legitimize an alternate narrative that the Ukrainian government is a U.S. adversary, and that Ukraine, not Russia, attacked us in 2016."

Hill had been in the White House since Trump became president, and she evinced a rueful familiarity with the rules of the game there. Her prior experience had been in parts of the government where there were clear lines of authority and chains of command. And according to the organizational chart nominally in place in the National Security Council, she had responsibility for Ukraine as well as Russia and its other eastern neighbors. For that reason, she was put off when Gordon Sondland swanned into the White House and announced that he was now in charge. Earlier in testimony, she recounted what happened.

"I actually had a very good relationship, I thought, at the very beginning with Ambassador Sondland," Hill said. "But the unfortunate thing was I had a blow-up with him in June, when he told me that he was in charge of Ukraine, because I initially said to him, 'You're not,' with that kind of, you know, surprise and probably irritation in my voice." But Sondland told Hill that the president himself had put him in charge, and that put an end to her protest.

As for David Holmes, it was through a strange stroke of fortune that he testified at all. When the hearings began, the Intelligence Committee staffers had no plans to call him because they had never even heard of him. After all, he was just a mid-level Foreign Service officer in the embassy in Kyiv. There was no reason to think that someone so far removed from the White House, and especially the Oval Office, would have relevant testimony in an impeachment proceeding. But on the eve of the public testimony, the committee released the transcripts of the private sessions. While still in Kyiv, Holmes read his boss Bill Taylor's transcript, and he realized that Taylor had not mentioned the story of the lunch that Gordon Sondland hosted in Kyiv on July 26, the day after the infamous phone call. Holmes called Taylor to remind him of the lunch. With his memory refreshed, Taylor mentioned the lunch in his public testimony and advised the lawyers for the Democrats and Republicans that Holmes was the embassy staffer with Sondland. In light of this, Schiff's staffers scrambled to bring Holmes to Washington for a private deposition and then public testimony, alongside Fiona Hill.

Holmes was a decade younger than George Kent, but they both had a certain State Department haughtiness along with similarly encyclopedic knowledge of their bailiwick. Their stories were complementary—Kent from Washington, Holmes from Kyiv. Both watched in mystification and horror as Giuliani, through Sondland, took over policy regarding Ukraine. Unlike the Amigos, Kent and Holmes (as well as the whistle-blower) actually had a rich understanding of Ukraine and its politics. They saw how corrupt Ukrainians like Shokin and Lutsenko manipulated Giuliani by telling him what he wanted to hear—as part of their own efforts to preserve or regain power. In all, Holmes's testimony was mostly cumulative of other witnesses, and the diplomat recounted his narrative in more detail than most members of Congress could absorb. But there was one more thing.

Trial lawyers know that the most important evidence doesn't necessarily come from the most high-profile witnesses. Sometimes there is a turning point in a case—an exhibit or a piece of testimony— that emerges from a relatively minor figure which serves to crystallize everything that the prosecution is trying to convey. So it was with David Holmes, who was testifying at all only because he happened to read what Bill Taylor told the committees in closed session.

It was about the lunch that Gordon Sondland hosted in Kyiv on July 26. The lunch was only four months earlier, and Holmes still had an almost cinematic recollection of the scene, which was perhaps unsurprising, given what an extraordinary experience it was for the young diplomat. Holmes described a pleasant summer afternoon in a quiet neighborhood. "The restaurant has glass doors that open onto a terrace, and we were at the first tables on the terrace, so immediately outside of the interior of the restaurant," he told the committee, which watched in rapt silence. "The doors were all wide open. There was a table for four, although I recall it being two tables for two pushed together. In any case, it was quite a wide table, and the table was set. . . . I was directly across from Ambassador Sondland. We were close enough that we could share an appetizer between us."

To Holmes's astonishment, Sondland whipped out his cell phone and placed a call to the White House and asked to speak to the president. After Sondland was passed through several intermediaries, Trump was on the line. After Sondland hung up, he provided a readout of the call to his luncheon guests, and he talked about the president's priorities.

"He said he doesn't really care about Ukraine," Holmes recalled.

Goldman, the investigator, asked: "Did he use slightly more colorful language than that?"

Holmes: "He did." In the earlier closed session, Holmes had quoted Sondland directly about Trump's view of Ukraine: "He does not give a shit about Ukraine."

Goldman: "What did he say that he does care about?"

Holmes: "He said he cares about big stuff."

Goldman: "Did he explain what he meant by big stuff?"

Holmes: "I asked him, well, what kind of big stuff. We have big stuff going on here, like a war with Russia. And he said, no, big stuff like the Biden investigation that Mr. Giuliani's pushing."

That was the whole case right there, stripped to its essentials. Trump didn't care about the people of Ukraine, who were fighting for their lives. (Nor, it was clear, did he care about American laws, norms, or national security interests.) All Trump cared about was the "big stuff"—which was, to him, his political and personal self-interest. From the day he declared his candidacy, through the Russia scandal and his endless solicitude toward Vladimir Putin, and on into his cruel manipulation of the struggling democracy in Ukraine, Trump didn't give a shit about anyone or anything but himself.

32

"In the Name of Itself and of the People of the United States of America"

On Saturday morning, December 7, the Democratic members of the Judiciary Committee straggled into a hearing room in the Longworth House Office Building. They wore casual clothes, but their task was anything but routine. It was not an especially happy time for the committee's liberal firebrands and especially for the chairman, Jerry Nadler. He was shuttling back and forth to New York, dealing with his wife's health crisis. He had also been sidelined. In the Nixon and Clinton impeachment investigations, the Judiciary Committee had taken the lead. But Pelosi had given most of the responsibility to Schiff and the Intelligence Committee. Many on Judiciary seethed, but they knew that protest was futile. The Speaker listened to her members, and was often guided by them, but once she made a decision, it was final and unappealable.

Pelosi had carved the Judiciary Committee's role down to a single thing, but it was an important one (albeit one subject to her veto and control). The committee would write and vote on articles of impeachment, which would then be sent to the floor of the House for a final vote. For the most part, history remembers impeachment as an up-or-down judgment. Everyone remembers that Bill Clinton and Andrew Johnson were impeached (and Richard Nixon resigned just before he would have been), but the precise framing of the charges against them is recalled by a relative few. Still, the members took great care with the articles, even though it was clear by this point that impeachment by the House in some form was going to happen.

In other words, the Judiciary Committee had to decide why the House needed to impeach Donald Trump. What, exactly, had the president done to deserve this sanction? The question was more complicated than the ones faced by the Judiciary Committee in 1974 and 1998. On those occasions, Watergate had already been investigated by a special prosecutor and a select Senate committee, and Kenneth Starr had already filed a detailed report recounting Clinton's misconduct. By the time the Judiciary Committee considered the Nixon and Clinton cases, their options were fairly clear. The charges were going to relate, in some central way, to Nixon's role in the Watergate cover-up and Clinton's lies under oath about his relationship with Monica Lewinsky.

This was different. Pelosi authorized a full-fledged impeachment investigation about Ukraine only in late September, and the House had pulled together an impressive investigation, with no cooperation from the administration, in just two months. But what, exactly, was Trump's impeachable conduct with respect to Ukraine? That was still undecided. And a hundred or so Democratic members of the House had endorsed impeachment even before the Ukraine story broke, based mostly on the allegations in the Mueller Report. Should those matters be part of the articles? And what about the other parts of Trump's misconduct—like his use of the presidency to enrich himself, in possible violation of the emoluments clause of the Constitution? Should those be included? All those questions were on the table as the members arrived on that Saturday morning.

They had gathered to question Laurence Tribe, the grand old man of the liberal tradition in American constitutional law. He had taught at Harvard Law School for five decades, where his student research assistants included Barack Obama, Elena Kagan, and Adam Schiff. (John Roberts was a student, though not an assistant.) After Tribe published the first comprehensive constitutional law treatise to appear in more than a generation, he became a likely Democratic appointee to the Supreme Court. But in 1987, he testified as a lead witness against Robert Bork's nomination to the Court; Republicans vowed, in revenge, to prevent Tribe from ever ascending to the Court. He became an effective advocate before the justices and a mentor to another generation of students. By 2020, Tribe was in his late seventies and shrunken with health woes, but his mind was sharp and his passion for impeachment limitless.

The previous week, the committee had held a public hearing with four law professors to discuss the constitutional basis for impeachment. Three of them—Noah Feldman of Harvard, Michael Gerhardt of the University of North Carolina, and Pamela Karlan of Stanford—were chosen by the Democrats; the Republicans called on Jonathan Turley of George Washington University. (In her opening statement, Karlan posed a notably prescient hypothetical: "What would you think if, when your governor asked the federal government for the disaster assistance that Congress has provided, the president responded, 'I would like you to do us a favor. I'll meet with you and send the disaster relief once you brand my opponent a criminal?' Wouldn't you know in your gut that such a president had abused his office, betrayed the national interest, and tried to corrupt the electoral process?")

There was unanimity among the four professors on one point—that an impeachable offense did not have to be a crime. This conclusion was based, in significant part, on Federalist No. 65, by Alexander Hamilton, which was the most commonly cited historical document in the debate. (The success of the eponymous musical appeared to render Hamilton's views especially authoritative.) In No. 65, Hamilton gave the most commonly cited definition of impeachable offenses, writing that they were "offenses which proceed from the misconduct of public men, or, in other words, from the abuse or violation of some public trust. They are of a nature which may with peculiar propriety be denominated POLITICAL, as they relate chiefly to injuries done immediately to the society itself." With characteristic foresight, Hamilton went on to note how controversial impeachment would always be, writing that it "will seldom fail to agitate the passions of the whole community, and to divide it into parties more or less friendly or inimical to the accused."

Even if it wasn't necessary for the House to charge that Trump committed a crime, what if he did commit one? The members put that question to Tribe. The Constitution defined impeachable offenses as "Treason, Bribery, or other high Crimes and Misdemeanors." Wasn't what Trump did to Zelensky a form of bribery? By this point, the

Democrats had mostly stopped using the phrase "quid pro quo." (This was wise because most of their constituents spoke English rather than Latin.) But the point was the same. Didn't Trump try to force Zelensky to produce dirt on the Bidens in return for American military aid and an Oval Office meeting? Why not charge Trump with bribery, since it was explicitly mentioned in the Constitution?

Tribe conceded that it was a tough call. It was tempting to include in the charges something that the Framers of the Constitution specifically described as an impeachable offense. But there were problems with the idea of charging Trump with bribery. For one thing, his interactions with Zelensky didn't *sound* like bribery. If the House was going to invoke the criminal law, Trump's behavior seemed more like extortion, which was not mentioned in the Constitution. And the Supreme Court had recently issued several decisions, notably one involving a former governor of Virginia, that made it harder to convict public officials of bribery. That raised questions about how to describe Trump's behavior. Zelensky never actually announced an investigation of Biden, so does that mean he was never bribed? Would the right charge be *attempted* bribery? And the payoff for Trump's bribe was going to be, in effect, opposition research on a political rival. Did that satisfy the current elements of bribery? All of these smaller issues led to a larger problem: Did charging Trump with bribery invite a niggling debate over the elements of the current federal crime of bribery rather than a focus on Trump's misbehavior?

What about the Mueller allegations? This was the issue on which the Judiciary firebrands felt strongest, and dozens of other Democrats in the House agreed with them. Mueller laid out a convincing case for repeated examples of obstruction of justice by Trump. In the Nixon and Clinton investigations, obstruction was at the heart of the charges. Four liberal stalwarts on the committee—David Cicilline of Rhode Island (who was also part of the Democratic House leadership), Eric Swalwell of California, Joe Neguse of Colorado, and Jamie Raskin of Maryland—had been pushing hard for impeachment on these grounds for months. After Barr sabotaged the release of the Mueller Report, and then Mueller himself underperformed as a witness, support for impeachment hovered around 35 percent in the polls. After the Ukraine story broke, support jumped to around 50 percent. Pelosi had passed the word that the Mueller allegations were old news. *Been there, done that.* She wasn't interested in reviving them in the impeachment proceeding. Tribe himself supported impeachment based on the Mueller allegations, but as he looked to the frontliners—and others who were seated to his left as he stared out at the members from the witness table—he saw their skepticism. Pelosi wanted a unified Democratic caucus, and her members were split about including Mueller-based charges. The calculus was clear. If the members won their seat with a narrow margin in 2018, they were unlikely to support a Mueller-based article; if the members had a safe seat, then they were gung ho for one.

That was especially true of Jamie Raskin, who was a law professor at American University before he was elected, as well as one of Tribe's former students. He was only in his second term in 2019, but his background and obvious intelligence gave him an outsized influence over his colleagues. Raskin pressed Tribe for a broad definition of Trump's impeachable conduct. He thought it was wrong to see any of the president's acts in isolation. It was a pattern: the campaign finance violations through the payments to Stormy Daniels; the profiting off the presidency through bookings at the Trump hotel in D.C.; the Mueller allegations; Ukraine. Pelosi and her team came to trust Raskin; they chose him to represent the Judiciary Committee before the Rules Committee when Nadler had to return to New York to care for his wife. But as for impeachment, Pelosi thought Raskin was too far in front of her caucus. Raskin and the other liberals were not naive. They knew the chances of conviction in the Senate were slim to nonexistent. In that case, they argued, why not load up the charges with all of Trump's misconduct, lay it all out in front of the country, and let the Republican senators explain why Trump should remain in office?

As Raskin pressed Tribe on the necessity of adding the emoluments clause charges to the bill of particulars against Trump, the professor could only smile at his former student—nice try, Tribe thought.

In the end, the final word on the structure of the articles came from Pelosi's office. She and her advisers had a strong interest in a bribery article because of the link to the constitutional text. The Judiciary Committee had hired Joshua Matz as a constitutional expert. He was young—just thirty-four—and a protégé of Tribe's, and they had coauthored a perceptive book about impeachment in 2018. Matz, known among the committee members as Doogie Howser, was sent off to do more research on the bribery issue. Was there any case—not necessarily an impeachment—that was anything like the Trump and Zelensky situation? His short answer was no—not in the United States or in Great Britain. The leadership decided it wasn't worth trying to defend a theory that was literally unprecedented.

In the end, Pelosi directed the writing of an article that made the most sense—one based on what Trump actually did. It was possible to contrive a connection to bribery or extortion, but the truth was simpler. Trump abused his power as president—engaged in "abuse or violation of some public trust," in Hamilton's words. So that's what they decided to say in the article. The actual writing was a group effort, but the main drafting was done by Matz and Maher Bitar, who worked for Schiff on the Intelligence Committee, with the supervision of Barry Berke and Norman Eisen, the outside lawyers who were acting as Nadler's impeachment counsel.

The preamble to the articles used the traditional language, which underscored the gravity of the occasion:

> Resolved, That Donald J. Trump, President of the United States, is impeached for high crimes and misdemeanors and that the following articles of impeachment be exhibited to the United States Senate:
>
> Articles of impeachment exhibited by the House of Representatives of the United States of America in the name of itself and of the people of the United States of America, against Donald J. Trump, President of the United States of America, in maintenance and support of its impeachment against him for high crimes and misdemeanors.

Article I was titled "Abuse of Power." As part of their effort to draw a contrast with the Mueller allegations, which involved the 2016 election, the authors of the article sought to make it forward-looking, to describe Trump's conduct as an ongoing threat to the Republic. The article said he abused his office: "Using the powers of his high office, President Trump solicited the interference of a foreign government,

Ukraine, in the 2020 United States Presidential election. He did so through a scheme or course of conduct that included soliciting the Government of Ukraine to publicly announce investigations that would benefit his reelection, harm the election prospects of a political opponent, and influence the 2020 United States Presidential election to his advantage." As the Democrats' investigation proceeded, this was a point that they came increasingly to emphasize—that all Trump wanted was for Zelensky to *announce* an investigation, not necessarily to conduct one. (In testimony and texts Volker, Sondland, and Taylor established the centrality of the announcement to Giuliani's and Trump's demands.) If Trump actually cared about corruption in Ukraine, as his supporters insisted he did, the president would have insisted that Zelensky conduct an actual investigation, not just announce one.

Article II—"Obstruction of Congress"—never had the same public resonance, but it drew on the institutional self-regard, and self-protection, of the House of Representatives. "Donald J. Trump has directed the unprecedented, categorical, and indiscriminate defiance of subpoenas issued by the House of Representatives pursuant to its 'sole Power of Impeachment,'" the article stated. The article represented a specific response to Cipollone's October 8 letter, with its refusal to produce any executive branch witnesses or documents. By doing so, the article asserted that Trump "sought to arrogate to himself the right to determine the propriety, scope, and nature of an impeachment inquiry into his own conduct, as well as the unilateral prerogative to deny any and all information to the House of Representatives in the exercise of its 'sole Power of Impeachment.'" It went on, "In the history of the Republic, no President has ever ordered the complete defiance of an impeachment inquiry or sought to obstruct and impede so comprehensively the ability of the House of Representatives to investigate 'high Crimes and Misdemeanors.'"

For the most part, the articles were straightforward summaries of the case against the president. There were, however, two sentences that stood out. They were cryptic, unelaborated allusions to . . . something else. The sentence in Article I read, "These actions were consistent with President Trump's previous invitations of foreign interference in United States elections." The sentence in Article II stated, "These actions were consistent with President Trump's previous efforts to undermine United States Government investigations into foreign interference in United States elections." These two throwaway references were all that remained of Robert Mueller's two-year investigation. They were scarcely even mentioned in the debate that followed.

Republicans were right about one thing. Pelosi was now jamming impeachment through the Judiciary Committee and through the House in a nearly frantic rush to complete the process by Christmas. On Monday, December 9, Nadler presided over a single day of testimony about the evidence in the case, with a pair of staffers as witnesses. Barry Berke of the Judiciary Committee testified for the majority, and Stephen Castor, a lawyer for the Republicans on the Intelligence Committee, spoke for the minority. Through a long day of surly exchanges, no minds were changed, or even, apparently, open. (The Democrats invited the president to participate in the hearing, to have his lawyers question or call witnesses, but Trump declined, having seen that his prospects were already doomed before the committee. Notably, too, there was another reason why Trump declined to call witnesses to refute the Democrats' factual presentation: no such witnesses existed.)

Two days later, Nadler gaveled the committee into session for what was known as the markup on impeachment—the vote on the articles. Again, the outcome was not in doubt, and the arguments were familiar, but Nadler allowed all forty-one members of the committee to make opening statements. Ted Lieu, a Democrat from California, was absent for medical reasons, so the Democrats on this day had a twenty-three to seventeen advantage in membership.

The plan had been for two days of argument and then a vote on the articles in the committee on Thursday, December 12. The Republicans did their best to prolong and complicate the proceedings with a variety of motions, all of which were voted down along party lines. They also came up with new explanations for some of the evidence. Since the July 25 call record was released in September, one statement by Trump had drawn the most attention. "I would like you to do us a favor though because our country has been through a lot and Ukraine knows a lot about it," Trump said, before asking Zelensky to investigate Ukraine's role in the 2016 election. Understandably, the statement was seen as nearly a smoking gun—proof that Trump wanted dirt on his opponents from Ukraine in return for continuing American support. But months after the release of the call record, Republicans on the Judiciary Committee decided that everyone had misunderstood the president's words. The key to this belated insight, it turned out, was understanding the difference between "us" and "me." "The Democrats talk about this one sentence the President said in the now-famous call transcript with President Zelensky—'I would like you to do us a favor, though,'" Jim Jordan of Ohio said in the committee debate. "The President doesn't say, I would like you to do me a favor, though, because I have been through a lot. He doesn't say that. Very clear. I would like you to do *us* a favor, though, because our country has been through a lot, and that is the understatement of the year. Heck, yeah, our country has been through a lot. This is the day after Bob Mueller sat in front of this committee, and we learned that there was nothing there, but two years he put our country through all kinds of turmoil because of you guys." (Once Republicans made this argument in the committee, Trump himself belatedly adopted this reading, tweeting, "I said I want you to do us (our Country!) a favor, not me a favor. They know that but decided to LIE in order to make a fraudulent point! Very sad."

Of course, the reason it took so long to come up with this explanation of Trump's meaning was that it was absurd. For starters, it was vaguely comic that it took Trump months to realize what he himself meant in his conversation with Zelensky. Moreover, there was no way that the prospect of Ukrainian investigations of the 2016 election and the Bidens served "us"—the United States. They served only Trump's personal political interests, which was obviously his only agenda for the phone call.

As for the rest of the impeachment debate in the committee, which spread out over two days, the members operated by the familiar congressional rule that *everything has been said, but not everyone has said it.* The proceedings went deep into the night on December 12, and Nadler—mindful that he could be accused of trying to hide the impeachment vote in the dark of night—called a halt before midnight. Reconvening promptly at 10:00 a.m. on Friday, December 13, Nadler moved to roll call votes on the two articles. The vote was the same on both articles—all twenty-three Democrats in favor, and all seventeen Republicans opposed. Nadler adjourned the committee after a session that was less than ten minutes long.

Pelosi kept up the pace, personally and politically. At seventy-nine, the Speaker worked and traveled more than virtually any of her colleagues. Her days were also longer than those of her male counterparts, because she began every day shortly after dawn with a visit to a Washington hair salon. As the Judiciary Committee was voting on the articles, Pelosi led a congressional delegation on a quick trip to Belgium for a commemoration of the seventy-fifth anniversary of the Battle of the Bulge. (She went to a similar event in Auschwitz the following month.) Always, though, she stayed in touch and remained in charge.

The Rules Committee met on December 17 to set out the rules for the debate the following day before the full House of Representatives. There would be six hours of debate, three for each side, with no amendments from the floor allowed. The Rules Committee also added another condition for the debate, which seemed at the time little more than a housekeeping matter. The committee said after the vote on the two articles, the full House would be permitted to consider a resolution appointing and authorizing the House managers for the impeachment trial in the Senate.

With his fate in the House a foregone conclusion, Trump threw one last punch in his own defense—a letter. The president was not known as a writer—ghostwriters wrote his books—but it was clear that he at least dictated a draft of his December 17 letter to Speaker Pelosi. It was five and a half pages, single-spaced, and it's unlikely any president ever wrote a more unhinged, inaccurate, or angry rant. It read like a four-thousand-word tweet, and for the most part the letter was received with the same kind of shrug as his shorter outbursts. *That's just Trump.* Still, the president of the United States did sign it, and it was fair to evaluate it as an expression of his true views. "This impeachment represents an unprecedented and unconstitutional abuse of power by Democrat Lawmakers, unequaled in nearly two and a half centuries of American legislative history," he wrote, ignoring that the Constitution explicitly authorizes the House of Representatives to impeach a president. "The Articles of Impeachment introduced by the House Judiciary Committee are not recognizable under any standard of Constitutional theory, interpretation, or jurisprudence. They include no crimes, no misdemeanors, and no offenses whatsoever. You have cheapened the importance of the very ugly word, impeachment!" As the Republicans' own witness acknowledged, impeachable offenses need not be crimes. Trump's presumption was remarkable, even on religious matters. He said Pelosi had declared "open war on American Democracy. . . . [Y]ou are offending Americans of faith by continually saying 'I pray for the President,' when you know this statement is not true, unless it is meant in a negative sense. It is a terrible thing you are doing, but you will have to live with it, not I!" (Many sentences in the letter ended with exclamation points.)

To the extent that Trump addressed the articles at all, he repeated his previous defenses—that his call with Zelensky had been "misquoted, mischaracterized, and fraudulently misrepresented," because the call was "perfect." As for the key sentence in the call record, Trump adopted his late realization: "I said do <u>us</u> a favor, not <u>me</u>, and <u>our country</u>, not a campaign." Besides, "never once did Ukraine complain about pressure being applied—not once!"—as if Zelensky were going to upset the hypersensitive Trump by complaining. "Everyone, you included, knows what is really happening. Your chosen candidate lost the election in 2016, in an Electoral College landslide. . . . [Y]ou will never get over it! You are unwilling and unable to accept the verdict issued at the ballot box during the great Election of 2016. So you have spent three straight years attempting to overturn the will of the American people and nullify their votes. You view democracy as your enemy!" He then went on to list his accomplishments as president and rehearse his complaints about the Mueller investigation and its cast of "18 angry Democrats." Sometimes Trump combined two obsessions in the same sentence, as when he complained (unjustifiably) about his denial of rights and (falsely) about the whistle-blower: "I have been denied the most fundamental rights afforded by the Constitution, including the right to present evidence, to have my own counsel present, to confront accusers, and to call and cross-examine witnesses, like the so-called whistleblower who started this entire hoax with a false report of the phone call that bears no relationship to the actual phone call that was made."

The letter reflected what Trump learned from his incessant

tweeting—that he could grind down fact-checkers and critics with sheer volume and repetition. No one had the patience to police all of his lies, especially when he repeated them, so they mostly stood uncorrected. For anyone who actually made it to the end of Trump's letter, the last sentence might not have had the meaning he intended: "One hundred years from now, when people look back at this affair, I want them to understand it, and learn from it, so that it can never happen to another President again."

On the morning of December 19, Pelosi spoke from the well of the House when she said, "Today, as speaker of the House, I solemnly and sadly open the debate on the impeachment of the president of the United States." Like everyone else, Pelosi knew what the result was going to be, and she had strict orders for her caucus—no gloating and no celebrating. She deputized Diana DeGette of Colorado to preside over most of the debate, because she was a trusted member of the Speaker's leadership team as well as an expert on the House rules. DeGette was to control the action on the floor in case the Republicans tried to derail the debate with procedural maneuvers. But that didn't happen, and the two sides took turns berating or supporting the president, mostly without even acknowledging one another's arguments. Few speeches stood out, except perhaps that of Barry Loudermilk, a Republican from Georgia. In his letter two days earlier, Trump had compared the impeachment proceedings to another famous American trial, writing (absurdly), "More due process was afforded to those accused in the Salem Witch Trials." But Loudermilk went Trump one better. "Before you take this historic vote today, one week before Christmas, I want you to keep this in mind," he told his colleagues. "When Jesus was falsely accused of treason, Pontius Pilate gave Jesus the opportunity to face his accusers. During that sham trial, Pontius Pilate afforded more rights to Jesus than the Democrats have afforded this president in this process." In addition to the self-evident lunacy of the comparison, Loudermilk was factually wrong. Trump was allowed to cross-examine and present witnesses, as well as to confront his accusers in the Judiciary Committee, but the president and his lawyers chose not to participate in the hearing.

There was just one element of uncertainty regarding the outcome—

the number of defections from each party. Impeachment served as a useful barometer of partisanship in the House. In 1974, the Judiciary Committee voted 27 to 11 for the first article of impeachment against Nixon, with 6 Republicans joining all 21 Democrats. (Nixon resigned before the full House voted.) In 1998, the Judiciary Committee voted 21 to 17, along party lines, to endorse four articles of impeachment against Clinton. But the story was different in the full House, where only two articles were approved. On the articles that passed, 5 Democrats voted for them, and 5 and then 12 Republicans voted against them. The other two articles went down to defeat with substantial numbers of Republican votes.

As it turned out, the partisanship was close to absolute in the House vote on Trump. For the final moments, when all the members cast their votes, Pelosi took the Speaker's chair and presided. Not a single Republican voted for either article. (Justin Amash, a Michigan Republican who had resigned from the party and would later launch a short-lived third-party presidential campaign against Trump, did vote yes on both as an independent.) Among Democrats, Collin Peterson of Minnesota and Jeff Van Drew of New Jersey voted no on both, and Jared Golden of Maine voted no on the second article. (Van Drew promptly announced he would become a Republican.) Tulsi Gabbard, a Hawaii Democrat who was then waging a quixotic run for president, voted present on both articles.

Still, there was clearly a sense of solemn occasion when Pelosi announced the result. As she often did, Pelosi dressed to fit the mood—on this day in a black suit adorned by a gold brooch of the Mace of the Republic, a venerable symbol of the House of Representatives. There is a real Mace of the Republic in the House, and it was used in the early days of Congress to keep order; it still sits in the chamber on a pedestal by the Speaker. Unlike the Senate, which has assigned seats, the members of the House mostly mill around on the floor, and they had gathered in rambunctious cliques as Pelosi prepared to announce the vote on the first article. "The yeas are 230; the nays are 197; present is one," she said. "Article I is adopted." And she banged her gavel. At that moment, a couple of members toward the back of the room started to cheer, and Pelosi made a gesture that immediately became famous. In less than a second, before the noise had a chance to build, she swiped an index card across her lips in an unmistakable demand to "zip it." The cheers stopped, mid-breath. Pelosi's control of her chamber was never more apparent, and she didn't even need the mace. The vote on the second article was 229 to 198, with one present.

In the drama surrounding the announcement of the results, hardly anyone noticed that Pelosi failed to take the planned third vote, authorizing her to present the managers to the Senate for the trial.

33

"Speaker Pelosi Wanted Leverage"

Most of the time, Nancy Pelosi and Mitch McConnell just circled around each other. The Speaker of the House and the majority leader in the Senate had little in common, except that they were both very good at their jobs. The caricature of Pelosi as a wild-eyed San Francisco radical amused those who knew her best. Sure, she had liberal views on the issues, but she ran the Democratic caucus and the full House with a clear understanding of the art of the possible. Impeachment was a classic example. After resisting for months, she turned into a supporter and said she wanted impeachment done by Christmas. It was. In a similar way, McConnell, the Kentucky senator, was a committed conservative, but he knew what he could and could not accomplish with his narrow, fifty-three to forty-seven majority. He could prevent votes from taking place in the Senate on the legislation passed by Pelosi's House; his success in doing so earned him the nickname the Grim Reaper, which he welcomed. McConnell could also force through the confirmations of scores of federal judges, because the filibuster, with its sixty-vote threshold, had been abolished for judicial appointments. That was McConnell's Senate agenda—obstruct the House and steamroll the judges. Other than that, pretty much all McConnell did was pass the federal budget, which he did after a wary annual dance with Pelosi.

Impeachment threw Pelosi and McConnell together. More to the point, impeachment allowed Pelosi to put a squeeze of sorts on McConnell. The Senate leader had known for weeks that the House was going to vote for impeachment, and he had to plan for a trial. The relationship between Trump and McConnell—between the bombastic president and the taciturn senator—was not warm or close, but they recognized that they needed each other. To that end, McConnell wanted the trial completed quickly. Like everyone else, he knew that there would never be anywhere near the sixty-seven votes needed to remove Trump from office. The point, then, was to conclude the trial with as little political damage as possible to the president and the Republican Party. If McConnell could embarrass the House Democrats in the process, so much the better. His preeminent goal was clear: get it over with. The Senate rules appeared to be in McConnell's favor. They said that when the House appointed managers, the Senate "shall immediately" inform the House of Representatives that the Senate was ready to proceed with the trial. As the schedule began playing out, McConnell's staff even thought about jamming through a trial in the days between Christmas and New Year's.

But Laurence Tribe noticed a quirk in the Senate rules. It was true that the Senate was supposed to start a trial "immediately." But the trial could begin only after the House passed a resolution naming its managers. In other words, only Pelosi—not McConnell—could trigger the start of the trial.

Shortly after the vote in the House, Pelosi announced that she would not name the managers, and thus allow the Senate trial to start, unless the Senate established "fair" procedures for its trial. Specifically, she said that the House Democrats wanted to make sure that the Senate conducted a real trial—with live witness testimony and the production of documents from the White House. As Pelosi knew as well as anyone, the Senate guards its institutional prerogatives, and McConnell would recoil at the idea that the House presumed to dictate how a Senate trial should unfold. "Speaker Pelosi wanted leverage—leverage to reach in to the Senate and dictate our trial proceedings to us," McConnell said. "Now I've made clear from the beginning that no such leverage exists. It is nonexistent." The standoff continued through the holidays. Pelosi knew that the Senate would never agree to her terms, but it was politically useful for her to keep the issue of witnesses in front of the public. Why didn't the Senate want witnesses? What were the Republicans afraid of? The delay served another purpose. It allowed the Democrats to put together their trial team, which meant that Pelosi had to select the House managers—the prosecutors in the trial of a lifetime.

The selection of the managers was a paradigmatic example of Pelosi's style in action. In a way, the stakes were not as high as they might have appeared. The outcome of the trial was never in doubt; the wrong managers were not going to cost the Democrats a chance to remove Trump from office. But the managers would provide a public face for the House of Representatives—and the Democratic Party—in an extraordinarily high-profile setting. This was theater as much as litigation, and Pelosi wanted a cast of stars. The only precedent for her decision was a negative one. In the Senate trial of Bill Clinton in 1999, the Republicans put forth as managers thirteen members of the Judiciary Committee, led by its chairman, Henry Hyde. They failed to divide the labor in a meaningful way and, as a group, impressed few people with their performances. Notably, all thirteen were white men.

In assembling her cast, Pelosi started with Adam Schiff as lead manager. This was not surprising, of course, given his role in the process to this point, but it was another slap at Jerry Nadler. Hyde was Nadler's counterpart, and he was the lead manager in the Clinton trial, and Pelosi did not even offer Nadler a face-saving deputy role. Pelosi made Nadler a manager, but he was just one of several on Schiff's team. Still, Schiff and Nadler were the only two more or less obligatory choices, and Pelosi had a free hand to select the rest.

There were lots of factors in play, but the first was choosing people who could do the job. It was still at least possible that there were going to be witnesses for the managers to examine, so it would be important to have lawyers with some trial experience. At a minimum, the managers would need to do some spontaneous thinking on their feet, so litigators were the most likely candidates. Diversity mattered, too, but not just in the traditional categories of race and gender. Republicans had been mocking Democrats as a party of the coasts, especially California and New York, which happened to be the home states of Pelosi's first two selections. So Pelosi wanted people from the center of the country, too. She needed lawyers, but it would be helpful to represent the national security world, too, in the way that the authors of the frontliners' op-ed piece did. Then, finally, there was the question of the experts, the impeachment enthusiasts, who had been pushing the issue since the Mueller Report was released. It was clear that they, more than any of their colleagues, could do the job. They knew the facts the best, cared the most, and had the most relevant skills. What was their role?

Hakeem Jeffries, whose district was in Brooklyn, was an obvious choice. As the number five Democrat in the House leadership, he was a Pelosi protégé of sorts and a possible successor as Speaker. He would be the first African American Speaker. He was a lawyer with litigation experience, and he had become a familiar spokesman on cable news against the president.

Zoe Lofgren, whose district included Silicon Valley, was also virtually certain to be picked. She enjoyed a unique place in American history as the only person to be professionally involved in all three impeachments in the modern era. She was a young congressional staffer in the Nixon inquiry, and once in Congress she served on the Judiciary Committee and voted against Clinton's impeachment. She had run unsuccessfully against Nadler for chairman of the Judiciary Committee and like many Californians was a close Pelosi ally.

So the first four were two New Yorkers and two Californians, which meant the others had to be from elsewhere. Val Demings was new to Congress—first elected in 2016—but she had a long career in law enforcement, which included a stint as chief of police in Orlando. (She was the first woman and second African American in the job; the first was her husband.) Demings was on both the Intelligence and the Judiciary Committees, so she was already familiar with the issues. Sylvia Garcia was a freshman in Congress, but like Demings, she was in her sixties, with a long legal career behind her, including time as a judge in Houston. She was the most soft-spoken in the group, and she took the smallest role in the trial.

At the time, Pelosi's selection of Jason Crow was seen as a surprise, including to Crow himself, but the choice made sense. He was also a freshman and the only manager who served on neither the Judiciary nor the Intelligence Committee. He was a frontliner who flipped a Republican seat in Colorado and one of the co-authors of the op-ed piece that persuaded Pelosi to proceed with impeachment in September. As a former Army Ranger who served in Iraq and Afghanistan, he met Pelosi's need for national security expertise among the managers.

He was just forty years old, the youngest in the group, and he was also a lawyer, with some litigation experience.

Pelosi could pick as many or as few managers as she wanted. (She briefly considered letting Schiff try the case by himself.) There was a broad consensus that the thirteen managers the Republicans used in 1999 were too many, but no one outside her inner circle knew how many she would select. She stopped at seven. The Speaker's omissions were notable. Several members of the Judiciary Committee had devoted months of their lives to impeachment, including Cicilline, Swalwell, Neguse, and Raskin. They all wanted to be managers, and they had arguably the best qualifications, and she picked none of them. In mid-2019, they and their liberal colleagues had complicated Pelosi's life by pushing for impeachment before she was ready. The savvy and loyal Jeffries was as liberal as they were, but he had never gotten in front of Pelosi on impeachment. The Speaker remembered those who did, not fondly, and she made the cold-blooded decision to leave them all by the side of the road.

Pelosi introduced the managers at a ceremony on January 15, where she also signed the official copy of the articles of impeachment. To do so, she followed a Washington tradition of writing tiny portions of her name with different pens and giving each pen to a different manager as a souvenir. Pelosi's gesture with the pens opened her to criticism from Republicans, who said the celebratory act violated Pelosi's pledge to treat impeachment as a solemn process.

As his impeachment moved from a likelihood to a reality, Trump spent some of his time trying to pretend that it never happened. On Twitter and elsewhere, he referred to the proceedings as the "fake impeachment" and the "impeachment hoax." When the House managers submitted legal briefs to the Senate, they were headed "In re IMPEACHMENT OF PRESIDENT DONALD J. TRUMP," but when Trump's lawyers filed papers, the heading was "IN PROCEEDINGS BEFORE THE UNITED STATES SENATE"—without use of the "ugly word," as Trump called it. As during the Clinton impeachment, tickets were required for admission to watch the proceedings from the Senate galleries. But unlike in 1999, the Trump allies who ran the Senate did not include the word "impeachment" on the tickets.

But the trial was going to take place, and Trump did have to make a plan for it. In public, he went back and forth on the issue of whether witnesses should testify. At times, he indulged his obsessions with the whistle-blower and Adam Schiff, so the president said that he wanted them to testify. But on this issue at least, cooler heads prevailed. If Trump was going to call witnesses, then the managers would have that right too. The overarching defense strategy was clear from the beginning. A boring, brief, and uneventful trial would certainly end in an acquittal, so that was the objective. Witness testimony would extend the trial and might disclose incriminating information, so there should be no witnesses. Thus, the strategy. *Quit while you're ahead. Don't make waves. Run out the clock.*

Trump understood this approach in theory, but it conflicted with the way he had lived his entire public life. He didn't want a boring defense, even if it was successful. (He always assumed he was going to be successful, and with reason in this case.) When attacked, he fought back. And in Trump's worldview, famous people were better allies than obscure ones. These principles led, in effect, to the creation of two defense teams. Cipollone, as White House counsel, was the de facto leader of the defense. (This was consistent with 1999, when Charles Ruff, Clinton's White House counsel, ran the defense in the Senate trial.) As his deputies, Cipollone picked Patrick Philbin and Michael Purpura, two quietly competent longtime government lawyers who were on his staff. This was more or less satisfactory to Trump, but he knew what these lawyers were not—celebrities.

So Trump went to his administration's unofficial employment agency—Fox News—and he recruited four of their regulars to serve on his defense team. Alan Dershowitz, the retired Harvard Law professor and celebrity attorney, had been defending Trump on television since Mueller was appointed. So had Ken Starr, the former independent counsel, as had Starr's successor in that job, Robert Ray. And Pam Bondi, who had recently completed her term as Florida's attorney general, was also recruited to participate. Except for Dershowitz, it wasn't even clear what these legal celebrities would do in the trial. But the fact that Trump hired them received a good deal of attention, and that might have been the whole point anyway.

In most respects, though, the most important lawyer for Trump was the one who had been with him the longest—Jay Sekulow. Back when Ty Cobb and Marc Kasowitz were running the show for Trump, in the spring of 2017, Sekulow had been hired in a fairly limited role, to give advice on constitutional law issues. But his role endured and expanded through each changing of the guard, through the John Dowd period and then for the Giuliani chapter and finally with Pat Cipollone in 2020. Of all the lawyers, Sekulow had spent the longest time in Trump's presence, listening to his self-pitying rants and rages against his enemies. Sekulow would make some legal arguments in the Senate, but he was there mostly to channel Trump himself, and Sekulow's words would be the best guide to the president's state of mind.

The standoff between Pelosi and McConnell ended in a way that was preordained. Pelosi relented and agreed to allow the House to vote on the managers on January 15, 2020, and thus to let the Senate trial begin. But in losing, Pelosi also won. She gave her managers time to prepare. She forced McConnell and his allies to defend the proposition that a meaningful trial could be held without hearing from witnesses. Still, the fact remained: the Senate, not Pelosi, would determine the procedures for the trial.

The contrast between how those procedures were established in 1999 and 2020 revealed a good deal about the two eras. Before the Clinton trial, all one hundred senators gathered in an unprecedented, informal session in the Old Senate Chamber to thrash out the plans for the Senate trial. They were united in trying to avoid the kind of brawl that had taken place in the House. After a few hours of discussion, they came up with a plan jointly sponsored by Ted Kennedy and Phil Gramm, who were ideological polar opposites. It was approved unanimously.

In 2020, the fight over the rules of the Senate trial was a partisan showdown, even though McConnell's plan was roughly similar to that at the Clinton trial. The lawyers on each side would have twenty-four hours of floor time to present their case, and then the senators would have sixteen hours of floor time to submit written questions to the lawyers on either side. Democrats pressed McConnell for a guarantee that both sides would be allowed to call witnesses, arguing that the Clinton trial, as the relevant precedent, did have witnesses. In prior impeachment trials, witnesses had actually testified on the floor of the Senate, as if it were a real courtroom. But in 1999, there were videotaped depositions of Monica Lewinsky, Clinton's friend Vernon Jordan, and White House aide Sidney Blumenthal. Edited excerpts were then played for all one hundred senators. (Robert Byrd, the veteran West Virginia senator and self-appointed guardian of the Senate's dignity, wanted to guarantee that the chamber was not sullied by the details of Lewinsky's account, so he insisted on a presentation limited to suitable excerpts.) Chuck Schumer, the Democratic leader, and his colleagues picked up Pelosi's demand for witnesses, as there were in the Clinton trial. They repeated the same theme: Was this going to be a fair trial or a cover-up?

But McConnell managed to finesse the issue and kick the can down the road. He correctly pointed out that in the Clinton trial the Senate voted on hearing witnesses in the middle of the trial, not before it began. And that was his proposal—putting off the vote on witnesses. Predictably, it passed along party lines, 53 to 47.

Even the most mundane activities in the Senate come barnacled with tradition. (For example, there is a rule that says it's always permissible to drink milk on the Senate floor, thanks to the example set by Everett Dirksen in the 1960s.) The traditions regarding impeachment trials go back much further. Indeed, most of the customs regarding these trials have endured, more or less intact, from the trial of Andrew Johnson in 1868. To start the proceedings, there was a formal procession of the House managers from their side of the Capitol to the Senate. For their part, the senators were required to take a special impeachment trial oath and then sign a form attesting that they had so sworn. In 1999, each senator was given a specially designed pen to sign the oath. (This commemoration turned out to be especially memorable because the Parker company inscribed "Untied States Senator" on the outside of the pen.) In any event, McConnell decreed that in 2020 the senators would all use the same ordinary pen to sign their oaths, to create a contrast with Pelosi's signing ceremony.

It is not just a tradition but a constitutional command that the chief justice of the United States preside at the impeachment trial of a president. Senate tradition mandated that the chief be escorted by an honor guard of senators the first time that he appeared in the chamber. (Patrick Leahy of Vermont served as an escort in both 1999 and 2020. Only fifteen senators who were present for the Clinton trial remained in office.) The Framers put the chief justice in this role for a practical reason. Under normal circumstances, the vice president serves as the presiding officer of the Senate. But in the trial of a president, the vice president has a conflict of interest, because he would take over if the president were to be convicted. Thus, the resort to the chief justice.

In 1999, there hadn't been an impeachment trial for more than a century, so there was a great deal of curiosity about the nature and extent of the role Chief Justice William Rehnquist would play. As it turned out, Rehnquist himself gave a characteristically pithy summation of his performance. "I did nothing in particular, and I did it very well," he said. Under the Senate rules for impeachment trials, virtually every ruling that a chief justice might make was subject to being overturned by a majority vote of the senators, so there was little incentive for the chief to inject himself into the proceedings. Through the weeks of Clinton's trial, Rehnquist made only one substantive ruling from the chair. Tom Harkin, the senator from Iowa, raised an objection early in the proceedings, when he asked Rehnquist to direct the House managers to "refrain from referring to the Senators as jurors." Rehnquist agreed, and the managers stopped using the word. (Later that day, Harkin boasted to his colleagues, "Hey! I won my first Supreme Court case!")

This was more than a semantic matter. Jurors in court cases are required to base their decisions only on the evidence presented to them. If the Framers had wanted that kind of impeachment trial, they could have assigned the cases to traditional courts and juries. But by giving the power to senators—all of whom have preexisting relationships with the president and well-established political affiliations—they made clear that they wanted a more holistic judgment about whether a president should be removed. Some senators found it convenient to dodge questions about impeachment by saying they were reserving judgment as "jurors." But they weren't just jurors. (In courtroom trials, of course, jurors can't vote to overrule the judge.)

The senators were nothing more, and nothing less, than politicians who were supposed to decide the president's fate based just in part on the evidence at trial but also on their overall sense of what was best for the country.

For the trial itself, the senators had to follow perhaps the simplest if also the most maddening rule about impeachment proceedings. They had to sit down and shut up. All one hundred senators were required to be seated at their assigned desks for the entire duration of the trial, and they were not allowed to utter a word—not to the participants or each other—unless they were recognized by the chief justice. The use of electronic devices, including phones, was also prohibited. To say this was unnatural behavior for one hundred politicians, especially U.S. senators, is a considerable understatement. For one thing, there are usually no more than a handful of senators on the floor at any time. And when the senators do visit the floor, they do so to vote (and then leave), schmooze with their colleagues, or give speeches. Silent attention to others, much less for hours, does not happen. To an admirable degree, as in 1999, the senators basically managed to comply with this mandate, with a minimum of talking or sleeping.

The lawyers on both sides spent a frantic few weeks preparing. It was a daunting amount of work. They had to prepare a massive trial brief, summarizing their arguments, and plan to present up to twelve hours' worth of arguments, which was a lot of time to fill. In addition to the seven managers, staffers from the Intelligence, Judiciary, and Oversight Committees pitched in for the Democrats. And about a dozen lawyers helped out for Trump. The themes for both sides were clear from the outset.

Schiff and Dan Goldman, his lead investigator, wanted to overwhelm the senators with facts. That was their advantage, they felt. Trump did what they said he did. True, their investigation was hamstrung by unavailable witnesses and unseen documents, but they still had accumulated thousands of pages from which to cull. In an advance from 1999, the Senate now had sufficient audiovisual capability to allow the managers to integrate excerpts from the earlier testimony and other graphics into their presentations. Schiff and the others were not naive. They knew they were never going to win sixty-seven votes.

But they wanted to rub senators' noses in what Trump had done. The managers weren't afraid to be repetitive, especially since the television audience would only dip in and out of the coverage. So they showed the greatest hits over and over again: Mulvaney's admitting to the quid pro quo at the news conference; David Holmes's hearing that Trump didn't give a shit about Ukraine; Taylor's anguished texts about the insanity of Giuliani's whole venture. The Republicans were going to vote to acquit, but they weren't going to be able to say they didn't know what Trump did.

But it was a mistake to think, as many did, that Schiff and the managers were focused on winning the votes of Republican senators, though they welcomed the chance to do so. The real focus of their efforts was to hold on to the Democrats, especially unpredictable moderates like Joe Manchin of West Virginia and Kyrsten Sinema of Arizona. The managers didn't want a "bipartisan" vote against their articles, so they kept a close eye on their moderates, both in the Senate chamber and in the senators' media appearances talking about the case. The managers pitched their case accordingly.

As for Trump's team, their approach was summed up in the trial brief they filed at the beginning of the case. The brief was 110 pages long, and 80 pages were devoted to procedural arguments—to assertions that the House had behaved inappropriately in investigating and filing the articles. These claims included "The Articles Fail to State Impeachable Offenses as a Matter of Law" and "The Articles Resulted from an Impeachment Inquiry That Violated All Precedent and Denied the President Constitutionally Required Due Process." The brief devoted little attention to defending Trump's actual conduct. Nor, really, did Trump's lawyers deny what he was alleged to have done. Instead, they just said that his behavior was legal and appropriate. "The July 25 Call Transcript Shows the President Did Nothing Wrong" and "President Zelensky and Other Senior Ukrainian Officials Confirmed There Was No Quid Pro Quo and No Pressure on Them Concerning Investigations."

So those were the plans for the trial. Cipollone wanted to talk about the House, and Schiff wanted to talk about Trump—if he could escape from the dentist's office.

34

"Moral Courage Is a Rarer Commodity than Bravery"

I t started with a loose filling, so Schiff dealt with it during the week before the trial started. But instead of solving the problem, the dentist's ministrations made the pain worse. To address the issue further, Schiff was told, might require him to refrain from talking for some period of time. This was unacceptable with the trial about to start. So he lived with the pain, alternating Tylenol and Advil in well more than the quantities advised on the packaging.

Schiff had to perform under demanding circumstances, even if his teeth had felt fine. McConnell's rules gave each side the same number of hours as the two parties received in the Clinton trial, but the majority leader truncated the number of trial days. That meant that the proceedings in the Senate, which began at 1:00 p.m., often went deep into the night, an exhausting proposition for everyone involved. On January 21, the day of the debate about the procedures, the Democrats filed a series of motions that extended the session until nearly 2:00 a.m. But everyone was back in the chamber by 1:00 p.m. on January 22 for opening statements.

On that day, the president greeted the beginning of the trial with a record frenzy of tweets. He posted 142 tweets and retweets, which broke his previous record of 124, which he set on the day that the House Judiciary Committee debated the articles of impeachment. Trump produced his usual collection of retweets of his supporters' tweets and his own citations of whatever he was watching on Fox News. As it happened, not one of the tweets concerned a news story that was starting to gain attention in the United States. Two days earlier, a man in Washington State, who had just returned from visiting family in Wuhan, China, became the first person in the United States to be diagnosed with the viral disease known as COVID-19. The first victim of the disease in South Korea was diagnosed the same day, and the coronavirus was spreading rapidly in China. Trump didn't mention the virus in any of his 142 tweets, but he was asked about the Washington man's illness in an interview with CNBC that day. "We have it totally under control," he said. "It's one person coming in from China. We have it under control. It's going to be just fine." For the next two weeks, Trump's pattern would recur—obsessive fixation on his political enemies and dismissive inattention to the growing threat of the virus.

House staffers prepared rough drafts of the opening presentations, and the managers customized them, based on their own interests and experiences. Schiff opened with an overview, and Nadler and Garcia then followed with detailed accounts of Trump's Ukraine scheme. The first manager to make any sort of personal connection to the evidence was Jason Crow, whose presentation concerned the withholding of military aid from Ukraine. "Ambassador Taylor testified that American aid is a concrete demonstration of our 'commitment to resist aggression and defend freedom.' He also detailed the many benefits of our assistance for Ukraine's forces," Crow said, and then he introduced a brief video clip from Taylor's testimony: "Mr. Chairman, the security assistance that we provide takes many forms. One of the components of that assistance is counter-battery radar. Another component are sniper weapons."

When Crow resumed, he drew an analogy to his own experience. "In 2005, I was an Army Ranger serving in a special operations task force in Afghanistan," Crow told the senators. "We were at a remote operating base along the Afghan-Pakistan border. Frequently, the insurgents that we were fighting would launch rockets and missiles onto our small base. But, luckily, we were provided with counter-battery radar. So 20, 30, 40 seconds before those rockets and mortars rained down on us, an alarm would sound. We would run out from our tents and jump into our concrete bunkers and wait for the attack to end. This is not a theoretical exercise, and the Ukrainians know it. For Ukraine, aid from the United States actually constitutes about 10 percent of their military budget. It is safe to say that they can't fight effectively without it. So there is no doubt. U.S. military assistance in Ukraine makes a real difference in the fight against Russia."

Val Demings followed with the story of the negotiations over Zelensky's hopes for a White House meeting. She played video from one of the memorable moments from Sondland's testimony:

> I know that members of this committee frequently frame these complicated issues in the form of a simple question: Was there a quid pro quo? As I testified previously with regard to the requested White House call and the White House meeting, the answer is yes. Mr. Giuliani conveyed to Secretary Perry, Ambassador Volker, and others that President Trump wanted a public statement from President Zelensky committing to investigations of Burisma and the 2016 election. Mr. Giuliani expressed those requests directly to the Ukrainians, and Mr. Giuliani also expressed those requests directly to us. We all understood that these prerequisites for the White House call and the White House meeting reflected President Trump's desires and requirements.

The presentations were dense with fact, if not always thrilling as theater. The managers operated by the venerable advice often given to writers: show, don't tell.

Hakeem Jeffries was an exception. He had experience in the pulpit as well as the legislature, and it showed: "George Washington once observed in his Farewell Address to the Nation that the Constitution was sacredly obligatory upon all. That means everyone. In fact, that is what makes our great country so distinct from authoritarian regimes and enemies of democracy. Vladimir Putin is above the law in Russia; Erdogan is above the law in Turkey; Kim Jong Un is above the law in North Korea, but in the United States of America, no one is above the law, not even the President of the United States. That is what this moment is all about." Jeffries's assignment was to walk the senators through the July 25 phone call, and he didn't hold back: "The conspiracy theory that President Trump advanced on the July 25 phone call is stone-cold Russian propaganda. . . . The idea that President Trump cares about corruption is laughable. It is laughable."

At one point during Jeffries's remarks, a protester in the gallery started screaming about God. Jeffries offered a deft ad-lib response: "And the scripture says, 'For the Lord loves justice and will not abandon His faithful ones.'" (The protester was removed from the gallery, but could be heard screaming in the background for some time. During the next break, Schiff quipped to Demings, the former police chief, "We could have used you out there." With a half smile, Demings invoked her credentials as a badass: "If you had, it would have been over a lot faster.")

Schiff then took the story from July 25 to September, when the whistle-blower came forward. Lofgren closed out the long day by describing the failed efforts by Congress to obtain information from the administration, which formed the basis for Article II. Just before 10:00 p.m., the Court of Impeachment, as it was formally known, adjourned for the day.

The managers' first day consisted, in effect, of a chronology of events, from the birth of the Ukraine initiative to the White House's obstruction of the congressional investigation. On the second day, they went through the constitutional law of impeachment and explained how it applied to Article I. Nadler began the day with a disquisition on the Constitution, drawing heavily on the testimony of the law professors before the Judiciary Committee. He also played a video of Alan Dershowitz from 1998 talking about the legitimate grounds for impeachment. "It certainly doesn't have to be a crime," Dershowitz said. "If you have somebody who completely corrupts the office of President and who abuses trust and poses great danger to our liberty, you don't need a technical crime." Half a dozen presentations took the discussion of Article I through the day and until adjournment at 10:30 p.m. The managers finished their initial presentation, with a similar recap of Article II, on Friday, January 24.

Schiff summed up. To date, he had not been known as especially partisan or eloquent. His speeches were functional and fact laden. But he found another gear in the trial. Schiff had come across a quotation from Robert Kennedy that summed up the challenge of the impeachment trial and, indeed, suggested a fundamental truth about the Trump era. "Moral courage is a rarer commodity than bravery in battle or great intelligence," Kennedy said. "Yet it is the one essential, vital quality for those who seek to change a world that yields most painfully to change." Schiff told the senators that he initially had misgivings about Kennedy's sentiment. He admired the courage of soldiers a great deal. But Kennedy's words continued: "Few men are willing to brave the disapproval of their peers, the censure of their colleagues, [and] the wrath of their society." Schiff explained, "I always tell my constituents that there are two kinds of jobs in Congress, and it is not Democrats or Republicans; it is those in a safe seat, and those in an unsafe seat. . . . Real political courage doesn't come from disagreeing with our opponents but from disagreeing with our friends and with our own party because it means having to stare down accusations of disloyalty and betrayal." In the trial and throughout Trump's presidency, there was never any doubt about his character or his conduct—his dishonesty, his arrogance, his ignorance, and his narcissism. Of course, Trump used the power and purse of the United States to exploit Ukraine for his personal political gain. *Of course.* Democrats saw it; Republicans saw it. As Schiff pointed out, the only real question in the trial was whether any Republicans were willing to admit what they saw.

The following day, Schiff found a dentist who would work over the weekend. He made the problem worse.

Trump understood television ratings, so he knew that few people watched on Saturday, especially during the middle of the day. He told his lawyers to offer just brief introductory remarks on January 25 and save the real opening statements for Monday, January 27.

Sekulow operated as master of ceremonies on Monday, but he laid out the theme, inspired by Trump, at the very beginning. "I don't think this was about just a phone call," he said. "There was a pattern and practice of attempts over a three-year period to not only interfere with the President's capability to govern—which, by the way, they were completely unsuccessful at; just look at the state of where we are as a country—but also interfere with the constitutional framework."

In Sekulow's telling (and in Trump's), the impeachment was not really about his misadventure with Ukraine. It was the culmination of events that began even before he was elected, when the deep state mobilized to try to help Clinton win and then, when she did not, to bring Trump down. Clinton to Comey to Mueller to Schiff—it was all one story, connected by Trump's utter blamelessness in all of their investigations and his unparalleled success in running the country. Other aspects of the defense began on this day. Starr talked about the history of impeachment; Purpura asserted that there were legitimate reasons to withhold the aid to Ukraine; Jane Raskin, a fine lawyer with a ludicrous assignment, made an argument asserting that Giuliani wasn't really that important—that he was just a "colorful distraction." Not surprisingly, Raskin's presentation did not include any quotations from Volker's texts or the July 25 transcript, since Giuliani was at the center of both. The day featured plenty of red meat for Trump's base, including an extensive (and misleading) description of Hunter Biden's role in Ukraine; a lengthy, if irrelevant, attack on Barack Obama; and most peculiarly of all, criticism of *The New York Times*'s "1619" history of slavery.

Alan Dershowitz, as was his custom, called a great deal of attention to himself, in part by asserting before the trial that he wasn't really one of Trump's lawyers. A longtime Democrat who had been trending Republican in recent years, he said he was just making a constitutional argument on the president's behalf. At the age of eighty-one, Dershowitz had become curiously obsessed with Justice Benjamin Curtis, who, after he retired from the Court, helped defend Andrew Johnson in his impeachment trial in 1868. In the Johnson trial, Curtis had asserted that only actual criminal offenses could be high crimes and misdemeanors. "Curtis argued that there must be a specific violation of preexisting law," according to Dershowitz. This was opposite to the opinion Dershowitz himself expressed in the lead-up to the Clinton impeachment, in 1998, and contrary to the view of basically every scholar of the subject, but Dershowitz put his singular interpretation to work for Trump. (Some Democratic senators, who were appalled by Dershowitz and starved for entertainment, sent notes to Elizabeth Warren, who was his former colleague at Harvard, teasing her about the quality of the faculty.)

Sekulow closed out the defense case the following morning, with a tour de force survey of Trump's grievances. His theme reflected the gulf between the worlds of the president's supporters and his adversaries. To Sekulow, Trump wasn't a flawed man but a martyr—as anyone could see. "I would like you to put yourselves in the shoes of the President," he said. "The President of the United States, before he was the President, was under an investigation." Then came the familiar litany of Trump's malign pursuers—Comey, the two FBI employees Page and Strzok (*the lovers*), Mueller, Christopher Steele. Sekulow repeated the same line over and over again: *Put yourselves in the shoes of the President*—as if the unfairness to him were chilling for anyone to contemplate. By questioning the July 25 call, the managers were interfering with the president's freedom of speech. "Do we have like a Biden-free zone? Was that what this was? You mention someone or you are concerned about a company, and it is now off limits? You can impeach the President of the United States for asking a question?" It was all just so monumentally unfair. . . .

The move to questions from the senators, on Wednesday, January 29, loosened the atmosphere in the chamber, by finally giving the senators something to do and forcing the lawyers on both sides to improvise, rather than read prepared arguments. For the most part, the questions were setups; that is, they were vehicles for the senators to display their own rooting interests in the case. The format called for Chief Justice Roberts to read the questions, and it was almost amusing to hear him read words so laden with partisan intent.

There was, for example, this question to the president's lawyers from Mike Lee and Ted Cruz, Republicans of Utah and Texas:

> The House managers have argued aggressively that the President's actions contravened U.S. foreign policy. Isn't it the President's place—certainly more than the place for career civil servants—to conduct foreign policy?

Answer from Patrick Philbin: Yes, it was the President's place.

Or this one, from Dianne Feinstein, the California Democrat, to the House managers:

The President's counsel stated that "there is simply no evidence anywhere that President Trump ever linked security assistance to any investigations"—is that true?

Answer from Jason Crow: No, it's not true.
Cruz offered what he thought was an easy one to the defense:

As a matter of law, does it matter if there was a quid pro quo? Is it true that quid pro quos are often used in foreign policy?

Dershowitz turned this softball into a fiasco, answering, "Every public official whom I know believes that his election is in the public interest. Mostly, you are right. Your election is in the public interest. If a President does something which he believes will help him get elected—in the public interest—that cannot be the kind of quid pro quo that results in impeachment." The absurdity of this position was self-evident—that the president had carte blanche to do anything to get himself reelected. His fellow defense lawyers quickly disavowed this view, Dershowitz tried to explain what he meant, and he left the next day for his retirement home in Florida.

Everyone knew that there was really only one major issue left to be resolved in the trial, and that was whether the parties would be allowed to call witnesses. Before the trial started, John Bolton had finally responded to the criticism he had been receiving for peddling a book and paid speeches but refusing to testify before Congress. His lawyer said he would testify in the Senate, if asked. There followed a series of leaks to the media that suggested his book contained incriminating information about Trump. This led to questions like this one, from Schumer, to the House managers:

John R. Bolton's forthcoming book states that the President wanted to continue withholding $391 million in military aid to Ukraine until Ukraine announced investigations into his top political rival and the debunked conspiracy theory about the 2016 election. Is there any way for the Senate to render a fully informed verdict in this case without hearing the testimony of Bolton, Mulvaney, and the other key eyewitnesses or without seeing the relevant documentary evidence?

Schiff: The Senate should hear from Bolton.

The managers and lawyers had been in the Senate for dozens of hours by this point, and they started to feel comfortable there. Some of the more outgoing lawyers, like Sekulow and Jeffries, managed to chat amiably with each other. (Cipollone remained grim-faced throughout.) After one of the House managers completed a speech, he went to the men's room that was just behind the Senate chamber, and he found himself at an adjacent urinal to the chief justice of the United States. The bathroom had a television tuned to Fox News, and at that moment Lindsey Graham was denouncing the manager's remarks. The two men watched in silence, until Roberts smiled and said, "Nothing like instant feedback."

The preeminent skill for any legislative leader is the ability to count votes—and win. When Pelosi endorsed impeachment in September, she knew she could deliver it in December. When McConnell, at the beginning of the impeachment trial, agreed to a vote on witnesses at a later date, he knew he would prevail. The moment arrived on January 31, when the full Senate voted on whether to allow each side to call witnesses, as they had in the Clinton trial.

In the days leading up to the vote, McConnell asserted—in public at least—that he wasn't sure if he had the votes to stop witnesses from being called. There was conflicting historical evidence on whether the chief justice had the authority to break ties during the trial. In his only substantive ruling during the trial, Roberts said he would not intervene to break ties, so a tie vote would fail. That meant that McConnell could afford to lose three votes from his fifty-three-seat majority to win on witnesses. He'd lost two of them already, because Susan Collins of Maine and Mitt Romney of Utah had already announced that they favored witnesses.

Most of the attention in advance of the vote focused on the prospect of testimony from Bolton. But Schumer actually called for four witnesses—Bolton, acting chief of staff Mulvaney, his deputy Robert Blair, and the Office of Management and Budget's Michael Duffey. McConnell used the breadth of that proposal to his advantage. He said the president's lawyers would then be allowed to call four of their own, including, presumably, Joe and Hunter Biden. This would have been a spectacle, of course, and it certainly would have delayed the end of the trial for weeks. McConnell knew that his Republican colleagues lacked the patience for such an extension, especially since the outcome of the trial was never in doubt. The day before the vote, McConnell got the lifeline he needed from his old friend Lamar Alexander of Tennessee, who said he would oppose witnesses. That gave Schumer's proposal a maximum of fifty votes—not enough.

By the time Schiff made his impassioned plea on the floor for witnesses, on the morning of Friday, January 31, he knew he was going to lose. The other vote in play, Lisa Murkowski of Alaska, went with her Republican colleagues, so the final tally was 51 to 49 against witnesses.

As the witness vote neared, Trump kept up his frenetic pace on Twitter. In the twenty-four hours around the Senate vote on witnesses, he tweeted more than a dozen times about Adam Schiff ("Schiff blasted for not focusing on California homeless. @foxandfriends") and dozens more times about the impeachment trial itself ("Washington Dems have spent the last 3 years trying to overturn the last election—and we will make sure they face another crushing defeat in the NEXT ELECTION"). Trump said nothing at all about the coronavirus on Twitter, even though on January 31 he began shutting down most travel from China to the United States. On a quick swing through Michigan and Iowa, also at this time, Trump did answer a question on the subject. "We think we have it very well under control. We have very little problem in this country at this moment—five. And those people are all recuperating successfully," he said. "But we're working very closely with China and other countries, and we think it's going to have a very good ending for it. So that I can assure you."

35

"A Lot of People Forget Abe Lincoln"

The Super Bowl took place on the last Sunday before the end of the trial. In an interview during the Fox broadcast of the game, Sean Hannity asked Trump about the coronavirus. "Well, we've pretty much shut it down, coming in from China," Trump said. "So, we're gonna see what happens." A few days earlier, his aide Peter Navarro had prepared a memo for the president about the developing coronavirus crisis. "The lack of immune protection or an existing cure or vaccine would leave Americans defenseless in the case of a full-blown coronavirus outbreak on U.S. soil," it said. "This lack of protection elevates the risk of the coronavirus evolving into a full-blown pandemic, imperiling the lives of millions of Americans."

On the following Monday morning, February 3, each side had two hours to sum up. The trial had taken two weeks, which was about half as long as the Clinton trial. By this point, the arguments were familiar. From Jason Crow, for the managers: "President Trump abused the extraordinary powers he alone holds as President of the United States to coerce an ally to interfere in our upcoming Presidential election for the benefit of his own reelection. He then used those unique powers to wage an unprecedented campaign to obstruct Congress and cover up his wrongdoing." From Jay Sekulow, for the defense: "This entire campaign of impeachment—that started from the very first day the President was inaugurated—is a partisan one, and it should never happen again. For three years, this push for impeachment came straight from the President's opponents, and it finally reached a crescendo."

Schiff (who finally had a root canal during Super Bowl weekend) had the last word: "He has betrayed our national security, and he will do so again. He has compromised our elections, and he will do so again. You will not change him. You cannot constrain him. He is who he is. Truth matters little to him. What is right matters even less. And decency matters not at all. I do not ask you to convict him because truth or right or decency matters nothing to him, but because we have proven our case and it matters to you. Truth matters to you. Right matters to you. You are decent. He is not who you are."

Under the peculiar Senate rules, the debate among the senators did not take place during the impeachment trial itself. Over the next three days, the Senate had to reconvene in regular sessions, to allow senators to give speeches announcing how they intended to vote. The Democrats mostly reaffirmed what the managers had been arguing, but the Republicans did not embrace all of the arguments raised by Trump's lawyers. Rather, the GOP senators displayed a distinct lack of enthusiasm, or worse, for Trump's behavior. Many Republican senators contented themselves with attacking the House's procedures rather than defending Trump's conduct. Even such conservative stalwarts as Chuck Grassley of Iowa couldn't bring themselves to say a word of either support or criticism about Trump. Speaking early in the debate and adopting a view that many Republicans followed, Grassley said, "The American people are more than adequately prepared to decide for themselves the fate of the President in November. This decision belongs to the voters." Lisa Murkowski, a Republican from Alaska with independent leanings, also didn't mention Trump's conduct in casting her vote to acquit, saying, "The voters will pronounce a verdict in nine months, and we must trust their judgment." (Rand Paul, the cantankerous libertarian from Kentucky, tried to ask a question during the trial that purported to name the whistle-blower. Roberts refused to read it, but Paul used the name during his speech explaining his vote.)

The next day featured a surreal clash of events. The debate continued in the morning. Susan Collins, the Maine Republican who voted in favor of witnesses, gave Trump a modest scolding. "It is clear from the July 25, 2019, phone call between President Trump and Ukrainian President Zelensky that the investigation into the Bidens' activities requested by President Trump was improper and demonstrated very poor judgment," she said. But she voted not guilty, saying, "We should entrust to the people the most fundamental decision of a democracy; namely, who should lead their country." This Republican argument, which was made so often, was political cowardice dressed up as democratic deference. Impeachment existed precisely because the Framers believed that sometimes Congress should not wait for the voters to make a change. To pass the buck to their constituents, as so many Republican senators did, was to shirk their constitutionally mandated duty. This was especially true when, as here, the president's misconduct was specifically designed to win the next election. To defer to the voters, as these Republicans did, was to reward Trump's misconduct, not to penalize it.

That night the hundred senators trooped across the Capitol for the president's State of the Union address in the House chamber. As it happened, Bill Clinton also gave his address in the middle of his impeachment trial in 1999. There were some similarities between the two, for both took place in times of considerable prosperity. Clinton in 1999: "Tonight, I stand before you to report that America has created the longest peacetime economic expansion in our history. . . . My fellow Americans, I stand before you tonight to report that the state of our union is strong." Trump in 2020: "I am thrilled to report to you tonight that our economy is the best it has ever been. . . . I say to the people of our great country, and to the Members of Congress before me: The State of our Union is stronger than ever before!" But where Clinton called for bipartisanship and healing, Trump gave a partisan stem-winder, which he highlighted by presenting "the country's highest civilian honor," the Presidential Medal of Freedom, to Rush Limbaugh, the reactionary radio figure. Trump also said, "I've also made an ironclad pledge to American families. We will also protect patients with pre-existing conditions"—at a time when his administration was attempting in court to invalidate the entire Obamacare law, with its protection for preexisting conditions. Trump refused to shake Pelosi's hand at the beginning of the speech; at the end, she tore up her copy.

The next day, February 5, was the final day of the debate and trial. Lamar Alexander, the Tennessee senator who gave McConnell his victory on witnesses, explained his reasoning: "There is no need for more evidence to prove something that I believe had already been proven. . . . There is no need for more evidence to conclude that the President withheld United States aid, at least in part, to pressure Ukraine to investigate the Bidens. The House managers have proved this with what they called a 'mountain of overwhelming evidence.' One of the managers said it was 'proved beyond a shadow of a doubt.'" But Alexander, too, said he would vote against impeachment and leave the final verdict on Trump to the voters.

Mitt Romney was nearly the last senator to speak. He occupied a peculiar place in both the Senate and the nation's politics. He had run a respectable race against Obama in 2012, but that earned him nothing but contempt from Trump, who frequently said of Romney, "He choked like a dog." As president-elect, Trump dangled the job of secretary of state before Romney and snatched it away. But Romney was the rare Republican with an independent political base, and in 2018 he won election to the Senate in Utah with no help from Trump and no need for it. As a seventy-two-year-old freshman senator, Romney didn't have to worry about a long political future. All he had to do was what was right.

When his turn came, Romney spoke with a bracing directness. "As a Senator juror, I swore an oath before God to exercise impartial justice," he said. "I am profoundly religious. My faith is at the heart of who I am. I take an oath before God as enormously consequential." He did not welcome this task, especially since the president belonged to his party. But the heart of Romney's remarks was his complete rejection of every element of Trump's defense. "The grave question the Constitution tasks Senators to answer is whether the President committed an act so extreme and egregious that it rises to the level of a high crime and misdemeanor," he said, followed by a dramatic pause.

"Yes, he did. The President asked a foreign government to investigate his political rival. The President withheld vital military funds from that government to press it to do so. The President delayed funds for an American ally at war with Russian invaders. The President's purpose was personal and political." Trump's lawyers had spent hours trying to refute each of these points, but Romney—quite properly—dismissed their contrived interpretations of Trump's behavior. Like Alexander, Romney saw through the obfuscations and rationalizations and recognized the simple truth: Trump did exactly what the managers said he did. But Romney, unlike Alexander, had the courage and independence to take that recognition to its appropriate conclusion.

Of all the customs and rules associated with an impeachment trial in the Senate, the most solemn concerns the vote itself. The room, as it had been throughout the trial, was silent. Each senator sat at his or her desk. On this day, of course, the outcome was not in doubt, but the Senate's duty at this moment still had the potential for a chilling finality. According to the Senate rules, when a sixty-seventh vote is cast for conviction, "such a vote operates automatically and instantaneously to separate the person impeached from office."

At 4:04 p.m., on February 5, Chief Justice Roberts returned to his post and said, "The Senate will convene as a Court of Impeachment." He called for the clerk to read Article I, which he did. Then Roberts, changing only slightly the words first uttered more than a century earlier during the trial of Andrew Johnson, said, "Each Senator, when his or her name is called, will stand at his or her place and vote guilty or not guilty, as required by rule XXIII of the Senate Rules on Impeachment. Article I, section 3, clause 6 of the Constitution regarding the vote required for conviction on impeachment provides that no person shall be convicted without the concurrence of two-thirds of the Members present. The question is on the first Article of Impeachment. Senators, how say you?"

In virtually all other circumstances, senators vote by saying "yay" or "nay," but here they must speak the language of the courtroom. Roberts concluded his instruction to the senators: "Is the respondent, Donald John Trump, guilty or not guilty?"

The votes took just a few minutes. After conferring with the clerk, Roberts said, "On this Article of Impeachment, 48 Senators have pronounced Donald John Trump, President of the United States, guilty as charged; 52 Senators have pronounced him not guilty as charged. Two-thirds of the Senators present not having pronounced him guilty, the Senate adjudges that the Respondent, Donald John Trump, President of the United States, is not guilty as charged on the first Article of Impeachment." The vote on the second article was 47 guilty and 53 not guilty—precisely on party lines, because Romney voted with his Republican colleagues. It was all over in less than half an hour.

As it happened, the following morning was the National Prayer Breakfast, which had long been an annual occasion for political adversaries to put aside their differences. The theme of the year was Jesus's command to love your enemies. The keynote speaker was Arthur C. Brooks, who left a conservative Washington think tank to become a professor at Harvard's Kennedy School of Government, with a specialty in building harmony among ideological antagonists. "I am here today to talk about what I believe is the biggest crisis facing our nation—and many other nations—today," Brooks said. "This is the crisis of contempt—the polarization that is tearing our society apart." He suggested that the audience "ask God to give you the strength to do this hard thing—to go against human nature, to follow Jesus' teaching and love your enemies." And he asked the crowd, "How many of you love somebody with whom you disagree politically?"

Many people in the audience raised their hands. Trump, sitting a few feet away from Brooks, did not.

Trump spoke next. "Arthur," he said, "I don't know if I agree with you. But I don't know if Arthur's going to like what I'm going to say.

"As everybody knows, my family, our great country and your President, have been put through a terrible ordeal by some very dishonest and corrupt people. They have done everything possible to destroy us. And by so doing, very badly hurt our nation," he said. "They know what they are doing is wrong, but they put themselves far ahead of our great country." Then he went after Romney and Pelosi, if not by name. "Weeks ago and again yesterday, courageous Republican politicians and leaders had the wisdom, fortitude and strength to do what everyone knows was right. I don't like people who use their faith as justification for doing what they know is wrong. Nor do I like people who say I pray for you, when they know that that's not so." Then he sort of drifted to a conclusion: "So many people have been hurt, and we can't let that go on. I'll be discussing that a little bit later at the White House."

Trump was referring to an event that afternoon in the East Room of the White House, where his lawyers, congressional supporters, and other allies gathered to celebrate his acquittal. The president was greeted with raucous cheers. "I invited some of our very good friends, and we have limited room, but everybody wanted to come," he said. "We kept it down to a minimum, and believe it or not, this is a minimum." Trump had a list of people to thank in front of him, but he mostly just extemporized for more than an hour. He spoke, as it were, from the heart.

This speech marked a fitting capstone to the Russia and Ukraine investigations, because Trump provided a perfect distillation of his character, with his pathologies on vivid display. As Sekulow said so often during the trial, his client regarded impeachment as the culmination of years of unjustified attacks, and that was how Trump began his remarks to his supporters. "If you go back to it, over the last number of years, we had the witch hunt. It started from the day we came down the escalator, myself and our future First Lady, who is with us right now," he said. "Thank you, Melania.

"And it never really stopped. We've been going through this now for over three years. It was evil, it was corrupt, it was dirty cops, it was leakers and liars, and this should never, ever happen to another president, ever. I don't know that other presidents would have been able to take it. Some people said, no, they wouldn't have.

"But I can tell you, at a minimum, you have to focus on this because it can get away very quickly no matter who you have with you. It can get away very quickly. It was a disgrace. Had I not fired James Comey, who was a disaster, by the way, it's possible I wouldn't even be standing here right now. We caught him in the act." (Trump apparently had abandoned his claim that he fired Comey because of his conduct of the Clinton investigation, and acknowledged that he fired him because of Russia.) "Dirty cops. Bad people. If this happened to President Obama, a lot of people would have been in jail for a long time already. Many, many years."

Through the sentence fragments and incomplete thoughts, the mid-sentence digressions and non sequiturs, Trump told the story of his investigation as he believed it unfolded. "We thought after the election, it would stop, but it didn't stop," he said. "It just started. Tremendous corruption. Tremendous corruption. So we had a campaign.

Little did we know we were running against some very, very bad and evil people with fake dossiers, with all of these horrible, dirty cops that took these dossiers and did bad things. They knew all about it. . . . This is a political thing, and every time I'd say, 'This is unfair. Let's go to court,' they say, 'Sir, you can't go to court, this is politics.' And we were treated unbelievably unfairly, and you have to understand we first went through Russia, Russia, Russia. It was all bullshit. . . .

"A corrupt politician named Adam Schiff made up my statement to the Ukrainian president. He brought it out of thin air. Just made it up. They say, he's a screenwriter, a failed screenwriter. Unfortunately, he went into politics after that. He said, don't call me, I'll call you. Fortunately for all of us here in our country, we had transcribers, professional transcribers. Then they said, well, maybe the transcription is not correct. But Lieutenant Colonel [Alexander] Vindman and his twin brother, we had some people that were really amazing, but we did everything. I said, what was wrong with it? They said, they didn't add this word. I said, add it. They're probably wrong, but add it." (The next day, Trump fired both Vindman brothers from the White House as well as Ambassador Sondland.)

"So I always said they're lousy politicians, but they do two things. They're vicious and mean. Vicious. Adam Schiff is a vicious, horrible person. Nancy Pelosi is a horrible person. And she wanted to impeach a long time ago when she said, 'I pray for the President.' She doesn't pray. She may pray but she prays for the opposite. But I doubt she prays at all. These are vicious people. But they do two things. They stick together. Historically, I'm not talking now. They stick together like glue. That's how they impeached, because they had whatever the number is, 220 people, so they don't lose anybody, they'll be able to impeach anybody. You could be George Washington. You could have just won the war and they say, 'Let's get him out of office.' And they stuck together, and they're vicious as hell."

He went on, "The spirit for the Republican Party right now is stronger, I think, than it's ever been in the history of our country. I think it's stronger than it's ever been. And that includes Honest Abe Lincoln. You know, a lot of people forget Abe Lincoln. I wish he were here. I'd give him one hell of an introduction. Right? But he was—he was a Republican. Abe Lincoln. Honest Abe. . . .

"They left Bob Mueller. He had the look but not a lot of other things. Always had the look, Mr. G-man. I love the FBI and the FBI loves me, 99 percent. It was the top scum. At the FBI, people don't like the top scum. So think of that, 100 million to 1, and he's investigating me. And then, 'God, Trump is a loathsome human being.' I'm really not a bad person."

Semper Fidelis

I t will take years to assess the full toll of the coronavirus. The cost in lives will be the most painful and important, and the economic wreckage left by the pandemic will be vast. The worldwide struggle for survival also obliterated all other news. For a time, understandably, nothing else mattered.

But there will come a time to view Donald Trump's presidency in full, and to take the measure of the conduct that prompted the Mueller and impeachment investigations—and of the investigations themselves. As is invariably the case with political scandals, the underlying facts in these probes became enmeshed with partisan politics, which happened to be especially toxic in this era. For many, the identity of the players mattered more than the facts on the ground. It's important, then, to view Trump's conduct through an unclouded lens—to make as fair-minded an assessment as possible of what he did and why.

Trump did, in short, exactly what Mueller said he did. The two men—president and prosecutor—were like photo negatives of each other. Trump could not tell the truth, and Mueller could not tell a lie. The Mueller Report, which Americans purchased more often than they read, laid out in sometimes excruciating detail what Trump did and did not do. As a candidate for president in 2016, Trump did not personally collude with Russia; as Mueller acknowledged, Trump engaged in no behavior that could conceivably be described as a criminal conspiracy. Of course, Trump gave every indication of *wanting* to collude with Russia, and he displayed no legal or ethical qualms about seeking or obtaining help from a hostile foreign power. But it takes an act, not just an intent, to commit a crime, and Trump did not commit any such act during the campaign.

It was different once Trump became president, because he now had more power to turn intentions into acts. This was most obvious, at first, in his efforts to undermine the investigations of him. The Mueller Report spelled it out clearly. Trump told Comey to lay off Michael Flynn; when Comey didn't, Trump fired Comey. Trump tried to undermine Mueller, and then he ordered McGahn to oust the prosecutor; then Trump told McGahn to lie about it. These were illegal acts—in conception and execution. These were crimes, even if Mueller stopped short of saying that they were.

Mueller said what Trump did, but he didn't say why Trump did it. He chose not to plumb Trump's psyche (or his bank accounts or tax returns) for the wellsprings of his actions. Still, Trump's character was at the heart of this story. To call the president a narcissist was accurate but incomplete. It was not just that he loved himself but also that he could never see the needs of others. His absence of empathy was as central to his being as his obsession with himself. He couldn't distinguish between his own needs and those of the country. There was never an internal monitor, a check, a superego that counseled him to restrain his own impulses. He could use his power—whether to control the Department of Justice or to conduct foreign policy—only to serve his own personal interests. That was all he saw.

Mueller, on the other hand, was all superego—always hyper concerned that his behavior remained within society's white lines as he saw them. Sometimes career prosecutors come to believe that their ends justify any means, and they bend the rules in pursuit of a good cause. Mueller went the other way. To enforce the law, he felt he had to comply with it—in a manner consistent with his own fastidious values. His team's accomplishments should not be underestimated. They won convictions and guilty pleas against important people, including Trump's campaign chairman and his national security adviser. They made disclosures about Russian interference in the 2016 election that provided unprecedented detail, and their revelations should have proved of staggering importance. In a less polarized environment, the president and Congress would have responded to these findings with bipartisan outrage, denounced this violation of our sovereignty, and taken steps to make sure that it never happened again. (Trump and his Republican allies did none of this, of course, and attempted instead to minimize or deny Russia's role in Trump's victory.) It took tremendous skill and effort for Mueller and his staff to conduct such an extensive investigation and produce such a comprehensive report in a very brief time. But Mueller's caution and respect for authority prevented him from taking the final, obvious, and even necessary step for his investigation—issuing a subpoena to the president. Mueller's report, as detailed as it was, contained a huge hole where Trump's voice should have been. True, the courts might ultimately have prevented an interview with the president, but that did not excuse Mueller's preemptive surrender on the issue.

Mueller's extreme isolation from the public and the press, it seemed, created a tendency to overthink. The OLC opinion barring an indictment of a sitting president fostered a kind of paralysis on Mueller's part. It led to the baffling not-guilty but not-innocent conclusion of the report. This contortion was unnecessary. Mueller could simply have told the truth about what was plain from his findings—that the president committed multiple crimes. In other words, if Mueller wanted to hear from Trump, he could have subpoenaed him; if Mueller thought Trump committed a crime, he could have said so. Instead, by hedging on both issues, Mueller undermined his otherwise remarkable work.

Like any bully, Trump was emboldened by the retreat of his adversary. This was apparent in the almost surreal confluence of events on July 24 and 25, 2019. Mueller's feeble congressional testimony gave Trump even more confidence that he could shake down Ukrainian president Zelensky with impunity. But even though the phone call was the linchpin of the impeachment case against Trump, it was far from the only evidence. The president found it convenient to describe the impeachment effort as based on a single call—which was, in his predictable opinion, "perfect." But Trump did a great deal more than that. He mobilized the entire executive branch behind his effort to use the nation's security relationship with Ukraine to help him win reelection in 2020.

Some of Trump's adversaries tried to define his behavior regarding Ukraine as a criminal offense, like bribery. Some of the president's supporters tried to excuse his conduct because it wasn't a crime. But both arguments missed the point. It was true that Trump did not commit a crime in his dealings with Zelensky; it was too much of a stretch to argue that his actions represented a technical violation of the criminal bribery or extortion statutes. Similarly, his stonewalling of Congress did not constitute a criminal offense. But Trump's behavior regarding Ukraine was *worse* than a crime. Anyone can commit a crime; only a president can undermine the Constitution. In the Russia investigation, Trump did commit a crime—obstruction of justice. But his ends in that effort, though contemptible, were merely seedy and personal—interfering with an investigation of himself. On the other hand, Trump's abuse of power regarding Ukraine had more grave consequences. He put Ukrainian lives at risk; he rewarded Russian aggression; he jeopardized American national security; he misled our allies; he undermined Congress's power of the purse; and he lied to everyone about what he was doing and why. The Framers created impeachment precisely to thwart this kind of conduct, which was, in Hamilton's words, "the abuse or violation of some public trust."

Under the circumstances, the congressional investigation of Trump's Ukraine initiative was a success. In the face of a complete blockade from the administration, and with a nearly impossible time deadline imposed by Pelosi for rational but political reasons, Schiff and his team put together an admirably complete and coherent story. Over time, of course, that narrative will be filled out with the testimony (or books) of the principals and the eventual release of the government's documentary record. (If the pattern with Trump holds, the more information that emerges, the worse he will look.) It was no insult to Schiff and the other House managers that they won only a single Republican vote in the Senate. History, if not the voters in red states, will be unkind to the senators who ignored or explained away the abundant evidence of Trump's misdeeds.

Trump followed his victory in the Senate trial not with magnanimity but with vengeance. Two days after the verdict, he had Alexander Vindman marched out of the White House, as punishment for his crime of testifying truthfully about Trump's Ukraine initiative. In a particularly sinister (and North Korean) touch, his brother Eugene, who wasn't even involved in the Ukraine matter, was also evicted from his job in the White House that same day. The hapless Gordon Sondland was quickly gone too, thrown out of an ambassadorship that he had no business having in the first place. Two months later, Trump gave a clear signal for how he envisioned the remainder of his presidency when he fired Michael Atkinson, the inspector general of the intelligence community. Atkinson's crime, too, was doing his job—that is, following the law by ruling that the whistle-blower's complaint should be turned over to Congress. Inspectors general exist to provide oversight, which frequently means criticism, of the operations of the executive branch. By firing Atkinson, Trump made clear (and boasted) that he cared most about loyalty—not to the rule of law but to him. After dismissing Atkinson, under cover of the coronavirus crisis, Trump also cashiered several other inspectors general. To be loyal to the principles of good government was to be dismissed as an operative of the deep state—and, likely, to be dismissed altogether.

Trump was always hard on his enemies, but what was especially distinctive about his presidency was that it was mostly disastrous for his friends, too. Trump endured; few others around him did. The roll call of unceremonious departures from his cabinet and senior White House staff was far longer than the list of survivors. Rudy Giuliani occupied a middle ground—neither fully in nor fully out of Trump's good graces. By the time the impeachment trial ended, he was still technically representing Trump, but he was too intimately involved in the facts of the Ukraine case to serve as one of his lawyers in the Senate trial. (At the victory celebration in the White House, Giuliani was noticeably absent, and Trump did not mention his name.) Giuliani's reckless statements and irresponsible Twitter feed had turned him into a fringe figure, a remarkable comedown for the man once known as America's Mayor. Giuliani was, apparently, too toxic even for Fox News; in 2019, he became affiliated with the One America News Network, which was devoted to cartoonish Trump adulation. Giuliani was also temporarily banned from Twitter because he was providing bogus medical advice for how to treat COVID-19. When I asked him whether he worried about how this chapter of his life would affect his legacy, he said, "I don't care about my legacy. I'll be dead."

Giuliani, at least, fared better than Lev Parnas and Igor Fruman, his erstwhile partners in the Ukraine initiative. In October 2019, they were indicted in the Southern District of New York for campaign finance violations, including funneling foreign money to organizations supporting Trump. One charge asserted that the two men hid the source of the $325,000 they paid to the America First Action political action committee so that they could attend the dinner with Trump in April 2018. (This was the one that Fruman secretly recorded.) Parnas and Fruman pleaded not guilty. The Southern District, which Giuliani once led as U.S. Attorney, is apparently also investigating Giuliani's role in the matter. In the end, though, Giuliani's association with Trump was more likely to cost him just his reputation, not his freedom.

Trump took vindictive joy in the fate of two of his main antagonists—Michael Cohen, his former devoted legal servant, and Michael Avenatti, who parlayed his failed representation of Stormy Daniels into momentary fame. Cohen was sentenced to three years in connection with his guilty plea for his involvement in an illegal campaign contribution (the payoff to Daniels) and his own various financial crimes. (He was released early, in May 2020, because of the coronavirus.) Avenatti was convicted for his role in a bizarre extortion scheme, where he threatened Nike and its lawyers and demanded a multimillion-dollar payoff. While Avenatti was in jail awaiting sentencing for that crime, he was also facing a much larger fraud case in Los Angeles, where he was charged with ripping off both his law partners and his clients. He was awaiting trial in still another case, where he was charged with defrauding Stormy Daniels of her book advance. (Avenatti was also released early because of the virus, but he faces the prospect of a lengthy return to prison after his trials are completed.)

John Bolton might have outfoxed himself. He dodged his obligation as a citizen to testify in the impeachment proceedings, thus protecting the commercial value of his book. But the Trump White House, which had the right of prepublication review, apparently exercised the heavy hand of the censor, leaving the former national security adviser with the choice of publishing a neutered work or starting a long court battle over the redactions.

Rod Rosenstein resigned shortly after Mueller submitted his report, thus completing his eventful tenure as deputy attorney general. His record was maddeningly contradictory. His embarrassing memo provided the pretext for Trump to fire Comey from the FBI; Rosenstein then redeemed himself by hiring Mueller, and he protected the special counsel and his staff and allowed them to complete their investigation; he endured years of abusive tweets from the president (including one that depicted Rosenstein behind bars); finally, though, he allowed himself to be used by Barr to whitewash Mueller's report. He then wrote a fawning farewell letter to the president, thanking Trump for "the courtesy and humor you often display in our personal conversations." After more than three decades of public service, Rosenstein became a partner in a law firm.

James Comey, the former FBI director whose actions set the investigation in motion, found himself, politically, a man without a country. Democrats reviled him for his last-minute sabotage of Hillary Clinton's campaign, and Republicans, especially the president, continued to defame him for doing his job in the Russia investigation. Comey gave speeches about "leadership" and exercised his powers of self-justification.

William Barr proved to be what Trump always wanted in an attorney general—a toady. Instead of following up on Mueller's findings and trying to protect the country from more foreign intrusions in our elections, Barr launched an investigation of the origins of the Russia investigation itself. In a shameful departure from the honorable traditions of the Justice Department, he devoted great public resources and his own energy in pursuing right-wing conspiracy theories. In March 2020, Judge Reggie B. Walton, a George W. Bush appointee, offered an apt postscript to Barr's partisan effort to undermine the Mueller Report. Walton rejected the Justice Department's attempt to dismiss a case filed by a public interest group, under the Freedom of Information Act, to obtain access to the unexpurgated Mueller Report. "The speed by which Attorney General Barr released to the public the summary of Special Counsel Mueller's principal conclusions, coupled with the fact that Attorney General Barr failed to provide a thorough representation of the findings set forth in the Mueller Report, causes the Court to question whether Attorney General Barr's intent was to create a one-sided narrative about the Mueller Report—a narrative that is clearly in some respects substantively at odds with the redacted version of the Mueller Report," Walton wrote, adding, "Attorney General Barr's lack of candor specifically call[s] into question Attorney General Barr's credibility."

It was not enough for Trump that he survived Mueller and impeachment, but he had to crush his adversaries—by proving that their efforts were a "hoax" all along. In particular, he wanted to wipe the special counsel's investigation from the history books, by undermining the convictions that Mueller won—especially those of Michael Flynn, Paul Manafort, and Roger Stone. (In November 2019, Stone was convicted of all seven counts against him, which included obstruction of justice, making false statements, and witness tampering.) It had been common in Washington scandals for those facing prison to cooperate with prosecutors in hopes of winning reduced sentences. But only Rick Gates, Manafort's deputy, provided genuine cooperation to Mueller. By dangling pardons in front of the other defendants, Trump made cooperation with Mueller look like a bad bet. Wisely, then, for their deliverance, Flynn, Manafort, and Stone put their trust in Trump—and in his instrument, Barr.

The attorney general delivered. In February 2020, Barr overruled the line prosecutors in Stone's case and asked for a lower sentence than had previously been requested. (In protest, all four lawyers on the case promptly dissociated themselves from the prosecution, and one quit the Justice Department.) Then, in May, Barr moved to drop the prosecution of Flynn altogether—even though the former national security adviser had earlier pleaded guilty to lying to FBI agents. It was an act apparently without precedent in the history of the Justice Department—surrendering a conviction when the defendant, a sophisticated man with highly capable lawyers, had already admitted his guilt. The Justice Department's main legal argument was that the FBI had no reason to interview Flynn in the first place—and that, accordingly, the subject matter of the interview was not "material" to an investigation. (The law allows prosecutions of false statements only when those statements are "material" to a pending investigation.) But the FBI's approach to Flynn was totally legitimate, and Flynn's lies were highly material to the Russia investigation. Indeed, at the time, there was so much concern about Flynn's behavior that Yates, the acting attorney general, went to the White House to express her alarm to McGahn, then the new White House counsel, about what Flynn was doing. Interviewing Flynn was a crucial step in that investigation.

In other words, Barr's proffered reason for dropping the Flynn case was an almost laughable pretext but one that conformed with Trump's belief that the investigation was illegitimate from the start. There was a sinister kind of symmetry to the evolution of Flynn's case. The most compelling evidence that Trump obstructed justice involved his meeting with Comey on February 14, 2017. On that day, the president shooed everyone else out of the Oval Office and said to the FBI director about the Flynn investigation, "I hope you can see your way clear to letting this go, to letting Flynn go. He is a good guy. I hope you can let this go." On May 7, 2020, by filing papers to conclude the prosecution, Barr finally did what Trump wanted all along. He let the Flynn case go.

For the most part, the prosecutors returned to their law firms. Mueller, Quarles, and Zebley resumed their partnerships with WilmerHale in Washington, but Jeannie Rhee struck out on her own, landing at the Washington office of a New York law firm. Andrew Goldstein, after many years as a prosecutor, also joined the Washington office of a national firm. Andrew Weissmann also left government service, returning to New York, teaching at New York University school of law, and becoming a partner in a law firm. Mueller made no public statements, but he did make an unpublicized appearance before a class at Harvard Law School in January 2020. He still had trouble hearing questions and was slow to respond and unsteady on his feet. He spoke little of the investigation, though he mentioned the continuing peril of Russian interference in our political system. The only subject he returned to several times was his service in the Marine Corps. Mueller said the values of the corps—honor, courage, and commitment—had been the driving forces of his life.

The coronavirus presented Donald Trump with a challenge unlike any other he had faced as president. As the pandemic deepened, some of his supporters asserted that Democrats were to blame for Trump's halting response, because he was distracted by the impeachment proceedings. If that was true, it was his own fault. No one told the president that he had to send 142 tweets on January 22, 2020, a key day in the virus crisis, when he might have devoted more attention to understanding the outbreak and halting its spread. That day was also the first time a case of COVID-19 was diagnosed in South Korea, which promptly began an orderly regime of testing that limited the immediate impact of the virus. In contrast, Trump that night addressed the growing threat with his customary salesman's patter. "We have it totally under control," he said. No, they didn't, and Trump's feckless indifference in those early days cost thousands of American lives.

Trump addressed the coronavirus the same way that he confronted his Russia and Ukraine scandals—with bluster, blame shifting, vindictiveness, and lies. Trump said, "I don't take responsibility at all," for the lack of testing for the virus. He blamed President Obama for lack of preparation, even though Trump's National Security Council, under John Bolton, disbanded the pandemic response team that Obama created. Trump blamed China, the World Health Organization, and especially the nation's governors for the magnitude of the crisis. In behavior reminiscent of his dealings with Ukraine's Zelensky, he demanded fealty from governors if their states were going to receive federal attention. At one point, Trump told Vice President Pence to ignore the governors of Michigan and Washington State because they had criticized the president.

Lies abounded in Trump's statements about the virus. "Anybody that needs a test, gets a test. We—they're there. They have the tests. And the tests are beautiful." (This was not true when Trump said it on March 6, 2020, and it remained untrue for long thereafter.) As for travelers arriving in the United States from Europe, he said, "If an American is coming back or anybody is coming back, we're testing." (They were not.) He said Google was building a website with the government to help Americans determine whether they needed to be tested. (Google wasn't.) "The Obama Administration made a decision on testing that turned out to be very detrimental to what we're doing," Trump said. (There was no such decision.) He said the Trump administration "inherited" a "broken," "bad," and "obsolete" test for the coronavirus. (Since the coronavirus did not exist before 2019, there was no test for it of any kind.) As for his news conferences about the virus, Trump boasted, as thousands of his fellow citizens were dying, that "the ratings are through the roof according to, of all sources, the Failing New York Times, 'Monday Night Football, Bachelor Finale' type numbers." In an apt symbol of his shambolic leadership of the response to the crisis, Trump suggested in one briefing that the virus should be treated by hitting the body with "ultraviolet or just very powerful light" and using "disinfectant, which knocks it out in a minute." (Characteristically, he later lied and said his statements about light and disinfectant were meant sarcastically.)

All of Trump's actions—regarding the Mueller investigation, the Ukraine initiative, and the coronavirus—took place against the backdrop of his campaign for reelection. Trump dodged the courts on Russia, and he won in Congress on Ukraine, and the people will render their verdict on the president and the coronavirus. Trump had no great passions on the issues, no policy agenda that he was determined to enact. For Trump, his presidency was more about him than what he could accomplish. For this reason, the only verdict that has ever mattered to Trump is the one rendered on Election Day.

AUTHOR'S NOTE

This book is based principally on my coverage of the 2016 presidential campaign and the first three-plus years of the Trump administration. For this book, I interviewed more than a hundred people, including members of Mueller's staff, subjects of and witnesses in Mueller's investigation, Trump's legal team, Trump administration officials, members of Congress of both parties, congressional staffers, and defense lawyers. The interviews were on a not-for-attribution basis; that is, I could use the information provided but without quoting directly or identifying the source.

The documentary record of these investigations is already enormous. The Mueller Report was an indispensable resource. Benjamin Wittes and his colleagues at lawfareblog.com performed a tremendous service to me and other researchers by posting all of the court filings in the Mueller investigation. Lawfare also did a useful timeline of the Trump-Ukraine scandal. Ryan Goodman and Steve Vladeck and their colleagues at justsecurity.org also posted a valuable timeline on Trump and Ukraine as well as a collection of public documents related to the impeachment proceedings.

I also steeped myself in the coverage of these investigations in the news media. I am particularly grateful for the extraordinary work of the journalists at *The New York Times* and *The Washington Post*. At the *Times,* as I note in the text, the work of Maggie Haberman and Michael S. Schmidt was especially important. At the *Post,* I thank the

White House team and especially Philip Rucker and Carol Leonnig for their terrific book, *A Very Stable Genius*. In longer-form journalism, I'd like to recognize my colleague Adam Entous's profiles of Hunter Biden and Yuriy Lutsenko in *The New Yorker* and Franklin Foer's profile of Paul Manafort in *The Atlantic*. As the story unfolded, I was fortunate to profile Rudy Giuliani, Roger Stone, Michael Cohen, and Adam Schiff in *The New Yorker*. As for books, I have inhaled the already vast Trump literature, but wish to point out my debt to Bob Woodward's *Fear*, James Comey's *A Higher Loyalty*, and Andrew McCabe's *The Threat*. My thanks also to the proprietors of the invaluable trumptwitterarchive.com. Other secondary sources appear in the notes to each chapter.

Anyone in the United States (or, say, the world) would recognize that these last months, as the coronavirus descended, have been an extraordinary time to complete and publish a book. At this stage in the process, I always take pleasure in thanking the many people who joined me in the endeavor. However, I realize that my circle of gratitude needs to be a great deal wider than for past books. This time, of all times, I need to thank the people in the news and book publishing business who run the presses, who work in the warehouses, who drive the trucks. From my television life, I am also aware of contributions of the people you don't see—the photojournalists in the field and the producers in the control room—and I salute them as well. In the same spirit, I express my gratitude to the folks who grow and deliver the food, and the grocery store workers who sell it, and everyone else who brings us what we order online (as well as our mail), so that authors and journalists can keep doing what we do. Today, work outside the home is heroism, and I thank all the heroes who made publication of this book possible. Closer to my quarantine home, many thanks from my family to Mike Luzi and the staff of the IGA in Sherman, Connecticut.

At Doubleday headquarters, I continue to have the good fortune to work with Bill Thomas, my editor, who steered this book to publication in such difficult circumstances. I am also grateful to the entire team at Doubleday, which included Todd Doughty (again!), copy editor Ingrid Sterner, Andy Hughes (head of a swift production), Bette Alexander (again!), Lydia Buechler, Michael Collica, Khari Dawkins, Chris DuFault, John Fontana, Michael Goldsmith, Kathy Hourigan, Lorraine Hyland, and Beth Meister. Julie Tate, the fact-checking legend, graced me with her efforts. Thanks also to Kris Dahl, Esther Newberg, Phyllis Grann, Ron Bernstein, John and Jordan Davis, and, once more, to Professor John Q. Barrett.

I remain grateful, too, to my colleagues at *The New Yorker,* especially David Remnick and Dorothy Wickenden, who have been my friends and bosses for many years. At CNN, where I spent so much time with this story, I thank Jeff Zucker and my remarkable and dedicated colleagues there.

Amy McIntosh—who is my wife for better and for worse and, during the virus crisis, also for lunch!—edited the first draft of this book with her usual intelligence and grace. I treasure the privilege of sharing my life with her. Unexpectedly, and not exactly voluntarily, Adam Toobin joined us for much of his first year of law school. I hope he was as happy to have us as we were to have him.

A word about the dedication. I began my professional life as a lawyer and did not come to journalism until I was in my thirties. Perhaps because of this relatively late start, I've always felt a special gratitude for being welcomed into the field and for the chance to make a living this way. In recent years I've been especially lucky because this has been a difficult time for journalists. The business—especially at newspapers and magazines—has been rough. To be honest, I don't have any particular idea of how to turn things around financially. It's not my field.

But I do want to say something about the value—in something other than money—of what we do. A defense of journalism sounds today, almost automatically, like an attack on Donald Trump. And it is true that the president has demeaned our work like no other figure in modern American history. Trump has used the epithets "fake news" and "enemies of the people" so often that they've become almost routine, part of the background hum of politics in the United States. But my purpose in saluting my colleagues is broader than simply standing up to Trump's attacks. The work we do is indispensable in a free nation; that was true before Trump's presidency and will be true after he is gone. Journalism matters not just because we speak truth to this particular president but because democracy will always require an informed electorate. Journalists, like everyone else, are imperfect; we make mistakes. But our country—and the world—is better off because of the work that we continue to do. I'm proud to be a journalist and to stand with my colleagues at this precarious moment.

June 2020

NOTES

Prologue: *The Forgotten Phone*

3 On the surface, the two men: Marc Fisher and Sari Horowitz, "Mueller and Trump: Born to Wealth, Raised to Lead. Then, Sharply Different Choices," *Washington Post,* Feb. 23, 2018, www.washingtonpost.com.

4 It later appeared that the doctor: Steve Eder, "Did a Queens Podiatrist Help Donald Trump Avoid Vietnam?," *New York Times,* Dec. 26, 2018, www.nytimes.com.

4 Trump sometimes bantered about Vietnam: Aaron Blake, "Trump's Flippant Talk About the Vietnam War," *Washington Post,* June 5, 2019, www.washingtonpost.com.

6 In his FBI days, he used the shirts: Garrett M. Graff, *The Threat Matrix: The FBI at War* (New York: Back Bay Books, 2012); see also Garrett M. Graff, "What Donald Trump Needs to Know About Bob Mueller and Jim Comey," *Politico,* May 18, 2017, www .politico.com.

1 *October Surprises*

28 Comey cost Clinton the presidency: See, for example, Nate Silver, "The Comey Letter Probably Cost Clinton the Election," FiveThirtyEight, May 3, 2017, fivethirtyeight .com. For a less definitive view, see Nate Cohn, "Did Comey Cost Clinton the Election?," *New York Times,* June 14, 2018, www.nytimes.com.

4 *"I Faced Great Pressure"*

59 what Russia did during the 2016 election: Shane Harris, Josh Dawsey, and Ellen Nakashima, "Trump Told Russian Officials in 2017 He Wasn't Concerned About Moscow's Interference in U.S. Election," *Washington Post,* Sept. 27, 2019, www .washingtonpost.com.

7 *"Do You Think Putin Will . . . Become My New Best Friend?"*

92 By one analysis, Trump and his businesses: Nick Penzenstadler and Susan Page, "Exclusive: Trump's 3,500 Lawsuits Unprecedented for a Presidential Nominee," *USA Today*, June 1, 2016, www.usatoday.com.

95 Dowd wanted the job: Philip Rucker and Carol Leonnig, *A Very Stable Genius: Donald J. Trump's Testing of America* (New York: Penguin Press, 2020), 97.

104 Trump raised it in an interview: "Transcript of AP Interview with Trump," Associated Press, April 23, 2017, apnews.com. See also Scott Shane, "How a Fringe Theory About Ukraine Took Root in the White House," *New York Times*, Nov. 26, 2019, www.nytimes.com.

104 a single months-old article: Kenneth P. Vogel and David Stern, "Ukrainian Efforts to Sabotage Trump Backfire," *Politico*, Jan. 11, 2017, www.politico.com.

104 Hannity spun that disclosure: Matt Gertz, "Sean Hannity Stoked Trump's Rage Towards Ukraine," Media Matters, Nov. 4, 2019, www.mediamatters.org.

8 *"This Dumb Meeting Which Your Father Insisted On"*

108 Ahmad had become almost famous: As an Assistant U.S. Attorney, she was profiled in *The New Yorker*. See William Finnegan, "Taking Down Terrorists in Court," *New Yorker*, May 15, 2017, www.newyorker.com.

112 Trump himself acknowledged in an interview: Peter Baker, Michael S. Schmidt, and Maggie Haberman, "Excerpts from the Times's Interview with Trump," *New York Times*, July 19, 2017, www.nytimes.com.

9 *"I Would Love to Speak, I Would Love To"*

124 It included this exchange: Tamara Keith, "Trump Under Oath: Sometimes Combative, Often Boastful, Usually Lacking Details," *Morning Edition*, NPR, March 27, 2018, www.npr.org.

10 *The $15,000 Ostrich Jacket*

136 When Paul Manafort joined the Trump campaign: The most thoughtful and extensive biographical treatment of Paul Manafort's career is Franklin Foer, "Paul Manafort, American Hustler," *Atlantic*, March 2018, www.theatlantic.com.

138 According to the Associated Press: Jeff Horwitz and Chad Day, "AP Exclusive: Before Trump Job, Manafort Worked to Aid Putin," Associated Press, March 22, 2017, apnews.com.

141 Manafort's true priorities: I am grateful to Marcy Wheeler, whose *Emptywheel* blog untangled many of the details about Manafort's role. See, for example, "Paul Manafort Violated Campaign Policy in Risking a Meeting with Konstantin Kilimnik on August 2, 2016," *Emptywheel*, April 29, 2019, www.emptywheel.net.

144 But the contents of the apartment: Marcy Wheeler, "Renewing My Obsession with Paul Manafort's iPods: Robert Mueller's 2,300 Media Devices," *Emptywheel*, July 16, 2019, www.emptywheel.net.

11 *"Being Patriotic"*

149 called itself the Denver Guardian: See Laura Sydell, "We Tracked Down a Fake-News Creator in the Suburbs. Here's What We Learned," *All Tech Considered,* NPR, Nov. 23, 2016, www.npr.org.

157 Miller would build a cage: To see Harry Miller's handiwork, see Donie O'Sullivan, Drew Griffin, and Scott Bronstein, "The Unwitting: The Trump Supporters Used by Russia," CNN, Feb. 20, 2018, money.cnn.com.

12 *Doing a Frank Pentangeli*

164 in Trump's July 2017 interview: See "Excerpts from the Times's Interview with Trump," *New York Times,* July 19, 2017, www.nytimes.com.

13 *Flipping Rick Gates*

183 backgrounds of Mueller's staff: For a good summary of the evidence on the partisan affiliations of Mueller's staff, see Louis Jacobson, "Fact-Checking Donald Trump's Claims About Democrats on Robert Mueller's Team," PolitiFact, March 21, 2018, www .politifact.com.

183 Starr himself was a partisan Republican: I wrote about the politics of Starr's staff in *The New Yorker.* See Jeffrey Toobin, "Clinton's Other Pursuer," *New Yorker,* April 6, 1998, www.newyorker.com.

14 *"Cut the Bullshit, Bob"*

189 His staff disagreed with the OLC opinions: Charlie Savage, "Can the President Be Indicted? A Long-Hidden Legal Memo Says Yes," *New York Times,* July 22, 2017, www .nytimes.com.

192 journalists investigated the way Sekulow: Elizabeth Williamson, "Trump's Other Personal Lawyer: Close to the Right, but Far from Giuliani," *New York Times,* Dec. 1, 2019, www.nytimes.com; Aaron C. Davis and Shawn Boburg, "Trump Attorney Jay Sekulow's Family Has Been Paid Millions from Charities They Control," *Washington Post,* June 27, 2017, www.washingtonpost.com; Jon Swaine, "Trump Lawyer's Firm Steered Millions in Donations to Family Members, Files Show," *Guardian,* June 27, 2017, www .theguardian.com.

15 *Michael Avenatti's Campaign for President*

201 "President Trump ordered the firing": Michael S. Schmidt and Maggie Haberman, "Trump Ordered Mueller Fired, but Backed Off When White House Counsel Threatened to Quit," *New York Times,* Jan. 25, 2018, www.nytimes.com.

208 including one to *Vanity Fair:* Rachel Dodes, "Michael Avenatti on His Style and Skincare Routine: 'I Own It,'" *Vanity Fair,* May 17, 2018, www.vanityfair.com.

17 *"Truth Isn't Truth"*

228 In keeping with the general ethical tenor: Joe Palazzolo and Michael Rothfeld, *The Fixers: The Bottom-Feeders, Crooked Lawyers, Gossipmongers, and Porn Stars Who Created the 45th President* (New York: Random House, 2020), 210.

234 They met daily, and became friends: See Russell Berman, "The Complicated Friendship of Robert Mueller and William Barr," *Atlantic,* April 28, 2019, www.theatlantic.com; David Rohde, "William Barr, Trump's Sword and Shield," *New Yorker,* Jan. 20, 2020, www.newyorker.com.

235 Barr traveled in never-Trump circles: Rohde, "William Barr, Trump's Sword and Shield."

18 *"There's Tears in Your Eyes"*

248 But a single juror held out: Matthew Haag and Sharon LaFraniere, "Manafort Jury Holdout Blocked Guilty Verdict on 10 of 18 Charges, Juror Says," *New York Times,* Aug. 23, 2018, www.nytimes.com.

19 *Friends in High Places*

260 In his debriefings with Mueller's team: See Sharon LaFraniere, Kenneth P. Vogel, and Scott Shane, "In Closed Hearing, a Clue About 'the Heart' of Mueller's Russia Inquiry," *New York Times,* Feb. 19, 2019, www.nytimes.com.

20 *"There's Nothing Ambiguous About Crosshairs"*

263 CNN journalists had been conducting: For an account of how the CNN journalists knew to be in position for the raid, see Jeremy Herb, "How CNN Captured Video of the Roger Stone Raid," CNN, Jan. 25, 2019, www.cnn.com. Here is the CNN video: www.youtube.com/watch?v=dWTzCNY7_YY.

21 *"The Immense Burden the Process Imposed on the President and His Office"*

272 Sekulow and the Raskins took charge: Rucker and Leonnig, *Very Stable Genius,* 323–24.

22 *"Thank You to My New Friend Rudy Giuliani for Your . . ."*

280 He was evicted for nonpayment: "Giuliani's Ukrainian Allies Racked Up Debts in South Florida," *Tampa Bay Times,* Oct. 1, 2019, www.tampabay.com.

280 Shortly before the 2016 election: Rebecca Ballhaus, Aruna Viswanatha, and Alex Leary, "Lev Parnas Paid His Way into Donald Trump's Orbit," *Wall Street Journal,* Jan. 19, 2020, www.wsj.com; Joe Palazzolo and Rebecca Davis O'Brien, "Giuliani Associate Left Trail of Troubled Businesses Before Ukraine Probe Push," *Wall Street Journal,* Oct. 31, 2019, www.wsj.com.

283 He even had to borrow $100,000: Erik Larson, "Giuliani Says He Had to Borrow from Trump Lawyer to Pay Taxes," Bloomberg, July 25, 2019, www.bloomberg.com.

284 he documented at least eight occasions: Vicky Ward, "Exclusive: After Private White

House Meeting, Giuliani Associate Lev Parnas Said He Was on a 'Secret Mission' for Trump, Sources Say," CNN, Nov. 16, 2019, cnn.com.

23 *Fraud Guaranteed*

289 the CrowdStrike theory was madness: For one of the many refutations of the Crowd-Strike conspiracy theory, see Brian Barrett, "Trump's Ukraine Server Delusion Is Spreading," *Wired,* Nov. 26, 2019, www.wired.com.

289 Trump was repeating Russian propaganda: See Thomas Rid, "Who's Really to Blame for the 'Ukraine Did It' Conspiracy Theory?," *Atlantic,* Dec. 5, 2019, www.theatlantic .com; and Julian E. Barnes and Matthew Rosenberg, "Charges of Ukrainian Meddling? A Russian Operation, U.S. Intelligence Says," *New York Times,* Nov. 26, 2019, www .nytimes.com.

291 Hunter Biden had a much rockier passage: The best summary of Hunter Biden's life, and his work in Ukraine, can be found in Adam Entous, "Will Hunter Biden Jeopardize His Father's Campaign," *New Yorker,* July 8 and 15, 2019, www.newyorker.com.

293 Trump sent Giuliani to Ukraine: "Trump Contradicts Past Denials, Admits Sending Giuliani to Ukraine," CNN, Feb. 13, 2020, cnn.com.

293 Shokin asserted he had been fired: Adam Entous, "The Ukrainian Prosecutor Behind Trump's Impeachment," *New Yorker,* Dec. 23, 2019, www.newyorker.com.

295 "Is there absolute commitment": Colby Itkowitz, Paul Sonne, and Tom Hamburger, "Parnas Used Access to Trump's World to Help Push Shadow Ukraine Effort, New Documents Show," *Washington Post,* Jan. 15, 2020, www.washingtonpost.com.

296 John Solomon, a veteran conservative reporter: For an internal review of all of Solomon's columns about Ukraine, see Hill Staff, "The Hill's Review of John Solomon's Columns on Ukraine," *Hill,* Feb. 20, 2020, thehill.com.

24 *"Ultimate Conclusions"*

303 It was a fairly relaxed meeting: See Rucker and Leonnig, *Very Stable Genius,* 375–78.

307 Trump's legal team gathered: Ibid., 388–89.

25 *"Talk to Rudy, Talk to Rudy"*

312 in was the power of the U.S. government: This period in U.S.-Ukraine policy is well documented in the House Intelligence Committee's "Trump-Ukraine Impeachment Inquiry Report," Dec. 2019, intelligence.house.gov.

26 *"I Would Like You to Do Us a Favor Though"*

329 the morning of July 25, 2019: For minute-by-minute examinations of the events of July 25, 2019, see Nancy Benac, "July 25 Forecast: Sunny, with Cloud of Impeachment for Trump," Associated Press, Nov. 30, 2019, apnews.com; Marshall Cohen and Will Houp, "What Happened on July 25, the Most Important Day in the Impeachment Scandal," CNN, Dec. 3, 2019, www.cnn.com.

333 He took the group to a restaurant: Adam Taylor, "What's on the Menu at the Trendy

Kyiv Restaurant Where Sondland Is Said to Have Phoned Trump," *Washington Post,*
Nov. 21, 2020, www.washingtonpost.com.

27 *"The Times Have Found Us"*

340 The Constitution needed a legal mechanism: There is, of course, a voluminous literature
on the history of impeachment. My summary is drawn principally from Laurence Tribe
and Joshua Matz, *To End a Presidency: The Power of Impeachment* (New York: Basic
Books, 2018), 1–9, 35–37. Another useful source is a history of the impeachment power
compiled by the staff of the House Judiciary Committee in February 1974, in advance of
the Nixon hearings. A principal author of this study was a young lawyer named Hillary
Rodham. See *Constitutional Grounds for Presidential Impeachment: Report by the Staff of
the Impeachment Inquiry,* House of Representatives, Committee on the Judiciary, 93rd
Cong., 2nd Sess., Feb. 1974, ia801902.us.archive.org.

344 Donald Trump almost had a point: For a look at these 2017–2018 impeachment efforts,
see Jeffrey Toobin, "Will the Fervor to Impeach Donald Trump Start a Democratic Civil
War?," *New Yorker,* May 28, 2018, www.newyorker.com.

348 At the St. Regis hotel that afternoon: Sheryl Gay Stolberg, "Pelosi's Leap on Impeachment: From No Go to No Choice," *New York Times,* Dec. 18, 2019, www.nytimes.com.

349 Cipollone had long practiced: Manuel Roig-Franzia and Josh Dawsey, "Trump Lawyer
Pat Cipollone Was a Camera-Shy Washington Everyman—Until Impeachment Made
Him a Star," *Washington Post,* Jan. 30, 2020, www.washingtonpost.com.

351 review the transcript in advance: Alayna Treene, "Some Trump Advisers Think Release
Was a Mistake," *Axios,* Sept. 26, 2019, www.axios.com.

28 *"It Reads Like a Classic Organized Crime Shakedown"*

360 the controversy about Schiff's "parody": For a close analysis of Schiff's remarks on September 26, and the controversy about them, see Lori Robertson, "Schiff's 'Parody' and
Trump's Response," FactCheck.org, Oct. 1, 2019, www.factcheck.org.

363 "Is you taking notes": Here is the scene: youtube.com/watch?v=hGo5bxWy2lg.

29 *"The Deep Disappointment and Dismay*
I Have Felt as These Events Have Unfolded"

377 "Have to get tougher and fight!": See, for example, Andrew Desiderio and Melanie
Zanona, "Impeachment Deposition Delayed After Republicans Storm Proceedings,"
Politico, Oct. 23, 2019, www.politico.com; Toluse Olorunnipa, Josh Dawsey, and Mike
DeBonis, "Republicans Storm Closed-Door Impeachment Hearing as Escalating Ukraine
Scandal Threatens Trump," *Washington Post,* Oct. 23, 2019, www.washingtonpost.com.

32 *"In the Name of Itself and of the People of the United States of America"*

406 It was five and a half pages: For a more detailed analysis of the letter, see the annotations
at "Read Trump's Letter to Pelosi Protesting Impeachment," *New York Times,* Dec. 17,
2019, www.nytimes.com.

33 *"Speaker Pelosi Wanted Leverage"*

418 traditions regarding impeachment trials: See Tribe and Matz, *To End a Presidency,* 130–38.

34 *"Moral Courage Is a Rarer Commodity than Bravery"*

423 first person in the United States to be diagnosed: See Ed Pilkington and Tom McCarthy, "The Missing Six Weeks: How Trump Failed the Biggest Test of His Life," *Guardian,* March 28, 2020, www.theguardian.com; Michael D. Shear et al., "The Lost Month: How a Failure to Test Blinded the U.S. to Covid-19," *New York Times,* March 28, 2020, www.nytimes.com.

35 *"A Lot of People Forget Abe Lincoln"*

432 "The lack of immune protection": Maggie Haberman, "Trade Adviser Warned White House in January of Risks of a Pandemic," *New York Times,* April 7, 2020, www.nytimes .com.

Epilogue: *Semper Fidelis*

450 Lies abounded in Trump's statements: See, for example, Christian Paz, "All the President's Lies About the Coronavirus," *Atlantic,* April 9, 2020, www.theatlantic.com.

INDEX

ABOUT THE AUTHOR

Jeffrey Toobin is chief legal analyst at CNN and a staff writer at *The New Yorker*. He is the author of several bestselling books, including *American Heiress, The Oath, The Nine,* and *The Run of His Life,* which was the basis for *American Crime Story: The People v. O. J. Simpson,* the acclaimed FX Networks limited series. *A Vast Conspiracy,* his book about the Bill Clinton–Monica Lewinsky scandal, will be the basis of the 2021 installment of *American Crime Story.*